LONAMA'S MAP

LONAMA'S MAP

Book 2
Portals of Tessalindria Series

F.W. FALLER

F.W. Faller

DPI
DISCIPLESHIP
PUBLICATIONS
INTERNATIONAL

Lonama's Map

Discipleship Publications International
2 Sterling Road
Billerica, Massachusetts 01862

Printed in the United States of America

ISBN: 1-57782-190-4

Cover illustration: Farley Vigneault
Interior design: Thais Faller Gloor
Interior illustrations: Rachel Faller

This book is fondly dedicated to my wife,
my best friend and companion forever,
and
written to the hearts of all beings
who stand at the crossroads,
seeking for the old paths
where the way is good,
who walk in them,
and find rest
for their
vorns
¥

Eshvallin stood on the peak Eliia and gazed back into history
To the dark stormy depths of times long forgotten.
Then, with a full turning, he faced into the haze of the future,
Churning and changing as a mist driven before the wind.

With upraised hands, he called to the Deep Sky,
"Is history but legend and the future but a fantasy?
Is history a fantasy and the future but a legend unborn?
And what of prophecy? Is it not but a dream
From which we will finally wake?"

And Mah'Eladra answered Eshvallin from the Margah
With a voice like a thousand mighty waterfalls
That shook the foundations of Tessalindria:
"The words of men, that tangle and divide the vorn,
That obscure reality and darken noble truth,
Are left behind in the ashes of eshandar.
For fantasy, legend, the future, the past
And the veil that men call prophecy
Are but small crossed threads in the weave
Of the vast tapestry of the Infinite."

—Karendo Marha

Contents

PART I

° Prologue °

The only one who truly fears nothing, is
he who does not fear death.

The Tessarandin, Book 3

Rindar was a dreamer…but as the most vivid dreams happen just before waking, he was suddenly aware that this was not a dream. He sat up, shook his head and shivered, partly because of the throbbing at the base of his skull and partly to wake himself into the gray dawn that filtered through the window to his left. He could not remember where he was.

He put his hands to his face, intending to sweep back his hair. There was blood everywhere. His hands were covered with it, and as he looked down, he saw that his shirt was caked and stiff to the touch. Spatters of it covered the rough wood floor where he sat sweating from the heat of the stuffy room.

He shook his head again and tried to stand up, struggling to remember any detail of how he had come to be where he was. He was on his

13

knees when the first flicker of remembrance darted through the clouds in his mind. The old man—

Rindar's memory descended on him suddenly, with violent urgency. In an involuntary motion his right hand went for the holster under his left arm where his hazarine should have been. It was empty. He rose to his feet, unsure where he wanted them to carry him. Thoughts of escape flooded his mind, but he was riveted to the floor, knowing that he could not leave the tiny kitchen without ridding himself of the blood. He reached for his hazarine again as an image of the old man flickered into his mind.

He scanned the small room from where he stood. The only door was behind him and it was still locked. In front of him was the table where he had confronted the old man, and the small carved box still sat on top of it where the man had offered it to him. The chair behind the table was pushed back carelessly, and beyond it, the tidy cupboards and sink seemed to be the only part of the room that had escaped the blood-bath, a bloodbath Rindar had no recollection of.

He moved carefully to the left of the table, past the empty waste bin on the floor; and as he passed the window, he glanced out onto the street two levels below. With the gray dawn had come the slow creep of the morning commute. Beings and vehicles pushed and shoved their way to some busy-ness that would occupy them for the rest of the day. Rindar would have to do his share, he knew, but not with blood on his hands; so he made his way to the small sink in the counter behind the chair. The faucet creaked as he turned on the water, and he scrubbed his hands in the cold trickle to remove the dried blood from under his fingernails.

The old man's eyes rose in his mind. There was something about them—the way he had stared, as if he could see Rindar's vorn in its entirety—deep into the very core of who he was. They had looked famil-iar and sad, but the most significant thing was the lack of fear. He had offered Rindar tea. Tea? At two in the morning with a hazarine leveled at his chest, the old man wanted to know if he wanted some tea.

Rindar hurried. As he scrubbed, he wondered where the old man could be. Perhaps he had gone for the marshals after knocking him out, or maybe someone had taken his body. He reached up to probe the lump on the back of his head. It was tender to the touch. If he had killed the man, how did he get the lump?

The smell of the half-dried blood was beginning to sicken Rindar. He carefully unbuttoned his shirt, stripping it off as if letting it touch any other part of his body would push him beyond his ability to restrain himself from retching into the sink. His thoughts slipped once again to his hazarine. He glanced over his shoulder as he dropped the shirt into the sink. Perhaps it was under the chair or the table. The hazarine had misfired—that had happened before, but what disturbed him most was that the old man somehow knew that it would. "Put your hazarine down," he had said. "It isn't going to work anyway."

The blood had not dried completely and softened under the flow of the tepid water from the spigot. Rindar scrubbed the cloth between his hands and wrung the water out of it repeatedly, letting the dark water run down the drain and disappear. The shirt would be wet but at least it would be clean.

His knife! He bent over to feel the sheath strapped to his left leg. That was gone too. A wave of panic overtook his vorn and reason slipped away. He grabbed the shirt and twisted it into a knot, trying to get the last drops out before he put it back on. He knew it would be cold, but still, he gasped involuntarily as he pulled it on. Moving quickly past the table, he went to his knees in a last effort to see if either the hazarine or knife was under something in the room. The blood on the floor stuck to his hands again. His heart raced.

To the sink again, scrubbing furiously as the nauseating smell overwhelmed his senses. Another wave of panic welled up inside. *Out!* it shouted. *Get out now!* He grabbed the carved box off the table. When he lifted it, he remembered the coins the man on the street had given him. He reached down and felt for them in his pocket. It seemed that they were all still there, but he did not have time to look at them. He shoved the carved box up under his arm and headed toward the door, noticing again through the fog of his fear that the door was still bolted from the inside. He worked the bolt free.

The hall was empty and quiet. The air seemed fresh compared to the stifling atmosphere of the bloody kitchen. Rindar moved quickly, descending the flight of stairs without a sound and running headlong through the small shop below the kitchen. He burst through the front door into the safety of the endless stream of beings.

Rindar moved east along the street, hugging the strange box. It smelled old, and its musty wooden scent wafted to his nostrils, mingled with the smell of the petrotruck exhaust and the peculiar odor of the city's sidewalks. The chill of the slight breeze that pressed his shirt against his body made him shiver, and he clutched the box tighter as he began to trot.

When he came to the end of the second block, he had to stop to wait for the traffic that swirled through the huge crossroads of the central business district of Vindarill. On the bank tower across the square, the huge calendar board was being changed. "Eveldar," it read across the top reminding anyone who watched that the third day of the week was just starting. Below that, the month and day were being changed to read "Ulrar 7." Rindar stared at the man who was changing the placard, high above the street on the narrow catwalk below the board, marking the march of days

amid the wonders of the modern city. The tradition of the manual changing of the calendar seemed suddenly ironic. Eveldar: Ulrar 7.

Rindar looked around at the throngs of commuters. No one else *was*
watching. The formal pronouncement of the new day was lost on the
crush of beings whose day had started several hours before. When the
traffic stopped, Rindar started trotting again, hurrying against the chill
toward his empty room at the boarding house where he could get a dry
shirt and several hours of sleep.

✠

In dreams we see the future, or maybe it's
the past,
Or maybe it's a tiny glimpse of insight
deep and vast.

Old Mythinian Rhyme

Rindar hadn't seen the sun for the entire day. The morning drizzle on
the window of his small compartment in the heart of Vindarill
remained as it was most of the day and had obscured what little view he
had of the brick wall across the alley.

Sleep had been nearly impossible, and what little he had managed
to get was fitful and full of opaque thoughts and twisted glimpses into
the events of the night before. Several times his dreams led him to the
docks where hundreds of gulls tore at the carcass of the old man who
sat without moving as they feasted on the flesh of his arms and back.
Each time the man looked up at him, he would beckon Rindar to join
him. Rindar would wake up shaking.

He got up just before dusk, stumbled down the hall to the bath-
room he shared with the other residents of the boarding house and
splashed his face with cold water to make sure he was fully awake. No
one else was home, and he reflected thankfully on his solitude as he
arranged his pack so that the strange box would fit into it.

He had not found the hazarine. Fortunately, he wore its holster
under his work tunic so that no one would notice it was missing. He
rarely needed it in the tunnels, and he knew that Minxa would have his
if they ran into any trouble that night. The missing boot knife bothered
him more, but he was not sure whether this was because he missed the
security of it strapped to his leg or because he did not know where it was.

Rindar trudged to the sub transit station in the dim evening fog,
going against the tide of beings heading back to their homes for the
night. It was a short ride from the station to the downtown tunnel
entrances where he planned to meet Minxa. Rindar found much com-

fort in his relationship with Minxa, though he often wondered why, for they were much the same and very different at the same time. Both were viddiks, a scurrilous epithet describing their ethnic heritage; and both were orphans, victims of the oppression routinely inflicted on indigenous Morlans by descendants of the Moorimans who had first come to Morlan hundreds of years before.

They had met in the boarding school where Rindar's mother had left him when he was seven. Minxa was a year older than Rindar, but their friendship had been immediate. All through school, they played together, studied together and then finally, had gotten a job together in the tunnels.

When they started working two years before, their supervisor had assigned them to the Search Detail, a band of young men whose task it was to search out the uncharted branches of the caves as the drillers discovered them. Each night, he joined the group, and they received their assignment to explore newly found passages. Minxa was his partner. They had spent countless hours together, charting the spurs to which they were assigned. It was dangerous work, but they were viddiks, and they considered themselves fortunate to have a job at all.

Along with the job came the hazarine. His handheld hazarine could deliver a bolt of energy sufficient to knock out or kill another being. Rindar was allowed to carry it legally for self-defense in the tunnels, but its use for any other purpose was highly illegal.

Minxa was leaning against one of the stone pillars at the entrance to the tunnels. "You feeling better?"

Rindar shook his head.

"You look terrible."

"I feel terrible."

"Can you work tonight?"

"I'm fine."

"You sure?"

"Get off my back, will you?"

"Did you bring it?"

"Shhhhhh—it's in my pack," Rindar whispered to Minxa, shoving his thumb over his shoulder at the battered leather detail pack he had been given as part of the gear used in the cave. "Later!"

They said nothing else as they walked down the long stairs to the tram that would take them to the latest drilling operation. No one spoke on the tram. Rindar was not sure why; it was just a custom. When they came to a stop, the ten searchers clambered off the tram, and it disappeared back up the tunnel. Somewhere down one of the tunnels to his right, Rindar could hear the drilling machines grinding their way into the solid rock that supported the city.

He and Minxa got their assignment from their supervisor without ceremony, then scattered with the group for their night's work. They had barely started down the first hole when Minxa broke the uneasy silence. "So—so what happened?"

"When?"

"Last night—this morning…"

Rindar took his time. He was not sure exactly where to start; he never was. He had learned that he could probably start anywhere and eventually pull it all together, and Minxa did have a knack for patience as he sorted out his feelings. "I'm not sure exactly. I went after that guy you picked out the other day."

"And?"

"It was strange from the very start—"

"Strange?"

"Well, as I was leaving the transit station in the square, a man sitting on the curb asked me for money. When I told him I didn't have any, he stood up. He was huge."

"Did you see his face?"

"No. He was in the shadows and it was dark. I started to reach for my hazarine, and he asked, 'Would you like to have some money?' I backed away, headed on my way. 'If you bring the old wooden box to me, I will give you so much money that you will never have to work again,' he said. I kept walking, but he followed me. I drew my hazarine and turned to face him."

"You still couldn't see him?"

"No. Then he just stopped, held out his hands and said, 'The only thing the old man has is a wooden box, Rindar. If you get it for me, you will never have to work again.' His accent was very strange. I had never heard anything like it. Then he bent down, set five silver coins on the curb and backed away. 'This is a deposit,' he said as he held up a bag of coins and shook them. 'The rest is for you, if you bring me the box.' 'Who are you?' I asked. 'I am Vashtor; I will find you.' He backed into an alley and vanished."

"You took the coins?" Minxa asked.

"Yes, but when I woke up, two of them were gone."

"What do you mean, when you woke up?"

"Well, let me finish—"

They were walking through the low tunnels, waving their lights back and forth over the floor, walls and ceiling, looking for fissures that might lead somewhere else. Their job was to explore anything and everything they could crawl into. They had not found anything yet.

"I got to the shop about one…pitch black…I figured he would be sleeping, so I went into the kitchen first. I pushed the door open silently.

As I stepped through the door and started playing my light…well, he was sitting at the table—in the middle of the kitchen."

"Sitting in the dark; just sitting?"

"It was almost as if he expected me…he knew my name."

Minxa stopped and Rindar turned to face him. "What are you saying?" Minxa's face was ashen and his jaw hung slack.

"I was standing just inside the door—I had shut it behind me—and he said, 'Hello, Rindar.' I started backing to the door and he said, 'Don't go, Rindar.'"

"What did you do?"

"C'mon, we need to keep moving." Rindar waved to Minxa to follow, and they started down the tunnel again. "I froze. After a moment, I found the light switch. When I saw him behind the table, he seemed bigger than when we saw him earlier. Maybe it was because of his shadow."

The clean floor of the tunnel was suddenly littered with fragments of stone. Rindar swung his light toward the ceiling. Directly above them, a fissure ran up and to the right; their first exploration for the night. "Help me get up there," he said. Rindar was smaller than Minxa, and whenever they needed to go up, it was Minxa's job to do the lifting. Rindar braced himself against the wall and stood up into Minxa's cradled hands, reaching up to the walls of the crevice with his hands on the freshly broken stone. The handholds were good. In a matter of seconds, he had hauled himself up far enough to get his feet braced into the walls. "Shadow me until I find a landing."

Minxa played his light up the crack ahead of him as Rindar toiled upward, stopping occasionally to use his own light. He was twenty feet above Minxa when he stopped. "I'm there," he called, pulling off his pack and setting it on the shelf beside him. He uncoiled a rope from his pack, made a sling around a corner of the fractured stone and dropped the free end down to Minxa. In less than a minute, his friend was sitting beside him on the shelf above the tunnel.

"Which way?" Rindar asked. "Up or flat?"

"I want to know more about what happened last night."

"I'll finish when we get a break—up or flat?"

"On the flat. Don't feel like climbing right now." Minxa swung his legs up onto the shelf and rolled over onto his belly moving like a snake into the horizontal crack, barely high enough for his body to get through. "Shadow me."

Rindar lay flat, cradling his lantern so the beam moved just in front of where Minxa wormed his way along about twenty feet in front of him. Minxa stopped suddenly and let out a low whistle. Rindar saw him scramble to his feet and watched Minxa's lantern playing around the walls briefly before Minxa bent down where Rindar could see his astonished face. "C'mon, you gotta see this."

He didn't need to be told twice. Rindar was good at this, and it was only moments before he had covered the distance to where Minxa stood. They were in a small room, perhaps five paces in diameter and just tall enough so that if they jumped they could have touched the stone overhead. They had been in many stone rooms before, but this was unusual in that it seemed to have been deliberately shaped. It was nearly circular and the ceiling was slightly arched. The floor of the room had fallen just enough to create the crack that they had used as an entrance. The crack continued on the other side. In the center of the room was a stone cylinder about the height of a small table and half the diameter of the room. It was difficult to tell whether it was a natural formation or not.

"This is just weird," whispered Minxa. "We're in the middle of solid rock!"

Rindar had a sudden thought. He slung his pack from his back and dropped it onto the stone table. He opened it, pulled the carved box from inside and set it carefully on the stone table, pushing his pack onto the floor. "Open it," he said.

"Me? Why me?"

"I don't know. Just open it."

Minxa flipped open the stand on his lantern and set it on the table so that the beam illuminated the intricately carved box. The angle of the light intensified the relief of the carved surface. He shook his head, "You're crazy."

"Maybe."

Minxa's hands lifted the cover of the box and slid it to the right, laying it gently on the table. "All right, it's open."

"Take out the paper—and unfold it."

"Why me?"

"It has to be you—c'mon."

Minxa sighed, "All right, but you owe me one." He worked his index fingers under the edge of the folded material in the box until he was able to lift it gently. Rindar watched as he unfolded it and laid it flat on the stone. Rindar lifted his own lamp into position opposite Minxa's.

It was clearly a map, perhaps three-feet long and two-feet wide. As it settled to the table, the folds almost disappeared, and it lay nearly flat on the uneven stone surface. Rindar had never seen anything like it in detail or decoration. He looked at it closely, and the closer he looked, the more detail there was, almost as if the depth of it was infinite.

Ancient symbols decorated its border, each perfectly inked onto the surface in small circles, but it was unclear what the proper orientation of it was since most of the glyphs were unrecognizable. In one corner was a simplified drawing of Asolara, Tessalindria's sun, and opposite it a globe that looked exactly like Tessalindria itself. In the other corners were perfect drawings of Tal and Meekar, the twin Tessalindrian moons.

"What is it?" Minxa asked.

"It's a map," Rindar replied, "and I have this vague feeling I should know more about it—something distant." Without thinking, he reached over and touched the image of Asolara in the corner. A wave of light swept over the map's surface. Minxa jumped back. A moment later Rindar touched the sun again, and another wave of light moved across its surface, leaving a faint glow behind it. Rindar turned off his lamp and reached across to turn off Minxa's.

Minxa caught his hand. "Don't."

Rindar looked up. "I know what it is, Minxa," he said, "and if I am right, what we have here—" He did not know what his next words should be.

"What?"

"It's Lonama's map." Even as he said it, Rindar felt a shudder run through him.

"Whose map?"

"Lonama's map. Do you remember any history—the legends—there was always this map that—"

"How do you know this is it?"

"It has to be. Turn off your light for just a minute." As Minxa reached for his light, Rindar touched Asolara again, holding his finger on it for a moment. The map glowed orange in the total darkness of the rock chamber. Rindar could see every detail.

"This is incredible!" exclaimed Minxa. The warm glow of the map illuminated Minxa's face and body enough so that his expression of disbelief was readily discernable.

Rindar looked back down. "Any idea what it's a map of?" he asked, leaning closer to see the details. Odd shapes and jagged pathways branched out from a small circular center, and two faint blotches of light emanated from the edges of the center circle. They both stared at the map, struggling to discern its contents.

It was Minxa who realized it first, but he had barely opened his mouth when Rindar suddenly knew what it was: "It's a map of this cave!" they said simultaneously.

Rindar was troubled. He felt a creeping fear inside as he looked up into Minxa's eyes. He saw it there too. He wondered how the old man could have had a map of this part of the tunnels. The tunnel below had only been drilled out yesterday while Rindar slept, after their encounter. It was impossible.

Impossible. The old man had said something about things that were impossible: "Sometimes the greatest truth is discovered when we are forced to accept the impossible."

Minxa interrupted his thoughts. "This is beyond strange. What did you call this thing? Whose map?"

It all came together in a twisted jumble of thoughts. "Lonama's map. Now it's coming back."

"What?"

"Lonama's map is a map of Tessalindria. It contains everything. If I remember correctly, it even contains information about different times. Most people do not believe it ever existed—but this fits—look," he said pointing to the center of the map. "When we opened it up, it centered on where we are. Right here in the middle is this little room we are standing in; that is the tunnel where we entered, and here is the crack down to the tunnel. Even the tunnel that was just drilled today is there!"

Minxa ran his finger over the jagged path leading in the opposite direction. "It looks as if it leads to another room just like this, and there's another beyond that, and—" His finger trailed off the edge of the map. "And it's oriented perfectly!"

Rindar grabbed the corner of the map and gave it a quick pull, rotating the entire piece slightly on the table. The twisting paths and rooms remained where they were. "Incredible! Turn on your light; we have some exploring to do." He picked up the map in the middle where it would fold as he lifted it. It yielded to his touch, and as he raised it from the table it folded perfectly, its light extinguishing as it did so. It seemed to Rindar that the map folded itself. As he laid it in the box, it fit perfectly into the shallow recess in the wood. "To the next room," he said as he slung his pack over his shoulder. "We'll check it again there."

✠

The brightest truth is often discovered in the darkness.

Sessasha
It Is Said

Rindar was already ahead of him, moving fast along the rough floor, confident in what he had seen in the map—that down the next crack was another chamber. Minxa was anxious. There was something about the map that unsettled him, and he still had not heard the details of how Rindar had acquired it. Something big had happened, and Rindar was reluctant to give up the story.

Minxa lay on his back this time. With the ceiling so close, he had to turn his head sideways to get through the lowest part. No matter how many times he did this, it still chilled him when he thought about the tons of rock resting an inch above his head.

"It's here!" Rindar's voice was full of excitement. "It's exactly like the other one." Minxa could see the splashes of light on the rock around him as Rindar shadowed him. In less than a minute, he stood beside his friend. Rindar opened the box and laid the map out so the corner with the sun was closest to Minxa. Minxa reached out and put his finger on it. Nothing happened.

Rindar looked up at Minxa, then reached across and touched the same spot. The map flashed orange and its light illuminated their faces. Minxa was not sure exactly what he felt, but it was something he didn't like and could not shrug off. It was some scramble of resentment, fear and anger.

Rindar bent to study the map, apparently unaware of Minxa's feelings. "Exactly what we thought," he said. "There's the chamber we came from—there's the next one—look at this!" Minxa bent to see what Rindar was pointing at. His fingertip touched the middle of the room they were in. "Those smudges of light—in the other chamber. They're *here* now."

Rindar was right. Before Minxa had time to think, Rindar ran around the table so that he stood beside him. One of the small smudges of light moved so the two smudges were right beside each other. "That's us—do you see it—that's us!" The excitement seemed to overwhelm his voice for a moment. "Never in my wildest—"

Rindar was interrupted by a faint sound echoing into the small chamber. It sounded like a piece of metal falling into a crevice in the rocks, and it came from where they had been. They looked at each other, and Minxa saw Rindar's index finger go to his lips as he reached into his tunic for his hazarine with his other hand. A frown swept over his face as he pulled his hand out a moment later. It was empty. Rindar started to pick up the map and then pressed it suddenly onto the stone again. Sliding his hand along the route they had taken to get where they were, he traced back to a point where he found two faint smudges of light, almost off the edge of the map; then quickly moving his hand the other way, he pointed to where they had to go: the next chamber.

Rindar grabbed the map and folded it into the box. As he dropped the lid into place, he signaled, *"Hand signs!"* Minxa and Rindar had developed a way to talk by pressing signs into each other's palms.

"All right, silent," Minxa signed back.

"Lights out." Minxa switched off his light as soon as Rindar had stuffed the map into his pack. They moved toward the passage he had indicated. It was dangerous to travel in the dark like this, but not a new experience for Minxa. The sensation was always the same. The difference

this time was that Minxa did not know why; he trusted Rindar's sense of
alarm, though he did not feel it. By agreement, Minxa followed. The
awareness of danger in the tunnels was something that was never ques-
tioned, and Minxa knew he would have to wait to find out what it was
about. For now, he followed.

Rindar already stood over the map when Minxa arrived in the third
chamber. It was barely glowing so that it cast no shadow, and Rindar was
only faintly illuminated by its glow. He stared down at it. The first of the
two smudges of light was in the crack leading to the first chamber and
the other was still on the shelf above the fissure. Rindar's finger was tracing a route beyond the chamber where they were. Several cracks led in
various directions; one of them was vertical and very narrow, leading off
at right angles to the direction they had been traveling.

"Where *hazarine*?" Minxa asked.

"*Later.*" Rindar folded the map and stuffed it into his pack again.
The darkness swallowed them. Minxa felt a tug on his shirt in the direction of the vertical crack. They squirmed into it. "*Up,*" Rindar pushed
into his palm. It was slow and difficult in the dark, but after about ten
feet, the crack opened onto a narrow shelf. The crack turned so that they
could not see back down into the chamber. "*Stop. Quiet. Hiding. Listen.*"
They were both breathing heavily.

"*Who?*" Minxa asked.

"*Listen!*"

They sat still on the narrow shelf. As they waited in the darkness,
Minxa's thoughts swirled through his mind. He wondered what the
sound was that they had heard originally. Perhaps one of their pursuers
had dropped a safety link. It would be unusual for the supervisor to
send two crews anywhere near each other without a good reason. He
knew Rindar would know that, which would account for some of his
suspicion, but the near panic of Rindar's actions seemed unwarranted.
Rindar did not have his hazarine, another reason for his fear. Minxa's
bigger concern was that this was somehow tied to something that
Rindar had not yet told him about the affair with the old man. Perhaps
it was the map. If it was as incredible and as old as it seemed to be, how
would Rindar have gotten it, and why didn't he know what it was if he
had bothered to take it?

A faint scraping interrupted his thoughts, and Rindar's grip tightened on his arm.

"They must have come this way." It was a faint whisper, but the
crack channeled it up to them.

"But where now?" whispered the second voice.

"Shhhhh."

Minxa and Rindar echoed their silence and for a long time there was no sound; perhaps it was a minute, perhaps two, until a deep sigh broke the silence. "I don't hear them, do you?"

"No. Not a sound."

"We were told they are two of the best. If they don't want to be found, it probably won't be us that finds them." Their pursuer spoke in a normal voice, as if the need for silence had been lost, and a sudden beam of light burst forth from the chamber. It really wasn't much, but in the darkness, it was profoundly bright. "And the other searchers won't help."

"Are you sure?"

"Not completely, but there is a certain code with these guys."

"Could we bribe them?"

"Doubt it."

Minxa felt Rindar squeeze his arm.

"And exactly why did we have to come after them in here? Couldn't we just pick them up later?"

"The Protag wanted him apprehended immediately."

"Why?"

"I actually don't know all the details, but the hazarine that was found belongs to this Rindar character, though it seems to have nothing to do with the crime."

"Do they know what really happened?"

"It's not very clear. The shopkeeper discovered it this morning, but it is very strange, and we don't even know if anyone even died."

"What do you mean?"

"Well, there was no body, but there was so much blood that if it was all from one being, he never could have survived."

"Maybe there was more than one."

"There *were* two bloods—probably enough of both of them for two deaths. They are being checked to see if there is a match to this Rindar character. The Protag said that there are no records for the tenant in the apartment."

"No records?"

"The shop owner didn't know him very well. She said he was a viddik who came into town a couple weeks ago and needed a place to stay. She was letting him stay in her third floor room as a favor to a friend."

"Where was the shop owner when all this happened?"

"She was out, but would not say where. The Protag suspects that she is Sessashian, so he is trying to find out. If she is, she was probably out at some secret meeting, and that would make it unlikely that she was involved in a murder. She said the door to the kitchen was locked and so were the windows when she came home. In addition, we don't think anyone could have removed a body that was bleeding that badly without other traces of blood on the stairs."

"Yevil Sessashians!" the second voice muttered. "And the hazarine?"

"Right on top of the desk—and a small knife on the floor with the dagger. We suspect the dagger was the weapon for the killing. They also found an old coin."

"What do you mean, 'old'?"

"A Tessamandrian twenty dragith in perfect condition. Pure silver from what I hear, right in the middle of the floor and covered with blood."

"Dragiths? They haven't been around since—very weird."

"Two others, exactly like it showed up the day before yesterday at a pawn shop on the waterfront in a raid that the Protag ordered."

Rindar's grip was cutting off the circulation in Minxa's arm. Minxa reached up his hand and pried his fingers open.

"*You?*" he pressed into Rindar's palm.

"*Yes. Later,*" came the reply.

"*No.*"

"*Yes.*"

Minxa's head swam. The voices from the chamber droned into the mundane conversation of two men who no longer had anything specific to talk about, and they faded from his awareness. He sat in a strange stupor, hoping that what he had heard was not what he thought he had heard.

✠

Distance and time twist every memory.

Hispattea
The Essences of Corritanean Wisdom

"I don't know how I lost my hazarine," Rindar explained, "but I know it wasn't on the table when I left." He was as frustrated as Minxa for an explanation. "And neither was the knife. I looked for it. The only thing on the table was the box with the map."

"What about the dagger?"

"There wasn't any dagger!"

"You think you're being framed?"

"By who?"

"How would I know?" Minxa shrugged. "Perhaps the old man was in on it."

"I don't know how he could have been."

"Maybe the big man you met on the street. What was his name?"

"Vashtor. I thought about that, but I got the map and he never came to find me. And why would he frame me? I'm just a viddik—there's nothing for anyone to get from me." As he said the words, he remembered the three remaining silver coins. He reached into his pocket, pulled one of them out and held it close to Minxa's lantern. "Look at this," he said.

Minxa bent in close to see the coin. "It's very old."

"I've never seen anything like it," Rindar mused. "It's thick too—a lot of silver here. I'm sure we can use it if we get out of here." He stuffed the coin back into his pocket.

Minxa shook his head.

"Like I said," Rindar continued, "it was strange from the first moment." He and Minxa were standing in the small room, having waited on the shelf for probably three hours after their pursuers had left. "Only one thing is sure right now."

"Yeah? What's that?"

"I can't go back—" He could see Minxa staring at him. "And neither can you."

"Why not?"

"Well, I'm sure not going back, and if you do, they will be all over you. You're just a viddik like me, and you know they'll clean you. You won't stand a chance."

"If you're not going back, what will you do? They'll have this place guarded like a prison, so how're we gonna get outta here?"

"They can't guard all the holes in this hill. Besides—" Rindar smiled as he spread his hand out over the map, "we have a map to everywhere."

"That's true—and we've found vent holes before," Minxa said, "and there must be others. You got any food?"

"Just some crackers I snagged from the cupboard this morning. You?"

"None." Minxa frowned. He was always hungry and he loved to eat.

"Well then, we better make it quick," Rindar said as he leaned over the map. "I don't think we should go back that way."

They stared at the map together. With a little more time to study it, Rindar noticed some of the other details. There were probably a hundred of the little circles with symbols in them around the perimeter of the map, varying in size from one another. The boldness of each symbol was different. Rindar guessed that they all meant something, but had no clue where to start, and the prospect of just pushing each one made him uneasy.

"If this is really a map of everywhere," said Minxa, "then there must be a way to move it around, wouldn't you guess?"

"Yes, but it's a bit scary, though I don't see much of a choice. I don't recognize any of this." He laid his finger on one of the circles that had a small black square inside it. Nothing happened.

"How about this one," said Minxa, pointing to a circle containing an arrow spiraling into the center.

Rindar touched it. The image on the map receded, leaving them in the center, but covering a much larger area. He touched it again and it receded further. "Incredible!" he muttered. The map now covered an area fifty times larger than before. They could see the larger drilled tunnels radiating outward from "Main Street" as they called the large vaulted cavern that formed the core of the system.

"How about this one?" Minxa had his finger on a circle with another small circle in it off to one side.

"Okay, you push it."

"I did, it doesn't seem to work for me."

Rindar moved over and touched the spot where Minxa's finger had been. The map shifted again so that the spot where they were on the map was off to one side. "That works," he said absently as he placed his index finger on the small circle representing the room they were in and dragged it across the map. The map obeyed and shifted to follow his finger. "Now we are getting somewhere." He smiled, then added, "That's enough for now. Let's find a way out." He dragged the room across the map so that the direction they had come from was almost off the edge, and the map showed all the cracks and crevices where they could go. He looked up at Minxa. "Pick a path."

Minxa ran his finger along one of the wider cracks carrying them away from Main Street. "That one!" he said.

Rindar folded the map into its case and slipped it into his pack. "Then that one it is," he said as he pulled the pack up onto his shoulder and plunged into the fissure before him. He was not at all sure where it would lead, but right then, that didn't matter.

✠

> The seed of discord is so small that it often cannot be seen until it has taken root.
>
> Old Tessamandrian Saying

Minxa sat on the cold stone floor of a small chamber and watched Rindar examine the map. It was envy, he had decided, with a twist of jealousy. He was envious of Rindar because of the map and jealous of his longtime friend as well. It was not so much that Rindar had the map and seemed to be the only one who could make it work, but that the map drew some kind of line in their relationship. Yet perhaps it was not the map at all, but just Minxa's own suspicion. Either way, he did not like the feelings that swept through him as he drained the last drop of water from his flask.

"We haven't been able to stand up for an hour," he said. "Haven't seen any water either."

"Hmmmm." Rindar had both elbows on the map, and his chin rested heavily into his palms. "We have been going up—which is good, and I'm thinking there has to be an opening somewhere."

"Why?" Even as he said it, Minxa hated the cynicism it conveyed.

Rindar looked up at him. "You know we can't go back," he said, "so the only hope we have is to find an opening. Problem is, we are not yet outside the rim of the city."

"How do you know *that*?"

"I think I figured out how to see different depths on the map, and right now, I think we are directly under East Wegan, and not far from the rim." Minxa watched him drag his index finger across the map as the features of the map transformed under the motion. Rindar went back to studying the map.

Minxa rubbed his knees. "My knees are killing me," he said, "even with these pads."

"Mine too."

Minxa could tell Rindar was only half there, absorbed by the map. Minxa sat silently, studying his friend. They had been through so much together. They were like twins in a hostile, hopeless world that gave them no quarter. He knew he could not go back. Even if he evaded the authorities, or if for some reason they did not care about him, living in Vindarill without Rindar would be lonely.

"Hmmm," Rindar intoned. "What do you make of this?"

Minxa rolled over onto his elbow to see where Rindar was pointing.

"We're right here," Rindar said, his left index finger placed on the map where they were sitting. "But look over here." His right index finger sat next to a place in the map that was completely black, almost like a hole.

"That *is* curious."

"I think we should go there."

Minxa wasn't so sure. They really did not know that much about the map. Rindar had figured a few things out, but the black spot just looked like a hole. "Holes have to go somewhere, I guess," Minxa said.

"My guess is that it does, but we don't know how to find out."

"Any clue from the map?"

"No."

"Makes me nervous," Minxa confessed.

"Me too, but we don't have a lot to lose, do we?"

Minxa had no answer to this, but that made him more nervous.

"Let's go," said Rindar. "It's not far and we can find out what it's about. When we get there, we can decide what to do."

"My knees are killing me," Minxa groaned again.

"So are mine, but they'll kill us no matter which direction we go, right?" Rindar said as he folded the map into its strange box. "You have any idea how long our lights will last?"

"Long time. I changed the power pack in mine before we left— whenever it was—my guess is it'll last a month. What we need is water."

"I have a little left, and there's got to be some here somewhere."

"If we don't die, or kill ourselves first," Minxa muttered. Rindar was already on his back, inching under a huge stone into the passage leading toward the blackness. As much as Minxa did not like it, he had no rational alternative. At least the first step didn't require him to be on his knees.

✠

Sometimes the only way out is through.

Oratanga
Passages

The route to the black spot on the map had been treacherous. In several places, they had had to take risks that, under ordinary circumstances, they would avoid, but these were not ordinary circumstances. As they had approached the location on the map, Rindar could sense a freshening of the still air of the cave, a sure sign that there was an opening to the outside somewhere.

"What do you think?" Rindar did not know himself, and he guessed that Minxa would not either, but it opened the conversation. For the first time in two hours, they were able to stand. Their backs were against a wall.

The room was small and flooded with fresh air. The high ceiling was out of their reach, and only the half of the room in which they stood was visible. Ten feet in front of them, the room disappeared into a blackness that defied description. Minxa had dropped his light into a crevice on their way to this room, so Rindar pointed his beam toward the nothingness.

"No clue," said Minxa as he bent down and scraped some dust off the smooth floor, "but I don't like it." He tossed the dust into the beam of Rindar's lamp where it met the darkness. The beam shone through the dust, but where it hit the darkness, it looked like someone had chopped it off with a knife.

"The fresh air seems to be coming out of it," said Rindar. "There must be an opening on the other side."

"Must be?"

"Well, where else could it be coming from?" Rindar could tell that Minxa was nervous, and he did not really expect an answer. He bent down and picked up a stone. When he tossed it into the blackness, it vanished at about the same point that the light stopped. There was no sound whatsoever.

"Try this one." Minxa bent down and grabbed a stone that filled both hands.

"Go ahead—"

Minxa lifted the stone to his chest and pushed it into the black wall. The darkness swallowed it in utter silence. He stood with his mouth open, staring at the spectacle in front of him.

"Here, hold the light," said Rindar. He bent down, took the rope from the back of his pack and uncoiled several arm lengths, then coiled the free end loosely before tossing it into the darkness. The coil disappeared. The point where the rope entered the blackness remained the same, as if the end of the rope had become weightless. He slowly pulled it. It came back toward him, hovering in the nothingness until the end came out. It fell slack at his feet.

"Can't the map tell us anything?" Minxa asked.

"I don't think so, but maybe now that we are closer—" He unfolded the map. The black spot on the map was almost in the center, and he could see both his and Minxa's light smudges standing before it. It gave no clue what was beyond it. "Nothing. Nothing at all."

"Maybe one of the buttons—"

"Maybe, but which one?" Rindar tried touching several of the circles around the perimeter of the map. None of them changed the appearance of the map or altered the black spot in any way that they could see. "Maybe one of us should try it."

"One of us?" asked Minxa.

Rindar stared at Minxa, who was staring back at him. "Have you ever noticed how often you answer statements with a question?"

Minxa smiled. "Well, one of us is sure not going to be me! Have you ever noticed how many times you make statements about something you think, assuming I also think it?"

Rindar reached down and grabbed the end of the rope and started wrapping it around his waist. "Maybe I should try it."

"Try what?"

Rindar stopped tying his knot and looked up, smiling. Minxa stared back. "You hold on to the rope. I am going to try something."

"You're crazy."

"Maybe. Do you have a better idea?"

"None, except—"

"Forget it. We can't go back."

"We?"

"*I'm* not going back." Rindar was testing the knot on the sling he had tied around his waist. He looked up. "You can go back if you want, but belay me through this thing before you leave, hmmm?"

"You *are* crazy."

Rindar had turned and stepped up to the blackness. When he put his hand up against it, there was no sensation at all, and his heart pounded as he slowly pushed his hand into the infinite dark wall. He felt nothing except his own hand and a slight cooling of the air around it. Fear suddenly overtook him, and he pulled it back suddenly. Nothing had changed.

"What does it feel like?"

"Nothing...nothing at all." Rindar got down on one knee, sliding his hand along the floor into the blackness. The floor seemed solid. "I think I can walk into it."

"What about the light? We only have the one."

"Give it to me for a moment—there is something else I need to try." Minxa handed him the light. Rindar turned it in his hand so it was shining back toward him. When he plunged it into the black wall, the light vanished. Rindar panicked, yanking his hand back toward him. The light seemed to turn on as it emerged into the chamber. "Somehow I don't think the light will be of any use in there," said Rindar slowly. "You keep it. If I find I need it, I'll come back and get it."

"You're not really going in there, are you?" Minxa was incredulous.

"You've got my rope, and you've never failed me before," Rindar said. "If I give three tugs, pull me out. Two tugs, tie the end around yourself and follow me in."

"Not a chance."

"Listen. If I am safe enough to give you two tugs, it will be safe enough for you to follow, right?" Rindar could see the doubt in Minxa's eyes. "I'm taking the map."

"Wouldn't do me any good anyway," Minxa said, his face suddenly overcome with sullen resignation.

Rindar turned to face the darkness. He stepped forward, pushed both hands into it and slid his left foot forward, feeling the floor as it disappeared from his vision. Glancing back over his shoulder he smiled into Minxa's terror. "See you on the other side," he said as he stepped forward into the unknown.

✠

The blackness of the portal is like none other, wrapping the vorn with a nothingness that defies words or thoughts.

Tristaron Harrista
The Kirrinath

Minxa was shaking. Rindar had completely disappeared from his view, and the rope, wrapped around his own waist, was slowly inching into the inky black wall in front of him. "Rindar!" he shouted. "Rindar!" His voice sounded shrill and tight in the stone chamber.

The rope crept forward, stopping now and then for brief pauses. The lamp lay on the floor beside him because he needed both hands for a safe belay. He knew that he could not resist a full fall of Rindar's weight, and there was nothing in the chamber to tie in to, so he braced himself with one foot on a protrusion of stone in front of him. He knew he had to be ready, but even so, it happened so quickly he could not control it.

The rope jerked tight. Minxa tried to play it out, but the force of it pulled him off balance, and he stepped forward into a loop of the rope. It pulled through his hands, and the loop pulled tight up between his legs, wrapping tightly around his left thigh; and in the next instant, he was catapulted forward into his greatest fear. The "No!" that tried to escape his lips was swallowed into nothingness.

For a brief instant, he felt himself being dragged along the floor of the cave; and then almost as quickly, he was free falling. He tried to yell, but the darkness swallowed his words. Then suddenly everything stopped swirling, and he found himself standing on solid ground. The total blackness surrounding him dulled all his senses, and he was paralyzed with fear, knowing that a move in any direction could be disastrous. His light was gone, probably still shining on the floor of the cave behind him. He stood for a long time, before the rope in his hand started moving again, slowly inching its way through his fingers.

He let it play. Rindar must have been somewhere ahead of him. He let the rope out slowly, a bit at a time until it stopped once again. Minxa waited. The only thing he could feel was the rope, idle and slack in his right hand.

Two tugs. He didn't want to believe it. The second two tugs were more urgent so he tugged back. The rope started moving again. He knew he needed to follow it, so he gripped it tightly and started inching forward. The last thing he wanted to do was to fall again.

It seemed like a long time, but Minxa probably only traveled about five paces. Without any warning, he stepped out into the semidarkness of a warm stone chamber to see Rindar sitting on a rock three feet in front of him. He was holding the rope and grinning from ear to ear in the weak natural light that filtered down from a crack in the ceiling.

Minxa frowned. "I lost the light," he said.

Rindar jumped up and threw his arms around him, hugging him tightly. "We made it! And look—daylight!"

Minxa was still confused because of what had just happened. "But isn't it close to midnight?" He swung his arm up to look at his watch. It was gone.

"That's what I thought, too, but look." Rindar pointed up into the crack above them. "Blue sky!"

It was true, but very odd. "You still have the map?"

"Yes. It's the only thing I still have. It was strange. I felt like I fell several hundred feet, and then suddenly I was on my feet, but still in the darkness. As I started to move, I felt the map box at my feet, so I scrounged around for my pack. I found it, but it was empty—nothing in it at all."

Minxa felt his pack. It was empty also. "What about the coins?" he asked.

He watched Rindar's hand reach for his pocket. He felt it briefly from the outside, then shoved his hand down into it. He pulled out one coin. "I guess two more are gone," he said.

"Let's get out of here. That darkness makes me nervous." Minxa thought he could feel the cool dark nothingness behind him. "I never, ever, ever, ever, ever want to do that again."

Rindar smiled as he shoved the coin back into his pocket. "It *was* a bit strange, wasn't it?"

"You're strange." Minxa looked up. "And that crack is too small to get out."

"Over here." Rindar was on his knees peering into a low passage. "There's some light at the far end. C'mon."

The room they were in was not a proper cave. It was more of a filled crevasse, where the boulders that formed the ceiling were jammed between the walls, forming a cavity beneath them. Here and there, thin shafts of light found their way through the cracks in the ceiling as Minxa followed Rindar between the two walls of the fissure. There were several tight squeezes along the way, and none of the openings to the surface were big enough to get through.

They took turns going first through each passage, and after passing through several small cavities where they could almost stand up, they came to one tall enough for them to stand. As they stretched, Minxa heard the first rumble. "What was that?"

"Don't know," Rindar said as a worried look swept over his face. They stood still and listened. It happened again: a low, rolling roar that lasted a few seconds, barely audible, even in the silence of the cave. "We'd better get out of here!" They moved quickly, and with their eyes adjusted to the dim light, they were able to make safe progress. The floor dropped down suddenly, and they had to wade through a pool of water that sloshed over their ankles into their shoes. As they climbed up out of the water on the other side, Rindar pointed. "There it is!"

Ten feet above them was a shelf of rock and a small passage leading directly to the outside. Almost by reflex, Minxa bent and cupped his hands. Rindar stepped up as Minxa's strength lifted him easily to bring the shelf within reach. Minxa watched Rindar disappear through the opening. There was silence for a brief moment and then a burst of incredulous profanity. Rindar's head appeared in the opening. "Get up here, fast!"

"What?"

"You gotta see this!" Rindar disappeared again.

"Right," Minxa muttered to himself as he started searching for hand and footholds to climb the few feet so he could reach the shelf. It was an easy climb, and within a minute he was wriggling his way through the shoulder-width hole up into the freedom of the surface. A pungent, aromatic smell greeted him as he emerged. Wherever they were, it was nowhere he had ever been before.

He pulled himself out of the hole and stood up. He looked back in the direction they had come from and followed the caved-in chasm until it disappeared into the trees.

"Up here!" He turned to see Rindar standing on a large rock, pointing urgently, silhouetted against the clear blue sky. Minxa climbed up beside him. Fifty feet below, the blue-green ocean pounded solemnly against the gray rocks that formed the base of the cliff on which they stood. His eyes moved involuntarily to the horizon. Far away, where the ocean met the sky, there was a thin line of land, punctuated with occasional mountains.

Neither he nor Rindar had ever seen the open ocean. Their experience was confined to the still, brackish water of Vindarill's harbor, awash with debris and film. He leaned forward and looked left around a clump of stubby thick evergreens where two gulls rode the rising air currents that flowed up the cliff from the ocean. The land was farther away in that direction. To the right, the ocean met the sky in a thin line of blue on blue, wrapping as far as he could see until it disappeared behind other rocks on the cliff. The smell of the water was different and filled all the senses. The vast flatness and distance to the eyes of a young man who had never left the confines of Vindarill was dizzying. Minxa stepped back.

Rindar smiled, sweeping his hand out toward the water. "It's amazing."

Minxa looked at him. He couldn't deny the statement, but his thoughts terrified him. "Something tells me we aren't in Vindarill anymore," was all he could think to say.

☩

Billy Billy, bub'n scrump, champy's in the cataroup,
Coppa Coppa attabump an' paaddi's got the misselsoup.
Atta filly, atta fro, Izzy harden uppen roar,
Misty is as Misty was, we'll be friends forever more.

Rindar Colloden † Minxa Maharan

Rindar had not seen the map in daylight. It looked the same, but the details were more striking. He had unfolded it onto a flat rock in the sun above the opening to the cave. Wherever they were, it was nowhere near Vindarill, and it was nowhere near anything that he could recognize. The initial scale of the map gave them no clue. It seemed they were on some kind of headland jutting out into the water.

Rindar found the symbol for reducing the map and held it momentarily until the map collapsed.

"We're on an island," gasped Minxa, "and not a very big one from the looks of it."

Rindar noticed that the map had no names on it whatsoever. There were circles on each of the edges of the map that were clustered in exactly the same way, but contained different symbols. Rindar placed his finger on the island and dragged it to the edge of the map away from the distant land on the horizon, then touched the scaling symbol again. He kept his finger there until the land appeared at the other edge of the map. "Well, however big this island is, it's a long way to anywhere else."

"We're not going to get off here in a hurry, so we may as well see what else is here." Minxa sat with his legs crossed in front of him and his head resting heavily in his hands as he spoke.

Rindar nodded and dragged the island to the center of the map. He scaled it until it filled the sheet. "Maybe we should just start walking, and we'll begin to figure out how big all this is."

"Which way?"

"Well, my guess is that if there is anyone on this place they will be somewhere over here, in the shelter of this other island."

Rindar could tell by the twitch of Minxa's hands that something was bothering him. He held a piece of bark between his fingers and was flipping it back and forth. "What's on your vorn, Minxa?"

"I don't believe in the vorn," Minxa said bluntly.

"I'm not sure I do either, but you know what I mean."

"Yeah, hmmm," Minxa responded. "I'm just a bit puzzled about what happened. I mean—where are we, and how did we get so far from Vindarill? We certainly didn't walk that far—and we didn't walk under the ocean either."

"I have a hunch. Do you want to hear it?"

Minxa looked down at the bark scrap in his hands. "The way you said that makes me wonder if I do."

"All right—"

"Don't be cute," Minxa retorted. "Go ahead. I'm gonna have to hear it sometime, I guess."

"Look," Rindar said, forcing Minxa to look up and make eye contact. "I'm not sure I like this any better than you. I didn't know what would happen. But we are far, far from Vindarill, and that has some of its own advantages."

"Really?"

"Nobody is hunting us. It's clean here…so far it seems pretty safe."

"And there's no food—"

"We can find food—and we have an incredible map… "

"Tell me your hunch."

"Don't jump on my head. It's just a hunch."

"I won't," Minxa grumbled.

"Well, do you remember *any* of your history?"

"You asked me that about the map. You know I never liked school."

"I never did either," Rindar said, "but for some reason, I liked history—you must remember some of the legends."

"Yes—and?"

"Well, part of the legend of Lonama's map is that it is a map of all places and all times for the whole of Tessalindria. It even shows the portals if you know how to use it."

"The portals? Do you believe that junk?"

"You got a better explanation for all this?"

"Are you trying to tell me that we went through one of the time portals?"

"It's the best explanation I have. Think about it. We walked through a cave for perhaps a day—several miles at most, wouldn't you say?" Minxa nodded. "And now we are miles and miles from where we started. If it was one of the portals, we may be years away as well."

"Great. That's just great," Minxa sulked.

Rindar hated Minxa's sulking, so he ignored it and continued.

"Judging from the emptiness of this place, we would have to be many hundred years before where we were. I mean, no place in Tessalindria could look like this in our time, do you think?"

Rindar could see Minxa thinking, trying to grasp their situation.

"Can't we just go back through it?"

"I don't know for sure, but I don't think they work that way."

"Maybe you better tell me what you do think."

"It's all a bit vague, but let's see: there are supposed to be eight portals, although, as I remember, there are only seven that have ever been found. Supposedly the eighth remains hidden until Mah'Eladra open it."

Minxa scowled. "Now you believe in Mah'Eladra?"

"I don't know. I'm just telling you what I remember of the legends."

Minxa retreated further into his sulk.

"They are nearly impossible to find without Lonama's map. But I think if you know how to use the map, you can go anywhere—to any time."

"It might explain why this Vashtor was so willing to pay you good money for it," Minxa said.

"I thought about that; but if he knew about it, why didn't he just go get it himself?"

"Good question." Minxa sat and brooded for a moment. "Wait a minute," he said as he sat up straight with an intense look of incredulity. "Did you *think* that the blackness was a portal before you went into it?" he asked.

"Well, I had no proof and—"

Minxa lunged at Rindar and grabbed the front of his shirt with both hands. "You stinkin' viddik—" He stopped in mid-sentence as if he had not thought further than that, and glowered at Rindar. His wild gray eyes stared into Rindar's for about ten seconds, then he pushed Rindar away and turned his back on him. "Don't ever do that again," he mumbled. "It's a violation of psadeq, and right now we have nothing else."

Rindar felt the twinge in his vorn at Minxa's words. In the world of the downtrodden, psadeq with another being was something to be carefully guarded, and his relationship with Minxa was the only psadeq he had ever known. He stared down at the map without seeing it. "I'm sorry," he said. "I should have told you, but whatever else happens, we have to stick together—I know that. Wherever we are—whenever we are—we have to work together, agreed?" He waited silently while Minxa pondered his words.

Minxa turned slowly and thrust his hand out, a gesture of acceptance and friendship. "Billy Billy, bub'n scrump, champy's in the cataroup, Coppa Coppa attabump an' paaddi's got the misselsoup," he said with a sober nod.

Rindar grabbed his hand and they pushed back and forth several times as he recited the second half of the verse that was the seal of their friendship, "Atta filly, atta fro, Izzy harden uppen roar, Misty is as Misty was, we'll be friends forever more." He dropped Minxa's hand by pushing it down and letting go. "Maybe it's a good thing," Rindar continued, "that we came through the portal—"

"Why?"

"The portals are supposedly guarded by the Eladra, and one does not get through them by accident. If we made it this far, there is probably a purpose."

Minxa rolled his eyes. "How do you remember all this stuff?"

"I dunno. If you had asked me yesterday, I probably wouldn't have. Seeing these things actually happen is bringing it all back somehow. C'mon, we need to make some kind of shelter before dark." Rindar stood up. "One last thing," he added as he stretched, "if we do run into anyone, anywhere, don't say anything about the map. I have a feeling it's a rare piece."

Minxa nodded. "Probably a good idea," he said, then added slowly, "we have no idea what we are in for here."

Rindar pondered Minxa's last words as they set about gathering goods for a shelter he didn't know how to make.

⚊ Islag ⚊

Sometimes there is only one path...

The Tessarandin, Book 3

M inxa stood up straight and looked out across the deadfall. "What was that?"

"What?" Rindar asked.

"I heard a voice."

Rindar looked at him and they both stopped, ears straining into the dead silence of the tangle around them. The damp, stuffy stillness was unbroken.

Minxa saw Rindar's smile and knew exactly what it meant. "I'm not crazy," he said.

"I never said you were."

"That bird makes me nervous," Minxa continued as he nodded up at the bird that had arrived shortly after they entered the deadfall. It sat preening itself on the top branch of a tall dead tree, bleached white from the sun. Its all-black plumage, set against the brilliant blue morning sky, arrested Minxa's attention. "I think it's watching us."

They fell silent as they resumed their berry picking. The close warmth of the deadfall in the sun was slowly driving out the chill that had overcome them in the restless night they spent near the cave. Despite having heaped the pine needles deep where they slept, Minxa had been able to feel the rocks beneath them; and with nothing for cover against the breeze off the ocean, they had slept little and risen early. Their clothes still smelled of damp soil and clung to their bodies with the sticky weight of the morning fog that followed them.

They had lost everything of value in the tumble through the portal. They had no matches for a fire, no lights, no compass; and Minxa had lost his hazarine and his bootknife. Both their water flasks were gone. It was as if the portal had stripped them of everything that might identify where they had come from,aside from their decrepit leather detail packs and their caving clothes.

Minxa still had his doubts about the whole portal idea, but everything confirmed that this unthinkable thing was true. He preferred to ignore the implications of having to believe in even a fragment of the legends: to accept the smallest part of them as true required that he open his mind to the possibility that all—or at least some—of them *might* be true. Even thinking about the task of sorting it out exhausted him.

They had nothing to eat and had left the cave behind, hoping to find something edible, but food was something that they had always bought or stolen from the stores in the Vindarill markets. After about half an hour of following a soggy woodland trail that wound along the cliffs, they came to the edge of the deadfall, brimming with small red berries that nearly fell off the thorny stalks into their hands. In desperation, Minxa tried one. Its sweet tartness reminded him of the boar berries one could buy in the stores in Vindarill. He had tried them once before when he had stolen a small box of them from a fruit cart in the open market. They waited several minutes to see if anything happened, but fear quickly gave way to hunger, and as they picked their way through the deadfall, they were feasting on the berries.

"There it is again!" At Minxa's words, the black bird dropped off the branch and glided down out of sight into the trees behind them. Rindar was listening.

They stood without moving until they heard it again, when Rindar leaned forward and whispered, "It sounds like someone singing."

Minxa nodded. *"Keep going. Quiet,"* he signaled with his hands.

Rindar led. From behind, Minxa watched him pick his way along, stopping to eat berries but placing each foot and moving each bramble with peculiar care. The voice grew louder. It sprang up intermittently, with each burst seeming to be a bit closer, but even that was hard to tell in the dense foliage. The strong voice of a woman rose and fell in strange combinations of notes that were foreign to their ears.

"*Woman,*" he tapped onto Rindar's back when they stopped.

"*Yes.*" Rindar bent to open the map on the ground. If she was near-by, they could see her on the map, but the sun was shining so brightly that it washed out the bright spots. Rindar pulled Minxa around so his shadow fell on the map, but even in the shade, the light was too bright to be able to see the faint smudges. He folded the map back into its case and stashed it in his pack. "*No map. Remember?*"

Minxa smiled. "*No map!*"

"*Wait.*"

The voice came closer. Minxa thought it unlikely that there would be more than one trail through the deadfall, so the safest thing was to wait and let her come to them. He found a small crook in the trail and crawled back into the undergrowth. Rindar did the same opposite him. They could see each other, but no one on the trail would see them unless they knew they were there.

Minxa heard the voice clearly:

"*...call the men from far and near.*
Let them seek and find—
From far away to let them hear
The voice that has no want to fear,
A quiet vorn, untroubled mind..."

It seemed unfinished, as if the singer paused for some private rest, then:

"*So sings the wisdom, clear and just.*
So sings the power of love and trust.
When all lies open, all is fair
And truth is laid and peace is there,
We find..."

Minxa guessed she was ten paces away when she suddenly stopped singing. Rindar lifted his index finger to his lips. The stillness of the deadfall made Minxa's ears ring as he sat and watched Rindar watching him.

What happened next was so sudden that he hardly had time to take a breath. "Don't move!" On one knee in the middle of the path a young woman with a drawn bow pointed an arrow directly into Minxa's eyes. He had never seen a real bow, but he knew what it was and knew he did not want the arrow loosed from her fingers. Her fierce gray eyes flickered as Minxa stared back. She was not very big, but it was hard to tell for sure in her kneeling position. Her dirty-blond hair was pulled back in a short ponytail. In her left ear was a single gold earring; a small gold ring ran through her nostrils.

"What are you doing here?" she demanded. Her voice was quiet but firm.

Minxa was not sure what to say. "Traveling."

"To where?" Minxa could not see Rindar, and he wondered if she knew he was there.

"South."

"Not much south of here."

There was a sudden movement behind her. Minxa never really saw what happened; but in the next instant, Rindar was flat on his back in the path, and she was standing over him, the bow still drawn. He could see her better now. She wore a short linen tunic that left her arms bare. The leather belt that drew it together around the waist held two knives and a small pouch directly behind her and one at her belly. Knee-length leather leggings tied around her calves nearly reached the moccasins that covered her ankles. A single black feather hung down behind her ponytail, and a slender quiver with several arrows in it lay close across her back.

"I knew there were two." She backed off a couple steps to let Rindar stand. "Get up! And tell your friend to come out." Rindar bent down and beckoned to Minxa who did not have to be told twice. "Why were you hiding?"

"Put the bow down," started Rindar. "We're not going to hurt you."

"I'll do as I please! Answer my question."

Minxa watched. He had nothing to say and Rindar was the far better diplomat. "We're new here and do not know this island very well—"

"Are you sure it's an island?"

Minxa thought that a curious question. Perhaps she knew less than they did.

Rindar continued, "Quite sure. We were heading south to the village." Minxa knew he was gambling on his knowledge.

"Did you stay out here last night?"

"Yes, a bit north of here—"

"Nobody stays in the woods here. What were you doing?"

"Look, I don't—"

"Answer my question!" She had not moved a muscle.

"We got stuck there. No way to get to the town in the dark. It was a cold night."

"Where are you from?"

"Vindarill."

"Never heard of it."

"It's a city—far away. And you? Where are you from?"

She paused a long time before answering. "Vindor."

The turn in the questioning seemed to be having a softening effect. Minxa listened.

"And what are you doing here on the island?"

"I came to Islag on my way to Tessamandria. I have a few days before the boat arrives."

"We're taking the same boat." Minxa was amazed at Rindar's matter-of-fact lie about something he knew nothing about.

"What is your name?"

"Rindar Colloden. And this is my friend, Minxa Maharan."

Whatever barrier the woman held vanished with the name giving. She dropped her bow and in a simple trained gesture, stowed the arrow in the quiver without breaking eye contact with Rindar. "My name is Rasler of Vindor. Now, if you will excuse me, I need to get my pack." She moved easily toward Rindar, and with a quick step, brushed between them, gliding up the trail and disappearing momentarily into the deadfall.

Minxa looked at Rindar. Rindar shrugged. Rasler was back in the next instant with a small leather pack slung over one shoulder.

"And where are you going today, Rasler of Vindor?" Rindar asked.

"I have business at the end of the island," she said as she passed between them again.

"There is nothing there except rocks, trees—and birds after you get out of this deadfall."

She turned to meet Rindar's eyes.

"No—there is something more—but one has to know it is there."

"May you find it quickly," Rindar offered, bowing slightly in a gesture of mock goodwill.

Rasler paused and smiled. "Thank you. You will find the village is not what you think." She turned suddenly, and without looking back, vanished around a turn in the trail through the deadfall.

"Let's go," Rindar whispered.

Minxa nodded and fell in behind his friend. It was obvious that Rindar wanted to put some distance between them before speaking. They had not gone ten steps when Rasler's voice broke the stillness:

"By guided star, by Tal's pale light
They trekked in darkness, night by night
'Til on the fated way they stood
As brothers in the common good—"

It was already faint in the thick still air around them. "C'mon," whispered Rindar. "This place is not that big. We'll see her later, I am sure."

☩

Eyes that refuse to see alternatives, see nothing at all.

Pratoraman
The Middle Way

"This is ridiculous," Rindar said. They were sitting back to back, bound so tightly with several coils of rope around the shoulders that it was difficult to breathe deeply.

"I know, but we lost our knives—there aren't even any sharp stones around."

"Can you reach my hands?" Rindar asked.

"It's no use."

"Try again."

"Forget it." Minxa's resignation filled his voice.

Their hands were between them, but they were stretched out in such a way that neither could reach the other, and their ankles had been bound with a tether to a tree in front of them so they could not move around.

"What was he trying to prove?" Rindar asked. "I mean, he seemed to think that we would be eaten alive or something if he left us here."

"He was an idiot."

"Yeah, well he got us both tied up, didn't he? And he went through our packs." Rindar nodded toward their packs, which lay on the ground a few yards away. "Wasn't much to find, though."

"You think he was looking for something specific?" Minxa asked.

"I have no idea. If he was, he didn't find it."

"Maybe the map?"

"Shhhh!"

"There's no one who's gonna hear us," Minxa said. "Besides, if that is what he wanted, he didn't know what he was looking for."

"We don't know who might be able to hear us."

"And what was that he said—something about a sacrifice to the Eladra?" Minxa asked, deliberately changing the subject.

"It seemed to me that he thought this place is haunted by the Eladra and that by leaving us here they would find us and—" A sudden movement above him interrupted Rindar. A black bird had landed on a limb of the tree to which he was tied. It looked like the same bird they had seen in the deadfall, but it was much closer now, and it was definitely looking at him. "Hello?" he said.

"Hello what?" said Minxa.

With a single flutter of its wings, the bird dropped down another branch, still looking at Rindar with one eye.

"That big black bird we saw in the deadfall," Rindar whispered over his shoulder, "—it's back."

Minxa groaned.

"Awww. That big black bird we saw in the deadfall—it's back." The bird's voice startled Rindar, and he felt Minxa stiffen behind him. "It's back. It's back. It's back." The bird called as it dropped to the ground and started strutting around them. "That big black bird. It's back." The nasal, raspy voice mocked them.

"It talks," Minxa blurted out.

The bird had moved around so that Rindar could not see it.

"It talks. Awww. It talks," mocked the bird.

"Get off me, you stupid bird!" Minxa yelled.

"Stupid bird. Stupid bird. Awww!"

"Ow!" yelled Minxa. "That hurts."

"What's happening?" Rindar asked over his shoulder.

"The bird dug its claws into my leg!" Minxa growled, "Get off me!"

The bird strutted around to where Rindar could see it clearly and stopped. It cocked its head and looked Rindar in the eyes. "Do *you* think I am stupid?"

Rindar was stunned. Up till then, he had thought that the bird was simply mimicking them. Now it stood still in front of him awaiting an answer to an intelligent question. "I—I—"

"Do you think I'm stupid?" demanded the bird again.

"No," Rindar said as confidently as he could. Stupid or not, this bird may be the only chance of escape they had. "It's just—I just never met a talking bird before."

Minxa groaned.

"Many birds talk. Many animals talk." The bird seemed surprised that he had never met a talking bird. "Your friend said I was stupid."

"Yes I know," Rindar confessed, "but I don't think he meant it the way it came across."

"Should I ask him again?" the bird asked.

"No, I don't think that is necessary."

"I have a name, don't you know!" stated the bird. "Do you have a name?"

"My name is Rindar."

"Rindar, Rindar, Rindar," the bird cawed as if repeating the name helped its memory. Rindar sat, intrigued by its odd mannerisms. From his memory of the legends, there was a time when the animals did talk. In Vindarill, there had been those that insisted it was still possible and even some who insisted they had heard animals talk. Rindar never had.

"Aren't you going to ask me my name?" the bird continued. "I have one, don't you know!"

"What is your name?" Rindar conceded.

"I am Ravensir Vakandar," the bird said as it puffed out its chest, "and I am not just a bird, I am a *raven*." The way he said it left little doubt that this was a matter of some pride.

"Well, Ravensir," Rindar said, "can you help us get out of this fix?"

The raven hopped up onto his shin. "Call me Vakandar. Awww." He dug his talons into Rindar's leg.

"Ow!"

"Sorry," Vakandar said as he hopped down onto the ground and turned toward Rindar's ankle bindings. He paused just above the knot of the rope. "Your friend called me stupid."

"You're not stupid," Rindar assured him.

"I want your friend to apologize, don't you know."

"I'm sorry I called you stupid," Minxa grumbled.

Vakandar paused to consider the apology, then began pecking at the knot on Rindar's ankles. "Very tight—very tight, indeed," he cawed between his tugs on the knot. He worked at it for several moments before he suddenly straightened as if he were listening.

"Must go," he said, "must go, sorry."

"Wait!" said Rindar.

Vakandar took a couple strides and was airborne, flying low before swooping up into the thick canopy of evergreens and disappearing from Rindar's sight. In the same instant, Rindar became suddenly aware of the dead stillness of the woods. Nothing moved and there was no sound. Out of the silence came a soft singular whistle of a lone bird somewhere to Rindar's left.

"What was that?" Minxa whispered.

"Shhhh!"

The whistle came again.

"A bird?"

"Shhhh!" Rindar wanted to hear, but he did not want to hear what came next. A low growl surrounded them, followed quickly by a blood-curdling screech and a sudden swift movement that caught Rindar's eye as something leapt toward them. Minxa swore by the NarEladra and rolled over pulling Rindar down with him onto his side. Someone laughed, and Rindar felt the rope that bound his feet to the tree suddenly fall slack.

"Need some help?" Rasler quipped as she squatted down beside them, sheathing her knives.

"You scared the fire out of us," Rindar said. He was trembling, and he could not see her very well from where he lay on his side. "Yes, we need your help. Can you untie us?"

Rasler didn't move. "Yes, I can."

"Ok—when?"

"I want to hear the one called Minxa speak first. He has not said anything to me yet."

Minxa turned his head, trying to see her, but he could not quite make it. "Can you please untie us? Please?"

"No tricks?"

"No tricks!" they said simultaneously.

Obviously amused by the situation, she remained still for some number of seconds, pretending to think about what to do. "All right," she said and moved to untie Rindar's hands. As she worked the knot, she asked, "Who did this?"

"We don't know. He was a big fellow with a black ponytail and beard—with dragons tattooed on his arms."

"Ahh, my friend Drofan," she said.

"You know him?" Minxa asked.

"I met him yesterday. Somewhat of a brute, I would say. Why did he do this?"

"Not sure. He surprised us," Rindar said. "Trapped us in some sort of net."

Rasler had worked Rindar's hands free and was working on the lashings between their shoulders when Minxa chimed in. "He seemed to think that if he tied us up, the Eladra would find us and eat us for their dinner."

"You're joking!"

"Not in the least. He was crazy," said Minxa.

"And he sure doesn't understand much about the Eladra," Rasler said.

"I guess not," Rindar echoed, not wanting to let her know that he knew nothing himself.

"Do you know much about Islag?" she asked.

"About what?"

"Islag—this island—do you know much about it?"

"No, this is the first time we've been here."

Rindar was free, and together they began working on the knots that held Minxa fast.

Rasler continued, "Islag is a very special place. There are many stories, and depending on who you listen to, it's either overwhelmingly haunted or especially endowed."

"In what way?" Minxa was genuinely curious.

"Well, there are supposed to be many Eladra here, and what you think about the Eladra and the NarEladra determines what you think of Islag."

"Hmmmm." Minxa's hands were free, and he was rubbing his wrists where the rope had been chafing.

"Supposedly, one of the Tessalindrian portals is on Islag," Rasler continued. "It would be guarded by the Eladra, so their presence here is somewhat expected—that is, if the portal story is true."

"Is that why you are here?" Minxa asked. "Looking for the portal?"

"Just curious actually. Even if I found it, my father told me that I should not go into it unless I had Lonama's map and knew how to navigate with it. You could end up anywhere—at any time—and you can't just go back through, either."

"What do you mean?" Rindar asked.

"I don't understand it completely," Rasler said, "but from what he said, the portals are constantly shifting. If you come through then turn around and go back through, you may end up somewhere completely different." She looked casually from Rindar to Minxa, and then looked up. "It won't be long before it's too dark to travel. Unless you feel like you have to go, it might make the most sense for us all to stay put for the night."

Rindar spoke. "We're in no hurry. We're just hungry—"

"And thirsty," Minxa assented with a grunt.

"Then it's decided," she said. "We'll stay here for the night. I have food and some water. I wasn't planning on company for tonight's dinner, but we can make it work. We may even see an Eladra." Minxa shifted as Rasler continued, "But probably not. They're not ones to show themselves for no good reason." Glancing around, she said, "First thing we need is a fire. If both of you can find wood, I'll get a flame—get the dry wood from the trees."

Rindar knew it would be totally dark soon, so he waved to Minxa; and they stood up, stretched and started scrounging for wood. The wood was everywhere on the ground, and the low branches of the thick trees were bare and dry, breaking easily with loud snaps as he and Minxa bundled them into their arms. Rindar watched Rasler as he worked. He saw her pull a small roll from her pack and unwrap it. A wisp of smoke rose from her hands, and she dropped something into the pile of dried moss and bark on the ground in front of her. As she blew on it, it burst into flames, and seconds later she had a fire the size of Rindar's fist.

By the time they were finished collecting wood, the fire was crackling gaily and illuminating the woods around them with its warm glow. The air was thick with the sweet, pungent smell of burning spruce needles. "How did you do that?" Rindar asked as they sat down on logs Rasler had rolled into place by the fire.

"I carry embers wrapped in my fire pouch. It can be tricky, but it's a whole lot easier than starting new each time." She stared into the fire. "Tell me about Vindarill," she said without lifting her eyes from the flames.

Minxa shot a glance at him, "*Be careful!*"

Rindar paused as he collected his thoughts. Rasler sat and waited, her gray eyes stared into the fire, and the tiny gold ring in her nose gleamed yellow like a star in the woods. Rindar found an odd pleasantness in being around someone who was not afraid and not in a hurry. She took each moment as it was without having to control it. "Vindarill is a big city," he started. "Perhaps it is ten miles or more across. There are too many beings there. They don't always get along, but since they are there together and don't have anywhere else to go, for the most part they learn to live with each other—"

Rasler looked at him across the fire. "I've never seen a city that big. Where is it?"

"It's on the coast of Morlan."

"Morlan? Never heard of it. How would I get there from here?"

Rindar knew that Rasler was probing. From what she knew about the portals, she probably suspected they had come through one. "I'm not sure you could," he said, "and probably not from *when* we came, either." He saw Minxa's jaw drop then snap up.

"You *did* come through the portal."

Rindar sat staring into the fire, poking at it with a long thin stick. "We did, but it was an accident."

"An accident?" Rasler's excitement choked her voice. "No one goes through a portal by accident!"

"Well," Rindar continued as he stirred the fire, "we did not go through it by accident, but we found it by accident, and we did not know what it was for sure." Minxa was staring into the flames, and Rasler waited without moving. "We were trapped, sort of—so we took a chance...had no idea what would really happen."

"You don't have a map?"

"A map? No." Rindar lied.

Rasler seemed convinced. "How were you 'trapped, sort of'?"

Rindar paused. He wanted it all to make sense, and he was not sure how to present it.

Minxa spoke before Rindar was ready. "We worked as searchers in the tunnels under Vindarill."

"Searchers?"

"Under the city there are huge tunnels drilled into the rock, so in case of a war, the inhabitants of the city could hide there," Minxa continued. "Searchers follow all the nooks and crevices that are exposed in the drilling to make sure they don't go anywhere."

"Yesterday we were following this one vein, and we heard someone following us," said Rindar. "We couldn't go back, so we kept going and we ran into the portal in one of the chambers."

"Why couldn't you go back?"

It was an innocent question, but Minxa looked up and answered before Rindar could fabricate anything. "Rindar killed someone. We were being hunted."

Rindar looked up at Rasler. She seemed curious, but completely unalarmed. "Who did you kill—and why?"

"It was some old being."

"You don't even know who he *was?*" Rasler's eyes flashed.

"No, he was new in town. That's why we marked him."

"What do you mean?" Her eyes had darkened in the firelight.

Rindar felt a twinge of shame; that same feeling in his vorn that he had felt when Minxa had accused him of breaking psadeq. He was suddenly aware that Rasler hadn't even flinched when he told her of killing someone, but when she suspected there was not a legitimate reason, she was visibly angered. He looked at Minxa, who avoided his gaze by staring into the fire.

"We think he had just come into town," he continued cautiously, "so we followed him. Later that night, I broke into the place where he was staying to steal whatever he had—"

Rasler leapt over the fire, and before he had time to lift his arms in self-defense, Rindar was flat on his back with a knife at his throat. She had him pinned with her knee putting a painful pressure on his belly. He couldn't move. "A murderer! A thief! Is there a reason I should not kill you now?" she hissed as she bore down with her knee.

Rindar knew his next words had to be chosen very carefully. "I didn't mean to—to kill him," he choked. Her face, full of fury and passion, was six inches from his. "Please—let me explain." Rindar almost choked again on the word "please." He could not remember the last time he had said it.

She held him tightly for several seconds, then relaxed her grip and stood up. "I rushed into judgment," she said, "but tell me what happened. I do want to know." She had slipped the knife back into its sheath on her belt and turned back toward her seat on the log.

Rindar sat up cautiously. Minxa had not moved, and Rindar could see the terror in his eyes. "You were about to kill me," he said as he brushed the pine needles from his shirt. "Have you ever killed a being?"

Rasler looked calmly into the fire. "Three."

"Three? Then how—"

"One wanted my bow," she interrupted. "He killed my horse, thinking he would make sport of me. His vorn was corrupted to where he had become less than a beast himself, posing as a man. When I learned his full intention, I killed him with this knife." The blade gleamed in the firelight as she slipped it from the sheath on her left.

"The other two were pirates on the coast of Vindor. They broke into an inn where I was staying and robbed the woman innkeeper, a considerably poor woman, eking out a life caring for travelers. I caught them on the shore, getting into their boat. One I strangled with my bolo, the other I killed with a stone slung through the back of his head." She looked up into Rindar's eyes. "Unpleasant business, it is, but corruption like this has to be eliminated before it is passed on. And you, my friend Rindar, with your quiet companion, Minxa—what was your reason for killing?"

Rindar had never felt shame for who he was until this. Sitting before him was a young woman, two-thirds his weight, with the strength and nobility of a lioness. He could not remember having met anyone like her. She had reasons for the way she chose to live, and principles...and the courage to live them out. Like a heroine from one of the legends, she was one of those ancient characters Rindar wished he could be like, but the dream of being a hero had died long ago on the streets of Vindarill. He continued picking at bits of twigs and leaves while he pondered his explanation for his coward's life. Deep inside, a choking feeling rose toward his throat.

"It was a matter of survival," he began when he had calmed the threat of crying. "Vindarill is a wretched place, and as a viddik, one doesn't stand a chance." Rasler stared at him thoughtfully. She sat in silence with the full light of the fire illuminating her face and hands. "We got paid for our jobs, but not much. Minxa and I took to looting in order to make ends meet. In a big city, it's easy to get away with."

"And there is no punishment? For looting?"

Minxa stirred. "If you get caught...but it's easy to get away with many things."

"Someone must know!"

Rindar realized that Rasler had never been in a city like Vindarill. Probably in this time, there were no such cities. "Yes, people know, but they do not know who you are, and they don't want to care. Many just ignore what happens around them. Most are simply afraid."

"Sounds ugly to me."

Rindar stared across the fire. He had never thought of it as ugly, but some vague corner of his vorn wanted to agree. Rasler's eyes penetrated deeply into his vorn. He looked down, feeling compelled to get to the heart of his story. "The old man was different somehow," he said. "He wasn't afraid." Something inside told him that this statement warranted a reaction. Rasler didn't move. Rindar looked into Minxa's eyes as it occurred to him that he had not yet told Minxa this story. Minxa was staring back with a mixture of fear and resentment. Rindar had never seen that look. He already knew what his next sentence would be, and he knew he did not want to be looking at Minxa when he said it. He forced his eyes back into Rasler's gaze. "I think—looking back—he must have been Sessashian."

Rasler sat up straight. "You know about *Sessasha*?"

Rindar felt a surge of caution: "Everybody's heard of Sessasha—at least in Vindarill," he added, sensing Rasler's tension.

"Sessasha hasn't even lived yet," she said flatly, shaking her head.

Minxa shuddered. "Then how do you know about him," he asked, looking up from the fire for the first time.

Rasler stared back at Minxa. "My father was in the circle—"

"With Sessasha?" Rindar interrupted. "I thought you said he hasn't lived yet!" They all sat and stared at each other as Rindar tried to piece together what they had just learned. There were too many questions. "You say your father was in Sessasha's circle?" he repeated.

"He was. He came back through the Krith Portal to Mythinia and made his way back to Vindor as an emissary for Sessasha. No one in Vindor had heard of Sessasha, of course, and my father was treated like a madman for teaching about the anthara who was to come." Rasler paused, staring into the fire. "Two years ago the persecution became so intense where we lived that he sent me on this journey to find Sessasha. He said Sessasha will need my help."

"But you said that Sessasha hasn't been born yet," insisted Minxa.

Rasler stared into the fire. Her eyes were far away as if she were seeing much more than the fire itself. "That's why I need to get through the portal," she said, "but I can't do that without Lonama's map. I thought that you might have one. My father said I would find the map when the right time came. Mah'Eladra told him so."

Rindar sat quietly, playing in the fire with his stick. Everything was a little too twisted, and he needed time to find acceptance for what was being said. Both Rasler and Minxa seemed to be content to do the same, so they sat in silence until Rindar changed the subject. "Where, exactly, are you going?"

Rasler stared into the fire. "I am searching for the map, and then for a portal to take me to the city of Kinvara at the time when Sessasha lives." She paused and continued staring into the fire. "But first, I am heading north to the Jualar Springs."

"The Jualar Springs?" Minxa asked. "What are they?"

"On the western slopes of the Crown of Tessalindria, there are seven springs. It is said that the water that flows from them is a source of healing and cleansing, so I am going there first to wash myself and make myself ready for Sessasha."

Minxa shook his head. Rindar knew what he was thinking by the way he pursed his lips. "How long will it take to get there?" Rindar asked.

"It's a day's journey to the southern coast of Tessamandria—by boat. Then one has to cross the NarEl Waste—four to five days, I think, and then another day or so to the Crown." Rasler had not taken her eyes from the fire.

"I've always wanted to see the Crown," Rindar mused. "Can we come with you?"

Minxa looked up. "Are you crazy?"

"Do you have a better plan?" Rindar asked.

"How about going back to Vindarill?"

"You want to risk going back through the portal?" Rindar asked. "It was weird enough the first time, and we have no clue where we might end up."

"That's what *she* says!" Minxa exclaimed, as he looked at Rindar and pointed at Rasler.

"Look, Minxa. There are eight portals and the range of times—it's mind-boggling. We might never get back to Vindarill, and if we did, who knows when, and we would still be stinkin' viddiks!" Rindar's anger flared with his last words.

"What is a viddik?" Rasler asked innocently.

Rindar turned to Minxa again. "See what I mean?" he said. He looked back at Rasler. "We're viddiks!" he said.

The anger in his voice must have convinced her not to probe further. "I thought I heard you say earlier that you were going on the boat—" Rasler said as she stared into Rindar's eyes.

"Yes, but just to get off this island. We really had no other plans."

Rasler nodded her head slowly as if she knew he was lying, but was not going to confront him. "I'll have to think about that and ask."

"Ask who?" Minxa blurted out.

"There will be conditions—" Rasler continued without acknowledging his question. "I will lead, and you—both of you—will follow," she said as she looked from Rindar to Minxa.

"Forget it!" said Minxa.

"We will all sleep on it one night before I decide. In the morning it will be clear."

"It won't happen!" Minxa continued, "And who died and left you in charge?"

"You don't have to come," Rasler said. "I will decide in the morning." There was something in her tone that made Rindar realize that there would be no more discussion. Rasler stood up, threw another bundle of sticks on the fire and said, "I have meager portions, but we will share them before we sleep." She leaned over to her small pack and pulled several parcels from its depth. After unfolding them neatly on the ground in front of her, she knelt before the small meal and covered it with her hands, then looked toward the sky with closed eyes and breathed deeply. Her lips quivered silently for several moments before she looked down at her hands and slowly removed them from the food. "There should be plenty."

Rindar had to look a second time. He was sure that there was more there than when she had covered it. He looked over at Minxa as Rasler busied herself dividing the portions into three. Minxa shook his head as he stared at Rasler's hands, his face overcast with a puzzled look.

Rasler looked up with a smile. She extended a handful of food to Rindar and the other to Minxa. "Dried tarlin and sweet pears. A little mirrin root will make your stomach think you ate a feast." Looking down, she took two slabs of some kind of dried bread and handed it to each of them before reaching into her pack and pulling out a flask of fresh water. "It's all I have," she said as she sat back and began carefully eating her portion from the parcels on the ground before her.

"Thank you," said Rindar, waiting for her acknowledgment before he began eating.

"Thanks," mumbled Minxa through the first mouthful of food. No one spoke further and Rindar found a quiet place for his mind by watching the fire as he finished his last pieces of this strange meal.

✠

Two can keep company, but three makes for a safer journey.

Old Otallan Saying

Minxa and Rindar plodded along the trail in the direction of the village. Rindar had refused to open the map because they were not sure what might have happened to Rasler or where she was. Although he had slept well enough considering the accommodations, there had been no breakfast, and the thick fog dripped off the boughs above them and licked their shoes. After a hundred paces, they were drenched.

"I don't know about you," Minxa grumbled, "but I'm just as glad to be rid of her."

"Why? She was kind enough to untie us, and she even fed us." Rindar was in front of him so Minxa could not see his face, and the words were almost completely swallowed by the silent forest.

"She's weird."

"Different."

"How can you defend her? You don't know her any better than I do."

"What I know, I like," Rindar said. "She has a very simple view of life."

"Simple? She's naïve."

"I guess that's a matter of perspective."

Minxa hated this side of Rindar: always the philosopher, always trying to see the better side of people. "What did you make of that little...thing she did over her food last night?" he asked.

"You mean *our* food?" Rindar looked back over his shoulder and smirked. "I could have sworn that there was more when she took her hands away than before, but it was probably a trick."

"Yeah, some trick—and that bit about her father and Sessasha's circle—" Sometimes Minxa wondered if he just liked to hear himself complain. Most of what he had just said was superficial, and he knew that deep inside there was a much bigger fear. Whatever it was, he could not make a conscious thought out of it: there were no words. No ideas surfaced in his mind. It frustrated him, but he hadn't the smallest clue what to do about it.

"I wonder where she went—and when," Rindar mused.

Minxa felt ignored. "She's weird," he said again.

Rindar stopped and turned around to face him. "You keep saying that."

"I think we should try going back through the portal, rather than following her."

"The portal scared you silly. You swore you would never do it again. Besides, as Rasler said, you don't have a clue where you might end up."

"We have the map!"

"That we don't know how to *use*! And don't say that word." Rindar looked around uneasily.

"Well, *I* certainly don't want to go with her after we get off this island."

"Why? We've got nowhere to go, no money, no idea what to do..." Rindar shrugged. "Might as well give her a chance."

As Minxa looked up at Rindar, he noticed a sudden movement behind Rindar's left shoulder. A huge figure loomed out of the fog, and without warning, Rindar was catapulted into Minxa. Minxa tripped as he tried to step back, and Rindar came crashing down on top of him. Rindar swore, but before Minxa could push him off, the figure was on top of both of them, chortling in amusement.

It was Drofan. He had rope in his hands and was already rearranging their limbs for a thorough lashing. Minxa had always thought himself to be strong and agile, but pinned under Rindar by this muscular giant, he was helpless.

"So you escaped somehow, eh?" Drofan snarled. "Now we can't have this, can we?" Minxa got the feeling that he was an expert at tying people up. "I'll find it this time," he growled as he wrapped another loop of rope around Minxa's wrist.

"Find what?" Rindar grunted.

"Shut up!" Drofan raised his fist to strike Rindar in the face, and as he did so, a low fluttering whistle interrupted him. The fist stopped. Drofan looked up and straightened above them, listening to the eerie howl that floated down from the small rise behind them and ended in a snarl like the tiger at the Vindarill zoo. No one moved.

A black shadow swept in over them. "Sesh!" Drofan swore.

The huge black bird braked suddenly in the air to avoid Drofan's flailing arms, and with an "Awwww" swept out of their reach. Drofan swore again and turned to watch the raven as it glided up into a tree behind him. "Watch this!" Vakandar said as he perched on the branch and spread his wings wide. A whistling sound and a soft thud interrupted Drofan's attention to the bird. He tottered and slumped over on top of Rindar, unconscious.

Minxa lay still. He didn't know what to expect next. Rindar was breathing heavily, but seemed in no hurry to extricate himself. At length, Rindar broke the silence. "Let's get out of here," he said as he squirmed out from under the unconscious man and helped Minxa roll their adversary onto his back beside them.

"Is he dead?" Minxa said as he stood up, trying to brush the damp dirt off his shirt.

"No—he is still breathing. Let's go."

"Where?"

"Toward the village is still best, I think."

Minxa saw Rindar jump, and his heart skipped a beat as Rasler stepped out from behind a tree not four paces from where they stood. The tree was hardly big enough to hide half of the woman who emerged from its protection.

"I warned this fellow twice. He will be out for a while and will have a serious headache when he wakes."

"Did you—"

"It was just a ball of clay: enough to knock him out without killing him. He'll be fine. Let's go." Rasler shouldered her pack and started down the trail.

"Just a ball of clay. Just a ball of clay." Vakandar the raven was strutting back and forth on the limb above them.

Rasler stopped and looked up. "Good work, Vakandar," she said. Her voice was matter of fact. "Now we need to get to the village." As she turned down the trail again, Vakandar dropped from his limb and swept down over her before wheeling off into the forest.

Minxa felt Rindar staring at him. When he looked up, Rindar shrugged and gestured for him to follow. As they fell in behind Rasler, it dawned on Minxa that she must have been following them. He realized that he would have to wait to find out why, and to understand her relationship to the strange Ravensir Vakandar.

✠

That faraway isle, that distant isle,
That tired and weary and desolate isle...

Hirandan
Ithrall to Islag

The inn on Islag sat prominently on the hilltop overlooking the harbor and the run-down houses of the small village. Dried sawgrass, browned by the sun and matted by the wind, filled the spaces between the gray bedrock that kept the island from being swallowed by the sea. The inn was as gray as the Islag rock, but lighter in hue. Its shabby facade spoke of neglect by its owner and abuse by the elements. Rindar had the feeling that it was a place to be avoided and at the same time, a place that one could not avoid if one desired to visit this strange, strangled ocean outpost.

They had arrived at the village in midafternoon. Having burned off the enshrouding fog, the sun beat down on the weary buildings. They walked the several hundred paces of the one dirt road that wound the length of the village, finding nothing of note save the strange secret stare of its few inhabitants. Rasler led them at last down the rocky incline that took them from the front of the inn to the small Islag wharf.

A rickety slip dropped to the starboard side of a long wooden boat that looked like something out of an ancient history book. Several of the crew were working on the deck, laying lines and carefully checking the rigging. They laughed and sang as they worked. "I'll be right back," Rasler said as she set off down the slip toward the short bearded man who sat on an old barrel smoking a pipe.

While she haggled with the old captain about the boat fare, Minxa and Rindar sat on a splintered beam facing the boats in the harbor and dangled their feet above the water as it slapped against the stone foundations of the wharf. The dock was as old and tired as the village and smelled of dead fish, pine tar and garbage. It was littered with remnants of the work it supported: bits of rope and worn glass, small shattered shells, smooth stones, rusty nails and stacks of buckets full of ropes and nets.

On the rocks where the wharf met the island, two seagulls were tearing apart the remains of a fish they had dragged from the water. They pulled at it as if each wanted all of it, and yet with each piece they pulled free, they paused only long enough to swallow before lunging forward to grab whatever was left. As Rindar watched, fragmented visions of his encounter with the old man floated through his mind. Why the gulls reminded him of the old man eluded him. Rindar shuddered involuntarily.

Minxa looked at him. "What?"

"It's the seagulls," he said. "They make me angry."

"Angry?"

"That's the closest word I have for it," Rindar answered.

"Angry at the gulls," Minxa prodded, "for just being gulls?"

"No. It's more than that. They just—I don't know. I—" Rindar's thoughts were interrupted by the huff of wings just to his right. He looked over to see Vakandar settling his pinion feathers against his body as he strutted toward them on the wood sill on which they sat.

"It's more than that—more than that," cawed the raven before he stuck his beak into one wing and carefully rearranged one of his sleek black feathers. "Nasty gulls," he continued. "Trouble the vorn, they do, don't you know. You feel it."

"I don't feel anything," Minxa mused.

Vakandar cocked his head to look at Minxa. "Not good, not good!" he crowed as he turned in a full circle and shook out his tail feathers. "Nasty gulls!"

"Shut up, you—" Minxa stopped in mid-sentence.

Vakandar turned his head to see Minxa in his left eye and then sprang into flight by dropping off the edge of the wharf. "Stupid bird, stupid bird," he cawed as he wheeled upward, passing low over Minxa's head. He came to roost on one of the pylons not far from where Rasler was finishing her animated barter with the boat owner.

"I didn't say it!" Minxa growled.

Rindar laughed. "You thought it though, didn't you?"

Minxa turned away without answering. Rindar could tell from the hitch of his shoulders that he was sulking. Rindar pondered what Vakandar had said. The gulls *did* disquiet his vorn, but he could not determine how or why exactly. He tried to think of something good, but his thoughts were overrun by clouded memories of the last two tumultuous days: of the gentle old man, the smell of the blood on his shirt and the grimy streets of Vindarill. The voice of the men who had pursued them in the cave rang in his ears as they described what they had found in the apartment, and he could feel the dark emptiness of the portal just before he stepped into it.

"Do you really want to go on this boat tomorrow?" Minxa asked.

Rindar sat for a moment and thought. "We still don't have a better plan, and besides, if this is all there is to this island, it doesn't interest me to stay here."

"Wouldn't you like to get back to Vindarill?" Minxa prodded.

"Yes—and no," Rindar said. "I feel like I need to find out what really happened—I still can't remember any of it, but Vindarill itself?—I'm not sure. You know what I mean?"

Minxa grunted. "I guess—for you, but if we went back, we could find this Vashtor character and sell him the map for more silver."

"I thought about that. We may not be able to find him, and even if we did—I got the feeling that he would not have to pay us anything, if you know what I mean. And, as I said earlier, I wouldn't know how to get back." Rindar stared out over the harbor and added, "Besides, I would like to see the Crown!"

"Why?"

"There are so many...stories about it," Rindar said as he looked at Minxa. "Aren't you the slightest bit interested?"

"You were going to say 'legends,' weren't you?" Minxa chided.

Rindar nodded. "And *you* don't want to find out about any more legends, do you?"

"Not really." Minxa paused before adding, "Not if discovering them has the same result as discovering the portal."

Rindar looked out over the harbor. It seemed like a good place to let the conversation slide into silence. He sat quietly on the gray wharf with his one and only best friend, staring out over the water of the harbor that sparkled brightly in the late afternoon sun. A strange iciness seemed to hang between them; a distance that Rindar could feel but could not name.

✠

What we see with our eyes, what we hear with our ears, is only a shadow of the fullness of reality.

Sessasha
It Is Said

"We'll stay in the woods again tonight," Rasler announced quietly as they sat down in the dining hall of the inn, "and keep the conversation light." She had insisted they sit at the table nearest the door.

The main dining area was not large: twelve tables, most of them occupied with men in pairs or threes who chatted idly over their dinners and flagons of mead, and glanced occasionally at the newcomers. Scruffy orange drapes hung loosely over the windows, bathing the room with an eerie glow that left its corners dark. The walls were decorated with decrepit bits of nautical nostalgia and rope, draped erratically between the knick-knacks. It gave the sense of an old fish house, as if the men there never had to leave their work.

"Why not stay here?" Minxa asked. "It's got to be better than the woods." He felt the quiet resentment that grew stronger each time Rasler told him what they were going to do.

"Do you have any money?" she asked.

Minxa felt his pockets involuntarily. When he looked up, Rindar was smiling. Something about the smile made him angry. Rindar was changing. In Vindarill he would never have mocked him this way. "I must have lost it in the—" Minxa stopped when he saw Rasler's finger on her lips.

"It's not safe to talk here," she said in a low voice.

"I think the woods will be fine," Minxa said as a bent old man approached their table with mugs of water.

The waiter nodded to Rasler as he set the mugs heavily onto the table. "What will it be?" he said through a sneer that was missing two teeth. His breath was thick with alcohol, and his blue eyes watered beneath the bushy eyebrows that drooped from his weathered forehead. The dirty white apron he wore looked as if it had not been laundered in weeks.

"A bowl of stew for the three of us and one of those loaves of bread you had the other night," said Rasler casually.

"No bread tonight," said the man, "only oatcakes."

"We'll take the oatcakes, then."

"Two and a half drags." The man held out his hand to Rasler as if he sensed she was in charge.

"We'll pay when we've eaten—and only a drag and a half."

The man hesitated. "A drag and a half now, or there isn't any stew left either."

Rasler reached down to her belt and removed a small leather purse. She dropped it on the table casually. It sounded like there was nothing in it, but she opened it and pulled out three small gold coins, placing them firmly into his gnarled hand. She looked up and smiled as he bowed stiffly and left.

"Everything is a bargain here," she laughed.

Minxa was curious. "Was that the last of your money?"

"My last half drag," she said. She looked from Rindar to Minxa and back again.

"How will you pay for the boat?" Rindar leaned forward as he spoke. "I have one silver coin that may not be any good here."

"We'll figure that out tomorrow," she said, "but we have other concerns right now."

Rindar followed her eyes as they rose toward the main door. Drofan had just come in. He glanced casually at the trio and headed for a table of younger men engaged in a boisterous drinking party at the far end of the hall. When he sat down, the men on either side of his stool slapped him on the back and laughed. Minxa's eyes slipped to the table in the corner next to Drofan. Several members of the boat crew that Minxa had seen at the dock were eating together. One of them leaned back in his chair with his back against both walls. He looked bigger than anyone else there, but Minxa wondered if that might have been an illusion created by the darkness of the corner. The man's arms were folded over his chest, and the food in front of him was untouched

"Keep talking," Rasler said, "but keep your wits about you. Drofan is trouble in a bundle, and I'm sure he's still got a headache. He just realized that the three of us know each other, and I don't think he knows what to do."

For a moment, Minxa felt the pull of wanting to be with Drofan's friends instead of where he was. When he turned back to the table, Rasler was watching him intently. "Things are not always as they seem, you know," she said as she smoothed the stained, wrinkled napkin on the table before her.

"What do you mean by that?" Minxa retorted. He looked at Rindar, who shrugged in feigned ignorance.

"What we see with our eyes is not always real—" she continued.

"So?"

She looked up from her napkin, straight into Minxa's face. He felt her thinking, her cool gray eyes flickering back and forth from one of his eyes to the other. Finally she looked down again. "That which is seen through the eyes, that which is sensed by the basa, is only a shadow of the fullness of reality," she continued. "You must—we must—be careful that we are not deluded by this shadow."

Minxa glanced at Rindar, who was listening intently to Rasler. Minxa knew that the basa was a part of the vorn, but even the vorn as a concept was vague. No one he knew would describe it as anything but that inner being that was responsible for feelings, emotions and thoughts. The Sessashians believed there was more to it than that, but he had never met a Sessashian he trusted and would not have dared to ask them what they thought of such things. As much as he had never cared to know before, he was sure he did not want to know now. He watched Rasler's hands as they continued to smooth the napkin.

Before she had time to continue, a young woman appeared at the side of the table with their dinner. Rasler smiled and said, "Thank you." The woman smiled briefly, then glanced suspiciously from Minxa to Rindar as she hurriedly set the bowl of stew in the center of the table and dropped the plate of oatcakes beside it. She smiled quickly to Rasler again and nodded, then turned away and disappeared into the kitchen.

Minxa turned to the single bowl of gray stew. Rindar tapped his bent spoon on the top of one of the three overdone oatcakes on the plate in front of him. It sounded like a block of wood. "We *paid* for this?" he asked as a pathetic smile curled his lips.

Rasler quietly broke her cake in half and laid it on the table. She repeated her little ritual from the night before, unrestrained by the crowd of beings in the inn. When she had finished she looked up into Rindar's eyes and said, "There are worse things to be eaten in this world, believe me," she said, then dipped one of the pieces of cake into the stew and began her meal.

Rindar followed, breaking his cake and dipping it in the stew. Minxa waited until Rindar had swallowed the first piece before reaching for the last remaining cake. Rindar smiled at him. Minxa shook his head, picked up his cake and pretended to struggle with breaking it.

Rasler smiled. "It breaks easier and tastes better if you are thankful—are you?" Minxa ignored her. "There's not a whole lot else to eat on Islag," she continued. "I've checked."

Minxa paused to think for a moment. "It'll do," he said as he dipped a piece of his oatcake into the stew. The stew tasted as gray as it looked, but as the first mouthful hit his stomach, Minxa suddenly realized how hungry he was.

Rasler continued, "Now, to answer your other question: we don't have to pay for the boat if we are willing to row."

"Row?" Minxa stopped eating as he said it. It had not occurred to him that the boat probably had no motor.

"Yes, row. This time of year the winds are from the northwest, and the only way to get the boat to Tessamandria will be to row it there."

"I've never been in a boat," said Rindar. Minxa watched as he stuffed a piece of the oatcake into his mouth before continuing. "And I wouldn't have a clue how to row."

Rasler laughed. "You don't have to know how, you just have to be willing to do it. The oars are linked together. They just need muscle to pull them."

"We can manage that," Rindar said. "How long a trip is it?"

"Not sure, maybe ten hours—uh oh."

Minxa looked up to see Drofan sauntering toward them. He approached with a grin and grabbed an empty chair from the table next to them, swung it around backwards and sat down with his legs straddling its back. "I didn't know you folks knew each other," he said. "Uh— may I join you?" His tone carried an emphasis that indicated he was not really giving them a choice.

Rasler was quick and civil. "Sure. We don't want any trouble."

Drofan put his fingers to his chest. "Trouble? From me?" he laughed. Rasler started to rise, and he raised his hands in a mock gesture of helplessness as his face and tone became suddenly serious. "No trouble—promise. Nice day in the woods, eh?" His dark brown eyes twinkled with mischief.

Minxa grunted. Rindar looked into Drofan's eyes. "Very nice, once the sun was up and our clothes dried. And how—"

"What do you want, Drofan?" interrupted Rasler without looking up from her meal.

"Well, I heard you were asking for a boat at the dock today. Where're you going?"

Rindar wanted to tell him it was none of his business, but Rasler intervened. "We are going to Tessamandria."

"We?"

"Yes—the three of us. Are you wanting to join us?"

Minxa looked up in disbelief. He saw Rindar open his mouth to speak but restrain himself when he saw Drofan's expression. It was a curious mixture of shock and disbelief with a twist of something Minxa couldn't identify.

"Where are you staying tonight?" Drofan asked seriously.

"In the woods," Rasler answered.

"I need to talk to you privately." Drofan's voice was hushed and his eyes darted around the room to see if any of the others were paying attention.

If Rasler was surprised, she did not let on. "Meet me at dusk at the point where the trail to the north end of the island leaves the road. No tricks."

"No tricks," Drofan echoed as he stood up. "It's been good to see you," he added for anyone who might have been listening. "See you later."

Minxa watched Drofan walk back to his comrades at the other end of the hall. As Drofan sat down, Minxa thought he saw him nod to the giant of a man sitting at the table in the corner. The man stood up and made his way out of the inn without even a glance at the table where the trio sat. He was huge, with a tired felt hat that shaded his eyes, and he was dressed in the same tattered gray clothing as the other men who crewed the boat. Minxa looked back at the table. The man's food remained uneaten. Rindar was dipping the last piece of his oatcake into the last stripe of the slushy gray stew. "What do you suppose that was all about?" he asked.

Rasler pushed back her chair. "I think he wants to come with us to Tessamandria." She stood up and nodded to the door. "Time to go. We will want to make camp before it gets dark."

As they walked out the door into the early evening sun, Minxa could feel the eyes that followed them. He was sure it was best to not be there any longer, but something inside him wanted to stay all the same. He felt he belonged there. In some small way, it seemed to be the place where he would feel most like being in Vindarill, but perhaps the feeling came from his resentment of Rasler's apparent control.

As Minxa emerged from the inn, he glanced around quickly to see what had become of Drofan's big friend. He could not have gone far in the short time since he had left the inn, but there was no sign of him anywhere. Minxa fell in beside Rindar as Rasler led them up over the slight rise toward the trail into the woods. The fresh salt air and the warm red sun breathed new vigor into him. He could feel the change but could not describe it. In any case, it was not enough to dispel the gnawing anger he held against Rindar for having dragged him into this strange place and time against his will, or the unease left by the man in the gray felt hat.

✠

Armatan about the outworld realities clarifies the provision of Mah'Eladra.

The Tessarandin, Book 4

The oar that had seemed so light in the exhilaration of boarding the boat on Islag had grown heavy and awkward after seven hours of rowing. Minxa's arms and back ached. The rowing had been arduous, but not very difficult. All the oars were linked with some kind of mechanism so that all Minxa had done for seven hours was pull when the oar started moving in the pulling direction.

On and off during the trip, Minxa had watched the big man he had seen in the inn. He was alone at the last oar on the left, and Minxa could see him straining powerfully with each stroke. He never turned or looked around, but just rowed. Something about the man intrigued Minxa and frightened him at the same time, but he could not identify the fear.

They passed between two points of land, in a channel that opened into the busy harbor of Karolil. Fishnets decorated the rocks. Many men, boys and women sat among them stitching and mending in the sun. They waved as the boat slipped past them toward the long pier directly in front of them.

Tall trees strode down almost to the edge of the water where the low sloping rocks ran in ridges to meet the waves. Unlike Islag, whose stark, craggy cliffs held its crown of deep blue-green trees far from the threat of the sea, the forest here was a light, shimmering green that glowed in the brilliant afternoon sun. In the calm harbor, the boat made a wake of its own that was not lost as it had been in the restless ocean behind them.

"Weighnuff!" All the oars lifted from the water, and the steersman used the momentum of the boat to coddle it to the low floating dock, as the starboard oars glided over its timbers. Two huge dockworkers threw ropes over the stout cleats in the gunwales and drew the boat to a stop against the wharf. "Drop oars!" The oars dropped to the deck with a heavy thump.

They filed silently off the boat and up onto the wharf. Rasler stepped to the side and sat down on one of the beams of the wharf to wait for Minxa and Rindar while the other rowers moved up the dock. Minxa saw Drofan pause briefly to speak to her. Rasler nodded without expression, but Minxa could not hear what she said to him. "What was that about?" he asked when he and Rindar caught up to her.

Rasler shrugged. "He wished us luck and I thanked him." She stood up and shouldered her pack. "We need to keep moving though," she added. "We don't have much time. I'll meet you at the top of the hill; I want to find out where Drofan is headed." She nodded up the wharf where Drofan was just disappearing around the corner of a low building.

As they walked, Minxa watched the groups of fishermen clustered on the wharf. Their hands were busy with the neat piles of fishing tackle that lay about the planking, and they alternately sucked on small clay pipes and joked with one another. They ignored the arrival of the boat except to nod as its rowers filed past.

The late afternoon sun shone warm on Minxa's back and cast a shadow twice as long as his height, illuminating the rich browns of the wharf with a peculiar radiance. It smelled like a wharf, but cleaner than the wharfs of Islag or Vindarill, and the water that slapped against the pilings was clear enough so that one could see the sand and rocks on the shallow bottom of the harbor. Neat houses lined the road that led from the wharf. They were bleached by the sun to the same gray as those of Islag, but were well kept and ornamented with flower boxes and surrounded by tidy white fences.

Where the road and the houses disappeared over the back of a small hill, a deep purple land mass rose to meet the violet northern sky. This purple wall ran to the east and to the west as far as Minxa could see. In either direction, it seemed to rise out of the ocean itself.

"Did you notice that the raven took off as soon as we entered the harbor?" Minxa asked Rindar, speaking low to keep the conversation private.

"He's a strange one," Rindar muttered back. "I thought it odd that he came with us. Maybe following us—or following Rasler."

"He gives me the creeps," Minxa said.

"Because he talks?"

"Don't know—"

"Because he's all black?"

"I told you, I don't know!" Minxa snapped.

"All right," Rindar said, "you don't have to take it so hard."

Minxa filtered his emotions as they made their way up the low hill toward the cluster of buildings that stood at the top. "I think I'm still angry at being here," he ventured after his thoughts calmed down. He nodded politely to a man who had smiled and tipped his hat to them as he passed.

"Maybe it's the bird's connection with Rasler," Rindar mused.

Minxa waited. "I don't like Rasler," he said at length. "Something about her...her style—and we don't even know what that connection is—to the bird, I mean. They know each other; that's clear."

"Do you still like *me*?" Rindar stopped in the road and was looking at him, waiting patiently for a direct answer.

Minxa turned to face him as a snarl of thoughts tangled his mind. "I think so—I mean—of course. You're my best friend."

"Really?"

"I'm just trying—something's different with you. Maybe it's this place; maybe it's whatever happened with that old man—maybe it's the map." Minxa stopped, pondering his next thought. "Maybe it's just me."

Rindar pursed his lips and bobbed his head as if he were weighing Minxa's options. "Maybe you're just hungry," he smiled. "Did you see where Drofan went?"

"No," he answered, "but I'm sure Rasler will find out."

Rindar shrugged. "Probably," he said. "He seemed very intent on coming with us last night; and then, in spite of Rasler's refusal to let him come, he came anyway—on his own." Rindar started up the hill. Minxa fell in beside his friend as they resumed their trek. "I think he is following us," Rindar continued. "From the things he said to us in the woods, I would guess he is after the you-know-what. We need to keep our wits about us."

"Did you see that big guy at the inn—the fellow in the corner?"

"No."

Minxa paused, then described to Rindar what he had seen. "He was the last rower; the one with an oar all to himself," he said.

Rindar nodded. "I did not see him get off the boat, did you?"

"No," Minxa admitted, "but I wasn't watching very closely."

Rindar changed the subject. "Have you thought any more about going with Rasler?" he asked.

"Yeah." Minxa had thought a lot on the boat. With each stroke of the oar, he had bullied his thoughts back and forth. "You're right. There isn't much of a choice."

"If you have a better idea, tell me."

"I don't." Minxa felt a sinking feeling in his stomach. It felt as if he was giving in to something that he knew would end up bad. For all the uncomfortable thoughts about what he faced in going with Rasler, thinking through all the details of another course of action was too much work. He smiled weakly at Rindar and shrugged. "Don't you have any desire to go back to Vindarill?" he asked. "Even just to find out what happened?"

Rindar stared up the hill. "Yes, I would like to know what happened." His words came slowly, full of the deep thoughts behind them. "I think I am afraid to try," he continued. "I didn't like coming through the portal any more than you did, and the risk of trying to get back and what might happen if we did is more than I want to face." Rindar's thoughts seemed unfinished so Minxa waited as they walked slowly. "I have dreams every night about the old man," Rindar continued. "They are strange—and vague, as if he keeps wanting me to talk to him, but I can't. He wants to tell me something, but I can never hear him. There is always something making too much noise."

"I still think you—we—were set up."

"I keep wondering that too. It might make sense if we were somebody important—but us?" Rindar laughed. "If we went back, we might be able to figure it out, but the way it happened—and the risk of trying to get back…it's too much."

"Someday, though?"

"Maybe," Rindar said, speaking into the distance, "but I have no interest in going back to being a viddik."

Rasler was waiting for them at the top of the hill. She sat on a large flat stone that formed one corner of a crossroads in the center of the town, talking with one of the villagers who sucked his small clay pipe and bent near to hear her. As they talked, he pointed and nodded in various directions. By the time Minxa and Rindar arrived and dropped themselves onto the stone, the old man had left.

"Did you find Drofan?" Rindar asked.

"He went straight to a bar just off the wharf," Rasler said. "Seems to know a lot of people there. The big fellow from the inn on Islag—the big rower—was there with him and several others."

"You saw him last night?" asked Minxa.

Rasler nodded. "I asked the captain who he was. His name is Vashtor. Been working the Karolil boat for about three years."

"Vashtor?" Rindar asked in surprise.

"Do you know him?"

"Never seen him before," Rindar lied. "We just got here remember?"

Rasler paused. "You just reacted to his name, that's all."

"It's just an odd name," Rindar said as he shook his head.

Rasler stared at him. Minxa was sure that she knew he was lying, but instead of pressing Rindar for more details, she changed the subject. "We'll be able to get all we need right here," she said, sweeping her hand around the intersection, "but we should do it quickly. Everything closes when the sun sets." She squinted toward the western horizon. "Little more than an hour at best, and we need to be on the road early. I don't like the way things are happening here."

"How're we gonna get what we need?" Minxa grumbled. "We only have Rindar's one coin."

Rasler fetched her purse from her belt. "We actually have a bit more," she said as she shook it.

Minxa could hear several coins. "You said last night at the inn—it was your last drag!" he growled.

"It was." Minxa detected no defensiveness in Rasler's voice as she poured several coins into her hand. "And Mah'Eladra gave us some more."

"Mah'Eladra?" Rindar beat Minxa to the question.

Rasler held out her hand. She held two silver coins, one larger copper coin and one gold one. "I knew we would not have enough, so I told them this morning that we would probably need more."

"Who? When this morning?" Minxa asked.

"Mah'Eladra. On Islag, before you were awake."

"And what happened?" Rindar seemed genuinely interested. Minxa felt irritated.

"Well, I found this in a crack in the floorboard of the boat, under my seat," she said, holding up the gold coin, "when we stopped rowing for lunch."

Minxa sneered. "Someone must have dropped it—and probably long before you asked Mah'Eladra."

"Perhaps so, but they told me to look there."

"When?"

"This morning."

"And the silver—the copper?"

"The copper one I found on the wharf at Islag, just before we got on the boat, and the silver I found behind this stone." She pointed over the back side of the stone behind where they sat.

"How did you know to look there?"

"I always look behind places where people are likely to sit."

Minxa pressed on. "So you think that Mah'Eladra just give you things because you ask for them?"

"Why not? Most anything you ever got in your life you got because

you asked someone who had it, right?—unless you stole it." Minxa
wanted to be offended by her afterthought, but her sincerity and intensity would not allow it. He looked down and shook his head in frustration. It was one more thing that he did not want to consider. He looked
up at Rindar, who shrugged and refused to defend him. Rasler continued, "Did you have children in—Vindarill?"

"How old do you think I am?" Minxa barked as he looked up.

"Twenty-two," Rasler answered without hesitation.

Rindar laughed.

"Seventeen," Minxa said, then shot back, "Do *you* have children?"

"I have a son."

Minxa could not identify the feeling that swept over him. He had
meant it as a comeback to her questioning, and now he felt waves of
compassion and frustration colliding inside him.

Rasler continued, "When you have children, you give them things
they ask for because you love them. You give them things they do not
ask for but you know they need—because you love them, and even
when they fail, you take care of them out of love."

Minxa was looking at the ground. This young woman spoke from a
place he knew he had never been. She spoke in a way that rang of profound truth but with a gentle acceptance of where he was, and he could
do nothing but listen.

"I have chosen to be as a child to Mah'Eladra. I tell them what I
need, and I look for their provision. If I don't find that for which I have
asked, then it is because I do not need it or there is a better alternative."
She flipped the gold coin over in her palm. "Today, by their provision,
we have just what we need, and you said you had one coin. Now is the
time to spend it. We have a long journey and we need several things.
Where is your money, Rindar?"

Rindar fetched the coin from his pocket and opened his palm to
show Rasler. She bent close to examine it. "Where did you get it?" she
asked in surprise.

"It was given to me in Vindarill—before we left. I still had it in my
pocket when we came through the portal."

"They use drags in Vindarill?" she asked.

"Sometimes," Minxa lied.

Rasler stared at him for a moment before she reached down, took
his hand and placed her gold coin into it before closing his fingers
around it. "Fifty drags," she said. "We will start up there tomorrow
morning," she continued as she pointed north toward the purple wall.
"You and Rindar find blanket rolls and food with this and the twenty
drag silver." She waved across the crossroads to the store on the opposite corner. The two-story building had a covered porch that ran the

width of it and was stacked with barrels and several wooden boxes over-
flowing with potatoes, carrots and onions lined up beside each other.
Two lines of dried fish hung between the rough beams that supported
the structure.

"Get two working knives at the—shop," she added as she nodded
toward the other corner at a low weathered building with unpainted
walls and two stout chimneys that rose from either end. Its sign swung
from chains: an elliptical iron ring that encircled a silhouette of a hammer and tongs. "Ironware" was all it said. "I will get some herbs and
other supplies we will need and visit the tailor—and the shoemaker. We
will meet back here at sundown."

Minxa sat still, not wanting to move. He just wanted to sit and
think, but Rindar prodded him with his index finger. "C'mon," Rindar
whispered, "we don't have much time."

ꙮ Across the Wastes ꙮ

Noble truth is the truth that stands
beyond personal experience.

Pratoraman
The Middle Way

It had taken most of the morning and half the afternoon to get to the top of the escarpment above the seaport of Karolil. Looking down, Rindar could see the village as a small cluster of dwellings with its light blue harbor and the cobalt sea stretching out away from it to the horizon. Islag was a gray crack between the ocean and the sky. As the air rose up the face of the escarpment, the smell of the water had been replaced by the warm odor of the soil and rock baked by the sun. Rindar sat with Minxa as they shared a snack of crackers and dried fruit with sips of water from their new flasks.

Three seagulls rode the rising air. As they drifted lazily back and forth, Rindar sensed that they were watching him, and it made him uneasy. "Do gulls usually come this far from the water?" he asked as he nodded at them.

"I don't know," Minxa answered. "I think that they want something to eat, but they're better than that raven."

"They make me nervous," Rindar answered, "like they're up to something."

"They're just gulls!" Minxa insisted.

"Why would they be this far from the water?"

"They'll go anywhere to find food. They probably think we have some."

"There's a lot more food in Karolil than here with us. I don't think that they are that stupid."

They sat for a while in silence before Minxa changed the subject. "Do you have any idea how long it will take us to get to the Crown?" he asked.

"Several days, I think," Rindar answered. "Rasler says she can find the way there. You should almost be able to see it from here." He swung around and pointed into the distance in the opposite direction. "You see those clouds on the horizon? They are probably sitting on the Crown."

"I found us a place to stay for the night," Rasler said.

"Sesh!" Minxa exclaimed as he jumped in surprise. Rindar felt the adrenaline rush through him.

"It's about half an hour from here," she continued, "halfway down to the plateau. We need to get there before it gets dark. The trail is not as clear as I'd hoped."

Rindar stood, and as he reached down to grab his pack, Minxa announced, "I'm not going yet."

"We'll eat after we have made camp," Rasler continued as she swung her pack onto her back. "Where are the gulls?" she asked.

Rindar turned around. The gulls had vanished.

"This is not good," Rasler urged. "We have to go!"

"I'm not rested enough yet," Minxa retorted.

"We agreed in Karolil that Rasler would be in charge."

"I'm tired. I'm not leaving until I'm ready."

"It's time to go," Rasler repeated as she hitched her pack. "You can stay here if you like—but I wouldn't if I were you." She started walking down the narrow trail toward the plateau below.

"Well, you're not me," Minxa said coldly as he started fishing in his pack for something else to eat.

Rindar was not sure what to do. He knew somehow that Rasler was right, but he did not want to leave Minxa alone. He had seen more of this dark side of Minxa lately, after arriving on Islag through the portal, but as he thought about it, he realized that it was not new. It had been there all along; but the isolation of their new and unfamiliar situation, their limited contact with other beings, coupled with more time together, seemed to bring Minxa's irritation to the surface more often.

"We cannot stay here long," he started.

"Why not?" Minxa droned.

"Rasler is right. The three of us need to stick together. We have no idea what kinds of dangers we face out here."

"Look at this place, will you?" Minxa swept his hand out over the plateau, down over the slope and then back to the village, far below them. "There's nothing here. No one for miles, and anyone would have to be crazy to come out here looking for us. We don't have anything except a bit of food. We don't have any money—we spent the last of what we had buying the meager supplies we are carrying. So what is the problem?"

Minxa was right, but Rindar knew he was also wrong. Truth was not always completely right, at least the kind of truth that Minxa saw; so Rindar hesitated, not being sure how to make his argument.

"Besides, Rasler gives me the creeps," Minxa continued.

"The creeps?"

"Have you noticed she seems to know everything, even when she can't possibly know it? She knows things are going to happen before they do."

"That's true, but so what? That's the kind of person we should like to have around, don't you think?"

"It's just weird…and did you notice that she spent her last few coins on dinner at the inn in Islag?"

"So? She did find the fifty drag golden—and the copper and the silver coins."

"I don't believe it and I don't like it…not a bit. There is something she is not telling us."

"It seems that way, sometimes."

Minxa just needed to talk. Rindar waited and looked out over the deepening shadows of the plateau. Nothing moved. Even the inevitable progress of the approaching darkness was imperceptible. The bright oranges of the rocks in the surface of the plateau were punctuated with the deep purple and blue lines that ran down the valleys.

Rindar knew that they had to go, but he wasn't sure what to say to Minxa. The infection of doubt crept through him, and though he knew that he had to trust Rasler's judgment, there was something in Minxa's presence that made him doubt anyway. He looked at Minxa, who leaned back with his hands folded around one knee. He was staring back in the direction of the town, deep in the shadows of the coast below them.

Minxa straightened and turned suddenly to Rindar as he felt the sense of danger that hit them at the same time. "What was that?" His voice was hushed and urgent.

Rindar moved into silent speak. "*Quiet. Danger!*" He held his finger to his lips as he looked around. Nothing moved in the vastness that surrounded them. "*We go,*" he tapped as he reached for his pack. Any trace of reluctance that Minxa may have had was gone as he shouldered his pack quietly and stood up.

The trail wound around the boulders and scrub brush that dominated the ridge. Perhaps the sense of foreboding altered his view from the ridge, but the vast comforting emptiness suddenly seemed darker. To Rindar's left, the small lights from the town twinkled in the distance, and only the very tips of the hills in the plateau to his right showed any reminder of the sun. In a few moments, they too would be lost in the deep purple-gray of dusk.

The wind picked up, and it whistled through the low bushes and moaned between the rocks. Minxa crowded close behind Rindar. He had not known Minxa to be a fearful person, but the new world in which they found themselves, its unfamiliarity and the distance in time from the crowded comfort of the city had begun to take its toll on both their vorns.

When they came to a place where the trail dipped suddenly to the right and started its descent into the plateau, Rindar stopped and pulled Minxa to the side. They leaned against a boulder with their backs to its warm face. "Do you still feel it?" he whispered in Minxa's ear.

"Following us—got to keep moving," Minxa whispered as he stepped in front of Rindar to take the lead. Rindar understood why Minxa had been crowding him. Minxa's suggestion of the danger being behind them melded with his own perception, and he did not like being in the back. The rough trail turned back and forth down the slope. This made their progress seem slow, but the switchbacks gave Rindar the slight comfort of being able to see the trail behind them and above.

Rindar wished that he had listened to Rasler's warning. He had no idea how far they would have to go before they caught up with her. They could barely see. Any hope of finding her would depend on her wanting to be found. If the danger they sensed was real, it would be foolish for Rasler to reveal her whereabouts and so endanger herself also. "Keep going," Rindar urged in a hoarse whisper. Neither Tal nor Meekar had risen, and Rindar vaguely remembered that the night before, neither of the moons had risen until much later.

Rindar had taken about ten steps when a long warbling whistle from above startled him. He froze and Minxa reached for his hand. Stars shone above the line of blackness formed by the rim of the plateau, but everything below the rim was a formless mass of pitch, moaning in the wind. Anything that moved there was invisible.

The whistle warbled again, this time at the turn of the switchback behind them. The darkness kept him from running, but Rindar's heart pounded with terror and his throat felt like dry paper.

A new sound emerged from the darkness: a whirring followed suddenly by a hum that shot over their heads into the dark above them and clattered against the rocks. A guttural curse echoed off the stones. Another whirring followed, then the hum and the ricochet of a second stone bouncing among the boulders. More cursing followed. This time it came from several beings at the same time. The third stone produced a howl of pain and hurried, angry voices tumbling down from the trail above them.

"Follow me," said a voice right behind Rindar and past him at the same time. Rindar looked down. Two small lights danced along the path in front of him. Rasler had tied something to her ankles that barely illuminated the path, and Rindar fell in behind her with Minxa holding onto his pack from behind. Rasler moved dangerously fast, but he followed closely with his eyes glued to the small bobbing lights.

They ran in the dark for about five minutes before Rasler stopped suddenly. "Wait here," she said. The lights on her ankles disappeared, and she vanished into the darkness back up the trail, leaving Rindar and Minxa sitting alone for about a minute. "We're safe now," she said when she returned. "C'mon, we don't have far to go."

The lights appeared on her ankles again, and the three of them ambled down the trail. Rindar tried to piece together what had happened, but the darkness and the fear occluded his ability to comprehend the sequence of events.

☩

True armatan has eyes that penetrate the darkest shadows in the vorn.

Hispattea
The Essences of Corritanean Wisdom

"We were being followed," Rasler said at lunch the next day. She broke her imposed silence with a casual statement of fact when they reached the floor of the plateau.

Minxa had removed his boots and the grass felt good between his toes. He had many questions. "Do you know *who* was following us?" he asked.

"No, but they were very good, and I tracked them for a while. They know what they are doing and seem to be very familiar with this trail, and my guess is that we are likely to encounter them again. They are not out for our best interest." Rasler's voice was low but firm, ringing with confidence in her knowledge.

"How many were there?" Rindar asked.

"Five or six. I could not tell exactly in the dark, but I wounded one of them with my sling."

"If it was dark, how could you see to use your sling?" Minxa asked.

"In the town where I grew up, my father made friends with a Pistisine guardian whose route passed through the town. The summer before I left home I traveled with her. She taught me how to see in the dark—and a few other things."

"Like how to lie to your friends?"

Rasler remained unfazed by Minxa's attack. "Do you feel I have been anything but honest with you?" she replied, looking straight into his eyes.

"You told us your change purse was empty when it obviously wasn't!"

Rasler reached down, and in a single quick motion, detached her purse from her belt. She tossed it into Minxa's lap. Minxa kept his eyes on Rasler as he slowly reached for the purse, rolled it between his fingers and shook it. A sneer spread over his face as he tossed it back. "Of course it's empty. You really did empty it at the lodge in the town."

"It was empty each time I said so."

"I suppose it was one of those 'Pistine' tricks you learned?"

"*Pistisine*! And yes, I *did* learn it from Fontara, but it is not a trick. It is a matter of armatan—one must believe."

Minxa snorted. As if dealing with Rasler's arrogance were not enough, her philosophical babble made it that much worse. He looked at Rindar. Rindar shrugged off Minxa's unspoken plea for support with a look of vague helplessness.

"When I need some money," Rasler continued, "I will find what I need. If I do not need it, there won't be any." Rasler focused on Minxa. "You scoff at my life, Minxa, and in your mind you deride my abilities as tricks or magic, as if I am a simpleton and an unsophisticated charlatan, and you are somehow better than me. Yet it is you who continually needs my intervention to even survive in my world. And you will need me again, so there is no sense to your irritation. Your mordage is thick, and it occludes your sense."

Minxa stiffened. "There is not any such thing as *mordage*," he grumbled, his eyes narrowing as the word came through his lips.

Rasler continued earnestly, "The mordage is very real. It infects the vorn, eventually occluding the nephus nearly into invisibility. But for those whose nephus is so jaded, it is indeed difficult to perceive its presence at all."

Minxa stared into the fog that had swallowed the trail in front of them. Rasler remained focused on him, so he turned his back on her in a gesture of contempt, hoping she would say no more.

In the quiet space that followed, Minxa was suddenly aware of the stillness and turned back to face the others. The same feeling of acute danger he had felt the night before returned. Rasler sat up straight, tipped her nose into the still air and breathed slowly, turning her head to one side and the other in quick, jerky motions. Her index fingers shot to her lips. "Get ready to run," she whispered. There was barely time to understand what she had said before she shouted, "Now!" She rolled nimbly to one side. A stone the size of her head smashed into soft earth exactly where she had been sitting. "Run!" she shouted again.

Minxa saw a second stone graze Rindar's shoulder before it shattered into pieces on the rock beside him. Rindar jumped to his feet. Rasler was nowhere to be seen. Minxa grabbed his boots as the rocks began to rain down around them. He started to run. Sharp rocks stabbed into his bare feet. He had barely taken three short steps when a stone creased his right cheek. He swore as he brought his hand up to his face and dropped one of his boots. Panic gripped him. Blood was running down his face, and he pressed his hand desperately against the wound, leaving his boot somewhere behind him as he stumbled onward in the fog.

As he passed the dim shadow of a large boulder, Rindar grabbed him by his arm and pulled him into its shelter. He held only one boot, and his feet were bleeding and bruised. They leaned against the rock breathing heavily. There was no sign of Rasler, and they could not see more than ten feet in the fog. They waited silently.

Suddenly the rocks stopped raining down, and the silence settled in around them again. Rindar motioned to him, *"Quiet."* He nodded and pulled his right hand slowly away from his cheek. It was bleeding badly from a deep gash, and Minxa quickly put his hand back over the wound to slow the flood of blood, wincing as he touched it.

Minxa held his hand to his face. Their enemy, whoever or whatever it was, remained unseen and unknown. Rasler was gone, and the hostility of the world around them lay like a stifling blanket on Rindar's vorn. He was breathing hard, and his heart pounded in his ears and chest. He knew they had to do something but had no idea what.

Minxa held his cheek against his shoulder as he struggled to put on his boot. When he finally got it tied, he brought his hand up to his cheek again and looked over at Rindar with a cold anger. Rindar had seen that look before, but not for a long time. He wanted to slap Minxa.

"Don't do it!" Rasler's telepathy interrupted Rindar's thoughts. He peered into the fog, but she was nowhere to be seen. *"His mordage is feeding yours,"* she continued. *"You must ignore his anger."* Rindar wanted to answer, but could not. *"Stitch his wound; it is safe for now, but stay quiet!"* Rindar removed his pack. *"When you have bandaged your friend,*

head to the left down the trail. We will meet later."

Rindar nodded as he dropped his pack to the ground. He bent to find the bandages, and it only took a moment to locate the small bundle that Rasler had purchased in Karolil. Minxa watched as Rindar unrolled it carefully on top of his pack. In the middle, he found a curved needle and a knot of fine thread. "I have to stitch that wound," he whispered. "Then we have to go."

Minxa removed his hand and quickly replaced it when he felt the blood flow down his cheek. He shook his head.

"We have no choice," Rindar insisted. He had never sewn anything in his life, and in Vindarill, he would not have dared to try. Here, there was no alternative. He waited insistently until Minxa relented and let him stitch the wound closed against the flow of blood.

✠

Friendship is measured with deeds, not words.

Mythinian Proverb

Minxa broke the silence with a hoarse whisper. "Thanks for helping out back there," he said as he walked along behind Rindar. He meant what he said. He knew Rindar was only doing what needed to be done, and his anger was not leveled at his friend. It was an anger that lay far deeper than the current situation. On the surface, it was about Rasler, but he had to admit to himself that she had done nothing but help.

The stitching had been painful. Rindar's passable attempt held the wound together and the bleeding had stopped, but they had no way to clean it properly. Minxa expected it to leave a nasty scar. He had winced every time Rindar ran the needle through the skin, and the wincing had caused more pain. When it was over, they had both sat back against the rock exhausted. The fog had thinned, and with Rindar's urging, they had left the shelter of the boulder and headed down the trail away from where they had come.

They had walked for about half an hour before Minxa felt free to speak. "You are a true friend," he continued in a hushed voice. "Sorry about my attitude."

"What happened to your boot?" Rindar whispered.

"I dropped it when that rock hit me. I was running and didn't stop."

"We should stop and wrap something around your foot," Rindar said. He paused and then seemed to change his mind suddenly. "Can you last a little longer," he continued, "until we get to a safe place?"

"Aren't we safe here?"

"No...not yet."

"How do you know?" Minxa whispered.

"Let's go a little farther," Rindar urged. After about twenty steps, Rindar waved to Minxa, signaling him to be silent. Rindar led the way into a narrow crack in the rock, which wound back about ten feet and then became too narrow to go any farther. They could hardly move in the narrow space. The angles in the stone cut the view so that they could barely see onto the trail where they had been walking. Minxa looked at Rindar curiously and signed, *"Why?"* with his fingers on Rindar's palm. Rindar put his finger to his lips and shrugged.

Minxa's impatience rose, and he started to move back toward the entrance. Rindar pulled him back. He shook Rindar's hand off his shirt, and as he turned to move again, he froze. A shadow passed the entrance to the crevice. It swept by in utter silence, followed by four others, perhaps two seconds apart.

Minxa held his breath as his heart pounded. There was nothing to do but wait.

A sudden shower of sand cascaded down from above. When it stopped, Minxa looked up cautiously. From ten feet above them, Rasler's silhouette peered down into their hiding place. "Climb," she whispered. He tugged on Rindar's sleeve and pointed toward the sky. They inched upward between the stone walls, bracing their arms, shoulders, back and knees to help in the climb. After several minutes, they emerged onto the stone platform above the crack.

Rasler motioned for them to sit down quietly. As they leaned against a protrusion of stone a few feet from the crack they had crawled out of, she handed them each a small stick of dried, salted meat. Then she reached into her pack and handed Minxa his second boot.

✠

Here we will build our fire and shed the weariness of this journey.

Erengnira
The Tiger in the Tree

Dawn on the fourth day found the travelers huddled at the back of a shallow cave facing north. It arrived slowly in sheets of driving rain from the east, fueled by a tempest that raged across the plateau and had forced them to stop and take refuge. They had no fire, and they hadn't spoken since they met on the rock after their separation. Rasler had forbidden both in spite of Minxa's nonverbal protests.

They followed Rasler because of their acute awareness of danger.

The nameless, faceless fear had driven them off the trail and had made their progress slow and painful as they scrambled over rocks and crawled through the dense undergrowth of the desolate wilderness. Each night she had managed to find them shelter in the unrelenting fog that surrounded them.

The wind howled at the mouth of the cave, and the pelting of the rain spat on them occasionally where they sat. Rasler spoke for the first time: "We're lost."

Minxa's first words were unrepeatable. He lowered his head between his knees where he sat and shook it in disgust. Rindar glanced up into Rasler's calm eyes. She didn't seem lost.

Rindar had a sudden thought, and it surprised him with its clarity and its obviousness. "I have a map," he said simply. He did not know why it had not occurred to him sooner to tell Rasler about it.

Rasler seemed unfazed. "I know."

"You *know*?"

"I guessed—and then I overheard you talking with Minxa about it on Islag. May I see it?"

A sudden wave of resentment crept into Rindar's hjarg. "Why didn't you ask me about it before?"

"I did. You lied to me."

Rindar looked down as the simple truth flowed into a realization that went far beyond the content of the single lie he had conceived on Islag when she had asked him about it. He was a liar. This lie had been lived out for several days and had jeopardized all their safety. Rasler knew it but had said nothing. If she had confronted him directly at any point until then, he would have been angry; he would have resisted the invasion of his private view of himself, and he would have resented her discovery. Now he found himself frustrated by Rasler's incredible capacity for acceptance, a frustration that made little sense in the current situation.

As he reached for his pack, Rasler's hand caught his wrist, and he looked up. "Where did you get this map?" she asked.

Rindar dropped his eyes. He sensed that a lie would only discredit him further in Rasler's eyes. "From the man...I killed."

Rasler let go of his wrist. "May I see it?"

Her question surprised him, partly because she had already asked it, but mostly because it carried no hint of a reaction to how he had acquired the map. He somehow knew that she wanted him to answer the question with his words and mind before he acquiesced with action. "Yes," he said. Rasler nodded and Minxa uttered another oath and spat on the ground between his legs.

Rasler waited patiently while Rindar pulled the small flat box from his pack. He marveled that in spite of the abuse of the last week, it looked exactly the same, and he breathed deeply as he opened it. Rasler remained still, and Minxa sat with his head still between his knees.

The map fell flat on the uneven floor of the cave and glowed faintly in the semidarkness of the dreary morning. Rindar saw Rasler's hands quivering as they moved above the map. "Do you know how it works?" she asked.

"Some," Rindar answered as he watched Rasler's excitement and awe.

"Where are we?"

"We're always in the center at first...right here," he said as he pointed to the small blotches of light in the middle. "This is the mouth of the cave..."

Rasler looked closer. "This must be that face of rock we climbed last night...and here is the stream." Her finger hovered over the map.

"You can touch it if you want," he volunteered.

She withdrew her hand quickly. "I shouldn't."

"What would you like to see?"

Rasler hesitated. It was the first time Rindar had seen her unsure of what to say or do. "What else is there to see?" she asked.

Minxa stirred and looked up. "You can see anything you want," he said, his voice was thick with aggravation. "At least *he* can," he added with a sneer, tossing his head in Rindar's direction and then turning away to stare out at the rain. Rasler ignored him.

"What would you like to see?" Rindar asked again.

"The other side of that stream." Her finger swept over the small stream in the corner of the map.

Rindar reached over and drew the details sideways so that the cave was in the far corner.

Rasler sat back in stunned silence. "How about over this way?" she said after a pause.

He pulled the details of the map in the direction she indicated.

"Can we see a bigger area?"

Rindar touched the small symbol he knew would make the details smaller and the coverage of the map larger.

"Incredible. Can you move it to yesterday?"

"What?"

"Yesterday. I want to see yesterday." Her voice carried a tone of insistence and frankness that made Rindar almost believe it was possible. It had not occurred to him that he might be able to move the map through time.

Rasler saw his confusion. "I have heard that you can see all time and all places."

"I...I have only had it for a week—only used it maybe five times,"

Rindar said. Rasler leaned close to the edge of the map examining the runes that lay within the circles in the border. Her eyes moved slowly around to the left. "Do you understand these symbols?" Rindar asked.

"Some of them," she said as she nodded. "They are very old. My father would know them—here!" she exclaimed, hovering her fingers over a string of connected circles. "These are the time controls." She leaned closer. "Forward...backward...day...hour...now...try this one," she added as she pointed to the one she called "backward."

Rindar touched it and nothing happened. She pointed to the "day" circle.

As he touched it, the map swirled for an instant and then stopped.

She leaned forward and stared for a moment. "There...there we are," she exclaimed, "and the spring—and that small hill that we climbed after we got up." Rasler sat up straight and looked at Rindar in surprise. "You can see other beings!"

Rindar nodded, then reached down and touched the circle to expand the view. The map drew down to where they could see about a mile around where they were. Rasler scanned the map rapidly. "More."

He touched it again. Rasler found what she was looking for quickly: seven small smudges spread out along the trail, perhaps a mile and a half from where they had been. Rindar looked up.

Rasler's eyes narrowed. "Touch 'now'."

The map swirled again under Rindar's finger.

"More," said Rasler calmly. Rindar touched the map.

"Again." After the swirling stopped, she pointed at the seven small dark specks. Two were on the trail together. The others were spread out, about halfway between the cave and the trail, perhaps a mile from where they sat.

"Does anyone know you have this?" she asked suddenly.

"No—but then, I didn't know that *you* knew we had it."

"Drofan," Minxa said.

Rasler whirled to face him. "What?"

"I think Drofan knows we have it," Minxa said. "I think that is why he tied us up. He just did not know what he was looking for when he went through our packs. You remember what he said the second time he caught us?" he asked as he looked at Rindar.

"Something about 'getting it this time'," Rindar conceded.

"If he came to steal it from you," Rasler observed, "but did not know what he was looking for, there must be someone else who knows."

"The big man at the inn," said Minxa.

"What?!" asked Rasler.

Minxa told her about what he had seen at the inn that night.

"It's worse than I thought," she said as she reached for her pack.

"What do you mean?"

"We have to leave soon."

"Sesh!" Minxa swore again.

Rasler looked over at him. "You may stay if you like, but I wouldn't if I were you. Whatever we face in this wind and rain, it is not likely to be worse than being captured by these beings," she said, pointing to the small smudges.

The onslaught of the rain chilled Rindar to the bone. They walked fast, following the course Rasler had charted into the wilderness using the map: first west, to separate themselves from their pursuers, then north toward the Crown of Tessalindria. Because of the fog, they had not yet seen it, but by Rasler's estimate, they were less than two days away. The peak should have dominated the view to the north. All Rindar could see were sheets of rain and fast-moving low clouds that sometimes dropped to surround them in numbing grayness.

Rasler led and Minxa brought up the rear. The thick undergrowth, coupled with the limited visibility, made their footing on the slippery wet rocks tricky. Rindar's fingers and toes grew numb with the chill. Small streams had become violent obstacles to their progress, and each crossing was at the risk of their lives. No one spoke except to the necessity of survival.

About noon, Rasler found an overhanging rock that sheltered them from the wind and rain. They crowded in under it and sat down on the cold stone, huddling together, wetter and more miserable than they had yet been on the journey. "May I see the map?" Rasler asked. Rindar slung off his pack and unfolded the precious map, opening it quickly before her and widening its range until they could see their pursuers.

Rasler inhaled deeply. The specks were all at the cave where they had stayed the night before. "We will build a fire and stay here. Right now we need firewood. Minxa, stay here and watch our stuff and prepare something we can cook. We're going to find some wood." She looked at Rindar and nodded her head out into the rain. "We'll be back soon. We won't have to go far."

Rindar did not want to leave Minxa alone, but he believed Rasler had a reason for everything she did, so he followed her out into the rain.

Rasler moved rapidly as if she knew that Rindar could keep up. They wound upward along the side of the hill. There were no trees here at all, and where she hoped to find wood was more than a mystery to Rindar.

They had come around the shelter of a bluff into the full frontal blast of the wind in their faces. Rasler stopped abruptly and held out her hands to the wind, looking up as if she were beseeching the clouds themselves. When she dropped her hands, she turned to him and smiled. "We passed it."

"What?"

"The tree," Rasler said as she slid by him and headed back and slightly up. Rindar followed her. She ran about forty paces before she stopped suddenly again. There, wedged into a crack in the rocks was an ancient tree, leafless and white with age and protected from the rain by the overhanging stone. She reached up and pulled off one of the branches. "Take off your cloak," she said. She stripped off her outer coat and laid it in the shallow cave and started breaking branches off the tree, snapping them across her knee so they would fit in the coat. Rindar did the same.

In a matter of minutes, they had enough wood to make a comfortable fire. As Rindar leaned over to pick up the bundle of wood on his cloak, Rasler moved under the overhang and sat down. "We have to talk," she said, motioning for him to sit down beside her. Rindar felt a strange fear. The place she wanted him to sit was uncomfortably close. Rindar hesitated. "You can stand in the rain if you prefer," she said.

The only place where it was not raining and not occupied by their collection of wood was right beside her. Rindar wondered at his hesitation. She was not particularly beautiful, but her confident manner and strength was something he had never seen in a woman. The rain had soaked her from head to foot, and her matted hair hung across her forehead and fell limply down behind her head. She sat with her knees pulled up to her chest and her arms wrapped around them. It made her appear small and weak.

It dawned on Rindar that he feared himself, not Rasler. He feared his emotions, so he turned and sat down beside her partly to prove that his fear was ridiculous and partly to get out of the cold rain. Rasler stared out into the gray clouds, and Rindar sat uncomfortably until she spoke.

"I think if we make it to the Crown, we will be safe. Until then we are in grave danger."

"What did you see on the map that made you so alarmed?"

She seemed surprised. Her eyes were inches away, and he could feel them probing him. "From the map...the dark smudges."

"Because they were *dark*?"

"Our spots were faint, light smudges. Theirs were dark—gray."

"You know something else about the map!?"

"My father had seen it. Someone in Sessasha's circle had it. He described everything he knew about it to me before I left home."

"Do you know how they are following us?" Rindar ventured.

"I have a suspicion."

Rindar sat for a moment hoping she would continue on her own. "What is it?" he finally asked.

She stared out into the clouds again. "I believe that they want the map, and they are drawn to our mordage."

Rindar remained silent, so Rasler continued. "The discussion we had the other day with Minxa—his mordage is deep. If he is not careful, he will be overcome by it. The NarEladra know the mordage—how to read it, how to follow it; and they find those whose mordage is close to overpowering them, and draw them away from Mah'Eladra—and others."

"NarEladra? You think they are NarEladra?"

"I am not sure, but we can take no chances."

Rindar shook his head in bewilderment. He knew little about the NarEladra, except from the legends, but from what he knew, it could not be good that they were on his trail.

"They feed the part of the being that breeds the mordage. At some point, the mordage becomes so strong that the awareness of the El disappears entirely and the vorn is crippled. The being is intelligent and ruthless in his pursuit of selfish goals—out of balance and destined for Oblivion."

Rasler looked at Rindar again. "Do you understand what I said?"

Part of Rindar wanted to be offended, but Rasler somehow made it impossible to do that. "I've heard the terms," he said, "but the way you connected them together slipped by me."

"For example?" She was staring at him with her gray eyes. He could not look back with her sitting so close.

"You said Minxa's mordage is deep, and you also used the word 'strong.' When we were talking, what was it—three nights ago?...you used the word 'thick'... I've never been given a good description of the mordage to know whether it is real, or to identify it. Minxa and I always made fun of people who thought the mordage was real."

"The mordage is like a wall between us and other beings. It is a wall that we build for defense, with our anger, our resentment—our jealousy, envy, fear...our actions—when we violate the laws of psadeq. It becomes something we hide behind to keep others from knowing what is really in our vorn. We build it a little bit at a time with each hurt, with each lie, with each angry word, each breach of trust. My father used the word 'thick' to describe the essence of the mordage that separates us from other beings. The word 'deep' he reserved for the effect it has on *our* vorn, how far it penetrates and how much damage it does to *us*."

She paused. It was beginning to make sense so Rindar nodded and she continued.

"Its 'strength' is a combination of the two, the overarching effect of alienating us from our own goodness, from the El that Mah'Eladra want us to have, from other beings, even those we want to be close to."

"And what is the El?" Rindar felt the embarrassment of his own ignorance, but if Rasler thought anything less of him because of it, she didn't show it.

"There are a lot of different ways to look at it, but the best description is that it is the piece of the vorn that can be connected directly to Mah'Eladra themselves. There is a part of the vorn that is empty, if you will, and can be filled only with a piece of the nature of Mah'Eladra. They fill it with the El. It is given to those beings who trust explicitly and are willing to take action based on its leadings—that kind of trust is the armatan of the Kirrinath."

"I think I need to sleep on this before you tell me much more," Rindar said, "but why do the NarEladra care?"

"The NarEladra are on a mission to destroy the man kind—out of envy. They were created to serve, but many have rebelled and want to have the freedom given to the man kind. Their goal is to destroy the vorn so that the person is destroyed when he or she dies. It does not satisfy them to kill a person whose vorn is not bound by its mordage."

They sat and stared into the rain.

"In either case," Rasler continued, "we must be very careful with your friend Minxa. He adds to his mordage daily and he hates me. I am not sure it was good to leave him alone, but I needed to talk to you about it."

"I don't think Minxa is a threat, but what should we watch for?"

"If we encounter our pursuers, I fear he will turn to them. They are clever—and very strong. I am also concerned they know we have the map, and it is essential they do not get it," she said, the emphasis punctuating her determined words. "Minxa trusts you—I sense his psadeq with you is strong; you are cymbic. You must confront him. You will have to protect him and strengthen him so he does not fall. Come, we need to get back."

Rindar hesitated. "I have some questions for you." Rasler settled back to the ground. Rindar waited to see if anything else was forthcoming before he broached his next question: "You mentioned that you had—you have—a son—"

Rasler shifted and continued staring out into the rain, and her face lost all but the faintest trace of expression. "His name is Lothandra," she said softly. "He lives with my father and mother."

Rindar watched her face. He was not sure whether it was a tear or a drop from her wet hair that ran down her face to her lip where she licked it off.

"I was a rebellious child," she continued, "and I disdained my father because of his armatan and the abuse he took for living it out. Life in Vindor was hard enough without the continual rejection of everyone because of my father. I made many mistakes—many, many mistakes. I was pregnant at seventeen, and we moved again to get away from the man whose child I carried." Rasler paused, picked up a pebble and tossed it into the rain. "My son was born in deep winter. Both of us nearly died. Throughout the ordeal, my father sought Mah'Eladra, and my life was spared in a profound miracle."

She turned and looked at Rindar. He could see the tears clearly now, brimming around her gray eyes. "That spring," she continued as she stared out into the rain again, "Fontara passed through our town. When she came through the village seeking a place to stay for three nights, my father was the only one who would take her in.

"She was a strong woman. Like none I had ever met, she knew where she was going, and she knew her destiny. She talked with my father long into the night and, I don't know why, but I stayed up and listened secretly." Rasler shivered.

"Are you cold?" Rindar asked.

"No," she said through clenched teeth, "but I have never told this story. It's hard."

Rindar nodded and looked away. It only seemed polite to let her continue without staring at her.

"When they were talking, I heard my father's truth for the first time. Fontara listened. She asked questions that dug deep into the wisdom my father had earned. They talked of Sessasha and his circle, of the Kirrinath and how it related to all life; of the Infinite—and Oblivion, of psadeq with men and Mah'Eladra. They talked about the future and the past as though it was real.

"I fell asleep at the door. I dreamt that Fontara had left, and I remember waking up and crying—crying because of me and who I was—and who Fontara was. When I discovered that Fontara was still there, I begged her to stay. She loved me. She taught me about armatan and showed me that it was possible to live as my father lived—that to live otherwise is not to really live at all.

"All that summer, she stayed. She taught me and helped heal psadeq with my father and mother. She was a Pistisine guardian. In the fall she had to leave, but she had already taught me so much." Rasler rocked back and forth gently, fighting to hold back her tears.

"For three more years, I lived with my parents, taking care of Lothandra and learning from my father and mother. Two years ago, as I sought Mah'Eladra, Visha'andar came to me. He told me he had spoken with my father, and it was time for me to go. He said that I had to leave Lothandra to find Sessasha—that he would watch over Lothandra in the care of my parents; when it was time, we would be reunited, but only if I left."

"Visha'andar?"

"Visha'andar is my father's guardian. He was given to my father before he came back to Vindor."

Rindar was confused.

"He is an Eladra," Rasler said.

Rindar nodded. Eladrim guardians were myths in Vindarill. "So you just left?" he asked.

Rasler waited to answer, and Rindar watched her struggle. "In words? I just left. In my vorn—it's been twenty months now—I often wonder if I really left at all."

Rindar didn't know what to say, so he waited. "What is the Kirrinath?" he asked after another long pause.

Rasler sat in a silent stare, lost, Rindar guessed, in thoughts of her journey and of leaving Lothandra. She began very slowly. "It is hard to describe," she said, "because it is many things and one thing at the same time…it's a way of thinking; it's a system of beliefs; it's a symbol and a series of symbols—

"The Kirrinath is as old as Tessalindria. Most who live within its guidance and adhere to the thinking that comes from it believe that the Eladra gave it to the man kind. It's a way to visualize the great truths and forces that create a life of psadeq with Mah'Eladra. It is not the life itself—" She paused and looked at Rindar. "There is no good place to start describing the Kirrinath," she said. "It is like a circle that has no starting point. One could start anywhere and by following the path, one will find it all." Rasler laughed. "I know that makes a lot of sense!"

"I was about to make that very point."

"Have you ever heard of noble truth, wisdom or vision?" she asked.

Rindar nodded. "I have heard them all, but probably wouldn't be able to describe them very well."

"You know psadeq, and I just told you about armatan. How about metnoga, kariis, raatsa or selkah? Kirrin?"

"I have heard of kirrin. The others of them are vague—like something the Sessashians would use."

"These words represent the great paths—or elements—of the Kirrinath. Since you know psadeq, you should start your search there," Rasler said. "It's a long journey. You will have to be patient, but I think I can help if you really want to understand it. My guess is that you do understand more than you think, but have never put names on your understanding."

Rindar shrugged. "Perhaps," he said.

"We don't have time now, but I will help as I can," Rasler said as she rose and gathered her bundle of wood. Rindar did the same. "I have much hope," she said as she started out of the cave. "I know that Mah'Eladra have a path for me, and I will see my son again, but not on my time." She headed out into the rain.

Rindar shouldered his bundle of wood. It was heavy but not unmanageable, and walking downhill they made quick time back to their stark shelter. As they walked, Rindar pondered what Rasler had said. "Confront," "protect" and "strengthen" were words she had used to describe his efforts with Minxa. He had never heard these words in the context in which she used them, and he marveled again at the strong young woman who led him. She had chosen her path and now, for some unseen reason, he was walking with her. His thoughts drifted back to the old man and the map. There was something that the man had said, something important, that stalked the shadows of his new understandings and held another fragment of truth about who he was and where he was going.

Tal and Meekar were directly overhead and cast deep shadows into the cave when Rasler shook Rindar from his shallow, restless sleep. The fullness of the twin moons meant it must have been nearly midnight. "Time to go," she said. "Our pursuers are on the move." She pointed at Minxa, and with a wave of her hand, asked Rindar to wake him. Minxa rolled over and grunted twice before Rindar could talk to him.

Rasler stood on the sloping rock in front of the shelter. Warm, milky moonlight bathed the landscape in a false daylight. "The Crown," she said in a low voice as she pointed north. Rindar looked up. The immensity of the looming horizon was overwhelming. The play between the gray shadows of the horizon and the inky, star-studded sky made it impossible to judge the distance to the silent snowcapped sentinel towering before them. It was not a single peak, but a cluster of jagged white teeth that rose toward the center. Rindar stood unmoving and watched as if he expected *it* to move.

"Is that where we are going?" asked Minxa.

"Yes, if we make it. The Jualar Springs lie somewhere on its southwestern slopes." Rasler bent down to finish packing. "If we travel hard, it may take us two days to get there, but I need one last look before you put the map away."

Rindar left the map open and finished stuffing his damp cloak and blanket into his pack. Rasler bent to scrutinize it. "They don't know where we are, but they are moving in this direction. The more distance we put between us, the harder it will be for them to track us."

Minxa rubbed his eyes. "How do you know that?"

Rasler slung her pack onto her shoulder before answering. "If they knew our trail, they would not be spread out, and if they had no sense at all of where we are, why would they be moving toward us and not back along the trail—or along the river?"

"If they don't have our trail," Minxa asked, "how would they follow us at all?"

"I believe they can sense where we are, but not very specifically," Rasler said.

Minxa cinched the strap on the back of his pack. "What beings can do that?"

"I'm not sure who they are, or how they do it, but I have no doubt that it is possible. Do you have a better explanation, Minxa?" She was looking straight at him.

Minxa shrugged. "No," he mocked, "but since I don't believe it, I don't have to explain it, do I?"

"As you wish," Rasler said as she started across the shadowy landscape that lay between them and the enormous majesty of the Crown of Tessalindria. Rindar and Minxa trundled along behind. Rindar wished he knew what Minxa was thinking, but this was not the time to ask or discuss his feelings. They needed to make good time.

"Do we know where we are going?" asked Minxa with a half grumble.

Rasler spoke over her shoulder. "We're heading down to the gully at the base of this hill. We will follow that to the west, and then there is a canyon heading north. This canyon will lead us toward the Crown. We can stop at the head of the canyon and plan our next move from there."

For a while they walked in silence, preoccupied with their own thoughts. Rindar was thinking about all the new questions he had for Rasler when Minxa interrupted: "Why do you think these...whoever they are...are following us?"

"I believe that they know about the map," said Rasler as she stopped and turned, purposely giving them a chance to catch their breath. She took a sip from her water flask.

"I've been trying to figure out how anyone following us could know about the map," Rindar said.

Rasler smiled. "You said you thought Drofan may have known something from what he said. Drofan came on the boat with us." She took another sip. "You said you saw Drofan again at the ironware store."

"Yes, we did," Rindar said. He thought back to the smithy where they bought their knives. "We had a brief discussion with the old man at the shop, and he insisted that we needed a map—a good map—and a tracker," he said. "But neither of us let on that we had it. Drofan probably overheard that conversation. You followed Drofan up the hill from the wharf. Where did you say he went then?"

"He went straight into the tavern—for a drink." Rasler smiled. "He may have been in league with the man with the ironware, and the discussion may have been a ploy to see if you would talk. There are far too many clever and ruthless people in this tiny world of ours," she continued. "It would not surprise me if Drofan is one of our pursuers. C'mon, we have to keep moving."

✠

The journey does not end until we despair.

Pratoraman
The Middle Way

"Now what?" Minxa asked.

They were sitting together on stones at the northern end of the narrow canyon. Tal and Meekar had moved west, and the near darkness of the deep shadows in the canyon had made the traveling treacherous and slow. The dry streambed they had used for a trail had risen only slightly, and after nearly an hour of careful navigation between the canyon's steep walls, they were boxed in about fifty feet below its rim.

"The map," said Rasler. "When I looked at it earlier, I was sure that there was a trail out of here."

Rindar handed her the box with the map.

"No, you open it," she said.

As Rindar lifted the cover off the box and spread the map out on a flat stone, Minxa realized that Rasler had never touched the map. She had come close, but had never even laid a finger on it.

"Widen it," she said. "I want to find our friends."

Rindar did as she asked, sliding the center away from where they had come so that the end of the canyon lay in the corner. They leaned over the map, which glowed with just enough light to see it clearly. Five small dark specks formed a loose line at the base of the hill below the cave where they had slept. "Only five?" She seemed puzzled.

"Where are the other two?" Minxa asked. "This doesn't look good," he continued as if he did not even need an answer to his own question. He had been in a good mood for most of the night. Perhaps it was the moonlight or simply the retreat of the rain and fog. Maybe the immense glimmering visage of the Crown before them had lifted his spirits, but the boxed-in canyon brought back the simmering resentment: Rasler had led them here and now they were trapped.

"Widen it further," Rasler continued.

The map shrunk beneath Rindar's finger. So did the gray specks and they could not find the other two.

"Get it down close around where we are," she said with an urgency that made Minxa nervous.

Rindar touched the map, and it obeyed. "Further," she said. "I want as much detail as we can get...more...that's good." Rasler scanned the details on the map. They were looking down into the canyon from above; three small smudges of light surrounded by three walls of stone.

Rindar gasped, "Look!" His finger pointed at another bright smudge of light perched on the canyon rim above them. Rasler stood up suddenly, and they all looked skyward.

A faint hint of dawn shaded the sky, dimming the stars so that only the brightest was visible, but the darkness, combined with the odd shadows of Tal and Meekar at the top of the stone canyon walls made it impossible to see any details. Rasler bent over the map again, orienting herself to the location of the smudge. It was moving rapidly around the end of the canyon, just far enough back from the edge so that they could not see it from where they were. She held her finger to her lips and beckoned the others to move quietly under a nearby overhang in the stone.

They sat in silence. Minxa half expected Rasler to get up and do something, but for the first time since he had met her, she seemed confused. The being at the top of the canyon stopped suddenly, then backtracked, before stopping again and then moving closer to the edge, as if looking for something.

Rasler rose. "Stay here," she whispered. She moved silently along the canyon wall like a shadow, heading down the streambed directly under the being above. In a matter of seconds, she had disappeared into the darkness toward the mouth of the canyon. Rindar sat motionless, watching the map. They could see Rasler's smudge moving slowly away down the streambed as the being started down the canyon wall directly above them.

It moved slowly and would stop for long periods, as if it were listening. A small stone clattered down the rock face, and Rindar saw Rasler stop. The climber stopped too. Rindar held his breath. The profound silence chafed Minxa's nerves.

It seemed like minutes before the smudge moved again. It worked its way slowly along the canyon wall, descending in a spiral around the end. Soon they would be able to see him. He came into view suddenly, moving along the wall as if he were descending stairs cut into the stone. When he was about ten feet off the canyon floor, he stopped and turned to face them, and with a sudden leap, landed on the floor of the canyon with a soft thud. He remained crouched and altogether still.

Rasler's sling whirred in the darkness, and with the hum of the stone, the being flattened himself to the ground. The stone shattered on the wall, and the fragments ricocheted into the darkness as the being stood up to full height. "Erinshava!" His voice was powerful and resonated off the stone.

The silence closed in around the canyon again as they waited. Minxa's heart pounded.

"Mora kant vor hinden sahlen, Erinshava," he said with a hint of gentleness, holding his hands out in a gesture of openness.

Rasler's smudge moved quickly. When she came into view, she was running headlong toward the giant. She threw herself into his open arms, and they embraced, speaking rapidly in the same strange language he had used. Then she backed up, grabbed him by the hand and led him toward Minxa and Rindar. When he noticed the map, spread out on the stone floor in front of them, he stopped still and stared at it for a moment before he turned to Rasler.

Minxa did not understand the rapid conversation between the giant and Rasler, except for occasional interjection of the word "Lonama." The animated discussion involved many gesticulations about the canyon wall and the map.

Finally, Rasler turned to Rindar. "Put the map away. It's time to go."

"Go where?" Minxa asked.

"Put the map away, Rindar." Rindar stooped and folded the map into its case and shoved the box into his pack.

When it was safely stowed, Rasler spoke again, "This is Visha'andar. He has found a stairway leading up to the rim of the canyon, but we have to hurry."

"We always have to hurry," grumbled Minxa as he bent to secure his pack.

"I'll explain later," Rasler continued, cinching a strap on her pack and slinging it onto her shoulder. "Can both of you climb?"

Rindar nodded. "Sure," said Minxa.

Visha'andar moved over to the wall where he had descended, beckoning them to follow. The dawn's light had begun to illuminate the canyon walls with subtle hues of green and ochre. Visha'andar reached high onto the wall, and with his left hand, found a handhold in the stone face and lifted himself with one arm. It was obvious that from there, he could see the steps.

"You sure you can do it?" asked Rasler, looking at Minxa.

Minxa scowled, his pride wounded by Rasler's doubt. "Like walking up a hill," he muttered as he motioned to Rindar to go ahead of him, the way they usually did. Rindar stepped to the rock face. The handhold that Visha'andar had used was beyond his reach, and the face below it was featureless. Minxa stepped forward and cupped his hands, boosting Rindar to the first place he could grasp. Rindar scrambled up until he could stand on the stairway. Hanging down, he gave Minxa his hand. Minxa pulled up until he was able to secure his grip. When Minxa had attained a secure hold, he reached back and helped Rasler up to the first step.

"This is incredible," Minxa whispered to Rindar as they worked up the wall. "We never would have found this thing."

"Perhaps when it got lighter, we would have seen it," said Rasler.

"I doubt it," Rindar answered. "The way these steps are cut make them nearly invisible from the bottom...as if it was done on purpose."

"Look at the way they are cut at the top," continued Rasler. "They would leave no shadow unless the sun were directly above them. We would have found them about noon." It was true. From the top, looking down in the early dawn, the progression of stairs followed a clear spiral along the wall and stopped just out of reach of an ordinary person near the bottom. "That would have been too late, I think."

"Probably," Rindar mused.

Minxa looked up. Visha'andar had pulled himself over the canyon rim. Minxa wondered who the giant was and how he had come to be here at this time. Rasler seemed to know him. It was all very vague and confusing, and now was not the time to ask for details. He focused on making it safely to the top. When they were all on the rim, Visha'andar turned and led them away from the canyon.

The advancing dawn was comforting and welcome. Soon the sun would drive the chill of the night out of the cold air that smelled faintly of smoke and river water.

A shadow swept in above them as Vakandar circled once then landed on Visha'andar's shoulder. The giant took no notice and continued leading the tired band. They had gone barely thirty steps when they rounded a bend in the trail to find a small fire, burned to coals and ready for cooking. Visha'andar sat down and beckoned to them to do the same. Vakandar hopped off his shoulder and with a shudder of wings, landed on the ground. "Glad you could make it. Glad you could," he crowed as he strutted behind Visha'andar and started preening himself.

With Vakandar's arrival, the irritation flooded back over Minxa's vorn. He wished the bird had not come back. He wished he could be somewhere else. The gash on his cheek started aching again, reminding him of the hostility of the world into which he had been thrown. He wished he were back in Vindarill.

They sat down on stones before their strange host as he roasted two fish on a spit. Minxa watched him as he pushed some small meal cakes closer to the fire for browning. He was a huge man with hair as black as the raven's feathers, whose eyes shone, almost as if the sun were behind them. He wore a loose gray tunic that left his muscled arms bare, with a wide belt of darker gray cloth. He had sandals with thick leather thongs that wrapped his huge feet. It was his feet that made Minxa realize how big he was, for all the proportions were right, and yet his feet were enormous.

Behind Visha'andar, the massive white peaks of the Crown of

Tessalindria, shimmering with the pearl pink of dawn, rose to frame his body like a god's.

No one spoke until Visha'andar looked up. "Are you hungry?" he asked. His speech in their language seemed out of place. Minxa nodded. "There is plenty," he continued. "It is ready—soon." His voice was strong and deep, and his accent was ancient in some way that Minxa could not describe.

"I am hungry for answers," Minxa said as he looked at Rindar. Rasler smiled.

"I have many answers," responded Visha'andar gently. "Do not be afraid to ask."

Suddenly, Minxa did not know what he wanted to ask. He flushed. It must have been obvious. "Um, did you know Rasler before?"

"Rasler?"

Minxa pointed in Rasler's direction.

Visha'andar looked surprised. "Erinshava? You call her…Rasler?" He laughed aloud and winked at Rasler. "It is such an ugly name." Rasler looked down as Visha'andar continued, "I know her when she is born."

"How?"

"I serve her father. I am his guardian."

The answer seemed too simple, but the clarity and directness of it left Minxa satisfied that it must be true despite its apparent absurdity. It felt odd, and Minxa felt like a child in his presence. "Then why are you here?" he asked.

"Erinshava needs my help. You cannot make it out of this without it." He waved in the direction of the canyon, looking down momentarily to turn the fish. When he looked up, his eyes asked for more.

"Do you know who is following us?" Minxa asked.

"Yes, I know them well."

"Who are they?"

"I cannot say. It is not my place."

Minxa could tell from the tone of his voice that he would reveal no more. "Why do they chase us?"

"They want…Lonama's map." The hesitation before he spoke the name jolted Minxa's memory back to the giant's unease when the map lay open before him on the canyon floor. Minxa watched him adjust the meal cakes on the rocks close to the fire. He looked up suddenly. "Now it is my turn to ask—do you own the map?" he asked as he looked directly into Minxa's eyes.

Minxa wanted to look away, but he shook his head and pointed to Rindar.

"For how long you have had the map?" Visha'andar asked Rindar.

"One week."

"Ahhh!" He smiled and turned the fish again. "What is your name?"

"I am Rindar Colloden."

"Rindar...hmmm...Colloden." Visha'andar looked up into his forehead, as if searching. "This name seems familiar—where are you born?"

"Vindarill," Rindar said.

"I do not know of...Vindarill." He looked suddenly at Minxa. "And you. Where are you born?"

"Vindarill also."

"Hmmmm, I must ask of this place, but now it is time to eat."

Visha'andar placed pieces of food into their bare hands. Each waited until he had served the others before they started eating with their fingers. The fish was hot, and flavored with spices Minxa had never tasted. The meal cake's savory sweetness was also foreign to his palate, but filled his stomach well. His mind spilled over with questions Minxa hoped he would have an opportunity to ask.

"I have a question," said Rasler when she had finished her meal.

Visha'andar looked up and nodded.

"When we looked at the map, we had seven pursuers. Now there are five. Where are the other two?"

Visha'andar looked up and cocked his head as if listening to the sky for a moment, then looked straight at Rasler. "They travel with two minions of Vishtoenvar—but no longer."

"NarEladra?"

Visha'andar nodded gravely. As with other revelations in this strange world, the mention of Vishtoenvar sent Minxa's mind reeling back to childish images of a dark-hooded figure that worked evil at will on people foolish enough to believe it. Here, however, it was not a joke. He saw Rindar startle slightly at the name.

Visha'andar looked at Rindar. "You are not sure you believe?" Just as quickly he turned to Minxa, and with a stern voice enjoined, "And your friend, Minxa, mocks understanding."

Minxa flushed and opened his mouth to say something, but closed it again without a word. Anger flashed inside him at Visha'andar's words, but anything he thought to say would surely bring more attention from one who seemed able to read his mind.

Visha'andar continued, "Your pursuers are in league with Vishtoenvar, though they do not know it. They do not know that their missing companions are NarEladra, nor that with each moment, they are slowly succumbing to their influence—and they do not know what has happened to them."

Minxa sat dumbstruck as Visha'andar looked down. "There is more to be eaten," he said, "and you must not be hungry on the journey ahead of you." He picked up one of the sticks. It seemed that there were more fish on them than Minxa remembered, and there were several more hot meal cakes. With a delicate movement, he held out more food to each of them. No one refused.

When he had finished serving, he stood up and looked east. "The sun is up soon. Wait here until you see it, then head north until you find a river. Follow it downstream to a ford where it joins another river and turns west." He paused with the same peculiar skyward listening. "Cross it, travel east along its northern bank—find a small island. Stay there for the night, but make no fire—eat only what you bring with you; pick nothing from the trees. You are saved there from any harm."

"Must you go?" asked Rasler.

"Time moves—I go," he replied and leaned forward to lay a hand on Rasler's shoulder. "Do you understand the path?"

"I do."

Visha'andar turned and looked at each of the companions in turn. "Stay together." His last words rang like a command rather than a suggestion as he turned and strode away. "Stay together. Stay close together, and do not pick anything from the trees!" He disappeared around a large boulder, not twenty steps from where they sat. Vakandar hopped off to follow him.

The giant's presence unnerved Minxa, and he was glad to see him gone. Minxa sat staring into the dying fire. No one moved or spoke until the sun crept above the horizon, its long orange arms chasing away the chill of the strange night.

✠

True belief often shows us that what we see is unbelievable.

Tristaron Harrista
The Kirrinath

To Minxa, the hour delay at the fire had seemed like an eternity. They knew from the map that their pursuers drew closer with each passing minute, and only fifty paces separated them from the box end of the canyon. Minxa argued with Rasler. She insisted that the group do exactly as Visha'andar had said. "I don't understand it," she said, "and he may not have either, but because he said it, it is best that we do it."

Minxa's attitude betrayed his scorn: "If he was a guardian, why did he leave, and where did he have to go? There is nothing around here for miles," he said. "If it is 'best' to do what he said, why didn't he explain it?" He leveled his endless whining questions at Rasler who refused to answer any of them, deflecting them with clever conversational diversions and return questions for which there was no plausible answer.

They left when the Asolara's fingers first touched their damp clothing, making their way north toward the river and the immensity of the Crown that towered in the morning sun ahead of them and captivated their vorns. Its eastern slopes glistened with white that faded into aqua and gray, then finally to ultramarine and purple to the west against the sky. To Minxa, the intense swaths of color rising from the dry oranges and browns of the mostly flat wasteland through which they trudged made it seem as if it had been painted on the horizon to delude him.

He finally broke the silence that had settled over them when they started walking. "He had a peculiar way of talking," he said. "What was that language he spoke when we first met him?"

"The Kor'Alura," said Rasler, "the original language. All the Eladra speak it."

"Eladra?" said Minxa. "He was an Eladra?"

"What did you think?" Rasler seemed genuinely surprised.

"Well, he seemed odd, but I would never have guessed…"

"They are very real," Rasler continued, as if in answer to Minxa's thoughts before they were spoken. "You may have encountered them before and never known it."

"There's something else I don't understand," said Minxa. "He said 'you are saved there from any harm,' you know—about the island. Do you think he meant 'safe' or 'saved' like he said?"

"We will only know when we are there," Rasler answered. "The Eladra speak precisely, and he would not make a mistake. If there is a failure in knowing what he meant, it will be because we did not hear it correctly."

"He always spoke in the present tense," Rindar observed. "Well—almost always."

"He lives in the present. Did you notice that when he spoke of the past or the future it was awkward for him?"

"Yes, that was strange."

Rasler smiled. "He uses the words because he knows that it is meaningful to us, but I don't think he understands them as we do."

"I don't get it," Minxa chimed in. "Are you saying he has no understanding of the future?"

"That's what I think," said Rasler.

Minxa frowned. "Then why did he tell us so precisely what to do? I mean—he must know something we don't."

"I doubt it. He told us what we need to know, but he probably could not tell you what it meant, even if you'd had a chance to ask him."

"And what was that business about servants of Vishtoenvar?" Minxa continued. "You expect us to believe that?"

Rasler turned stern. "Vishtoenvar is as real as that stone," she said, pointing at a large orange boulder sitting by itself to the left of her.

"Says who?" Minxa's tone was surly.

Rasler looked up. Rindar saw her catch her words before she answered in kind. After a brief pause she began again: "Minxa, do you believe that Mah'Eladra are real?"

"I'm not sure, but their existence is plausible."

"You don't believe then."

"I wouldn't say that."

"So you do believe."

Rindar saw Minxa hesitate. "Look," he said, "I would not be the one to deny that Mah'Eladra are there. I mean—there are many who believe. They may be right…"

"And?"

"Well, I have never seen any proof…"

"But you are afraid to take a stand against such a belief." Rasler drove hard, but Minxa stood his ground.

"I would not be afraid if I knew for sure."

Rasler switched the course of the conversation. "Are Mah'Eladra good or bad?"

"Why, good, of course."

"How about Vishtoenvar? Good or bad?"

"I'm not sure he exists, but if he does, I have heard that he is—bad," Minxa admitted.

Rasler let their thoughts settle as they walked a few paces in silence. "I have found in my travels that most beings want to believe in Mah'Eladra because they are afraid of the consequences of being wrong."

"What!?"

"They want to believe that somehow, Mah'Eladra's goodness will transcend their own unwillingness to believe. About the same number do not want to believe that Vishtoenvar is real because of the consequences of being right, that his evil will overshadow their shallow goodness. It is a very convenient, but flawed way of thinking."

"I don't understand," Minxa said thickly.

"You look into your own vorn, and you hope Mah'Eladra exist and will overlook what you see there. What you see causes you to fear that you may actually be more like Vishtoenvar, if you admit he exists."

They were walking with their heads down, watching each step and engrossed in the debate. Rasler stopped suddenly and exclaimed, "The river!" When Rindar looked up, Rasler was pointing to the thin ribbon of water about two hundred yards in front of them. The empty stone wasteland ended abruptly at the edge of the water, and the far side was thick with trees and undergrowth, as if someone had drawn a line in Tessalindria and forbidden the forest to cross it.

Rasler started running and Rindar followed close on her heels.

✠

The great river captivated his vorn. Whence it came he could not tell, and where it flowed, he could not see, but the hope of life flowed in it and strengthened his vorn.

Arafinda
Irhandarin (The Journey)

The word "river" to Minxa meant the Harvan River, which drifted sluggishly through the heart of Vindarill. It carried with it the detritus and filth of a hundred thousand beings who had, long before, lost a sense of the natural order and cleanliness of a world untainted by their selfishness. Minxa had spent many hours perched on the piers of Vindarill watching the harbor above the river's putrid waters. It had never occurred to him what the Harvan had been before the cities were built, so he was unprepared for the emotion of seeing an unspoiled river for the first time.

The river had cut deep into the stone, so when they reached its edge they were standing about ten feet above its flow. Rasler stood with her eyes closed and her head tilted up as if the smell of the river or its sound was enough to fill her with its presence. Minxa could not close his eyes to the feast before him. "Unbelievable," he exclaimed.

The river was about two hundred feet wide where they stood. Its far side marked the edge of the carpet of trees that rose gradually behind it into the blue-green majesty of the Crown, now overwhelming in its enormity. The water, clear as crystal, flowed toward the northwest, where it disappeared into the details of the landscape.

"Look, fish!" said Rindar, pointing excitedly. Minxa looked down at the swarms of silver and orange fish swimming up the current, racing its torrent, perhaps seeking its source far to the east and south.

Minxa had not bathed since he left Islag and suddenly, in the pristine presence of the river, he felt his uncleanness. There was at the same time, both a great and a seemingly forbidden desire to jump into the water and wash himself of Vindarill, Islag and the wastes. This was never a feeling he had sitting on the piers above the Harvan.

"We need to check the map," said Rasler, breaking the spell of the glory that lay before him and bringing Minxa's awareness back to their stalkers. "There is a ford somewhere downstream," she said. "We'll be able to get to the water there."

Rasler looked up from the map. Her finger pointed to their pursuers, trapped in the end of the canyon. "They will see the steps in about half an hour," she said. "Then they will be chasing us again. We must make it to the island before nightfall."

The hike along the river was long and wondrous. With the barren stony wasteland to his left and the far riverbank with its thick vegetation sloping up the foothills to the Crown on his right, Minxa felt overwhelmed with continual amazement. Occasionally, flocks of yellow birds would rise suddenly out of the trees, warning one another of the travelers' approach with the cacophony of their cries. He marveled again about the river. Its surface sparkled like crystal, and its depths were alive with the schools of bright fish. Occasionally the trail would dip closer to the water, but the rocks were slippery and steep, making any attempt to get into the water far too dangerous.

They traveled fast and spoke little as the sun inched its way down into Minxa's face, turning the rocks to a warm orange and the hills to the right into a potpourri of purples and blues.

Rindar was the first to see the island. "There!" he said, pointing, "close to the other side, with the huge stone in front of it." Minxa squinted to see. The river had widened and slowed somewhat where another river flowed into it. The far shore was several hundred yards away, and just below where the rivers joined lay the island, barely visible against the wall of trees.

"The ford must be close," said Rasler, "and we do not have long before dark."

"Why do we have to stay on the island?" asked Minxa. The surly tone had returned in his voice, and he made no effort to soften it.

"We don't have to," said Rasler casually, "but it's what Visha'andar said to do, and we would be fools not to listen to him."

"We'll probably get wet getting there, and he also said 'no fire,' remember?" continued Minxa.

Rindar intervened. "Everything else he told us has been right so far, so I think we should do as he suggested."

"Can we at least consider other alternatives when we get there? It looks pretty small," Minxa protested.

"That's fair," said Rasler over her shoulder, "but the alternatives will have to be pretty compelling to make me not follow Visha'andar's plan."

Rasler's small concession was good for Minxa's frame of mind. He knew he had changed no one's mind, but just the sense of having them consider an alternative to Rasler's plans satisfied something inside him, and he said no more about it.

He had been wondering how one would ford a river of this size and power, and when they came to the place, the ford was a stunning and terrifying thing. The river was wider, but with the water from the adjoining river, it was still too deep to wade safely in the swift current. Strewn across the river in a wide swath were large boulders that stuck out of the water. They were not far apart, but the narrow gaps between them boiled with foaming water, whose deafening roar drowned out all communication. To ford the river, one would have to jump from stone to stone over these roaring chutes of water.

It was slow, tricky work. Several times, they found themselves at a dead end and had to go backwards to find a route that led them in the right direction. After half an hour, with several close calls, they arrived safely on the far shore. The sun was only half its diameter above the stony wastes of the horizon, so they rested for a few minutes and watched it sink out of sight before donning their packs and heading east along the northern bank toward the island.

Δ   The Margah in the River   Δ

There is not always a reason—especially when we are dealing with beings that reason.

Mortag of Horrinaine
Of Beings

Rindar sat in the small circle where they had laid out their bedrolls. They had waded across the twenty-five feet of swift water that separated the island from the bank of the river, and they were soaked from the waist down, with no fire and no sun. It was cold.

Minxa's mood was foul. "What is this place?"

"I am not sure," said Rasler, "but it is very odd indeed."

"Is this an altar of some sort?" Rindar asked, pointing to the small stack of stones with a flat top in the center of the low clearing in which they sat. Rasler shrugged.

"We could have quite a fire here if we wanted to." Minxa pointed to the neat stack of wood piled against the monstrous boulder that formed the upstream wall of the clearing.

"Yes," mused Rasler, "it is as if we are being tested to see if we will listen. It's very tempting, isn't it?"

Everyone nodded.

"But it is safe here, I think," she continued. "It all looked rather ordinary from the shore, and one would never guess what is here—from there. We are well hidden."

"And look at the fruit!" exclaimed Minxa. From the riverbank, the low bushes created the illusion that the island was an overgrown rock pile, but within the clearing, the bushes were laden with berries. Upstream from the stone altar was a singular huge tree, whose branches spread like a canopy, drooping down from the tallest point in the center to touch the bordering shrubs all around the edge of the circle. Rindar had never seen anything like the peculiar, bright orange fruit that hung down through its leaves. It was perfectly round, and its aromatic fragrance dominated the ambiance of this secret place.

"Just make sure you don't pick any," Rasler reminded them as she bent to open her pack.

"I don't like it," said Minxa. "I think we are trapped here if they ever figure out where we are."

"Good point." Rasler sat thinking. "But there may be a reason for all of it. There usually is a reason—though not always," she added with a shrug.

They didn't have much time to explore the tiny island. The upstream end was a mammoth stone. It stood as the barrier against the relentless flow of the river, and was probably the genesis of the island that formed in its wake over hundreds of years. The clearing in which they sat was five paces in diameter, and to the west, the downstream end trailed off into the river.

Tal and Meekar had risen over the boulder, and their light filtered through the canopy of the great tree. The moonbeams danced about as the leaves fluttered in the light breeze. Rindar's eyes had adjusted somewhat, but there was little else to see, and he shivered from the chill of the air flowing around his damp clothing.

They had just shared the last of the meager food from their packs when Rasler sat up straight. She listened briefly and then leapt to her feet, disappearing into the darkness of the undergrowth on the river side of the clearing. In less than a minute she was back. "They are on the other side of the river, heading for the ford," she whispered.

"Traveling in the dark?" Rindar said softly.

"Shhhhh…no more than whispers," she urged. "Stay here and stay down out of sight. I will watch them."

Cooperation with Rasler's suggestion made sense. She seemed to have the energy and the capability to do what she said, and the day had started for them in the middle of the night before. With little else to do anyway, sleep seemed worthwhile. Rindar suggested that they move their bedrolls closer to one another for warmth.

Rindar laid quietly in the shifting darkness and stared up at the moonlit canopy of leaves above him. Distant as it was, the dull roar of the river, pressing its way through the rocks of the ford, eclipsed the subtler sounds that would warn of danger. Their safety lay in the secrecy of their hiding place and the vigilance of one person. Rindar found it impossible to sleep.

Minxa tossed and turned beside him. After several minutes he rolled over and whispered, "Sesh! This is insane!"

"How do you know?"

"I feel it!"

"You can't feel this sort of thing," Rindar said. Even as the words left his lips, he doubted his own assertion.

"I can," he said. "They're headed for us, and they're going to find us…in a way, I hope they do."

"What!?"

"How do we know that they are all that bad?" he asked. "We have never met them…"

"They tried to kill us with the stones! Don't you remember?"

Minxa ignored him. "If all they want is the map, maybe we should just give it to them."

Rindar's anger stirred in a way that it seldom did with Minxa. "No, we can't!"

"And why not? It isn't really yours anyway…perhaps we are supposed to give it to them."

The flow of Minxa's reasoning was becoming clear, and Rindar had no evidence to refute it, except for an intense fear of the risk of finding out. "You've left your loga," Rindar said, deciding suddenly that he did not want to talk further.

They lay quietly for a while before Minxa rolled over suddenly and sat up. "I'm going to see for myself."

"Don't…" Rindar reached out to grab him, but he moved away, and Rindar's hand barely touched his shirt.

"I'll be back soon."

"Minxa!" He was out of earshot of Rindar's forced whisper. Rindar watched him move to the edge of the clearing and hesitate before he slipped into the blackness of the perimeter foliage toward the shore side of the tiny island. There was nothing to do. Rindar was alone with his wakefulness, trapped in the endless churnings of a mind full of fear.

Exhaustion must have taken over, for the next thing Rindar knew he was being gently shaken. "Where's Minxa?" It was Rasler.

"I don't know."

Rasler put her hands to her face as if some unspeakable horror confronted her. She leaned closer. "Did you see him go?"

"I tried to stop him, but he said he wanted to see for himself. He disappeared over there."

"This is not good," she whispered shaking her head. "When?" she asked.

"I haven't any idea." Tal and Meekar were directly overhead.

"They passed by here about half an hour ago..." Rasler sat crosslegged on the ground beside Rindar, leaning over to whisper to him. She was obviously agitated. "They were heading east along the bank of the river...very quiet...they move like shadows." She was thinking between her phrases. "I watched them...until they were out of my sight—around the next bend."

"Do you think they saw us?"

"They hesitated on the shore opposite me. They pointed and whispered, but moved on...I don't think they saw me. I was well hidden."

"Do you think they still track our mordage?"

"I don't know. When the NarEladra were with them, I am sure that is what they were doing, but there were only five." She sat still for several moments before continuing. "I think I know what this place is."

Rindar waited as she formed her thoughts.

"I think it is an Eladrim stronghold," she whispered. "If this is true, it would be suicide for anyone to assault us here."

Rindar hoped what Rasler said was true, but he had no basis for believing it. They sat silently, absorbed in their own thoughts until Minxa returned.

He appeared silently out of the dark in the same general place he had vanished and made his way quickly to his bedroll without acknowledging Rasler's presence. "They've passed by," he whispered as he pulled the blankets around him and rolled over. Rindar could smell the pungent fragrance of the orange fruit on his breath.

"*Say nothing,*" Rasler spoke to Rindar's mind. "*No arguments now. We need to sleep.*" Her hand pressed firmly on Rindar's shoulder as she rose quietly. The roar of the ford seemed to rise in intensity around their silent hiding place on the tiny island. Rasler was right. There was nothing for Rindar to do except try to sleep.

✠

We should be thankful that few people know the fist of Mah'Eladra.

Colloran
Outworlds

For several moments Minxa could not separate reality from his fitful dream about being attacked as they lay in their hiding place. He fought to wake up from its clutches. Rasler yelled. Minxa tried to sit up and found himself covered with a heavy net. "Sesh! Wake up...wake up!" he yelled.

"Shut up!" someone growled.

"Sesh!" Minxa swore again.

"Shut up!" the voice yelled. It was an ugly voice, one from a distant memory that Minxa thought he should know somehow.

Minxa was awake now and fully aware that he was trapped. He lay still while the attackers moved around them, extracting each from the net and binding them one at a time. With the moons low to the west, little light made it to the clearing, making it impossible to see, but their voices were guttural and cruel. One of them was a woman.

"Bind the Pistisine first—this one." Minxa heard Rasler struggling valiantly, but there were too many hands. "Put her against the tree—the big one."

"Now the one on the right." Minxa was still too groggy to resist effectively. He reasoned that obedience was the wiser choice, so when they hauled him up and tied his hands behind his back he didn't struggle. They dragged him over to the tree and propped him up beside Rasler. It only took a moment before Rindar was dropped beside him.

"Light a fire."

"I wouldn't..." said Rasler.

A huge form filled the darkness in front of her, but Minxa could not make out the face. "Ho, she speaks." It was followed by an ugly chuckle. "And why not?" came the leering question.

"We were warned not to light a fire here."

"Light the fire!"

The woman spoke. "Perhaps we should listen..."

"Light the fire!"

Minxa watched helplessly in the darkness like a child's doll dropped in the corner of the room. Their captors set about making the fire. The first strikes of the steel were like needles in his eyes, but the first flame was like a beacon. Suddenly, the world had form, and details became visible as the fire grew.

Four men and one woman comprised the group. They were dressed in gray and brown clothes meant for hiding in the wastes. Two of the men had been posted as guards and had their backs turned to the captives, facing out into the dark perimeter of the clearing. The woman was the fire starter.

"Well done, Sereline, it is a welcome light." The apparent leader of the group spoke with genuine appreciation. "Build it high; there is plenty of wood over there," he said as he waved to the neat pile against the stone.

"I wouldn't," said Rasler.

The leader turned and moved in front of her. "Why not?" he asked.

"The fist of Mah'Eladra."

"Here is your fist, ashtemba!" He punched her hard. She turned slightly so the blow came to the side of her face rather than straight on. As he continued staring at her, she slowly turned her head to expose the other side, but instead of striking her, he spit in her face. She didn't move. He studied her for another moment and then withdrew to the small fire burning brightly beside the stone altar in the clearing.

Minxa got a good look at his face. It was young, handsome and clean-shaven with penetrating dark eyes and long, chiseled features, full of purpose and crowned with a carefully cut shock of reddish-blonde hair. As misguided as the vorn behind it might have been, it was not the evil face Minxa had conjured in the dark, but these were brutal beings, as Rasler had suggested.

With the movements of his arms against his shoulders, Rindar was busy trying to untie his hands behind his back. His efforts were futile, and after several minutes he stopped with a deep sigh.

The three captors at the fire talked quietly as they continued to pile wood onto the fire, but the roar of the ford still dominated the background noise. Minxa couldn't hear their conversation. The fire crackled and sparked, and the flames leapt upward, causing the leaves of the great tree to shiver as the smoke rose through them.

Suddenly, from far away to the south and east, a low rumble rolled across the river. Everyone turned. Thunder! In an instant, Rasler rolled to her right and onto her knees, and in a single quick movement she was on her feet and hopping toward the edge of the clearing.

"Stop her," commanded the leader. The guard on the side of the clearing turned, took four bounding steps and enveloped her in his arms as she squirmed and wriggled in a desperate effort to be free.

As he turned toward the fire, Minxa saw his face. Drofan!

"Sorry, princess," he said, "you didn't have permission to do that."

The distant thunder rolled again as Drofan forced Rasler back into her place against the tree. "If any of them try that again, tie them all to the tree," said the leader.

"Do what I did!" Rasler whispered to Rindar.

Rindar didn't move, but she spoke again with new urgency. "Do it now!"

Rindar did the best he could, but was no match for Rasler's performance. Rolling into Minxa's lap, he managed to get onto his knees, and as he struggled to stand, Rasler moved again. Rindar never made it, but Rasler was on her feet again. They caught her before she had hopped four times, and both of them were thrown back against the tree. Drofan and the second guard held them as the leader tied them all together to the trunk of the tree.

"Great," Minxa muttered to Rindar. "What were you thinking, viddik?"

Rindar didn't answer. Minxa looked over at Rasler who stared back with a faint smile, as if she had purposely provoked them and her trick had succeeded, though it landed them in a greater fix than before. The thunder rolled again.

The five captors sat down around the fire. They talked and laughed, glancing over their shoulders at their three captives while they ate and drank. Occasionally, one of them would break from the circle to get a handful of fruit from the various shrubs and from the tree. The thunder rolled, and Rasler shook her head in disbelief each time they did so. Watching them made Minxa angry, and the minutes dragged by, leaving him with no hint of what time it may have been because the bright fire eclipsed any light from outside.

When their meal was done, they started rummaging through Minxa's pack, throwing things around the clearing. They were looking for something. The leader picked up Rasler's bow from the ground by her bedroll. She snapped at him, "Don't touch that."

He laughed. "Watch me." He drew one of the arrows from her quiver and took aim. The shaft hissed through the air and buried its head in the trunk of a tree on the far side of the clearing. "Nice bow," he said. He hung it and the quiver on a small broken branch a few inches above Rasler's head.

The thunder continued to tumble in over the island, more frequently, but no nearer than when it had first started. At one point, Drofan disappeared into the undergrowth and returned laughing. "It's miles away. Lots of lightning, but nothing to worry about."

They rummaged through Rindar's pack. When Rasler's had been torn apart, the leader came over and squatted down in front of Rasler. "All right, Pistisine, where is it?"

"What is your name?" asked Rasler in return.

The man sneered and nodded, as if he were trying to outthink the brave young woman tied to the tree before him. "We haven't been properly introduced, have we?"

Rasler sat motionless, staring into his eyes.

"Come, all of you," he called, "we have to introduce ourselves to our guests."

They stood in a loose line, looking down on the captives. "I am Marhan, the leader of this crowd. This is Sereline, our tracker and fire starter. On her right is Drofan, whom you know. Parata is our historian and guide, and Silara—my one-man army."

Minxa thought that Silara looked the part. His face was that of a cruel warrior, as quick to kill as to save and a man not to be trusted—ever.

"And you? Who are you?" Marhan asked, sweeping his hand across the three of them.

"I am Rasler," she said, then nodded to her left, "Minxa—and Rindar."

"A sorry lot, to be sure," said Marhan, smiling. "And where are you going?"

"We are headed for the Jualar Springs."

"Too bad you will never reach them." The others laughed, except for Sereline, who seemed disturbed by the treatment they were receiving. "And how do you plan to find them? The Crown of Tessalindria is a large place."

"I will find them," said Rasler. Her confidence was contagious and it gave Minxa a fleeting hope that she was right.

"Yes—yes, I suppose you will. But perhaps not...if you do not have the map. Now where is it!?"

"It's in Rindar's pack," said Minxa suddenly.

"So you do have the map, but it's not in any of the packs." Marhan stroked his chin in mock thoughtfulness. "We have looked—so where could it be?" He bent down suddenly and peered into Minxa's face and asked, "Aren't you the one we saw when we passed by on the bank?" Minxa looked down between his legs. "And now you play the traitor again...you may be useful to us. Would you rather sit by our fire—or stay lashed to this tree?" he mocked as he continued his questions: "Have you any better idea about this map—where it might be?"

Minxa wanted to confess to hiding it, but he had no clue as to where it could be. He decided it was best to say nothing. The thunder rolled in again, but it was almost unnoticed by now, having become a backdrop to the scene being played out before him.

"Rindar must be its current guardian," continued Marhan, "but he does not seem smart enough to hide it...and Minxa—" He stared into Minxa's eyes. "Minxa has no vested interest in the map; otherwise he would not have told me where it was. So it falls to the Pistisine." He bent over until his eyes were a few inches from Rasler's face. "Where is the map?" he growled.

"Run, Marhan. It's the fist of Mah'Eladra!"

Marhan's eyes boiled. He raised his own fist to strike Rasler again, but stopped suddenly, and his face turned from surprise to horror. Everyone heard the sudden roar that swallowed all the sound of the island. In the next instant, there was a thunderous crash as a wall of water struck the boulder behind them.

Minxa barely had time to take a deep breath before the fury of the huge wave crashed around them. Everything vanished. The five beings before him were swept away instantly. Had he not been tied to the tree, Minxa would have been taken with them. He closed his eyes tightly.

The water churned sand and stone into a holocaust of terror and tossed logs around them like toothpicks, snapping branches off the trees with explosive force. The trunk of the mighty tree to which they were tied shivered under its impact. Minxa's lungs burned for air. The water dropped suddenly, swirling down around them to leave their heads above the surface so he could breathe. Rasler was crying—or maybe laughing.

Rindar was in near hysteria. In the rush of strength that accompanied his panic, he struggled helplessly to free himself. As the water receded, Minxa noticed for the first time a deep pain throbbing in his shoulder. Rindar started crying. There was nothing to do but sit and wait.

✠

The boundaries of outworld mercies are not drawn by men.

Tristaron Harrista
The Kirrinath

Rindar wanted to wipe the mud and tears off his face with his shoulder, but his shirt was caked with mud. The wall of water had ripped the canopy from the island, and as the gray light of dawn illuminated the wreckage, he saw that the whole landscape had been rearranged. Boulders had shifted, and the bushes along the bank had disappeared. The tree to which they were still tied had been stripped of numerous branches, and everything was caked with mud. Only a stump remained of the tree into which Marhan had shot Rasler's arrow, and a mud-caked body was wrapped hideously around it, impaled on the arrow. Rindar could not tell who it was.

The water had shrunk their bonds, and they cut into Rindar's wrists and ankles, making it painful to even try to escape. Rasler worked to free herself, but Minxa sat, staring vacantly at the destruction surrounding them. The sun climbed slowly, and as the edge of the shadow from the massive boulder inched toward them, the landscape steamed. They sat without talking and Rindar fell back asleep.

He woke suddenly. A body, covered with mud, crawled slowly toward him along the ground. The left leg dragged behind as she crawled to within three paces of him, when she collapsed on her face and lay still. "Sereline!" he shouted. "Sereline!"

Rasler looked up. "We can help you, Sereline," said Rasler, "but you must help us first."

Sereline looked up. Rindar could see her eyes filled with pain and tears. With a mighty effort, she pulled herself toward him; and as she got closer, he saw that her leg was broken. It was amazing she was alive. She inched closer, moving around him to get at the ropes that bound them to the tree. Rindar could not see what she was doing, but suddenly he felt the ropes spring loose.

His legs were stiff with cold, but he rolled over and wriggled to where Sereline lay half dead in the mud. She had a knife. "Can you free my hands?"

"I think..." was all she could say. Rindar felt the knife working perilously close to his wrists. There was no alternative. It was a valiant effort, with long pauses. "Don't die, Sereline," he whispered.

"Almost..." she gasped.

The ropes loosened suddenly. He pulled his hands around in front and turned to face the young woman. She lay still, but breathing. Rindar grabbed the knife and sawed through his leg bonds. "I'm coming, Rasler," he said as he crawled to Rasler with the knife in his mouth. She rolled over silently to expose her bound wrists. Rindar cut through the rope and crawled to where he could free her feet.

She was up in an instant and moved quickly to Sereline's side. "Don't go," she was saying over and over. "Don't let yourself go." She stripped off her tunic and rolled it under the head of the dying woman. "Rindar, come here." Rindar was busy freeing Minxa, who did not seem to care one way or the other, so he crawled around to where Rasler crouched over Sereline. "Hold her hand and give her your life. I will be right back."

She handed Sereline's hand to Rindar. Give her his life? Rindar had no idea what that meant. He held Sereline's limp hand in both of his and tried to concentrate—tried to understand what Rasler meant. Rasler bounded up into what was left of the tree. A few seconds later she dropped back to the ground carrying one of the orange fruits. "There was only one left," she said as she plunged the knife into its thick skin and gave it a quick twist and a squeeze. The orange liquid oozed to the surface. Rasler held the fruit carefully above Sereline's lips and dripped the juice slowly into her mouth. "Hold her head up a little." Rindar obeyed and they sat and waited.

Sereline coughed suddenly and swallowed. "A little more now," Rasler urged, speaking to Sereline and squeezing the fruit again. She swallowed again, then again. Rasler stopped and set the fruit to the side in the crook of a forked stick to keep it out of the mud. "Now to this leg!" she said, moving quickly to attend to the twisted limb. With the knife, she stripped the leggings to expose it, and with a sudden swift yank she straightened it. Sereline groaned and lurched, then her weight fell back into Rindar's hands as agony twisted every muscle of her face.

Rindar sat amazed as Rasler splinted the leg with a branch and strips of the leggings. "Stay with her, Rindar; she needs you." She sprang around the tree and freed Minxa. "Get up!" she ordered. "We have a lot to do." Minxa groaned. "Get up!" She pushed him with her foot, and he fell over on his side. Blood soaked through his torn shirt near his right shoulder. She knelt beside him, her voice suddenly tender and full of concern. "Bite on this," she said as she placed a stick up to his lips.

He looked up into her eyes and reached forward with his teeth and bit hard into the muddy wood. "Hold still. It's going to hurt." Rindar watched as she reached down and grabbed the end of the object and worked it from his shoulder. Minxa groaned, and passed out. Rasler covered the wound with her right hand and threw the shard of bloody stone out into the river, then turned and bound Minxa's shoulder tightly with his shirt. With a valiant heave, she lifted his limp body from the mud and carried him to where Rindar sat cradling Sereline. "Stay here, I'm going for help."

Rindar finally had time to think as his best friend lay unconscious beside him and he cradled the life of an enemy in his arms. Visha'andar had warned them not to light the fire and not to pick the fruit. Or was it eat the fruit? Rindar thought he said pick, specifically, and either way, the rogues had done both. Rasler had told them not to light the fire just as she had told Marhan not to touch her bow.

It was all becoming clearer as the sun warmed his numb body. He tried to piece together the facts: Rasler had specifically provoked Marhan into tying them to the tree. She jumped up the first time when she heard the thunder. The distant thunder was from a storm far upstream, and somehow she knew it would create a flood. The huge boulder shielded them from the direct impact of the flood's powerful wave, but Rindar could not imagine that anyone who was not tied down could have survived. He wondered about Sereline and why she had not died and why she came back to help them. He and Rasler had remained untouched, except by the exhaustion of the whole strange night, but Minxa had been seriously wounded by a shard of stone in the back of his shoulder.

How had that stone missed Rasler, and where was the map?

There were too many questions, and it was not long before exhaustion overtook his determination to remain alert. He fell asleep beside Minxa with Sereline's head in his lap.

✠

They sang and the stars leapt to their places,
They sang and the trees sprang forth in fruit...

The Tessarandin, Book 12

Rindar opened his eyes and looked up. To his right, a fire burned brightly in the darkness, and he could smell the fish Rasler was cooking on a makeshift spit. Across the fire facing her was Visha'andar, playing in the fire with a stick.

Rasler looked over and smiled as Rindar raised his head. He dropped it back onto the roll of soft, dry cloth which served as his pillow and asked, "Where is Minxa?" His voice was hoarse.

"He is over here—still asleep." Rasler waved to the other side of the fire.

"And—the other?" He could not remember her name.

"Sereline is here also—and doing well, thanks to you."

"Yeah? What'd I do?"

"You gave her your life."

Rindar still did not know what that meant. It did not seem like he needed to get up yet, so he lay still, staring up at the sky. Rasler and Visha'andar picked up the conversation that he had interrupted when he woke.

"Two days?" Rasler asked.

"If you travel quickly. Longer if Sereline needs to go slower."

"And the others?"

"The other three are alive, but they are far downstream."

Rasler sat deep in thought, and she waited before speaking again. "Silara's death seemed fitting enough."

"Guard your vorn, Erinshava. It is not your place to make a judgment on a being's death. It is his time."

"You are right. I'm sorry—I forget my place sometimes." She sat still, as if reflecting on her world and her role in it. "I am glad she was spared..."

"Yes. She—will tell you her story when she is stronger. It is different than one would believe from the company she kept."

Rindar watched the sparks leaping up from the fire as Visha'andar poked it with his stick. He suddenly became aware of the roar of the ford somewhere downstream in the darkness and the stillness of the endless sky above him.

He remembered them starting to talk again, but he faded quickly into sleep, and their voices became vague murmurs in senseless fragments of sentences. The night sky disappeared with the smells of the river, and finally, the utter silence of deep sleep drowned out the roar of the ford as Rindar slipped into the world of dreams.

He had many dreams, as varied and odd as the fabric of the dream world itself, and behind the frenetic visual story line of the dreamscape, there were voices singing. They sang in a strange sonorous language that Rindar had never heard. The chorus rose and fell in verses and pitch, combined into harmonies he had never heard and could never describe. Sometimes they broke through with a reality that made them seem as if it was not a dream at all; that they were there with him, all around him, singing songs of rebirth and rebuilding, with words that he thought he understood, but could not remember or repeat.

Finally, he dreamt again of the old man. Rindar saw him standing on the corner of one of the busy intersections in Vindarill waiting for traffic to stop and let him cross. Rindar wanted to talk to him. As Rindar approached, the old man turned and looked at him, and the singing was drowned by the roar of the traffic. Without speaking, the man asked how Sereline was. Rindar was too surprised to speak so the old man asked him again.

"She is asleep," Rindar said.

"Where is she?" he asked.

"She's asleep," Rindar shouted to make sure he was heard, "over by the fire."

"Walk with her, Rindar," the man said.

"She has a broken leg."

"The leg will heal. Walk with her, Rindar." The man smiled and turned slowly, stepping into the traffic.

"Stop," Rindar shouted, but the man had disappeared into the flow of the vehicles. Then Rindar remembered that if he never left Vindarill, he would never meet Sereline. He stood on the edge of the traffic searching for the old man as its roar grew louder and louder.

The sound of the dream traffic dissolved into the river roaring through the rocks of the ford, and when Rindar opened his eyes, it was light. His first sight was the canopy of green leaves of the great tree, dripping with the fragrant orange fruit. He sat up in disbelief. Bright sun filtered through the leaves and splashed on the ground, illuminating the glade with its warmth. The small altar was intact in the middle of the glade, and behind him, stacked against the huge stone, stood the neat pile of wood. Minxa lay on the ground beside him. Rasler and Sereline lay two paces away, under clean dry blankets. No one else was awake.

Rindar stood up, confused. Almost everything seemed to be just as it was when they arrived on the island, but not quite. Some of the bushes around the perimeter were smaller so that he could actually see over them, but there were no signs anywhere of the destruction wrought by the flood.

"Rindar!" The high shriek came from above. He looked up, squinting against the sun into the leafy ceiling of the island. "Rindar come." One of the yellow birds they had seen in the flocks the day before fluttered its wings above him. "Come, stand on the rock."

"The rock?"

"Come," she shrieked again, "come stand on the rock." She flitted down and swept toward the huge boulder that had shielded them from the impact of Mah'Eladra's fist, and with a flick of her wings, shot upward, landing gracefully on top of the boulder. She paused there briefly before flitting away across the narrow stretch of water into the woods on the riverbank.

The face of the boulder was too smooth and too steep to climb, so Rindar walked to one side and slid along between the stone face and the thick berry bushes that pressed against it. He finally found a place where he could scramble upward. When he emerged from the tangle of foliage into the brilliant glare of the sunlight, the surface of the rock rose before him. At its summit, twenty feet above the floor of the clearing, sat Visha'andar, his arms wrapped around one knee and his other leg resting comfortably on the stone. Vakandar perched on his shoulder preening his wings. Visha'andar stared up and to the northeast. Rindar turned to follow his gaze.

Rindar had often wondered how the mind absorbs the panorama of vision, and how it communicates what is seen to the places in the vorn that shape one's perception of life, but to deny the emotion of what he saw would have been to deny reality. The Crown of Tessalindria shone in the morning sun like a glittering diadem of the world. In that instant Rindar understood where it got its name. He could not take his eyes from it as they roved back and forth, absorbing the images and embedding them deep in his memory.

"Come, Rindar. Sit with me," said Visha'andar. His voice was gentle, but would not be denied. Rindar turned and moved cautiously up the sloping face of the stone to where the Eladra sat. Visha'andar motioned for him to sit and looked solemnly into his eyes. "We must talk."

"Aww. We must talk. Talk we must," Vakandar said as he shuddered his feathers.

Rindar sat down, and Visha'andar waved his hand out over the stone toward the spectacle before them. "Behold the Crown of Tessalindria."

They sat for several minutes. Rindar was not sure what to say. He let his eyes feast on the enormous vision surrounding him. On one side, the Crown commanded every thought and feeling, but to the right was the bleak reddish desolation of the wastes through which they had come. The wastes faded far to the south against the rim of the plateau, visible only as a gray line against the blue sky.

"Why are you here, Rindar?" Visha'andar asked suddenly.

Rindar turned to face him. Visha'andar was still staring at the Crown. "I...I don't know."

"Where do you go, Rindar?" he asked without moving his eyes.

"I don't know that either," Rindar confessed.

Rindar was not uncomfortable. Visha'andar, though threatening in size and strength, had a manner of talking that disarmed all fear.

"You are here for a purpose. You must cleanse yourself in the Jualar Springs. Then you must go to Kinvara, for you will find your purpose there."

"What is Kinvara?"

Visha'andar turned slowly to look at Rindar. "Kinvara is the capital of Tessamandria," he said. "It is some journey north of the Crown of Tessalindria, and you are needed there."

"For what?"

"It is not my place to say."

"Then why do I need to know this?"

"You need to know that you must go there. You will understand— when it is time to understand. I can tell you no more."

They sat still. Rindar felt like he did not have permission to leave and no reason to stay. "I have several questions," he ventured.

"I have many answers," Visha'andar said smiling, indicating that Rindar should ask.

"What is this place?"

"This is Pellith, one of the many Margahs of the Eladra."

"Margah?"

"A meeting place; an encampment; a haven. The Margahs are created so that we have places to go where we find refuge. They are protected by Mah'Eladra themselves."

"So why did you tell us to come here."

"No one is allowed to enter the Margahs without permission from the Eladra. I sent you here for your safety. If the NarEladra traveling with Marhan had been with him, he would never have set foot on the island."

"We nearly died here!" Rindar felt an anger rising in his throat.

"Near death is not death."

"Minxa was seriously injured." Rindar knew he was being antago-
nistic.

Visha'andar seemed ambivalent to his emotion. "He should have
died. He picked and ate fruit from the island."

"Then why didn't he?"

"It is not my place to say."

"Who can say, then?"

"Mah'Eladra."

"And Sereline?" Rindar shot back.

"She—will tell you her story."

"And Silara?"

"I did impale him on that arrow myself."

"You were there?" Rindar asked incredulously.

"There are many of us there."

Rindar's head was spinning. He was getting a glimpse of the complex fabric of the world around him, getting to know things that he had
never been aware of; he found himself reluctant to know more, but not
reluctant enough to stop asking questions. "After the flood, Rasler—
Erinshava picked the fruit…"

"She picked it to save another's life."

"The tree…the big one in the middle. I've never seen anything like it."

"They are only in the Margahs. No one may eat their fruit."

"Even you?"

"No one."

"Sereline?"

"She is not aware she ate. Erinshava fed it to her."

"Will she die?"

"No."

His answers were so commanding that Rindar found it impossible
to doubt them, but they flew in the face of all logic. He opened his
mouth to say "Ever?" but the word never came.

"You have more questions!?" Visha'andar said.

"The island was nearly destroyed by—the fist of Mah'Eladra…now
it's…"

"We worked through the night while you slept, for there was much
to do, much healing."

Rindar looked over at him. Visha'andar gazed back at him with a
curious passivity.

"Did you heal Sereline?"

"Mostly."

"Minxa?"

"His mordage is too thick; his nephus too damaged, but his basa heals; that is the promise of Mah'Eladra to all beings. You give help to him, Rindar. He is close to giving in to Marhan."

Rindar stared up into the glistening Crown. How could he help Minxa if he didn't even know how to help himself? Visha'andar must have read his thoughts and said, "You must find a way."

Rindar pondered Visha'andar's last statement for several long moments until his thoughts shifted suddenly.

"You have another question?" the giant asked.

"The two NarEladra that were traveling with Marhan—what happened to them?"

"I engaged them in battle. I vanquished Vissaron to Oblivion; I wounded Vashtor, but he escaped."

"Vashtor?"

"His name was Vishator before he rebelled with Vishtoenvar. He changed his name as many did, as part of their rebellion."

"Vashtor is a NarEladra?"

"Yes, and one who is close to Vishtoenvar. He is treacherous and clever."

Rindar was not sure whether he should probe further. He felt comfortable in Visha'andar's presence, but did not want to ask further so he changed the subject. "What can you tell me about the Kirrinath?"

"The Kirrinath is the province of the man kind," Visha'andar said. "I do not understand it, nor can I teach it."

Rindar was confused. "Ras—Erinshava said it was given by the Eladra."

"We serve Mah'Eladra. They gave it to us to give to you."

"She said it represented a way of life—paths on which to walk."

"Yes—for men, but we serve Mah'Eladra and are bound differently. The Kirrinath does not govern us, but there are those of our number who rebelled, who wanted the freedom of your kind and wanted to know the Kirrinath; they were cast out.

"Do you see the wastes?" he asked as he swept his hand toward the south.

Rindar nodded.

"The NarEl Waste," he said, "destroyed by my kind when they were cast out of the Grand Eliia Margah in the Crown." Visha'andar's eyes stormed. Vakandar hopped off his shoulder onto the stone a safe distance away. "They traveled south and west," he continued, "leaving this destruction, from which there has never been healing." His voice rose like the storm in his eyes. Rindar felt the emotional force of the giant's anger pressing on his vorn; but almost as quickly as it rose, it subsided, and Visha'andar sat still, staring at the horizon.

They sat in silence as Rindar tried to assimilate his new understanding and fit it into the way his world had seemed. All around him, the bright glory of the physical world gleamed with freshness and vitality. Perhaps it was Visha'andar's presence; perhaps it was the Margah itself or his slowly awakening vorn, but a new vigor coursed through him.

Visha'andar stood up. "Time is moving, I go," he said. "The others awake soon. They need your help, and you must not fear, Rindar." Visha'andar's eyes bored into Rindar for several seconds before he turned, strode to the end of the rock and dove into the river. Rindar never saw him come up.

"You go to the springs, to the springs," Vakandar repeated as he strutted back and forth in front of Rindar. "You must go to Kinvara, Kinvara you must."

"How will I find them?"

"Rasler knows. Rasler will lead you. Rindar must follow Rasler." With a single huff of his huge wings, Vakandar was aloft, riding the air currents that rose around the boulder from the spruce-scented air that flowed off the Crown. "Follow Rasler," he cawed as he dipped out of sight over the edge of the stone.

Rindar sat for a long time. It was the first time he had been warm and dry in days. The light breeze carried the scent of the thick, rich greenery of the slopes of the Crown to his nostrils and out over the river toward the NarEl Waste. The breeze brought hope and confidence, and Rindar wanted to breathe it deeply for as long as he could.

⚡ To the Crown ⚡

There is much healing when death is properly grieved.

Karendo Marha
Journey to the Infinite

"I would never have agreed to do it if I had known what was going to happen," said Sereline. The four travelers were walking up the gently ascending trail into the foothills of the Crown from the ford at the river. "They needed a tracker. 'Two days,' they said, 'maybe three at the most.' To find three friends that had hiked to the plateau and not returned."

They walked two abreast because of the width of the trail. Rasler and Sereline were in front, and Minxa and Rindar walked behind as Sereline told her story over her shoulder. Rindar watched her from behind as she occasionally turned to speak to him and Minxa. She was taller than Rasler and more feminine, not only in her appearance, but also in her movements and bearing. She had copper-colored hair that covered her ears and hung halfway down her back in a loose braid, tied at the bottom with a tight binding of leather. Her head was round, as was her face, with ruddy skin and dark eyebrows that accentuated her coal-black eyes.

From head to foot, she was dressed in grays and browns. The soft moccasins on her feet had leggings that rose to trap the bottom of her trousers around her calves. While the others scuffed along the trail, she glided silently, limping slightly, her eyes darting about incessantly to capture details of the foreign world around her.

"We left Karolil, five of us, and spent most of the day ascending the escarpment, but it did not become apparent what was happening until we met the others at the lip."

"The others?" Rasler prodded.

"Vissaron and Vashtor. I knew something was wrong from the way they looked at me, but I didn't know what…and I hadn't bargained to lead six—only the four. When we sat down to eat, I could tell from the conversation that I had been misled."

"How?" Rindar asked.

She glanced back over her shoulder. "I had been noticing signs of someone coming up that trail only hours before. It troubled me. It suddenly became clear that those whom I was being asked to track had not been lost for days, but were these people. 'They can't be more than a couple hours ahead,' said one of them. I confronted their deceit and they laughed. When I told them that I was leaving unless they told me what was going on, Vissaron grabbed me by the hair and threw me down. He threatened me with a knife. 'We hired you for a job, and you will not leave until you finish it.'

"I have seen this kind before," Sereline continued, "and I think they were NarEladra. It took me less than an instant to realize that my only course of action was to cooperate and hope to escape alive. Soon after, I discovered that the real objective was the map. They would stop at nothing to get it. They forced me to track for them, and on several occasions, I tried to lose your trail, but they always knew somehow that I was deceiving them. Had it not been for Marhan, Vissaron would have killed me at the cave where you spent that night."

The trail they were following was not well traveled, but was easy enough to follow. It meandered back and forth along the contours of the terrain, and they had come to a place where they could look out over the trees and see the progress of their ascent. Rasler suggested that they stop for a rest. Minxa's shoulder was not healing well, so Rindar was carrying both packs, and the stop afforded a welcome respite.

Rindar was surprised how far below them the river seemed. He could see the ford and the Margah, a little to its left, as small details in a vast carpet. The contrast of the slopes leading to the river and the vast eroded landscape of the waste beyond it was even more startling from this vantage point. He sat on the rocks and ate some dried fruit and crackers and let his eyes gather whatever tidbits he could of the vastness below.

Sereline continued, "That morning, Vissaron and Vashtor disappeared. Marhan was mad. He said he had been betrayed, and he was sure they would try to get the map themselves. Then we got caught in that canyon—how did you ever see those steps without the sun to make the shadows?"

Rindar opened his mouth to speak, but Rasler got there first. "Perhaps I shall tell you later," she said smiling.

"Fair enough. They wanted to lynch me there. I barely convinced them that as a tracker, I did not know all the details of the wasteland, just how to follow someone through it. We had given up, frankly, and were just resting before we headed back when we saw them."

"Why did Marhan call me a Pistisine?" asked Rasler in the lull that followed.

"I'm not sure. Are you a Pistisine?"

"No. I don't think so, though I have had some experience with one of them."

Sereline nodded and then shook her head. "I never thought they actually existed," she said. "They were always legends to me."

"You will find that most of the legends have a basis in truth."

"Like the map? Is it really able to do all those things?"

Rasler smiled. "What things?"

"Well, I had heard of Lonama's map, I mean, who hasn't, but the way they talked about it, it seemed that it can do anything...show you anything; if you know how to use it."

"What were they going to do with it?"

"I don't know, but I'm sure it wasn't good, and I secretly hoped we would never find it. It seemed that Vashtor was the one who really wanted it. They made some kind of deal to get it, but I think they couldn't touch it for some reason, and they needed someone else to use it for them. They seemed convinced that Marhan could do that."

"Would you like to see it?" asked Rasler, grinning impishly at Rindar.

"You have it!?" Rindar gasped.

"I hid it."

"When?"

"While you slept the first night."

"Where did you hide it?"

"I won't tell you." She reached over and carefully pulled the treasure from her pack. It looked like it had not even been wet, and there was not a trace of mud on it. She handed it to Rindar. He hesitated. "Go on," she said, "Sereline wants to see the map. I suggest you show her while I take a look at Minxa's wound."

"Why didn't you say anything when I asked about it at the Margah?"

"You didn't really ask. You mentioned it, but seemed satisfied that it was gone with the flood, and I was not sure the danger of it being discovered was past."

As Rindar took the box from her hand, he felt a strange joy stir in his vorn. Part of it was the joy of finding the map, and part of it was the opportunity to show it to Sereline. He looked up at her as he set the box on the ledge on which they sat. Sereline sat to his right, partially facing him. She was looking back with a peculiar intensity and looked down suddenly when their eyes met. It startled Rindar, though he didn't know exactly why.

Sereline sensed his hesitation and looked back up. "What?" she said gently.

"How did you survive at the Margah—I mean, all the others…Silara got killed, and the others were swept away, but what happened to you?"

Sereline looked down again. "I don't know," she said. "It all happened so fast that there was not time to think. I remember the roar just before the crush of the water hit us, and I remember being lifted up with nothing to grab on to." Sereline rubbed her left leg with both hands before she continued. "I hit something, and my ankle caught in the fork of a tree branch. The swirl of the water wrenched me over, and I felt the bone snap, but the limb would not let go. It was almost as if it held me for a purpose. I passed out."

"When I woke, I was lying in the mud on my back, my ankle still caught." Sereline looked up as she described freeing her foot. "When I was done, I was exhausted with pain and I lay back down. I did not know at that time that anyone else had survived, and all I could remember were Rasler's last words about the fist of Mah'Eladra. Somehow, I knew I was being punished and yet spared at the same time. My father always taught me that there was a reason for everything. I'm not sure I think that is true—always—but this time, I struggled to sit up and look for the reason. Maybe it was just that I knew it was not my time to die, and that's when I saw the three of you, still tied to the tree. I knew that was why I was still there."

"It's a good thing," said Rasler. "We were in quite a fix."

Rindar looked over at Minxa. He sat with his back against a warm flat stone, and his head was slumped over in sleep. Rindar looked at Rasler and nodded toward Minxa. "He's exhausted," he said.

"Why don't we stay here for the night," Rasler said as she looked up at the sun. "We'll be able to watch the sun set. Check the map, Rindar— show Sereline how it works, and make sure we are not being pursued. Cover Minxa so he does not get chilled, and I'll get wood for a fire."

✠

Those who hung the stars, each in its place,
gave a great gift to all Tessalindria.

Colloran
The Outworlds

They had made camp for the night a few feet back in the woods in the saddle behind the outcropping on which they had stopped. Rindar watched the last touch of darkness settle onto the horizon to the west behind the fire that burned brightly on the stone slab as one by one the stars came into view.

Rindar and Rasler had consulted the map, and there was no danger where they were, so for the first time since leaving Karolil, they thought they could rest safely. The night air was mild, and the fire was not so much for warmth as for comfort. Rasler had cleaned Minxa's shoulder wound again. He was gripped with pain every time he tried to move, so he sat still and stared into the fire as if he were the only one in the camp. Rindar studied his face in the stillness. The gash on his cheek had scarred over, and his eyes seemed dull and lifeless, even as the firelight danced on them.

Rasler broke the silence. She burst forth in a song, and the first word startled Rindar:

"High above the world we stand.
The quiet night is now at hand
To settle deep on hill and dale,
To blanket all within its veil,
To shelter those whose weary vorns
Seek respite from the day.
And thus we breathe the breath of life
And lay aside our wrath and strife
To seek one psadeq, fair and good,
With those around us, as we should,
And ask forgiveness, seek kariis,
In Mah'Eladra's way."

Rindar had heard her singing in the deadfall on Islag, but now, so close and powerful, it stirred something deep within him. She sang with her eyes closed, and when she stopped, she sat perfectly still, breathing as if she tasted something far beyond the fire and the starlit sky. Then she looked down and opened the small book that she held in her hands. She tipped it forward into the firelight and selected a certain page:

"You are to respect one another. To do this you must speak only what is true and listen only to that which produces psadeq. In psadeq we find healing and acceptance. Treat each other with conscious kindness, for in such effort of the loga there is healing for the basa and a softening of the nephus. Share everything you have, even with those who have more than you. Do not withhold goodness out of jealousy, for goodness is grown by the giving of goodness. Do not hold onto things that can be taken away, for that leads to bitterness. Hold tightly to that which cannot be taken away, for this leads to greater joy."

Rindar looked from Sereline to Minxa as he sat quietly and listened to Rasler. The fire slowly died as the small pages turned, and the wisdom flowed through the deep poetry of her words. Rindar stared into the coals as her voice enchanted him. When she stopped and looked up, Minxa stirred. "What is that?"

"The Tessarandin."

"The whole thing?" asked Sereline.

"No, only a few of the books."

"Where did you get it? It looks like it is handwritten," Rindar observed. He could barely make out the fine handwriting on the pages.

"I wrote it out myself—copied it from the one that Fontara carried— a few pages at a time. Before I left home, I had it bound by the bookbinder in the city."

"May I see it?" Rindar asked. Rasler leaned forward and handed it to him. It was worn soft with use, and each page was perfectly composed in neat lines of text. He held it closer to the fire. The lettering was in an old style with several additional characters that he did not recognize, and there were no visible mistakes. It reminded him of pictures of ancient manuscripts he had seen in school. "Are copies of this rare?"

"Very rare. It is a lot of work to make one."

"Why don't you just buy one?" Minxa asked.

"Buy one?" Rasler's surprise was evident. "No one makes copies to sell! Part of the experience of the Tessarandin is to copy it oneself."

"Where we come from, we could buy copies," said Minxa, "if you wanted one, that is. We had to read part of it growing up."

"Do you remember what you read?" asked Sereline.

"No, not really. All I remember is being forced to read it."

"Why?"

"I'm not sure. Everybody had to do it."

"That which is written in the Tessarandin is meant to be absorbed, not just read," Rasler interjected.

Rindar continued glancing through the pages. There were tiny marks here and there that were not part of the text and occasional scribbles that looked like illustrations. "That part that you read," he said, handing the book back to Rasler, "said something about the effort of the loga bringing healing to the basa. I have heard all these terms about the vorn, but never understood them very well..."

"You mean the basa, the loga—like that?"

Rindar nodded.

"The basa is that part of the vorn that is totally bound to this soil and stone," she said as she patted the ground. "And it is more than that. It was described to me as that part of us that defies the natural order of nonliving things."

"What do you mean?" asked Rindar.

"Well, things that are not living, behave in certain ways, and for the most part, they are all sinking. Water runs downhill, rocks fall and break, dead trees fall and the wood burns—the heat goes away and there is less left when it is all over. None of these things have the power to defy the sinking.

"But things that are living can make water go up, like trees. As the tree grows and becomes larger, it pushes the water even higher. Flowers turn brown earth into brilliant purple, yellow and red blossoms. We pile rocks up into walls and bind them together with mortar, and we build houses, boats, towers...if you take away the life, these things may look the same for a while, but without life to maintain them, even they begin to sink. The basa is your body with its life, but even that sinks without the loga. When we use our loga purposefully, it helps to keep the basa from sinking."

Rasler stopped and they all sat, lost in their own reflections. Sereline put another bundle of sticks into the fire, and the twigs crackled as they burst into flame.

"The loga is that part of the vorn that understands and absorbs knowledge," Rasler continued. "It allows us to think, act and make decisions."

Rindar looked up. Tal's light could be seen to the east on the horizon, so the stars shone in the blackness. He did not recall ever seeing a sky like that before. In Vindarill, he never looked up, and even if he had, the tall buildings, with their lighted windows illuminating the streets until late into the night, would have hidden the canopy of the sky. Here, except for the fire, lost in the vast shadow of the Crown, there was nothing but sky. He sat and looked, retracing the little steps that had brought him to this strange and dangerous place, to end up perched on a rock under the enormous open sky. For the first time he wondered about the Deep Sky: whether it was truly there. The legends spoke of it being behind the stars—behind the night sky.

Sereline must have seen him looking up. "Do you see Miseratta?" she asked.

"Miseratta?"

"The stars—just up there." She leaned close and pointed with her left index finger so that Rindar could look along her arm into the stars. "See the two bright horizontal stars?" Rindar nodded. "They are her shoulders," she said, "and her water jar; those three stars along the bottom—it's said that she is tasting the water of life for the first time and she now lives forever in the stars."

"The only constellation I really know is Elgatora," Rindar admitted.

"Right over there." Sereline pointed to his left at the two horses galloping along the horizon. Rindar had never seen them so bright, and it dawned on him why the ancients put so much imagination into watching the stars. "Over there is Vitorinda," Sereline continued. "They say that if you are at the equator, Vitorinda stands on the horizon at the equinox."

"Have you ever seen Hellscor?" Rindar asked.

"In midsummer we could see three stars in the ring, but no more from Karolil," Sereline admitted.

"I have," said Rasler. "The ring of fire we call it. They are the southern guide stars."

They sat for a long time as Rasler and Sereline pointed out the constellations they knew: Alizar, the huge turtle, in whose left rear leg was the northern pole star, Nolaran; Bolandar the great raven; Kendoran; Hissoth and Viznarkan. Just on the western horizon, sinking out of sight was the great Pasidalla cluster that reminded Rindar of one of the bright smudges on Lonama's map. Directly overhead Cozzaall, the serpent, lay coiled and ready to strike. Beside Cozzaall and to the south, was Ferinaak, the shark, turning on his side. Sereline pointed out her favorite star: Linzora. The green sky gem sparkled in the east, in the curve of the Great Horn. "There is none other like it," she said.

Rindar had never thought to have a favorite star, but perhaps now was a good time to do so. Somehow, it suddenly seemed very important. "I should have a favorite star," he said, hoping that Sereline might point one out for him.

"You should," she said. "Before this journey is over, you will find one."

They fell silent. Rindar could almost feel Tessalindria turning in the vast tapestry of the night sky, immersed in a stunning beauty that he had never seen before. There was nothing to do but to be still and wonder at the enormous quiet world around him.

Sometime during his pondering, Rasler started singing again. This time it was gentle and interspersed with periods of silence. She sang about heroes of old and about the mighty conflict between the Eladra and the NarEladra; about the arrival of the spirit of Vestin and the defection of Vishtoenvar. She sang stories of the Great Fathers, of The Beginnings and how Tessalindria came to be. Sometimes the words were in the strange Kor'Alura, and sometimes in an ancient Vindorian dialect that Rindar had never heard before, yet understood with surprising clarity. She sang about the end of things, some of it so strange that it made little sense, and every so often she paused and read words of deep wisdom from her tiny book.

The fire died slowly, and when the night chill overtook its warmth, Rasler stopped singing. "It is time to sleep," she said. Sereline sat with her arms wrapped around her knees and her eyes closed. Minxa was already asleep on his blanket. Rasler stood over him for a moment watching, then pulled the remaining folds carefully to cover him from the night. "He can stay here," she said.

That night Rindar slept well and did not remember any of his dreams.

✠

When we understand kirrin, we understand that there is no such thing as luck.

Tristaron Harrista
The Kirrinath

The trail continued to rise, and by midmorning Minxa began to feel the effect of the thin air and the chill induced by the altitude. They moved as fast as they could, and Minxa struggled to keep up. He was thankful that Rindar was carrying his pack and staying with him. The extra day's rest at the Margah had helped his wound to heal, but he still felt weak.

He remembered little of the night before. Rasler had read from her book, but most of it did not make much sense to him, and he had vague recollections about some singing. The pain of his wound after a day's journey up the slope had made his head feel like it was full of the dried leaves that littered the path, and many of the things that Rasler had said required a clearer mind to understand.

Six small specks had appeared on the map that morning. They were on the north side of the ford near the Margah when Sereline first saw them, and Rasler wanted to take no chances even though they were a day behind them. "Marhan must have found someone else to help him," she had muttered as Sereline pointed them out on the map. "Three others…one more night and we can make it to the springs. C'mon, we need to start."

Sereline and Rasler were a hundred paces in front of them, alternately visible on the long, straighter stretches of the trail and hidden by the trees and foliage where the trail turned back on itself as it zigzagged up the slope. Minxa could hear them talking and laughing faintly, but they were far enough away that he could not understand their words. "Did you fall for any of that blither blather Rasler was spouting last night?" he asked.

Rindar took a deep breath before he answered. "I'm not sure what to think, honestly," he said. "This world is so different from Vindarill—but I wouldn't call it 'blither blather,' nor would I use the word 'spouting' to describe what Rasler was doing. When you use phrases like 'fall for' it, you insult my intelligence."

Minxa felt the rebuke. He had been strong in an effort to make a point. "All right," he said, "maybe I could have used better words, but I don't see it. It seems to me that this is all so primitive—backwards—like she is living out all the superstitions that...that we have learned are just that."

"Superstitions?"

"Yes, superstitions."

"For example?"

"This thing about the Kirrinath," Minxa said.

"What about it?"

"Don't you remember in school they showed that it had no basis in truth? They taught us about how it sort of worked, and to actually think like that may have been essential when people did not understand much about their world. They came up with the Kirrinath to describe how it might work. It gave social order and allowed the various cultures to survive and communicate and thrive. Do you remember that?"

"I remember all that."

"Well, here we are. I mean—we actually get to see where it came from," Minxa concluded.

"And?"

"That doesn't make it any less a superstition."

"That is one way to look at it," Rindar said as he paused to lean on his knees and catch his breath, "but there are other ways to see it."

Minxa was thankful for the break. It was easier to talk when they were not walking. "What do you mean?"

"Well, suppose this is what is really true."

"You're crazy."

"Maybe, but humor me for a moment," Rindar said as he pointed up the trail. "We have to keep up." Rindar started walking. Minxa winced as he fell in beside him. His shoulder was very sore, and he had to be careful with every movement.

"The other day," Rindar began, "you accused me of breaking psadeq with you, which was true, remember?"

"Yes."

"And I have heard you use the word 'wise' more than a few times in your life, and kirrin is something we all strive for, even if vaguely."

"So?"

"Well, wisdom is one of the paths in the Kirrinath; psadeq and kirrin are sort of the result of all the paths converging."

"They are just part of our culture—they describe…" Minxa suddenly realized what he was about to say and was not sure he wanted to continue.

"Describe what?"

"They describe ways—no, patterns—that we follow that seem to…to make sense in our lives," he conceded.

"Right," Rindar said. "And we believe that they actually work and that they are important concepts in our lives. But suppose in the year 2747 they have concluded that psadeq and wisdom are foolish superstitions; that kirrin is a vague cultural striving, and all of it should be abandoned in a modern world where they teach that *we* were backward superstitious people that needed them in order to make sense out of our backward, superstitious lives."

"I doubt that would happen," Minxa said. Somehow, if he did not admit he could be wrong, he did not have to deal with being wrong, which he hated.

"Actually," Rindar posed, "I think that it would be foolish to abandon these ideas. They give us a manageable way to look at our relationships with others and the scope of our life, and I actually think that it would be a bad thing for our world to get rid of them."

"I would probably agree with you."

"Probably?" Rindar was smiling.

"All right, all right…I do agree with you."

"Good. Now suppose," Rindar continued, "that there is such a thing as noble truth."

"I didn't get what she meant by that."

Rindar thought for a moment as they walked. "Truth can be somewhat relative, sometimes," he said. "I mean, some things that are true for you are not true for me."

"For example?"

"For you it's true that you think you would be happier if you were back in Vindarill, right?"

Minxa nodded.

"That's probably not true for Sereline or Rasler, wouldn't you guess?"

"Probably not."

"Noble truths are truths that are true for everyone, at all times, under all circumstances. They don't depend on opinions or situations; they just are."

"Name one."

"Well, let's see…" They shuffled through the leaves that covered the trail as Rindar sifted through his thoughts.

"Can we sit down for a moment?" Minxa asked. "My shoulder is throbbing." A boulder big enough for both of them to sit on was beside the trail.

Rindar dropped the packs and sat down beside Minxa. "You gonna make it?"

"I'll be all right. Just need a rest." Minxa took a deep breath and exhaled in a sigh. "It hurts a lot," he said. "It tires me out just trying to keep it from hurting." He was not sure whether the throbbing pulse of pain with each heartbeat was any better than the pain of walking, but it did feel good to rest. He sipped water from his water flask.

"I saw Rasler pull that shard of stone from your shoulder," Rindar said. "I am amazed you can even walk. Anything I can do to help?"

"Just let me rest."

It comforted Minxa that Rindar did not feel compelled to talk. He closed his eyes and sat still, trying to allow every part of his body to rest. The sun warmed him on his left, and the fragrant breeze that flowed down the hill cooled him on his right, so he sat and enjoyed the sensation of experiencing these extremes. He felt lucky to be alive.

Minxa believed in luck. Even though his life had been hard, luck had served him well through the hardest of it. He was only a viddik, but he was a lucky viddik. Somewhere down inside, he also knew that the conversation he was having with Rindar was leading to conclusions that would challenge whether he was really as lucky as he had always thought, and he was not sure he wanted it to go in that direction. From what he had heard, luck was not a path in the Kirrinath, and if there were no such thing as luck, he would have to come to a new understanding about what he called luck in his life. He could see dimly that it led to belief that Mah'Eladra were more involved in all of it than he wanted to admit. Mah'Eladra were sentient and would demand he pay attention, but luck demanded no attention at all. It just happened.

"We have to keep moving." Rindar's soft admonition shattered his near-dream thinking.

Minxa shook his head and opened his eyes. Rindar shouldered both packs again. When Minxa tried to stand up, the throbbing pain returned. "It hurts," he said.

"I don't doubt that," Rindar said. "We'll sleep well tonight."

"And I don't want to hear your answer about noble truth," Minxa grumbled. "At least not now."

"Does it make you afraid?"

Minxa wished Rindar had not asked it that way. He prided himself on fearing few things, but he was finding that having to reexamine the basis on which he chose to live his life was one of those things. The consequences were too grave or altogether unknown. "No, I'm not afraid," he lied. "I'm tired."

Rindar changed the subject. "It seems that this Vashtor character is a NarEladra," he mused.

"Maybe," Minxa mumbled, "but he's probably not the same guy you met in Vindarill. It's got to be a coincidence."

"Quite a coincidence—both of them are after the map," Rindar observed and then fell silent. Minxa did not want the discussion to continue so he said nothing. The name could easily be a coincidence, but the pursuit of the map pushed it a bit too far. The twenty drag silver was the most troubling, but Minxa preferred to ignore it rather than deal with the consequences of believing in the NarEladra. He kept his head down, slogging along the trail behind Rindar.

They found Sereline and Rasler waiting for them at the next turn in the trail, and they continued their trek together with quiet, unthreatening idle chatter. Suddenly Sereline gasped and Minxa looked up. The trail had turned around an outcropping of stone to reveal an enormous gateway.

Huge white stones formed an arch thirty feet over the trail in front of them. Its flat top rose above the trees where the white stones gleamed in the afternoon sun, and each stone was fitted into the perfection of the arch. Over its top, chiseled in deep letters, was the phrase:

⅋Ⅲⴸ<Uⅴ

Rasler stood with her hands on her hips. "The Ransom Gate," she said as she turned to face the others. "This is good. It means that we are farther than I thought." On either side of the arch, remnants of a massive stone wall disappeared into the woods in both directions.

"What is it?" Sereline asked.

Rasler started walking toward the arch. "It was built thousands of years ago. It is one of eight gates through the Elarha Wall that surrounds the Crown. The Eladra built it."

"Why is it called 'The Ransom Gate'?" Rindar asked.

"Not sure," Rasler tossed over her shoulder. "It had something to do with the spirit of Vestin and Vishtoenvar's rebellion. When he and his followers were banished from the Crown, the Eladra built the Elarha Wall as a barrier around the entire Crown. As far as I understand, no NarEladra may walk the land inside the wall."

"Even now?" Sereline queried.

"I think so...I hope so, too," Rasler smiled.

"Ransom—ransom." Sereline tumbled the word over in her mouth. "What a strange word." Minxa had never heard it, but perhaps it was an old word from the Kor'Alura that meant something special.

The travelers were standing under the stone gateway. The carved stone surfaces were covered with intricate glyphs and scenes from ancient battles. The white stones themselves were nearly cubic, perhaps eight feet on a side, fitted together so perfectly that even a leaf from the trail would not fit between them. They rose up on either side, getting smaller as they closed over the top where they were crowned by an oversized capstone that kept the two walls of stone from collapsing on one another.

"Look at this!" Sereline's voice floated down from the top of the arch. "Up here...you have to see this!" Sereline peered over the edge of one of the stones. "There are stairs up the back!"

Minxa trudged through the arch. A broad set of steep steps came into view on each side of the road. They spiraled upward until they were high enough to join into the slope of the arch. Rasler bounded up the steps to join Sereline, but Minxa sat down heavily on the first step. "I'll stay here," he said. "I'm too tired." Rindar looked down at him. "Go ahead," he continued. "I'll wait for you."

Rindar slipped off the packs and dropped them beside him. "You sure? I'll help you up."

"I'm okay," Minxa smiled weakly. He knew he needed to save his strength because as soon as the others came back down, they would be on the march again, staying ahead of their pursuers. He leaned against the stone. It was warm from the sun and felt good against his shoulder. The pain eased slightly with the warmth, and Minxa let himself drift into a shallow sleep.

⊠

The future is also a part of history.

Karendo Marha
Journey to the Infinite

The climb to the top of the arch thoroughly winded Rindar. When he got there, Rasler and Sereline were standing on the huge capstone staring up the hill at the Crown. They had been walking through the trees since leaving the river, and with the exception of several places where they could see through breaks in the trees, Rindar had not been able to see the Crown itself. From the capstone, which rose above the treetops, he could see everything.

The brilliant early afternoon sun cast deep shadows on the towering peaks. The carpet of trees rose from in front of him and turned yellowish before succumbing to the ridges of bare stone funneling upward to where the snow began. The shades of blue and white, peculiar to deep mountain snow on the peaks, spiked into the deepening blue sky.

Rasler pointed up the hill. "Just up there," she said, "perhaps two hundred paces; do you see the line in the trees?"

Rindar squinted. There was an almost imperceptible break running along the slope, following the contours of the mountains. "Yes, I see it," he said. Sereline nodded.

"That is the Harhazian Road. According to Visha'andar, it runs just inside the wall surrounding the girth of the Crown. When we get there, we will head west. It will be easier traveling and about a day's walk to the trail leading to the springs."

Rindar looked south. They had come much farther than he had imagined. To the south, the warm browns, blacks and oranges of the wastes shimmered in the sun. They were high enough now so that he could see a strip of ocean over the rim of the plateau before it all dissolved into the sky. He stood and stared, breathing deeply of the cool wind that flowed down the mountain.

Sereline's eyes were closed, and her face tipped upward to the sun, facing south across the wastes. She posed like a statue, as still as the stone on which she stood. Rindar could see her breathing deeply as if she tasted the world around her in long, slow draughts.

The arch was about ten-feet wide at the top, and the mammoth capstone was twice that in length. In the very center of its rectangular surface was a carved bench of pure white stone that was long enough for all three of them to sit together. Rindar sat down facing the wastes and Rasler sat beside him. "We have come far," she said. Her voice was low as she deferred to Sereline's private communion with the wind. "We should be safe inside the wall, but cannot take any chances." She looked around. "Minxa didn't want to join us?"

"He is very tired," Rindar said. "His shoulder is healing slowly and the walking doesn't help."

"Thanks for carrying his pack for him."

"We've done harder things," Rindar mused.

"How long have you known Minxa?" Rasler asked. She was staring out over the wastes.

"We met each other when we first started school."

"School?" Rasler's tone indicated that she had never heard the word. "You used the word last night, but I do not know what it means."

Rindar was surprised, but he tried to respect her lack of knowledge.

"Where we come from, children are sent to a place called a school where we are taught things—all together."

"How many children?"

"All of them—I mean everyone. We are put in groups of twenty or thirty and taught to read. We are taught subjects like history and math—"

"By one person?" Rasler seemed incredulous.

"Usually," Rindar said, "but sometimes we have different teachers for different things."

"Do you think that one person can teach you all the things you need to know to be—complete? To be wise? To be kind?"

"I don't think that is their job. They just teach us things like history and reading."

"And who teaches you to be wise and kind; to be respectful and full of kariis?"

"Usually, that's left to the parents."

"Why don't the parents teach you to read and write and to be wise, kind and full of kariis at the same time?"

"I don't know," Rindar said. "I didn't have a choice and never thought about that."

Rasler seemed to realize that she was treading into areas in which Rindar did not have answers. "It just seems odd," she continued. "What about you? Did your parents teach you anything?"

Rindar felt a ball of emotion rolling around inside his belly. He held up his hands so that Rasler could see his wrists. "Do you see these tattoos?" he asked, indicating with a nod the narrow blue band that completely encircled both wrists.

Rasler nodded. "I was wondering what they were. You both have it."

"We are viddiks. 'Born viddik and marked as such.'" He felt like gagging as he repeated the phrase that cursed his life, a phrase he had promised he would never say out loud.

"That's another word I have heard you use that I don't know."

"Have you heard of Mooriman?"

"Yes. It is a source of great evil in this world."

"Sometime in the future from now, about six hundred years before I was born in Vindarill, Mooriman invaded the continent of Manna. They overran those living there and made them slaves. In Vindarill, the descendants of the slaves are called viddiks, bred and raised to serve the Mooriman invaders. In my time, according to the laws of Morlan—the country where Vindarill is a city—it is against the law to have slaves. But we still live in slavery. As a viddik, there is little hope of doing much more than surviving. These tattoos,"—Rindar shook his fists at the sky—"condemn me everywhere I go. Minxa and I were taken from our parents when we were barely old enough to remember them. They put us in orphan homes full of other viddik kids."

Rasler was silent. Rindar simmered with an anger that he had not felt since coming through the portal, but that was ever present in daily life in Vindarill. Rasler glanced at Sereline, still standing motionless in the light breeze, then turned back to Rindar. "So why does Minxa hate being here so much?"

Rindar shook his head. "I don't know," he confessed. "I think he hates the idea of being here more than he hates the place. He came here unexpectedly. I also think that this place makes him look at himself. In Vindarill it was easy not to examine yourself. It was so busy and so hard that life was full of just surviving, so we never had time to stop and think, and there was no one who would teach us. And—" A thought crossed his mind that he had never thought before. "And now that I think about it, perhaps they deliberately left out the part about teaching us to think about it."

"Sounds like an ugly place."

Rindar had been offended the first time Rasler said this, but this time it seemed to fit. Overwhelmed by that realization, he had nothing to say; he needed some time before he was ready to talk further. They sat quietly for several minutes, listening to the immense silence of the forest, the sky and the hulking noble peaks of the Crown of Tessalindria.

✠

When the basa feels pain, it should fore-shadow in us the agony of Oblivion for the El.

Pratoraman
The Middle Way

Minxa thought the voices were part of his dream, whispers in the shadows behind the trees at the Margah, and he couldn't quite make out what they were saying. It seemed as if they did not want to be heard. Someone dropped something and a voice whispered, "Idiot!"

Minxa tried to lean forward, but a hand clamped over his mouth, and another hand pressed his shoulder against the stone. He groaned. "One more sound out of you and—" The one he remembered as Marhan held the tip of a knife in his left nostril. Minxa blinked.

"You're coming with us," Marhan whispered as he slid his knife into its sheath. He pulled several cloth strips out of a pocket and forced a wad of it into Minxa's mouth, then tied another across his mouth so Minxa could not talk or yell. "Get up!"

Minxa had not seen the other man with Marhan. "You got the map?"

Marhan whispered as the man finished the task of looting the packs.

Minxa saw the man nod. "And look at this," he said as he held up Rasler's little book. After turning it over once or twice, he dropped it into his pack, which he immediately slung up onto his shoulder.

"Stand up!" commanded Marhan. He grabbed Minxa by the upper arm and hauled him to his feet. Minxa groaned as the searing pain shot through his shoulder. He felt the wound open under his shirt, and tears rolled down his eyes as he tried to choke back the sobs on the wad of cloth in his mouth. "C'mon, move it!"

Minxa wanted to protest, but the two men held his arms and hurried him up the trail. The blood was running down his shoulder. "Usheth! He's bleedin'," the other man said.

"Can't stop now," hissed Marhan, "—when we get some distance!"

The two hundred yards he had to run with his captors seemed like miles to Minxa. Pain shot through his upper body, and he stumbled several times to the curses and yanks of Marhan and the brute with him. After a sudden steep rise in the trail, they found themselves on a stone road. It was paved with the same white stone as the arch and was tufted with grass and moss that forced its way up between the stones, but it was perfectly flat and stretched into the distance in both directions.

The two horses tied to a tree snorted when the men approached. They hoisted Minxa onto the larger horse. Marhan swung up behind him and whispered, "Lean forward around the neck and hang on. We'll leave you to die if you fall off."

Marhan set the horses to a gallop. Minxa expected it to be jarring, but the huge neck of the horse swayed in a rhythm that allowed him to hold himself half upright, rocking to the motion of the horse's gait. He held tightly to the horse's mane with his left hand and tucked his right hand and arm close to his body. Marhan's hand held Minxa's shirt in the middle of his back.

They galloped on for some time, the endless woods gliding by in a painful green blur with the steady rhythm of the horses' hooves on the hard road. After a while, they slowed down and then stopped. Marhan whistled. A whistle answered from out of the trees, and in the next instant they were galloping again. Minxa closed his eyes and held on. He had no other choice.

✠

The gulls. The gulls that swoop and turn
And bring the darkness with their shadow.

Ramonmara
The Legend of Mishla Mira

Two gulls floated below them. Rindar watched their black backs from the top of the arch. They sailed on the rising air currents created by the sun beating down on the warm slopes that rose from the wastes. Sereline turned from her pose. "Something is wrong!" she said suddenly, opening her eyes wide. As she limped toward them, Rindar saw a dark spot out of the corner of his eye, moving rapidly in from the west above the treetops. As it approached, the gulls suddenly dipped and headed down the slope. The black bird came in above them as they dove and twisted to evade its attack, screaming desperately above the still forest.

"C'mon," said Rasler as she bounded for the stairs. "It's Vakandar." Rindar tried to keep up, but Sereline and Rasler both reached the bottom before he did. As he rounded the last corner in the steps, Rasler was stringing her bow, and Sereline was standing over their open packs looking into them. Minxa was gone.

"He cannot have gone far," Rasler said. Rindar had never seen such wildness in her eyes. "He took the map...and he took my book."

Sereline crouched near the ground, scanning the trail. "There are at least two others," she said, "and they are headed up the hill."

Rindar opened his mouth to ask why they would do that, but Rasler interrupted him. "There is no time for questions. Come on."

Sereline led. The lingering hint of her broken leg was suddenly gone as she headed up the road from the great Ransom Gate. Rindar wished he could ask how she followed the trail, but there was no time. The thin air burned in Rindar's lungs as they ran. Every fifty feet or so, Sereline would stop at some invisible sign that only a tracker could understand and then begin running again, following the invisible trail through the woods.

It was not long before they emerged onto the Harhazian Road. It was very old and not well used. Rindar stopped to catch his breath as Sereline bent down. She ran her hand over the stone where they had emerged from the woods. He had just leaned over with his hands on his knees when Sereline stood up, holding out her hand for Rasler and him to see.

"Blood," she said, "and horses!" A faint red smear that she had wiped off the white stone ran across her finger. "Minxa must be bleeding again."

"Do you think they kidnapped him?" Rindar gasped. "Or—did he go voluntarily?"

Rasler was grim, "I don't know. Either way, his life is in danger." She bent over and looked into Rindar's eyes. "Are you going to make it?"

"I think so," he gasped, "but I cannot go this fast forever."

Rasler straightened. "At least they are inside the wall and headed in the direction we want to go, but the horses worry me. Let's go."

They started running again, but it was more of a trot. Rindar's pack banged around unmercifully, moving one way when his body was going the other and coming down when he wanted it to be going up. He held the straps on his shoulder and tried to keep up. The road was smooth and level, and the weeds were the only impediment, so they made good time. "Wait," said Rasler, stopping suddenly. Sereline looked back and stopped as Rasler stood up straight and closed her eyes.

Her bow was in her left hand and she slowly raised it, slipping an arrow from her quiver and bringing it down to meet her bow in a single motion. They waited for what seemed like a long time to Rindar; the utter silence of the woods around him was threatening. *"Don't move."* Rasler spoke to Rindar's mind.

The words had barely reached Rindar's consciousness when Rasler ducked and rolled over on her shoulder. A hissing arrow glanced off the stone behind her and skipped up into the trees on the other side. Rasler came up on one knee and her bowstring sang. The arrow disappeared into the canopy of trees to Rindar's left, snapping through leaves as it sped toward its unseen target. Someone yelled and cursed. Rindar heard a branch break, followed by a thud, as Rasler and Sereline plunged into the undergrowth, leaving Rindar standing alone on the road. Another curse followed, and he heard Rasler say, "On your feet, scoundrel."

"Don't shoot." It was a man's voice, filled with anger and fear.

"On your feet then," said Rasler, "and no tricks."

Rindar heard them moving toward him. As they emerged onto the road he could see what had happened. The man beside Sereline was a little shorter than Rindar with a full red beard and angry gray eyes. Rindar guessed he was one of Marhan's new recruits. He wore a cap and clothing of forest green and brown, unremarkable except for Rasler's arrow protruding from his right shoulder. His hands were behind him as if they were tied. His legs were hobbled with rope so he could walk, but little more, and Sereline escorted him by holding onto his left arm.

Rasler stepped from the woods behind him, her bow drawn and the arrow aimed between his shoulder blades. When he saw Rindar, he spat at his feet. Sereline stopped, and Rasler stepped around in front of the man, lowering her bow and slipping the arrow into the quiver over her shoulder without losing eye contact. She moved in close. "Where is our friend?"

"Find him yourself."

Rasler's hand shot to the arrow in his shoulder and yanked it from his shoulder. He howled in pain, but before he had time to recover, Rasler had maneuvered the bloody arrowhead into one of his nostrils and had forced his head back. He winced, but stood perfectly still, knowing that a false move would mean greater pain. "I don't want to do this, but I will. Where is our friend?!" She slowly twisted the arrow as the man raised his head, trying to escape the sharp tip turning in his nostril.

"I…I don't know. He is…with the others." With his head thrust back from the arrow's threat, the man choked as he tried to speak.

"How many others?"

"Five."

"How many horses?"

The man hesitated and the arrow twisted again.

"Stop…stop—there are four…horses."

"Who is in charge? Marhan?"

The man tried to nod. It was enough for Rasler, so she pulled the arrow down and wiped its tip on his green shirt. "You should be thankful my aim was good. I might have hit your heart. Your shoulder will heal, but your heart would not have."

She slipped the arrow back into her quiver. "Let's go."

"Where are you going?" the man asked.

"To find our friend," Rasler muttered as she shouldered her pack.

"What about me—what are you going to do about me?"

"You are free to go."

"What about my hands? Can you untie my hands?"

"No."

"I'll die!" the man pleaded.

"You won't die." Rasler moved in close to look him in the eye. "The arrow you sent for me—if it had hit me, would you have left me to die?" They stared at one another for a moment. "I thought so," she said. "I am letting you live, but I am not letting you follow us."

She turned and started jogging. Sereline and Rindar caught up to her, leaving the wounded stranger howling threats after them as he lay bound on the shimmering white road.

⊞

Every being has a thread of goodness that forms the fabric of the vorn.

Mortag of Horrinaine
Of Beings

Between the screaming pain and the exhaustion of trying to remain on the horse, Minxa had no idea how far they had traveled along the road when Marhan reined in the horse and slid to the ground. "Wait here," he commanded in a hoarse whisper. The other horseman pulled up beside Minxa and took the reins. Minxa looked at him through half-closed eyes. He did not look any crueler than Marhan did, but looks were not the measure of a man in this world any more than they were in Vindarill. Minxa wondered why he had to keep discovering this over and over. He closed his eyes and let the warmth of the still horse comfort him.

"The others are down in the gully to the left, not far from the wall," Marhan said when he returned. "Well hidden—a good place for the night. I do not think they will find us."

"But the Pistisine—" protested the other rider.

"She will be dead." Marhan took the reins and started to the side of the road. Minxa held on, not wanting to move.

"How do you know?"

"Faranda is the best hunter I know. She's no match for his skill."

They eased down the bank at the side of the road and picked their way through the woods until they emerged in a small clearing with a large boulder to its left. As they came around the boulder, Minxa saw the fire. Drofan was one of the three other men that rose to meet them.

Minxa still lay on the horse's neck as Drofan approached. "You look bad, friend," he said.

"I feel bad," Minxa grumbled.

"You're bleeding!"

Minxa nodded.

"Let me help you down, and we'll take care of that." Minxa felt Drofan's strength as he helped him down from the horse and led him gently to a place where he could sit down with his back to the rock. He was not far from the fire.

One of the other men took the two horses and led them away, and the third squatted down beside Minxa. "Can I see that wound?" he asked.

Minxa nodded. He was perplexed. He wondered why they had bothered to capture him and why they had not just taken the map and either killed him or left him. If they had left him, he would have alerted the others. Some shadow in the back of his mind said there was more to this than he could perceive. "What is your name?" he mumbled as the man began unbuttoning his shirt.

"Tarlin, from Riverton," he said, "but don't speak now; you need to rest." Tarlin worked carefully. When he had exposed the wound he said "Sakah!" From the way he said it, Minxa guessed it was an oath of some sort. "Wait here," he said.

Minxa closed his eyes and waited. He could hear hushed and hurried conversations but did not have the energy to care what was being said. When Tarlin returned, he opened his eyes. "I need to wash that wound—it's likely to hurt."

The warm water made Minxa wince, but he knew he had to endure it. He clenched his teeth each time Tarlin touched it. "How did this happen?"

"The flood—at the island," he gasped. "A shard of stone—"

"And no one cleaned and dressed it?"

"No, they did. It was beginning to heal before—" He gasped again as Tarlin applied a poultice of some sort. "Before the ride here."

"You need to rest now," Tarlin said. "When you wake you will feel better."

Minxa nodded and leaned back against the stone, his eyes closed. The fire burned to his right, and he could feel its heat and the pungent wisp of smoke that wafted his way when the breeze shifted. The men were talking, but they made no sense, their voices rising and falling. There was psadeq here. He could feel it, and even in the half-awareness of his pain and desire for sleep, he began to wonder if it could be shared with him.

✠

If a man shouts in the forest, and there is no one to hear him, did he say anything?

Oratanga
Passages

"There may be others," said Rasler. "Stay alert." They had slowed to a fast walk because Rindar was having trouble keeping up. Sereline scanned the road and the woods, and Rasler carried her bow with an arrow nocked in it.

They had been traveling a long time and had not stopped to eat or even drink since they left the arch. They had passed at least a dozen of the ornamental white stone markers that lined the road. Rindar guessed that they were mile-markers but had not had time to examine them or ask.

The sun hung low in the trees when Sereline whispered in Rasler's ear. Rasler turned and touched her index finger to her lips, then leaned over and whispered, "They are near. We will hide behind that marker until it's nearly dark."

They moved silently. Rasler dropped her pack behind the marker and sat down, so Rindar and Sereline did the same. No one spoke. Rindar wanted to ask how Sereline knew where they were, but he knew it was not safe to talk. Rasler closed her eyes and leaned against the rock. It felt good to sit, but Rindar could feel the fear rolling like waves through his vorn. How did they expect to win against five men? Rindar knew Rasler was cunning and quick, but he was not as sure about Sereline. From what he had observed, she could have been Rasler's twin,

and it comforted him to know they were on his side. They made formi-
dable enemies.

As the sun set, dusk settled into twilight. Rasler and Sereline sat up
simultaneously and moved in close against Rindar, who sat in the middle. They drew their knees up and pressed against the stone. Rindar did
the same. He held his breath, and as he did so, he heard voices.

"We should have heard from Faranda by now."

"Seems that way, don't it?"

"Do you suppose he's all right?"

"Dunno. He was going after the Pistisine. He's a good shot."

"Do you think he'll turn?"

"Who?"

"Him!"

"I dunno. He came willingly enough."

"He was hurt—didn't have much of a choice, eh?"

"Why didn't Marhan just get the map?"

"That's a good question. That's what we came for."

They were standing right on the other side of the stone.

"What are we supposed to be doing?"

"We're supposed to hide and keep an eye out for them, but it will
be an hour or so before they could possibly be here—without horses
and all."

Rindar could hear them relieving themselves on the stone.

"If they stop here—" There was a pause as if the speaker had made
a hand sign. "If they pass by, we just let them go?"

"Something about this doesn't make sense."

Rindar suddenly realized that the voice belonged to Drofan.

"Yeah, I was thinking the same thing."

"I mean, Marhan was just supposed to get the map and bring it back
to Riverton. Then we'd get what Vashtor promised." There was a long
pause and the same voice continued. "Instead, he captures this Minxa
character and heads away from the Riverton Road." More silence followed. "I think he wants the map for himself, and Minxa knows something about it."

"Maybe," said Drofan, "we haven't seen Vashtor since he abandoned
us in the wastes."

"I think Marhan found him in Riverton when we got the horses…
either way, something doesn't make sense."

"Marhan's treating Minxa awful nice. I mean, you heard his order
for us to treat him nice, didn't you?"

There was another pause before Drofan spoke. "Listen, I don't want
to mess with Marhan."

"Neither do I—but I don't want to mess with Vashtor either."

"Good point," Drofan admitted. "I bet we won't get paid if Marhan doesn't get paid."

"So what do we do?"

"Well. Right now we need to make sure that whoever is left doesn't stop here. C'mon."

✠

Even good things can happen in the darkness.

Old Mythinian Saying

"Rindar, stay here," Rasler mindspoke, and in the next instant, she and Sereline rolled out around the stone from each side.

All Rindar heard was a "Wha—" and two thuds, followed by the sound of the two men falling. Rasler and Sereline dragged the bodies around the stone and propped them up against the back of it. Rasler pulled a couple of leather thongs and two bandages from her pack, and Sereline tied the men's hands while Rasler stuffed the bandages into their mouths.

"Drofan!" whispered Rasler. She smiled at Sereline. "Not real bright, this one. Let's go."

They shouldered their packs and moved out onto the road. Neither of the moons was up, so there was little light, but the road shone white by the light of the stars. Sereline led them across the road and into a gully on the downhill side. As they crouched low, Rasler whispered in Rindar's ear. "They are on the other side of this rise, and we need you to walk over the top pretending you are lost and that you smelled their fire. Start calling for help."

"Me?"

"Yes, Rindar. It's the only way." Rindar couldn't believe what he heard; they were using him as bait. "You need to go now. Take your pack—and convince them you want to join them. Remember that they may not know that Sereline is with us, unless Minxa told them."

"I can't do it."

Rasler would not listen. She pointed. "Go—now!"

Rindar had to trust. In spite of all his fear, he stood up. "Go!" said Rasler urgently, so Rindar turned and headed up out of the ravine.

As he came over the top of the ridge, he could see the firelight dancing on the trees from behind a large boulder. Rindar had been through moments when he thought he might be crazy, and this was one of them as he walked slowly toward the camp of his enemies with a lie on his tongue. When he was about thirty paces away, two men appeared around either end of the boulder. "Who is it?" they called.

"Rindar," he said without breaking stride. The third form appeared as the first two started toward him, their drawn knives glinting in the light. Rindar kept walking. They met him about twenty paces from the fire.

"What are you doing here?"

"I've come for my friend."

They grabbed Rindar by the arms, and one of them held a knife to his throat. It was the one that Marhan had called Parata. "How did you get past the guards?"

Rindar sighed as if he was weary. "What guards?"

By this time, Marhan had approached, and he stopped in front of Rindar. "What happened to the Pistisine?"

"Rasler?"

"Yeah, that one." Marhan's eyes gleamed, even in the near darkness.

"She was shot dead on the road."

"How did you escape?"

"I ran. Your archer was in a tree. By the time he got down, I was too far ahead."

Marhan's eyes narrowed. "That's enough. How did you get here so fast; how did you find our camp?"

"Look, I'm tired. I ran most of the way trying to find Minxa. He's my friend. When I smelled smoke, I figured you were here."

Marhan looked suspicious, and he stroked his chin as he considered what to do. "Tie him up, Parata, then go get Drofan and Tarlin. If they fell asleep, scare 'em good." Rindar did not resist being led back to the fire. In his mind, he knew that Rasler and Sereline would make quick work of Parata but he wasn't so sure how they would save *him*.

"Tie him beside his friend," commanded Marhan as he sat down by the fire. They led Rindar to a tree on the far side of the fire where Minxa was sleeping peacefully, facing into the fire as he leaned back against a slope in the boulder. They shoved Rindar down and bound his feet and hands. Minxa groaned when Rindar's shoulder bumped him, but he did not wake.

By straining, Rindar could see the fire over his right shoulder. Marhan and the one whose name he did not know sat close to it, talking rapidly in low voices so that Rindar could not understand what they were saying. Rindar turned away because it was making his neck stiff to watch, and nothing else seemed to be happening.

A horse snorted in the darkness somewhere in front of where Rindar sat. He looked back to the fire to see Marhan standing, listening intently. The other one was still and listening also, but remained seated.

"Something's not right," said Marhan.

No sooner had he finished the words than he suddenly crumpled to his knees and pitched forward onto his face. The other man jumped up and glancing first right then left, headed toward the horses. He had not taken ten steps when a shadow leapt from behind one of the huge trees right into his path below his knees. He yelped as he tripped, careening headlong down the slope. Another shadow moved, followed by a groan from the man and then total silence.

Rindar waited. Marhan lay still by the fire, its shadows doing an eerie dance against the quiet trees. He dared not speak. The next sound was that of horses, walking slowly up the rise. Rasler and Sereline led them. They found Minxa and Rindar quickly.

"He's asleep," Rindar said, "maybe unconscious!"

"I'll take care of him," said Rasler. "Find the map—and my book. Make sure we have them."

Sereline and Rindar searched the saddlebags. "Found the book," said Sereline. "It was tucked into one of the pouches."

"No map?"

"Not here."

"Look around the fire."

The map box was beside the log where Marhan had been sitting. Rindar checked to see that the map was still inside. "It's here," he said.

"Good! Let's get out of here."

"Should we take anything else?" Rindar asked.

"Only the horses," said Rasler in a low voice. "Help me get Minxa up onto one of them."

They led the horses up to the road before mounting them. Rindar had never ridden a horse, and the experience exhilarated him. Rasler led and held the reins to Minxa's horse, with Sereline and Rindar following behind. Once the horses sensed the safety of traveling on the road, Rasler set them all into a canter, and they moved swiftly into the darkness toward the trail to the springs.

Rindar never learned how Rasler found the trailhead to the springs in the dark. She didn't consult the map, and there were no false stops in the search. Perhaps she knew from the mileposts. They had passed three of them on the horses before she stopped. "We go right here," she announced and turned up the trail.

They spent the night about a mile from the road, another night with no fire. "How far is it to the springs?" Rindar asked. She shrugged, snapped out her blanket and lay down to sleep without giving him an answer. Minxa was still unconscious. Rindar had laid him down and covered him with extra blankets to make sure he was warm. Rindar lay down close beside him. He did not want to lose his friend, and he determined to do whatever he could to make sure Minxa was still with them in the morning.

ᛞ The Jualar Springs ᛞ

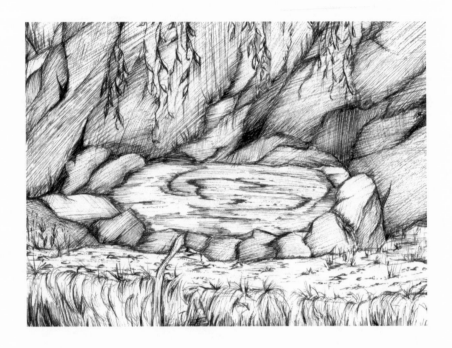

The seven jewels of the Crown of
Tessalindria are the springs that feed the
Verillain flow.

Mordestal
O Tessalindria

Minxa was still confused about exactly what had happened. When
he had fallen asleep the night before, he was in the camp with
the men who had kidnapped him, and now he was back with the others, and they had the horses. Rindar had explained all of it, and Minxa
vaguely remembered parts of his dreams that agreed with Rindar's story,
but it was all jumbled in his mind. He had been roused from a fitful
sleep by the distant pounding. Rasler said it was the hammer of the
Eladrim smith who lived in the dale.

The horses seemed particularly alert when they mounted them.
Rasler led them up the trail beside the stream that flowed past their
campground. Perhaps it was the daylight and they did not have to be as
cautious, but Minxa sensed the overall lightness that seemed to surround

the small group as they moved upward toward the springs.

"Am I dreaming," asked Sereline, "or is something different here?"

"What do you mean?" Rindar asked.

"Well, everything seems to be brighter, maybe sharper, fresher—it just seems—I'm not sure how to describe it."

"I think that there is less mordage here," said Rasler, looking back over her shoulder.

Minxa was directly behind her. "I thought mordage was something that is attached to people—at least that's the way you have used it before." He purposefully injected an edge of ridicule into his voice.

"It's used in two ways," she said. "Yes, individuals carry their own mordage, but the accumulated effect burdens our entire world. In certain places, the mordage of our world is held at bay, and it is said that in the Crown, it's removed altogether."

"What do you mean 'in the Crown'?" Rindar asked. "Do you mean here?"

"No. Within the ring of peaks that form the Crown, there is a place, at least the legends attest to it, where there is no mordage, and no one with mordage may go there."

"Sounds like a nice legend," grumbled Minxa. On the surface, his companions seemed sincere, but inside they were trapped by their beliefs. He hated the way Rindar was being suckered into their foolishness.

"Why do you always have such an attitude, Minxa?" Sereline asked.

Minxa looked back with a sneer on his lips. "Rasler thinks it's my 'mordage.'"

"Maybe it is," Sereline continued. "If the effect of your mordage is to keep you from realizing you have it, how would you ever know it was there if you don't trust anyone else to see it for you?"

The question hung in the air as they rode along. Minxa pretended to ignore it altogether, as if it had never been asked at all. It was a worthy question and something that he should consider, but the issue demanded assumptions that defied all reason. It was as if it had been invented to sustain itself. A person started believing part of it, and the logical conclusion was to believe all of it, even though it had no basis in truth.

With each turn of the trail, the heavy blows of the hammer grew stronger and more distinct in their content. A new smell filled Minxa's nostrils. It was pungent and reminded him of rush hour in Vindarill. "What is that?" he asked.

"What?" said Rasler, turning suddenly in alarm.

"That smell!"

"It's coal smoke," she laughed, "and you'd better get used to it."

Minxa realized that it was the same smell from the smithy in Karolil, but here it was full smoke, not just the lingering scent of a day's work.

As the party came up over a small rise, the land leveled out into a clearing. On the far side, snuggled against a sharp rise in the hill was a low building. At the right end of the structure, a tall stone chimney rose high above the roof, and a spiral of gray smoke curled into the still morning air, before spreading out and flowing down the valley behind them.

The building was long, with regularly spaced doors and windows that indicated a number of small rooms, all side by side. A porch ran its length, allowing a person to walk from door to door without getting wet in the rain, and it was all wood, including the dark layers of lapped shingles that covered the roof. It spoke of great antiquity and great care.

The hammering stopped as the travelers approached on the horses. They were ten paces from the door when a man emerged from the dark interior. He stooped as he stepped through the door, and when he straightened, Minxa could see that he would tower above all of them. "Hullo! Are you friend or foe?" His voice boomed full of confidence, as if the answer didn't matter. He carried a huge hammer in his left hand, and tongs hung limply in his right, and his completely bald head was smeared with black soot, as was his old wrinkled face. The smudges accentuated his piercing blue eyes. In each ear he had a gold ring that Minxa could have put his hand through, and he was clothed in a heavy gray tunic from head to foot with a long leather apron that hung almost to his enormous shoeless feet.

He continued to walk toward them. "Well?"

"We are friends," said Rasler.

"And where be you from?"

"My name is Rasler; I am from Vindor."

"That's a long way, missy." He grinned and his perfect teeth flashed white behind his sooted face. "And you," he continued, pointing to Minxa with the tongs, "you would be—?"

"Minxa—"

The giant cocked his head as if he had not heard.

Minxa leaned forward and raised his voice. "Minxa. From Vindarill."

The old man nodded slowly as if he were thinking. "Hmmm, that is a very long way from here—and a very long time, and you are wounded. How are you wounded?"

Minxa looked at Rasler. "I have been told it was the fist of Mah'Eladra."

"To wound so slightly is unlike Mah'Eladra's fist."

Minxa opened his mouth in surprise, but the giant turned to Rindar. "And you?" he asked.

"I am Rindar, sir, also from Vindarill."

He leaned forward and looked up through his bushy eyebrows that he raised to see better. "Rindar...Rindar...Mindar from Vindarill. Yes...yes. You, too, are a long way from home, are you not?"

Rindar nodded.

"And Copper Hair—do you also come from some other-time?" he cocked his head toward Sereline without moving otherwise.

"I am Sereline. I have lived in Karolil, south across the wastes, by the sea."

He nodded. "I understand. Beautiful place by the ocean, do you not think?"

"It is beautiful, sir."

He stood up straight suddenly, stretched his arms wide and called in his booming voice, "I am Vishortan, the guardian, the smith. You are welcome as friends. Come, I will show you to your rooms."

Minxa looked at Rasler. She nodded, and they all dismounted and led their horses after the huge hulk of a man who still held his hammer and tongs. "These horses, they are fine, are they not?" he called over his shoulder. "You got them, where?"

"We borrowed them to save our lives," said Rasler.

"You stole them," Minxa interjected.

Vishortan kept walking. "You did not help in the stealing, Minxa of Vindarill?"

"I was unconscious."

"Your life was saved by this 'theft', was it not?"

"I...I'm not sure—"

"You should make sure, yuh? Tie the horses here," he said as he waved his hand toward the railing in front of the building, "Rasler and Copper Hair, you will stay in this room. Minxa and Mindar; this room shall be yours." He turned and smiled, waving his hammer and tongs this way and that as he described where they could get water and refresh themselves; that they were free to walk about, but were not to go to the springs, which were further up the valley. "You are safe here. If you need anything, call my name."

He started to walk away, then turned back. "Minxa of Vindarill, come with me. You want healing, do you not?"

Minxa hesitated.

"Do you want healing? I will be in the smithy," Vishortan said as he turned and headed back to his work.

"He may not offer again," whispered Rasler. Minxa looked at her. He was not sure which was greater, his pride or his pain, and he could not rationalize his pride because the pain was so great that it should not even have been a question. "Go ahead. Go now!" she urged. Minxa looked at Rindar for help. He nodded after the giant.

Minxa dropped his pack and hesitated again. He looked up at Sereline. She looked down. Finally, he threw his tunic down onto his pack and turned to follow Vishortan into one of the small rooms of the long building.

The door was hardly shut when Rindar heard Minxa howl in pain. He started to move, but Rasler stayed him by grabbing his arm. "Wait," she said.

Everything was silent for about a minute before the door opened slowly and Minxa came out through it. He was rubbing his shoulder with his left hand, and he wore a scowl. He was halfway to them when Vishortan appeared at the door. The giant was smiling and carrying his tongs and hammer. He eyed them all briefly, then turned and headed back to his shop.

"What happened?" Rindar asked.

"Never mind, ashtemba! He healed it somehow, but not all the way," he said, "and it hurt when he did it."

"We heard," said Sereline, smiling.

"What do you mean, 'not all the way'?" asked Rasler.

Minxa was still rubbing his shoulder. "It's sore."

"It's sore? You had a hole an inch-and-a-half deep in the back of your shoulder!" Rasler exclaimed.

Sereline picked up her pack and turned to go into her room. "It seems to me you should be more grateful," she tossed over her shoulder.

Minxa uttered something rude and picked up his tunic and his pack. "I'm going to take a nap," he snapped, and walked to the door that Vishortan had indicated for him.

Rindar looked at Rasler. She shook her head in disgust. "I'm going for a walk."

There are times when individuals need to be left alone, and this was one of those times for Minxa. Rindar put his pack by the door and headed toward the sound of hammering from the other end of the building.

The acrid smell of hot iron and coal smoke filled the dark smithy. The only other time Rindar had been in a smithy was just a few days before in Karolil, and preconceptions built on other preconceptions filled his mind so that he did not know what to expect. As his shadow fell across the threshold, Vishortan looked up.

"Come in, Mindar," he boomed, "come, there is a stool here with no one to sit on it." He turned back to tend his fire as he continued. "There are few smithies in Vindarill, yuh? And you have never seen one?"

"Yes, that's right," Rindar said as he sat down. The four-foot-square stone forge was covered in layers with nodules of coal the size of his thumbnail. Toward one side, near the chimney, the fire burned brightly as the air roared up through it, creating bright fingers of flame that burst through the coal. The fire swept sideways with wisps of smoke trailing from the edges of the fire toward the chimney.

"There are two rules for visitors to my smithy," Vishortan said. As he looked up, he raked hot coals around a piece of iron that lay buried in the fire. "First, no one enters without my permission; and second, no one is permitted to speak or move when my iron is out of the fire. This is clear, is it not, Mindar?"

Rindar nodded. He was curious why Vishortan kept calling him Mindar. He had said Rindar twice the first time they met, but now it was Mindar, as if Vishortan thought that Rindar was someone else or that he knew something that Rindar didn't know himself. Rindar knew that the Eladra thought differently, but Visha'andar had never called him Mindar. "You have come to visit the springs?" His odd habit of turning statements into questions was something Rindar had to get used to.

"Yes and no," Rindar said. "Rasler suggested that I come with her since I had nowhere specific to go after coming to Islag. So here we are."

"You came through the portal on Islag, did you not?" He was looking down and pushing coal with a small rake that he held in his hand.

"Yes."

"And Minxa of Vindarill; he came with you?"

"Yes."

"He does not want to be here, yuh?"

Rindar opened his mouth to speak as Vishortan pulled the iron from his fire and tapped it on the anvil. It was a short sword, perhaps fifteen inches long. It glowed bright orange with the heat. Vishortan looked at Rindar, who closed his mouth: no talking with the steel out of the fire.

Rindar didn't see how Vishortan got the hammer to his hand, but the thunderous blows that followed shocked Rindar's unsuspecting ears. Five strokes to one side and then five strokes to the other, back and forth the sword danced, rolling quickly between the blows so that the cadence of the hammering was never interrupted. When the blade had cooled to a dull orange, Vishortan pulled it from the anvil and thrust it rapidly back into the fire.

He looked up as he tidied up the coal around the blade with his fire rake. "Well?"

Rindar hesitated.

"Minxa—here," Vishortan reminded.

"Right. Minxa was with me when we went through the portal. We didn't know what it was—well, I guessed, but Minxa did not know."

Vishortan's eyes were glued to the fire, but he nodded slowly. "His mordage is thick and exceedingly deep, and it is not easy to heal him. I do not think he wants to be here, and I sense that he would be somewhere else if he could."

"Where?"

"I cannot know." He bent over and fiddled with something at the back of the forge, and the roar of the fire decreased.

"What did you do?" Rindar asked.

"The fire is too hot so I slowed the flow of air."

"Where is the air coming from?"

Vishortan looked at him and smiled. "It comes from the Crown itself. Come and see," he said, beckoning Rindar to the window behind the forge. "See the log? That is my air."

A long log extended out the back of the smithy and disappeared into a rock wall built against the side of the hill that rose steeply behind the house. "There is a cave there with a flow of air from high on the mountain. I walled it so the air is forced into my forge."

Rindar was still standing by the window when Vishortan pulled the blade from the fire. He stayed there until the hammer and the blade had played out their ritual and it was safely back in the coals.

"That is why I built the smithy here. The supply is endless, yuh?"

Rindar knew that, in his ignorance, he could not appreciate Vishortan's innovation, so he simply nodded.

"You met Rasler when?"

"On Islag."

"Hmmm—and Copper Hair?"

"Sereline?"

"Yes, the one with copper hair."

"We met at the Margah, by the ford at the river."

"Ahhhh…after the fist?" The way he asked made Rindar think he knew more than he was letting on.

"Yes."

"How do you come to the Margah?"

"A friend of Rasler's—Visha'andar told us to go there when we met him in the wastes."

The giant raised one bushy eyebrow in surprise. "Visha'andar? A friend of Rasler?"

"It seems that way."

The blade slid out of the fire. It was as if Vishortan needed the time to think as he pounded and flipped the steel. The shape of the blade was being slowly perfected under the brutal blows of the hammer. When it was safely back in the fire he looked up. "Visha'andar called her something else, yuh?"

"Yes…I'm trying to remember—he called her—Erin…"

"Erinshava?"

"Yes, that was it!"

The giant stared into the fire. His forehead was furrowed in thought, and he muttered something that Rindar could not hear. Somehow Rindar knew it was not time to interrupt, so he studied Vishortan as he sat and waited. His hands were larger than they should have been, and his bare forearms bulged, built up by the hammering and gripping required in the blacksmith's trade.

"Someday you will try smithing?" he asked, stirring suddenly from his strange reverie.

"I...I would like that."

"I sense that you would be a fine smith."

"I wouldn't know."

"What do you know about the springs?"

"Very little. Rasler—Erinshava, told me that they heal the vorn. Other than that—" The blade slipped from the fire to interrupt Rindar. He waited until Vishortan buried it in the coal again. "Other than that, I know nothing," he said, finishing his sentence.

"Your vorn needs healing, yuh?"

"Well, I think so—can the springs really heal?"

Vishortan smiled. "Yes and no. It depends on you. Do you think they heal?"

"I want to think that they do, but I am not sure. And I am not sure what I need to be healed of either."

Vishortan leaned over and adjusted the air a little and stood up. "We will see, yuh?" he chuckled. "Tomorrow." Then as if there were no more to be said about the springs, he changed the subject again. "Soon it will be time to eat. You are hungry, yuh?"

Rindar nodded, "Yes."

Vishortan pulled the blade from the fire one last time and hammered it down, straightening it and flattening it with precision strikes until it barely glowed; then he turned and thrust it into a large bin full of gray dust. "Wood ashes," he exclaimed. "They will keep the blade warm and let it cool slowly. Come here. I wish to show you the fire."

Rindar moved to where he could see down into the bright heart of the coals. "I want to come back after we eat, and I do not want to have to light the fire again." He leaned over as he spoke and came up with a piece of wood the thickness of his forearm, which he thrust into the heart of the fire. It flamed as he pushed the coal around it. "Without the air, the fire will die," he said, "and this log keeps it alive. Come, your food is waiting, and the others are here soon."

"The others?" Rindar asked.

"You do not think that you are the only ones here, do you?"

Rindar hadn't thought about it at all, but it made sense. He followed Vishortan out of the smithy and two doors down. The giant stopped by the door before opening it. "Go get your friends. There is a lot to eat."

✠

One who comes in peace does not come to steal.

Mythinian Proverb

From the outside, it seemed impossible that the building could contain the room where they sat in front of a fire following dinner. It burned brightly in the mammoth fireplace at one end of the hall. The long table behind them had been cleared by Vishortan, who traveled back and forth to the kitchen carrying the bowls and trays that remained from dinner before joining them in the soft leather chairs.

Three others had been there for dinner. Tarantor was their leader. "I came here hoping to find a respite from the endless boredom of life," he was saying. "Phonda and Dolar came along to watch!" He laughed as his friends smiled and shook their heads.

Rindar guessed that his age was close to fifty, though it was hard to tell in the dancing light of the fire and the dim candles that lit the perimeter of the hall. His hair was light and perhaps graying, and he carried the slight stoop of a body on which gravity had begun playing its tricks.

Phonda smiled and spoke slowly. He was a short man with thick arms and a full beard that hid his neck, leaving the impression of stout strength. "We knew he would need help once he was here."

"And we wanted to make sure he got here and got back safely," said Dolar.

"Where did you come from?" asked Rasler as she swirled a mug of hot cider absently and stared into the fire.

"We arrived from Kinvara—three days ago," said Tarantor.

"Is it far from here?" Rasler continued.

"It took us four days on foot," said Phonda, "but those were long, full days of walking."

"Why didn't you come on horses?" asked Sereline. She was sitting to the side of the fire, and her copper hair shone in the dancing light as she leaned forward on her seat.

"Too conspicuous. Tarantor wanted something a little less attention-getting," responded Phonda, "and you—where are you from?"

As Rasler opened her mouth to speak, Vishortan sat up suddenly and cocked his head. In an instant he was on his feet and heading for the door, with Rasler close on his heels. He bolted into the darkness. "What's going on?" Rindar asked.

"The horses," Rasler called over her shoulder as she plunged through the door. Rindar jumped up. Sereline was in front of him and Minxa just behind. Tarantor, Phonda and Dolar followed as they launched themselves into the darkness.

Rindar heard a horse whinny and several hurried shouts. A sudden pop and a flash of light lit the sky above the field. An eerie blue lit the figures that cast stark shadows on the gray-looking grass. "Stop!" Vishortan bellowed, his booming voice rolling across the field like thunder. Rindar saw the four figures start to run as they struggled to pull horses behind them.

Vishortan moved like a dart, heading off the leader. "Stop, now!" he roared again. The horses stopped suddenly, and the figures dropped the reins and started for the trees. Vishortan was in front of them before they got there, and with a swift side step, dropped his shoulder and flung his massive weight into the leading figure. The body lifted from the ground and flew back into those that followed, and they collapsed together in a heap. Vishortan leapt on them and pinned them to the ground amid a flurry of snarls and epithets.

Rindar knew who it was before he got there. "The horses are ours!" Drofan whined.

"Shut up!" growled Marhan. "Let me do the talking!"

"Get the horses!" ordered Vishortan. By the time Rindar got hold of the reins of two of the horses, Vishortan had all four of the brigands bound and on their feet, headed for the house. "No one comes to Verillain Dale to steal!" Vishortan said, his voice calm but rumbling with power.

"We did not come to steal. They are our horses," said Marhan. "They were stolen from us last night."

Vishortan stopped suddenly. He looked over at Rasler, who was leading the other two horses. "Is this so, Erinshava?"

Rasler stopped and turned to Vishortan. "We took them to escape from these men after we rescued Minxa from them. They had kidnapped him."

"But you did steal them, did you not?"

Rasler looked down. "Yes."

Vishortan started untying the men. "Take your horses and go," he said sternly as the thongs fell from Drofan's wrists. "If I find you in Verillain Dale tomorrow morning, I will hunt you down and throw you over the wall personally!" Marhan rubbed his wrists and looked up at Rasler with a sneer.

Rindar stood speechless as Marhan headed for the horses. As he reached out to take the reins of the lead horse, the horse stepped forward and brought his hoof down hard on Marhan's foot. Marhan cursed. The horse reared up thrashing his front hooves as Marhan backed away, and when the horse landed on all fours, he looked over at Vishortan. "I ask to not go with these men," he said clearly. Rindar looked at Minxa. His mouth was open and he stood gaping at the horse. Rasler smiled, shaking her head. Marhan stopped nursing his foot and stared.

"Ho," called Vishortan as he stepped forward. "Speak and tell us why, good friend, and tell us your name, will you not?"

"I am a Mythinian Cortimane and my name is Drogataffonamantar. My master and I were on a trading mission along the western shore of the NarEl Waste." The horse's voice had a nasal tone, and it rose and fell with quite a different intonation than a human's, but his speech was clear and concise. He moved his head back and forth as he spoke, looking directly at Vishortan from different angles. "We were making our way up the great river and had stopped at a trading outpost there when we were nearly washed away in a flash flood. We pulled two of these men from the river, nearly dead they were." He snorted and pawed the ground, and his ears swept back against his head. "When they had revived and become stronger, they recruited two others there, killed my master and stole me and the others." He nodded at the other horses.

"Do the others speak?" asked Vishortan.

"I do," said the second horse. "What Droga says is so. These men are the true thieves," she said, tossing her head in the direction of the offenders.

Vishortan stood up straight and strode over to Marhan, lifting him off the ground with one hand by his upper arm and set him down so he landed on the foot that Droga had stepped on. Marhan winced in pain and fear.

"Get out of Verillain Dale!" Vishortan growled. "And don't ever come here again!" As Marhan turned and started moving away, Vishortan whirled to face Minxa suddenly. "You want to go with them, do you not?"

Minxa looked down. "No, I don't," he said bluntly. Rindar felt for Minxa. He could tell Minxa was offended that Vishortan should ask, but he said nothing else.

Vishortan raised his hands into the milky blue light and thundered, "Vissa ortaga ontala vata mokar!" Rindar looked up and noticed a nearly imperceptible swirling in the direction of the retreating quartet. Turning to the horses, Vishortan said, "Come, Droga, and bring your companions. I will make sure you are stabled and well fed. It honors us to have you here. A Cortimane!" He reached up and snapped his fingers, and the blue light overhead disappeared, wrapping the group in darkness. Rindar heard Marhan swear angrily, followed by a sequence of hurried voices behind him in the dark.

✠

The eyes of the vorn are always shaded by the mordage that stands between one's vorn and what he sees.

Sessasha
It Is Said

Vishortan sat brooding by the fire after they had returned. "He was a Mooriman," he rumbled at length, looking up and scanning the other faces.

"I wondered about that," said Sereline, "but how did you know?"

"I could feel his mordage. The light hair, the gray eyes, the clean, angular face, but mostly the mordage."

Rindar looked over at Minxa who stared back angrily.

Vishortan continued, "There are many lately, passing by the Crown on the way into Tessamandria."

"They have been passing through Karolil also," said Sereline, "and causing trouble as they come."

Tarantor looked up. "We saw many coming and going through Kinvara—traders, mostly, but a few warriors also. The king is watching carefully. We do not feel that it is a threat yet, but the change signifies an ill wind, especially because of the reports from Morlan."

"Drofan was from Islag, I think," Rindar volunteered.

Vishortan looked at him thoughtfully. "That is odd, is it not? The Moorimans will not go to Islag."

"Why not?" asked Minxa.

"Although Islag is not a Margah, we protect it. It is a special place for the Eladra, and the NarEladra will not go there, and neither will the Moorimans."

"Then how did Vashtor go there?" asked Rindar.

"Vashtor? Vashtor traveled to Islag?" There was genuine surprise in Vishortan's face.

"Seems he worked the Karolil to Islag boat for nearly three years," Rasler interjected.

Vishortan furrowed his brow in a worried thought. "I must speak with Vishanthrall," he mumbled.

"What is happening in Morlan, Tarantor?" asked Rasler.

"Mooriman is on the move. They have been raiding the cities and expanding their influence along the whole coast and moving inland in a number of places. Several of our commercial vessels have been prevented from trading with the cities there, and the Mooriman navy is roaming the Vorsian Sea from Mooriman nearly to the northern ice floes. Although there have been no attacks, our merchants are afraid."

Rindar sat staring into the fire. The world around him seemed threatening. It was not the immediate threat of physical danger he had lived with for the past week, but a pervasive, invisible darkness that seemed to settle down over him. Somehow, his friend Minxa was part of it, but he could not and did not want to know how or why. He didn't want to talk to Minxa about it because every attempt to do so ended in vague arguments that further separated them from each other and left Rindar feeling helpless and angry. The anger of each episode would dissolve with time because of their relationship, but the helplessness grew, and it alarmed Rindar in the deepest part of his vorn.

Vishortan looked up. "It is late now," he said, "and tomorrow is a busy day. Everyone must sleep so it can be lived well."

Rindar stood up, stretched and walked away from the fire out into the night to find his bed. "See you in the morning," he called to Sereline and Rasler as they made their way into their room.

"Until then," Rasler said. Rindar heard the door close behind her.

Minxa was lying on his bed. A single candle on a hook in the middle of the room between their cots cast flickering shadows on the bare walls and ceiling. It reminded Rindar of the kitchen with the old man. He shuddered and began arranging his blankets. Minxa had a stick in his hand and was twirling it back and forth between his fingers. "What's up?" Rindar asked.

"I'm trying to figure out what you like so much about all this," he said as he continued to stare at the ceiling.

Rindar sat down to take off his shoes. "I'm trying to make the best of a situation over which I have little control."

"You have the map, Rindar!" Minxa spun the stick around his thumb and caught it with his fingers.

"I'm not sure I know what you mean—or at least what you are trying to say." Rindar didn't like Minxa's tone, but in his frustration, he left it unchallenged.

Minxa sat up, uncrossed his legs and swung them over the side of the bed. He was facing Rindar squarely. "You can go anywhere you want."

"Like back to Vindarill?" Rindar pulled off one sock.

"Yes, like back to Vindarill!"

"Minxa, I barely know how to use this map. I don't even know if I could use it to navigate through a portal if we could find one—"

"We could go back to Islag. We know there's one there!" Minxa's eyes shone brightly in the candlelight.

"Somehow I think we are supposed to be here," Rindar responded. "There have been too many things that have happened for me to believe otherwise."

"You mean coincidences—or just dumb luck. We were always lucky, you and me; you know that."

"That's what we called it, but now I'm not so sure."

"See what I mean? You're losing your sense."

"Look Minxa, do you remember what life was like in Vindarill? We were viddiks!"

"We *are* viddiks."

"Not here! Here they have to ask us what these mean." Rindar held out his hands. "And they are appalled when we tell them. Here we are treated the way we always hoped we would be in Vindarill, but there we knew that we never would. The air is clean. The water is clean. You can see the stars! Here we do not have to be afraid of everyone. We don't have to steal to get food, and everywhere we go—things happen." It was the only way he could think of to end the sentence.

"Luck?"

"I don't think so. No one could be this lucky—not even us."

Minxa stared at him.

"There are forces at work here that go way beyond luck, Minxa. Perhaps they even eliminate it altogether, but you have to open your eyes to the possibilities. Just open them a little. You are my best friend, Minxa. Please—open your eyes."

Minxa continued to stare. Rindar tried to read his face and what he saw was anger. "They are wide open, Rindar, and I am not seeing what you are seeing, so would you help me get back through a portal?" he asked. "Even if you don't want to?"

Rindar breathed deeply. "I can do that, I think," he said, "but I can't promise when."

Minxa pursed his lips and nodded. "I'll take it," he said as he extended his hand. Rindar slapped it. "Now put out that light; I'm tired." Minxa swung his feet up onto the bed and pulled his blankets over himself.

"Aren't you gonna take your boots off?"

Minxa pushed off each boot with his other foot, and they fell on the floor of the cabin. "Satisfied?"

Rindar stood up and pinched out the candle and slipped under his arranged blankets in the darkness. It was the first bed he had slept in since leaving Vindarill. He knew it would not be long before sleep would slip over him, so he lay on his back staring up into the dark silence of the ceiling, so far from home, so deep in time. The night took him in and swallowed him without a sound.

✠

We call something arbitrary when we cannot see the reason behind it.

Pratoraman
The Middle Way

The trail to the springs started at the eastern end of Vishortan's camp and rose steeply into the notch between the two peaks that formed the valley. In places it switched back and forth but remained close to the swift stream and waterfalls that roared to Minxa's left. Rasler led with Sereline, and Minxa took turns bringing up the rear with Rindar. Tarantor, Phonda and Dolar had left early. Vishortan had mumbled something about them needing to be alone.

"How far is it to the springs?" Minxa wanted to know.

Sereline looked back over her shoulder and said, "Vishortan said it would be about three miles to the first spring."

"As the raven flies?" asked Minxa.

"Not sure," she tossed over her back.

"We have to do this every day?"

"One day for each spring," Rindar said. "At least, that's what Vishortan said."

"Why can't we visit them all in one day?" Minxa grumbled.

"He was very explicit," Rindar said. "You heard him tell us as well as I did: one spring each day, but only if you are ready for it. Even the way it's done was explicit."

"Yeah. You'd think it was some kind of mystical experience."

"Not mystical," chimed in Rasler, "but certainly a vornal one."

Minxa pressed his case. "Look," he said, "Vishortan's whole explanation smells like a whole bunch of bad ceremony. You have to be nearly drowned by someone else—all the way under the water, all at once. Then when you come up, you have to go bathe in the waterfall by the spring—I mean—what for? And why naked? It all seems a bit weird to me."

"Maybe we'll understand better when we get there," suggested Sereline.

Minxa continued like he had not heard her. "And that part about metnoga—and the whole, what was it? The armatan thing; if you don't believe it's going to do something, why would you bother with it in the first place? And what is it supposed to do anyway? And why does it have to be done on different days in all seven springs? What happens if I stop at six—or five—or one for that matter? What would happen if I don't do it at all, just change my mind—without the bath?"

Minxa's rant had the desired effect. He really did not want an answer to any of the questions, but was just throwing them to the wind in an effort to vent his feelings about the whole affair. Inside, he was still not sure whether some if it might be true, or even all of it. One reason for his raging was to temper Rindar's apparent acceptance of the whole thing. Rindar was his only friend, and his enchantment with this odd world they had fallen into annoyed Minxa.

They walked on in silence, back and forth, higher and higher, winding up through the trees that still dripped with the morning dew. They passed deep basins of boiling water where beautiful cataracts plunged into the solid stone of the mountain. Fragrant laurels tangled their roots with the towering hemlocks. The deep shade of the trees made the occasional shaft of sunlight that found its way to the ground hurt their eyes. Minxa wanted to enjoy the beauty surrounding him, but his irritation surrounded him like thick fog.

At one point the trail led them out onto a flat rock overlooking a beautiful funnel of water, as smooth as poured glass, plunging through a fissure in the rocks on its way into a stone cauldron far below. It was quieter here and Rasler stopped. Minxa stepped up beside her to see the spectacle, not ten feet away.

They were all staring at the cataract when Rasler spoke. "I will try to answer your questions, Minxa, but only if you really want an answer." She said it gently, but with a certainty that left no doubt that she was genuinely concerned about his feelings on the matter.

Rindar was standing beside him, and Minxa felt him shift his weight from one foot to the other. Rindar said nothing and did not even look over at Minxa. This was a battle Minxa needed to have in private—to come to terms with his attitude. No one moved. It seemed like a long time before he spoke.

"Sorry 'bout the attitude," he maundered, "but I *do* want to know— I mean, some of it just doesn't make sense."

Rasler sat down cross-legged on the stone with her back to the water and waved for the rest to join her. They sat down in a small circle on the stone. Rasler was deep in thought, and they waited for her to start.

Minxa was impatient. "Well?"

Rasler looked up. "Are you willing to concede that there are things that are true, even if you do not understand them—perhaps even if no one understands them?"

Minxa was suspicious, knowing that this concession might lead to conclusions he was not ready to make. "For example?"

"Well—the way we eat. We know that we have to eat a wide variety of foods to stay healthy, but we do not understand how it all works, and we do not have to understand it to admit that it is true."

"Where I come from, they understand it!" Minxa scowled.

"That's not entirely true, Minxa," Rindar pointed out. Minxa glared at him.

"'They' understand?" Rasler continued. "How about you? Do you understand how it all works?"

Minxa looked down and shifted as Rasler pressed on: "It's okay to not understand, Minxa, and still receive the benefit of someone else's knowledge. We all do this every day. That is why groups of people accomplish more than as many individuals." She was looking around at all of them as she spoke, but she concluded by focusing again on Minxa. "So are you willing to concede that this is true, Minxa?"

"All right, yes, but what does this have to do with Vishortan's instructions?"

"Well, the first step in accepting his instructions is admitting that there might actually be a reason for every instruction, and it is not necessary for you to understand it in order for it to work." Rasler paused, looking intently at Minxa.

Minxa looked up and then reached up with his arms, stretched and yawned. "All right," he said. "All right," he said again, "what else?"

"Is that a 'yes'?" Rasler pressed.

Minxa was annoyed, but he saw her point and knew he had not truly answered her question. "Yes—yes, it's a yes," he said, with a bit of scorn curling around the end of the sentence. "I concede that there are things that work—and that I do not have to understand them in order for them to work."

Rasler continued looking at him.

"What?" he said.

"If you don't fully accept this and open yourself to its truth, you will not accept what is next."

Minxa looked over at Rindar and wondered if Rindar understood his struggle or not. It was the struggle of knowing your opponent and knowing that they will probably lead you where you don't want to be if you concede even the first point, yet desperately wanting to know how they are going to do it before they do it.

"Yes?" Rasler pressed.

"All right. All right, yes!" Minxa conceded.

Sereline smiled and looked toward the water so Minxa would not see her face. It made him angry inside, but Rasler seemed to be satisfied and continued, "Are you willing to concede that there are things that are completely arbitrary, but are still important, or significant?"

"You'd better clarify that."

"Suppose you are very thirsty, and you find a well. The owner of the well says that he will only give water to people who are wearing blue tunics and have bare feet. Your blue tunic is in the bottom of your pack and it is winter, so you think it is reasonable to argue with him, but his mind is made up. Eventually you have to decide how badly you want a drink from this arbitrary man, do you not?"

"That's stupid."

Rasler was unfazed. "Stupid or not; arbitrary or not; how badly do you want the drink?"

Minxa did not answer.

"Minxa," Rasler continued, her tone persuading him to look into her eyes. "We live with the recognition of the arbitrary all day long and think nothing of it, because it costs us nothing. It's all around us. The arbitrary that offends us usually does so because it forces us to give up something, maybe something as simple as our control or our pride, but we give in to the arbitrary when the value of accepting it outweighs the value of our pride or control."

Minxa was uncomfortable. He stared at some unseen feature of the stone in front of him. "All right," he said, "I can accept that some important things are arbitrary." He continued staring as Rasler pursued her course.

"A third concession you must make is that preconceptions often lead us to the wrong conclusions."

"Well, that's a little more obvious. It happens all the time."

"Yes," Rasler paused, "but are you willing to concede it may be happening right now?"

Minxa shook his head and clenched his teeth, covering his face with his hands and rubbing it vigorously. "For example?"

"What is the picture in your mind of the spring we are looking for?"

"Uh...I guess it's a...it's a flow of water, coming out of the side of the hill."

"And where does it go?"

"I don't know for sure... "

"In your mind, Minxa, what do you envision?"

"Well I guess it's flowing into a pool that is big enough for someone to get into."

"Is it hot or cold?"

"Cold."

"Clear or murky?"

"Springs are clear," Minxa said. "At least the ones I know of."

"Suppose that this one is filthy, hot water pouring into a pool full of mud and old leaves and that anyone with an ounce of sense, when dunked in it, would want desperately to jump into something else to get cleaned off."

"And why would anyone insist that I be dunked in such a slime hole in the first place?"

"It could be arbitrary," said Rasler. Sereline tried to hide her smile again, but Minxa did not think it the least bit comical. "On the other hand, there could be a lesson in it. If the object of the dunking is to remove some of your mordage, which is a vornal effect, what would be more dramatic than having to wash in the filthiest slime hole on the mountain so that there would be no illusion of physical cleanliness?"

Minxa was frustrated. "I give up," he said, shaking his head.

Rasler reached forward and touched his arm, and Minxa looked up into her eyes. "Don't give up like that," she said gently. "Give up your frustration, your pride. Give up Minxa's way, but don't give up trying to understand. We all have a lot to learn, and we must be open to life being different...and surprising." Her tone was soft and accepting.

Minxa exhaled forcefully and shivered. Shaking off her touch, he scrambled to his feet and stretched. "All right," he said, "let's go find this filthy spring."

✠

Metnoga is the active state of changing one's wisdom, vision and armatan according to the greater principles of virtue and noble truth.

Tristaron Harrista
The Kirrinath

Rindar was not sure if Rasler knew what the springs actually were, but he smelled the first spring a hundred paces before they got to it, and the stench grew with every step.

"It smells like something died around here," said Minxa when he first noticed it.

"I think it is sulphur—mostly," said Sereline, "but it's worse."

"Maybe it's the spring," added Rasler. Rindar was behind her so he could not see if she was smiling.

Minxa must have thought that she was. "That's not funny!" he groused.

Sereline laughed. "It's getting worse, so we'll find out soon enough."

As they came around a bend, the trail branched onto a wide log laid across the chasm at the top of one of the waterfalls. The top side of it had been flattened with an axe so one could walk across it with some care. They could see the spring on the far side, and it was about midway across the log that Rindar realized that it was indeed the spring that was the source of the vile odor.

"This is unbelievable," Minxa moaned. "Did you know about this before, Rasler?"

"No," she responded, "what I said back there was purely conjecture."

Several things became apparent as they approached the small pool. A fine mist, condensing in the cool morning air, rose from the surface of the gray-black spring. Crudely laid stones formed the perimeter of the spring that was barely wide enough for a person to lie down in. To its right was a pure white stone with one of the Kirrinath runes carved neatly into its face. The stone was a strange contrast to the mucky pit in front of them. Rindar stood staring at it.

"How deep is it?" asked Sereline. To Rindar, it looked like there were only a couple of inches of water, but where the water stopped and the muck started was difficult to tell. The slight rippling of the surface indicated that the water rose up from somewhere in the middle. Rasler stepped away and picked up a stick about five-feet long. She slid it slowly into the pool, which nearly swallowed it before meeting any resistance.

"Ugghh," said Minxa.

Rasler pulled out the stick, and the stench intensified momentarily. "Unbelievable," she muttered as she tossed the stick into the waterfall.

On the side of the pool nearest the river, a small trickle of the black water spilled over the stones and dribbled down the bank before dropping over the edge of a stone slab into the waterfall. The surge of water swallowed the ooze as it plunged into the deep pool below.

Rasler smiled. "I guess you jump in there after you get out of here," she said. "And look, there are steps so that you can climb out." She pointed to the far bank where several uneven stones set into the bank formed crude stairs to the other end of the log bridge. She turned back to them with a half grin. "Who wants to be first?"

All the way up the trail Rindar had been planning on being first. Now he was not so sure, but he knew someone had to do it, and he had little doubt that Rasler would volunteer if no one else did. "I will," he said.

"Sesh! You're an idiot," said Minxa, shaking his head.

Rindar tried to ignore him. He looked at Rasler and said, "Tell me again what is supposed to happen here."

"Well, according to Vishortan, you are to strip down. It makes more sense now. This muck would ruin any clothing, but I don't think that is the real point—"

"What is the real point?" interrupted Minxa. The snide, angry tone had returned.

"I think part of the real point is that this is what we were told to do," said Rasler bluntly, "and that should be sufficient. However, if I had to think of a reason, my guess is that it has something to do with our attachment to clothing. It hides who we are, for good and for bad, if you think about it."

Rindar had never thought about it. "What do you mean?" he asked.

"Clothing is something we add to who we are to protect ourselves; to cover ourselves. Clothing is something we hide behind. We use it to make us seem more than what we really are. If you took a king, and took away all the clothes that make him appear as a king, he would quickly become just an ordinary man, would he not?"

It was a new idea, and it made Rindar uncomfortable. He looked down at his clothes. They had been drubbed and beaten, rained on, sweated in and slept in numerous times. He had had one opportunity to wash them since the morning he left Vindarill, and that was in the river at the Margah, without soap or warm water. They were nothing to be proud of, but they did their job, and he had not given them a second thought until just now. Suddenly, they became very important.

"I have been pondering this a while," continued Rasler. "To remove my clothes for this moment is to remove all pretense, all protection, everything that hides me and everything I hide behind. I have to stand before others as I really am, as Mah'Eladra see me anyway. This is the kind of courage it takes to open oneself to the true metnoga needed for the springs. I mean—if I am afraid to take my clothes off, which are purely physical, what does that say about my willingness to have my mordage removed?"

Minxa was rubbing his face with his hands again. "This is idiotic!" he said, and then, looking up at Rindar he asked, "Are you really going to do this?"

"I don't know—but Rasler is right. I can't think of a good reason not to do it except that I'm uncomfortable—my own fear—my own exposure; and Vishortan was very specific."

"And maybe crazy," retorted Minxa. "Look Rindar, you would be arrested in Vindarill if you did this."

"We are not in Vindarill any longer, Minxa," he said.

"It's the principle of the thing. It would be considered lewd."

"Being nude is not the same as being lewd, except in your mind, Minxa," Rasler interjected.

"I don't see you walking around without clothes very often," Minxa shot back.

"Yes, because of my mordage—because my vorn is corrupt, and so are the vorns of those around me—it would not be right. But here we have been commanded to do it, by the very ones who command our modesty. A strange paradox it is, where psadeq demands we cover ourselves for the sake of others, it also demands we uncover ourselves for this one moment to restore psadeq with the ones who are the authors of psadeq. Will it make me uncomfortable? Yes. Is it odd? Yes. Is it lewd? No. If you are not ready to do it, you shouldn't—I think I can do it."

"I would feel more comfortable if it were just Minxa and I," Rindar volunteered. "No offense, but I do have a sense that it would be improper in the presence of women. That seems right to me."

"I was feeling the same," added Sereline. "Rasler and I can go across the bridge and wait. I think that would be best, don't you?" she said, looking at Rasler.

Rasler nodded. "We will explore up the trail a bit farther. Give a yell when you are ready."

"Wait," Rindar said, "I need to understand a little better about the metnoga. I thought I understood when Vishortan explained it, but I want to go over it again."

"Metnoga is a state of thinking," Rasler said. "It implies that a change has taken place. In a way it's a decision to look at yourself differently, to look at the world around you differently. It's a decision to put your trust in the noble truth that surrounds us rather than the truths we find convenient, and what we perceive at the simplest level."

Rindar must have been staring blankly as he pondered her reasoning. Rasler waved her hand in front of him gently to get his attention. "As an example: when you lived in—"

"Vindarill?" Rindar asked.

"Yes, Vindarill. You were a thief, a liar—" She paused as if she were unsure whether to continue, "and a murderer, right?"

Rindar looked down. "Yes," he confessed, "and more than that, to be sure."

"The paths of Mah'Eladra do not allow such. Metnoga, in this case, is simply acknowledging this and deciding that the way of thinking that you tolerated in Vindarill is no longer acceptable. Start there. There are six more springs." Rasler turned to Minxa. "I think that is why there is more than one spring, and that is also why they must be done on different days. The fullness of metnoga for anyone's life would be overwhelming to realize in one day. Come on, Sereline, the trail picks up over here." She waved toward where the trail disappeared uphill into the thick undergrowth overhanging the stream.

"And don't forget to wait until you hear the voice," Sereline tossed over her shoulder with a grin.

"That's another thing I didn't get," confided Minxa as the women disappeared. "How in the world would you hear anything in that muck?!"

"I'm not sure, but I guess we'll find out."

"Maybe you will," Minxa said, looking at Rindar to see his reaction.

"You're not going to do it?" Rindar asked in surprise.

"It depends—on what happens to you."

Rindar had grown tired of arguing with Minxa about everything. "Whatever you want," he said in disgust. "I'm going to put my clothes over there by the stairs so I can get dressed when I get out. Wait here. I'll be right back."

✠

Death is a sinking down. Life is a rising up.

Oratanga
Passages

The self-consciousness of nakedness, even when the women were not around, made Rindar feel weak and exposed, and getting into the mucky pool was a relief of sorts, in spite of the stench. He slipped in, with Minxa watching dubiously from the edge, and as he sank down he had the uncomfortable feeling that there was no real bottom. Instead, it just got thicker and stickier. He lay back, still holding on to the stones on one side. The instructions were to lie on his back. Minxa was to push him under, face up. With a deep breath, he was to stay there as long as he could, thinking about the metnoga, until it was time to come up; he would know it was time by "hearing the voice."

The mud was hot, but comfortably so, and Rindar felt the slight rising of the water out of the spring around his legs. He lowered himself until his head, left shoulder and arm were the only parts out of the spring. Sooner or later he would have to let go and trust that if he were to be pushed down, it would be possible to come back up. Fear was not a strong enough word. "Are you sure you are ready for this?" Minxa's face looked as terrified as Rindar felt.

Rindar knew if he waited, he might not make it, so he closed his eyes, leaned back and took a deep breath. When he felt Minxa's hand pushing him down, he let go of the rock and pulled his left hand into the putrid morass. The world became silent and then dark as the slime closed over his face.

The only sound there was Rindar's heart pounding in his chest. The black ooze filled his nostrils and covered his eyes. Concentrate! Memories of his life flooded around him. Minxa's touch was completely lost in the thick warmth of the mud and water, so Rindar could not tell if Minxa was still holding on to him. He was totally alone with himself, perhaps more alone than he had ever been in his life, and cut off from everything else that was living. *Perhaps this is what death is like,* he thought. Suddenly, he realized that he could no longer tell which way was up. *"What do you want from me?"* he cried in his mind, trying to move, but not being sure that he was actually moving.

"Orten vana, tukanam?" It was not a single voice but many, a strange blend of male and female, spoken in complete unity from all directions at once, and he understood it perfectly. *"Do you want to live?"*

"Yes!" Rindar shouted in his mind.

"Stand up from this pool of death, and wash yourself in the flow of life." It boomed around him and through him in the original language. Rindar could feel Minxa pulling. Up, up, up! He broke the surface and Minxa pulled him from the swamp. He did not dare to open his eyes, and his nose was plugged solid. Rindar gasped for air and felt some of the slime slip into his mouth. He felt Minxa push him, and then he fell without warning. The icy water of the waterfall flashed over him as he tumbled down into the basin and the twenty-foot torrent of descending water plunged him deep into the bowl, scrubbing him with its effervescence.

Rindar needed air and started for the surface. He came up gasping. He had barely broken the surface when he saw Minxa jump from the ledge by the spring into the torrent. He was covered with muck and he disappeared into the cataract on his way down. Rindar swam toward the staircase. Minxa surfaced beside him. "Whooie!" he yelled. He was fully clothed, perfectly clean and grinning from ear to ear. "You should have seen yourself!" he yelled over the roar of the falls.

Rindar pulled himself onto the flat stone at the water's edge. "What happened to you?" he called to Minxa as he brushed the hair back from his forehead.

"What? Do you think I was going to stay covered with that muck after I pulled you out?" Minxa yelled. He pulled himself up on the rock beside Rindar, still fully clothed. Minxa started examining Rindar. "Incredible," he kept saying, "there isn't a trace on you, not even in your ears. But, whooie! You should'a seen the water turn black when you hit the pool."

Rindar was shivering. It was then that he first noticed a subtle lightness all around him. At first, he thought it was the cumulative effect of the strange sequence of warm silence followed by the cold roar of the falls. Or maybe it was the transition from the absolute blackness of the mud to the brilliant whiteness of the waterfall, but as he sat he was becoming aware that it was more than all that. When he looked around, he could see fleeting patches of brightness. If he looked directly at them, they were not visible, but his entire peripheral vision swam with light.

He turned to Minxa. "How did you know to pull me up?" he asked.

"You told me to!"

"Me?"

"It sounded like you!" He looked at Rindar suspiciously. Rindar decided that it was best not to point out that he had no way of speaking from under the surface of the spring.

"Your turn," Rindar said.

Minxa turned to him and frowned. "I'm not ready for this."

"You can do it, Minxa." Rindar felt a sudden urgency; not for himself, but for Minxa.

"I don't know—I...I'm just not ready."

"You sure? If you really aren't going to do it, then I will call Rasler and Sereline."

"That would be best," Minxa said quietly.

They sat for a long time, listening to the roar of the falls and drying themselves on the sun baked rocks. "You sure?" Rindar asked again.

Minxa looked down and nodded. "I'll get the women," Rindar said as he stood up and put his clothes back on. He left Minxa sitting alone on the rock. An uneasy feeling crept in around the edges of his new-found lightening as he headed up the trail to find Sereline and Rasler.

It was midafternoon when the hikers got back to the lodge. Rindar was still feeling the effect of his experience with the spring, and he guessed that Sereline and Rasler had similar feelings. Minxa had sunk into one of his funks, and when they arrived, he had gone straight to their room.

No one had talked much on the way down, and Rasler and Sereline seemed preoccupied with their own thoughts, so Rindar headed toward the smithy where he could hear Vishortan's hammer. He was pounding when Rindar reached the door, so he stood still and waited until Vishortan had gotten the piece back into the fire. "May I come in?"

The giant looked up and smiled. "Come in, come in," he said as he beckoned with his tongs. "You enjoyed your hike, did you not?"

"I did," Rindar answered as he sat down on the stool by the forge. "What are you making today?"

"I am finishing the forging on the sword I started yesterday. You found the spring, did you not?" he said as he rearranged the coal in the fire.

"We did. It was hard to miss."

Vishortan raised one eyebrow, furrowed his brow and looked straight at Rindar. "Something troubles you?"

Rindar nodded as he looked out the window. The horses were grazing in the field in front of the lodge. Rindar let himself be distracted by them for a moment.

"You can tell me what it is, no?" Vishortan asked.

"It's Minxa. He refused to go in the spring."

"Hmmm." Vishortan nodded as he pulled the sword from the fire. He laid the blade across the face of the anvil and with a light hammer started rapidly hammering along one edge, deftly flipping the blade back and forth between strokes at measured intervals. As the blade lost its color, he worked his way from the tip to where the handle would be. When he was done, he lifted if off the anvil and held it toward the window, sighting along the length of the blade, turning it several times to see it from different angles. When he was satisfied, he slid it back on top of the fire and stooped to turn down the air blast. "It is not good," he said as he looked up.

"I didn't think so either," Rindar echoed.

"Is he angry?"

"No, sad I think; disappointed. He said that he wasn't ready." As he stared into the fire, Rindar could feel Vishortan watching him from the other side, and he did not want to look up. "Last night," he continued, "why did you ask him if he wanted to go with Marhan and his—henchmen?"

Vishortan sighed. "His mordage is thick and deep; it keeps him from understanding and makes him think that he cannot do things he needs to do. Part of him thinks that joining with Marhan will allow him to escape the need to face himself. It is a great deception." Vishortan watched the blade carefully, turning it occasionally, and sliding it back and forth in the fire.

"What should I do?" Rindar asked.

Vishortan seemed absorbed with his blade, but in reality he was just taking time to think. "You can only encourage him. The further you progress with your changes, the more it will challenge him, unless he also begins the process. Tomorrow, see if he will stop at the first spring. It is the best you can do, but the decision is his alone."

Rindar nodded. He was not sure that he understood what it all meant, but it seemed clear enough and required no further discussion. "I have another question," he said.

"Ask. I have many answers. But first—" He smiled and pulled the blade from the fire and carried it across the space to the long wood ash bin and plunged it in, moving it back and forth until it was buried three or four inches down. When he looked up he said, "The ashes—but you had a question, did you not?"

"When I came up out of the waterfall—and for a few minutes afterward—it seemed that the whole area was filled with light; fleeting light, that I could not really see if I looked directly at it…"

"They were escorts."

"Escorts?"

"*Eladrim* escorts. They surround the mountain. They live here, as I do."

"You are an Eladra, aren't you?"

"Yes, but I am time-bound. That is why you see me as you do. The escorts are not time-bound, so you can only see them when they stand still, and then only briefly."

"And why were they there?"

"Oh, they flock to the springs when anyone is washed in them. It is a celebration."

"Do the Eladra go in the springs?" Rindar asked.

"It is forbidden!" Vishortan's voice raised in intensity and conviction. "No Eladra may touch the waters of the springs or the Verillain flow."

"Have any ever tried?"

"Only once," he said darkly. "When Vishtoenvar rebelled, several of those following him bathed in the springs. That is why they are dark. They—were—clear as crystal, but they are defiled by the disobedience of the NarEladra." He paused. Rindar could tell he was remembering something that touched him deep inside.

"I'm sorry," Rindar said. "I would like to have seen them clean."

"They are beautiful!" he said sadly as he stooped and cut the airflow to the forge. "Come! It is nearly time for dinner, and Tarantor is almost here. He is at the third spring today."

✠

Darkness begets a still greater darkness.

Sessasha
It Is Said

Minxa lay on his bunk, staring up at the ceiling. The lodge lay in the shadow of the mountain ridge that formed the southern side of the dale, so the light was already failing in his tiny room. It was quiet. Rindar had gone off to the smithy, and Rasler and Sereline had disappeared. The only sound was the distant, occasional hammering from the forge. A gray spider crawled across the yellowed white ceiling, upside down to Minxa's world and traversing the large flat empty expanse, headed to somewhere for some purpose that Minxa would never know.

He felt like the spider. The world around him seemed upside down, and he had nowhere to go, so he was just traveling through. None of the discussions with Rasler made any sense to him at all. Rindar was grow-ing distant with his infatuation with this upside-down world, and the only respite he had had since coming through the portal was the few hours by the fire with Marhan and his crew.

Minxa couldn't identify what had been so comfortable. The ride had been hard, but once there, he had been well taken care of. Tarlin had cleaned and bound his wound, and after he had rested, they served him some of the stew they had been cooking. He couldn't describe the taste in words, but even the memory of it made his mouth water. It was the first hot meal he'd had since the inn on Islag, and they sat around the fire afterward talking until Drofan and Tarlin had been sent off to guard the path to their camp. The talk was easy and unfettered, the kind of talk that he and Rindar and their schoolmates had often had. It rambled around the ordinary and didn't seem to have any purpose except to help each other feel a part of what they were.

When Drofan and Tarlin had left, Marhan sat down beside him after pulling the map box from the horse's saddlebag and setting it on the ground. "You know much about this thing?" he asked.

"I have seen Rindar use it," Minxa answered, "but it didn't work for me when I tried it."

Marhan smiled. "Maybe you should try it now."

"Why?" Minxa remembered feeling suspicious, but something about Marhan's easy manner made him feel ashamed of his own suspicion.

"Well, since we don't know much about it, maybe it works for the person who seems to own it."

"Maybe."

"You don't really want to be here, do you?" Marhan had said.

"I didn't ask to come here, if that's what you mean."

"I guess I meant that if you could figure out how to use the map, we could find a way to use it to get you back where you came from."

It made sense. It was the first ray of hope that Minxa had had. What Marhan said was true. It dawned on him how much he loathed his sit-uation, and this was the first offer he had had to do something about it. "Did your friend ever offer to help you get back?" Marhan had asked.

"Not yet."

"Don't you think that's strange?"

Minxa had felt very tired after his dinner and wanted to sleep again, but he did remember asking Marhan why he wanted the map. "Well, I was hired to get it for someone else; someone very important. He has promised us a lot of money if we bring it to him," he said, "but Parata has convinced me that if we keep it, it will be worth far more."

"If it is worth so much, why did you attack us to get it? I mean—why didn't you just offer to buy it?"

"Ho, my friend," Marhan had answered, "do you think that this Rasler character and your friend, Rindar, would just hand it over? They want it for themselves, don't you see? You just happened to be with them, but they don't really care about your dreams, do they? Think about it!"

"Rindar is my best friend!" he had protested.

"He may have been, but the map changes things. You've seen it yourself, haven't you?"

It had not occurred to Minxa that maybe the map's effect on Rindar was the problem and not the passing through the portal; that it had some kind of spell on him, that it had attracted Rasler to it and that together, under that spell, they were conspiring and not including him. Minxa didn't believe in spells. Spells were another heap of hokum from the ignorant ages into which he had been thrust, but he had seen the magic of the map and had to admit he did not know enough to argue with Marhan.

The conversation had droned on until Minxa had fallen asleep, and he could remember few other details. Looking back, however, he believed that Marhan's view made much more sense than all the nonsense that Rasler was trying to put over on him.

The spider made it to the wall and had nestled itself into a corner. Minxa wanted the security of some corner, but with Rasler, Sereline and Rindar, he felt more alone than he had ever felt. He wanted to be back in Vindarill. In Vindarill his aloneness could be lost in the familiar, so at least he did not have to feel alone. Marhan was right. If he were to take the map to Marhan, he might have a better chance of getting back to Vindarill, even if it was without Rindar.

With this last thought lingering and the now vague distant hammering as the only reminder of his strange situation, Minxa looked up to the ceiling with the spider tucked into the corner, and fell asleep on his cot.

✠

The small flower of bitterness has very deep roots.

Hispattea
The Essences of Corritanean Wisdom

The next two days at the springs were the same as the first. It took them longer to walk to the second and third springs, and they got back later each day. Minxa hesitated on the way past the first spring. "Do you want to do it?" Rindar had asked.

"No." Minxa's voice was sad and full of resignation, and he refused to talk further. Each spring was fouler and deeper than the one before, and after each immersion, Rindar felt lighter, and Minxa seemed more distant and detached.

Dinner was a larger-than-life affair, as it had been each night before. Vishortan brought food out of the kitchen to the long table that stretched nearly the length of the great hall. There were berries and fruits, the likes of which Rindar had never seen, with fresh vegetables and savory sauces for the delicate meat dishes he served. When asked where he got it, all he said was, "From the kitchen." He cleared away the dishes as fast as they used them and kept bringing more until no one could eat any more.

More long sessions by the fire followed the dinners. Rasler read from her beloved book as everyone stared into the fire and let the words wash over them. Rindar watched Vishortan. He had an expression of rapt joy, as if he had never heard the words before.

Tarantor told stories about life on the island of Tophan, growing up far to the north, and how he had come to Tessamandria on a trade ship to hide from the Mooriman navy patrolling the Vorsian Sea. As Rindar listened, he noticed that Tarantor seemed to be younger each day. It was hard to tell because Rindar did not know him very well, but his hair seemed less gray, and he was more animated.

Vishortan began to tell of the history of the Crown, from the very beginning when it was formed, and the huge celebrations of the Eladra as they returned each day from laying the foundations of Tessalindria. He sang about digging the seas and tracing out the rivers, of laying down the forests and the fields and forming the islands and the great northern and southern ice fields. It was a beautiful song, full of strength and pathos, alternating between the Kor'Alura and old Tessamandrian. He told them more about the Vishtoenvar rebellion, the building of the Elarha Wall, the flight of the NarEladra to Mooriman and the desolation of the NarEl Waste in their flight.

Phonda and Tarantor shared more tales from the north and their exploits in the northern kingdoms of Vann, Doth and Portman, and out onto the northern ice field. Rindar even tried his hand at explaining what life was like in Vindarill, with a little help from Minxa who, for the most part, sat staring at the fire and left early for bed each night.

Rindar woke on the fifth day with a strange sense of ill ease. All that lived slept in the quiet stillness of the early dawn, so he slipped out of bed, dressed quietly, and stepped out into the chilly shadowland of the dale, leaving Minxa asleep on his bed. The sky was overcast with thick clouds that seemed as if they wanted to rain but couldn't, and the chill wind flowing down the dale drove a light mist before it. Rindar looked

across the field in front of the lodge. The trees on the far side were nearly hidden by the mist, but he could see the horses grazing by the trailhead that led down the valley.

Droga looked up as he approached them. "You all are up early,"
Rindar said.

"The grass is sweeter in the early morning," said Droga in the distinct tremolo that was somewhere just short of a whinny. "You are up
pretty early yourself, Master Rindar," he said as he bent to snatch another tuft of grass.

"I couldn't sleep."

"But not as early as Master Mink-sa."

"What?!"

Droga looked up at Rindar's surprise. "He passed by here—perhaps
an hour ago—down the trail."

"Which trail?" Rindar asked, knowing the answer already, as Droga
tossed his head in the direction of the trail by which they had first
entered the dale.

Rindar turned and headed back to the lodge at a full run. He burst
into the room. What he had mistaken for his sleeping friend was a rumpled roll of blankets, and there was a note on the bed, scribbled onto a
scrap of torn paper. He carried it out into the gray dawn to read it.
"Don't bother following. I couldn't do it. Had to try something else." It
was signed with an "M."

Something else? What else was there to try? He didn't even know
where he was going, unless Minxa had the map. Rindar ran to look
under his mattress where he had hidden it. If Minxa had taken the map,
he could not have gotten it during the night. As Rindar put his hand
underneath the mattress, a double sickness swept over him. It was gone.
He rose and turned out through the door into the field. His best friend
had stolen the most valuable possession he had.

Rindar bolted across the field, and as he headed down the trail,
Droga galloped up beside him. "I can carry you faster, Master Rindar."

Rindar was breathing hard. "You have no saddle," he gasped, "and
I...am not a rider."

Droga stepped in front of Rindar to cut him off. "I am a Cortimane.
I will keep you on my back if you get on. Grab my mane."

Rindar reached up and grabbed the back of his mane as tightly as he
could. As he tried to pull up, Droga shifted his weight, and Rindar found
himself lying on Droga's back. "Hold tight with your knees—wrap your
arms around my neck."

As Droga turned and started down the trail, Rindar could feel the
horse's neck and shoulder muscles moving under his arms. The smell of
Droga's damp hide mingled with the fragrant woodland air that whistled

past his ears, and the trees swept past them like a dream. The trail wound along the stream, and it seemed that with every turn he would be hurled from Droga's back, but with each movement Droga swayed and twitched so that Rindar remained firmly in place. The horse never broke stride as he navigated the roots and the rocks of the trail with Rindar clinging desperately to his back.

After fifteen minutes the ground began to level out, and Droga slowed to a walk. "What's happening?" Rindar whispered in his ear.

"Ssssss." The horse could not pronounce a true "sh" sound.

Rindar could hardly hear the horse's steps as they glided silently through the woods. Droga's head swayed this way and that with his ears cocked forward, alert to the tiniest sound, and sniffing the air in short breaths. As they rounded a bend in the trail, Droga stopped. Rindar looked up to see the slight rise leading up onto the Harhazian Road. Droga nodded to the left. Rindar looked over to see Minxa sitting on a stone by the side of the road about thirty paces away, with his back turned toward them. His pack was beside him, and he was leaning forward with his elbows on his knees as if he were thinking.

Droga twitched and Rindar slid off his back. It was not abrupt, but just enough so that he landed softly. With a toss of his head, Droga indicated that Rindar should approach Minxa, so he started quietly down the trail toward him.

A twig snapped under his foot when Rindar was about fifteen feet behind Minxa. Minxa whirled to look at him, then scowled and turned away. Rindar walked up onto the road in front of him. "What do you want?" Minxa asked gruffly.

Rindar was angry and hurt. "I want an explanation and I want the map."

"How did you get here? Were you following me the whole way?"

"No, I woke after you left, I—" Rindar was about to say he had come on a horse, but when he looked up, Droga had vanished. Minxa looked up suspiciously and glanced back over his shoulder.

"Leave me alone."

"You're my friend—you always have been."

Minxa turned away and looked south down the road without answering.

Rindar wasn't sure what to say. Minxa had never seemed helpless to him, but sitting on the stone in the vast gray emptiness of the fogbound woods, he looked lost and hopeless. "Look," Rindar said, "this is a huge place, and we are many miles from anyone. You will never make it—"

"I have the map!" he interrupted.

"Which you can't use," Rindar pointed out.

"But you can," Minxa insisted

"And you will," said a voice behind Rindar.

Rindar wheeled to see Marhan on the far side of the road, holding the map box in front of him with both hands. He wasn't alone. "You know Drofan," he said as he nodded his head to his left. "And I heard that you met my archer, Faranda, on the road. Pity you had to be so hard on him." The others laughed as they started toward Rindar. "Tarlin and Vormin have a score to settle with your girlfriends. Too bad they aren't here to defend you."

Rindar turned to Minxa. "What are you doing?" he demanded.

Minxa looked down. "He's doing the smart thing," said Marhan. "Joining us."

"Minxa, look at me!" Rindar said. "This is insane!"

"Insanity would be for you to resist right now, or to try to convince our new friend to leave," said Marhan as he came along beside Rindar. "We are now just getting reacquainted. Sit down, little man," he added shoving Rindar backward. As he tried to step back, he tripped over Drofan's foot and fell onto the stones.

What Marhan had said was true. It would have been insane for Rindar to try to extricate himself from this situation alone. He lay on the ground as the others leered down at him. Faranda kicked him in the shoulder. "Sit up!" he growled.

Rindar sat up as Marhan squatted in front of him, holding out the map. "My friend Minxa here says that you know how to use this map," he said. "I want to see you do it."

"Try it yourself," Rindar said.

Marhan slapped Rindar's face. "I am not bargaining with you," he growled. "Open the map."

Rindar was trying to think. He needed time. "What good is the map to you if you can't use it?" he asked as he held out his hand to receive the box.

"Let's just say—there are others who need it. Open it!"

Rindar didn't like the way he said "others," so he tried to ignore the comment as he carefully laid the box on the white stone of the road. The five men formed a tight circle around him. Minxa remained on the stone outside the circle, so Rindar could not see his face. Before he opened the box, he looked into the faces of each of them, and as he did so he was suddenly aware of the circle of fleeting light that formed a ring around them. Escorts! He was still inside the wall, so this had to be a good sign.

Rindar looked up at Marhan. "I'm not sure you really want me to do this," he said casually.

Marhan leaned forward. "Quit stalling and open the box!"

In that instant, they all heard the hoofbeats. They were coming fast along the road, and the others stood up to peer into the mist. Faranda had an arrow nocked in his bow, and as Droga appeared, he raised it. "No!" Rindar shouted, lunging up at him. Faranda instinctively turned his bow on Rindar, and in that instant of hesitation Droga was upon them. Rindar flattened himself to the ground. The bow twanged and the arrow clattered off the stones. Drofan cursed and Marhan yelled. Rindar felt Droga's body pass over him as it collided with several bodies, scattering them like twigs.

Rindar grabbed the map box and scrambled to his feet. Faranda was unconscious on the ground. Drofan and Tarlin were running for their lives. Vormin lay on the ground gripping his shoulder. Marhan was on his feet too, and had drawn a knife. He lunged at Rindar, swinging the knife toward Rindar's heart. Rindar tried to move out of the way, but the blade caught his left shoulder. Shooting pain wracked his arm. As Marhan pulled the knife back for a second stroke, a high thin hiss and a slight pop behind Rindar arrested Marhan's arm. An astonished panic swept over his face as he dropped the knife. It clattered to the stones as he turned and started running. There was another hiss behind Rindar. He turned to see Droga moving toward him. "Get on!" the horse said urgently.

Rindar held the map in his right arm. His left was nearly useless with pain from the wound. "I—I don't know if I can," Rindar stammered.

"Try. You must! Put the box in your tunic."

Rindar shoved the box down into the front of his shirt. It was awkward there but it was the only way. He reached up, grabbed Droga's mane and tried to pull up with his right arm. Blood flowed down his left, and pain wracked the whole left side of his body. "Pull!" said Droga and Rindar pulled. Rindar didn't know how it happened, but he had a sense of being lifted onto Droga's back. Droga moved quickly. In an instant they were on the trail to the Verillain Dale, moving like the wind, upward toward the lodge and Rindar's true friends.

⊞

The stop at a crossroads in the journey of life is often brief by necessity.

Oratanga
Passages

"Sesh!" Minxa said. "Did you see that?"

"I saw it," Marhan growled as he picked his knife up from the white stone road. He examined its edge carefully before wiping Rindar's blood off on his sleeve.

"Why'd you have to stab him?" Minxa said. His voice was high and strained.

Marhan leaned toward him and shouted in his face, "He had the map! Did you see that? He took the map!" The anger in his voice sent chills into Minxa's vorn.

"But—but you didn't have to stab him."

Marhan hammered the knife back into its sheath with his palm before looking up again. "I'll do what I need to do. I lead this group, and if you want to be with us, you will not question whether or not I stab anyone, is this clear?"

Minxa looked down. He had few choices. He could run away, but he doubted he would get very far. His bargaining chip, the map, was back in Rindar's hands, and there was little reason for the group to accept him now. If he cowered before them or showed his fear, they would use that to enslave him in the worst way, and he did not doubt that Marhan was serious about his leadership in the group.

As the other men returned, Marhan turned his wrath toward them. "Sakah!" he yelled as he kicked at a stick that lay on the road. "Cowards!" His words were leveled at Drofan and Tarlin. "You got no guts! Now what're we gonna do?"

Drofan's face told Minxa that he was insulted. "The horse—we had to get out of the way."

Marhan grabbed his shirt. His knuckles turned white as he pulled Drofan's face up close to his own. "You ran!" he yelled. "You ran like a mouse! You let him just take the map and leave."

Drofan eyed him coolly. "So did you," he said without blinking.

Marhan did not know what to say. He stared into Drofan's eyes for several seconds, and then shoved him away. "We gotta leave here," he said. He turned to Minxa. "You still wanna come?"

Minxa had to think quickly. He was sure that he had stepped over a line with Rindar that could never be recrossed. There would be no psadeq if he went back. "Where're we going?"

Marhan paused. "I don't know right now," he said, "but we are not finished with this yet."

Minxa knew what he meant. "They can see you on the map, you know," he said.

"I guessed as much, ashtemba!" Marhan said as he eyed Minxa. "We will have to come up with some other plan 'cause I can't send you home unless you help me get the map, and you'll never get it from them if you go back." Marhan paused. "Stick with us and we'll think of something." He extended his hand to Minxa and pulled him up off his seat in an effortless display of pure physical strength.

As Minxa stooped to get his pack, Marhan continued, "We work in partners. Your partner will be Parata," he said as he tossed his head toward Minxa's new compatriot. Parata acknowledged Minxa with a grim nod. "We work as a team. We keep no secrets, and we share equally in all we do and all we receive. Is this clear?"

"I think so," Minxa said. He shouldered his pack and fell in behind Parata.

"First we need to get outside the wall," Marhan announced to the entire group. "Then we'll figure out what we do next."

It made sense to Minxa. His recent introduction to the group had been scary, but now he seemed well enough accepted. It would take time for him to know what this decision meant, but whatever it was, it could not be any worse than his ordeal with Rasler and Sereline. They trudged off along the white road heading north, walking in pairs or three abreast, talking quietly to keep from irritating Marhan further.

✠

> The spark of life that animates the basa is a profound mystery, defying the deepest science and the wisest minds.
>
> Fillaranda Darenton
> Science and the Vorn

Consciousness came slowly. There was a glimmer of light and then a sense of warmth and chill. Rindar heard falling water and birds, and the sweet, thick fragrance of hemlock filled his nostrils before he was suddenly aware of being alone, very alone. The surface he lay on was hard, warm and sloping.

He opened his eyes and sat up, shaking his head involuntarily to clear the thoughts. This sick, woozy feeling was something he had experienced before—the night he had killed the old man in his apartment.

Fragments of memory were returning, but Rindar was sure he had never been here before. The large flat stone on which he sat sloped gently into the cauldron of water at the base of the falls in front of him, and he was naked. His clothes were piled on the rock behind him, and he was still dripping, as if he had just been pulled from the water; as if he had just come through another one of the springs, but not one he had seen before.

Rindar shook his head again. The last thing he remembered was the endless vague ride up the dale on Droga's back, hanging on desperately and trying not to let go of the map as his consciousness faded in and out of the darkness. He recalled nothing else.

"Hello?" Rindar called. "Anyone else here?" He reached for his clothes. Asolara bathed his body, but the wetness chilled his skin, and his nakedness made him uncomfortable. As he swung his shirt over his head, he felt a twinge in his left shoulder, and his eyes moved instinctively. The thick purple scar, though still tender to the touch, was completely healed.

His clothing added a sense of warmth and security. Rindar was beginning to understand better what Rasler had said that day at the first spring, how much he depended on his clothes for the definition of who he was. Even with no one around, he felt better being dressed, more confident and more eager to be with others.

"Hello!" Rindar called again, with more intent. He moved away from the falls and found the deserted trail. The elevation of the sun suggested that it was late afternoon and probably time that he head down to the lodge, assuming he was still in the Verillain Dale, so he started walking.

"Rindar!" He turned to see Tarantor behind him. With each trip to one of the springs he had been looking younger and younger, and now as he faced Rindar, they seemed to be nearly the same age. Not a trace of gray appeared in his hair or beard; his face was youthful, and he stood erect, like a man of about twenty. He was alone. "You're alive!" Tarantor said exultantly, as he stepped forward and placed both hands on Rindar's shoulders.

"Yes," Rindar said, nodding and trying to think how he should respond. "Should I be dead?"

"You were dead!" Tarantor said. "By the time Droga got you back to the lodge, you had lost so much blood that we thought you would never make it. Vishortan did everything he could but—" He paused, staring at Rindar in amazement.

"So what happened?" Rindar asked.

"Well, you were barely alive. Vishortan didn't think you would make it, but Sereline insisted that we try to get you here. The problem was how."

"I'm confused," Rindar admitted. "Can you start by telling me where we are?"

Tarantor turned. "Follow me," he said as he started up the trail.

As Rindar fell in behind him, he was struck again at the transformation of Tarantor from the middle-aged man he had met some days before to the figure of youth and bearing that walked in front of him. It suddenly occurred to Rindar that he did not know how long he had known Tarantor. "Was I out for a long time?"

Tarantor smiled over his shoulder. "Three days, my friend. And you weren't just out!"

"What do you mean?"

"You were dead."

"Now you've really got me confused," Rindar said. They had scrambled up a steep bank of rocks and then over a dome of solid rock. As they came over the crest, the forest opened up. Rindar stopped and stared. They were standing on the lip of a huge stone bowl, perhaps twenty-five paces across, and in the center was a wide pool of water. It had no visible source to fill it, and no visible depth, but the surface was rolling with movement, and out of the downhill side it spilled like glass through a spout down into the pool where he had awakened. This was the source of the Verillain flow.

Rindar looked at Tarantor who smiled again. "This is the headwaters, the upwelling. It is the source, and no one knows where the water comes from. The legends say that it flows here from the bowl in the Crown through a thousand pathways in the rock." Rindar wished he could have seen his own face. Tarantor laughed and continued, "Sit down, and I will do my best to explain everything."

They sat at the edge of the pool on the smooth black stone that had been warmed by the morning sun. "Can you start with my arrival back at the lodge?" Rindar asked.

"That's as good a place as any," Tarantor said. He stared into the pool as if his mind was drifting back over the sequence of events. "Vishortan met Droga as you came out of the woods. He seemed to know what had happened. He carried you to your bed, laid you there and closed the door. I know he tried, but when he emerged from your room, his face was grim, and he was carrying you."

"Was I dead then?"

"I'm not sure. Vishortan said nothing. He carried you around to the back of the lodge where there is a cave in the side of the mountain. We followed him, but he would not allow us to go in with him. He laid you in there somewhere. After a long time he came out. 'We must wait,' he said. 'Three days, by the word of Mah'Eladra.'

"Sereline asked if there was something else to be done. 'We will not eat until we take him out,' Vishortan told us. So we waited. Sereline cried most of the time, and Rasler stayed at the mouth of the cave, guarding it. In spite of our fast, Vishortan encouraged me to continue my progress up the springs. 'We need your help later,' was all he said, so I did not go that day, but started again the next."

Rindar thought for a moment when Tarantor paused. "So you must have finished with all seven springs."

Tarantor nodded. "Yesterday. Today I was to come here and go into this pool, but three days had passed for you in the cave, and I wanted to see what would happen. Vishortan retrieved your body. It was very cold, but the death stiffness never happened. Vishortan seemed confused."

"You speak as if it was not me," Rindar mused.

"It wasn't. You must have been somewhere else. It was Sereline that suggested that we bring you here. 'But there are rules,' Vishortan explained. 'Simple rules: no living person can approach the pool of life without first having been cleansed in all seven springs. Tarantor can go, but he is not allowed to bring another with him.' In other words, I had to make the journey alone, for it has always been that way. 'Besides,' he said, 'Mindar is dead.'

"Sereline argued with him. 'Do your rules apply to dead people?' she asked. Vishortan seemed unsure. He asked Sereline how it would be possible for me to carry you all this distance without help. Of course, that would be ridiculous. 'What about Droga?' Sereline asked, 'Do the rules allow animals?' She was relentless. In all the ages, Vishortan had never dealt with a death in the dale or the peculiar circumstances surrounding yours. Somehow, Sereline knew that the rules could be bent. She also recognized that she needed permission from the rule maker to bend them. She argued that Mah'Eladra had set you on the path of the springs, and it was ridiculous that they would not let you finish, just because of the rules. 'Besides,' she pointed out, 'he's been dead three days, and the death stiffness never overtook him; doesn't that violate the rules?'"

"I would never have taken Sereline to be so aggressive," Rindar smiled.

"She is quite something. She kept pushing. She argued, and quite convincingly, that rules are good because they give a sense of order—and structure for ordinary situations, but under extraordinary circumstances, all rules can be changed, especially arbitrary ones, if the rule maker allows it."

"Vishortan asked her how she knew these rules were arbitrary. 'If the rule maker gives no reason for them,' she replied, 'they perhaps are arbitrary; and if you cannot give me a rational reason for them, then you, too, should admit that they are arbitrary.'"

"She has a good point," Rindar admitted. He had never thought it through clearly, but it made sense.

"Quite good," Tarantor continued, "but Vishortan's response was rather curious."

Tarantor had an amused smile on his face. "In what way?" Rindar asked.

"Well, he seemed to retreat into polite name calling. 'You are a woman,' he said, 'and young—and you come from Karolil.' As if any of that mattered, 'And you seek to challenge me on what is allowed in the dale?'"

"No kidding," Rindar said. "How did she respond to that?"

"She seemed completely unfazed. 'Were I a Mooriman sewer slave born in the gutters of Farhantra, would the rules be different? Does ignorance invalidate the force of clear thinking?' She was sincere and she said it in full respect. You should have seen Rasler's face. 'Besides, Rindar was innocent. Doesn't this count for anything?' she added.

"It was interesting the way Vishortan accepted the challenge. He kept eye contact, but I could see his mind take a step back. He waited a moment and then responded. 'Innocence is a state of being, weighed over a lifetime. Mindar's innocent actions on the Harhazian Road do not make him innocent in his death, do they?'"

"Why do you think," Rindar interrupted, "that he insists on calling me Mindar instead of Rindar?"

Tarantor shook his head. "That's very odd, isn't it? I haven't any clue." He paused and stared into the rolling water in front of them as if the puzzlement of the question deserved a few moments of thought; then he abruptly looked up and continued his story. "Sereline kept after him. 'Does a man's mordage cling to him forever? Isn't that the point of washing in the springs? Wasn't Rindar on that path, and do you have any doubt that he would have continued thus, had he not been interrupted by the violence of evil against him?' She had taken a step forward so she was staring directly up into Vishortan's face. 'Surely, if we help him complete his journey, his intent will be recognized, even in death.'"

Rindar sat still, marveling at Sereline's courage and clarity of reasoning. Three days of thinking had probably clarified her perspective, and the additional clarity that is gained in fasting probably helped.

"Suddenly, Vishortan relented," continued Tarantor. "'Sereline,' he said, 'you have great wisdom and hope, and your armatan is to be commended. We will do as you say.'"

"He called her 'Sereline'?" Rindar asked.

"First time I heard him say it," said Tarantor. "And he smiled. It was as if he had known all along, but wanted to see how far she would go to save her friend."

The next instant was one Rindar would never forget, as the realization of what had happened dawned on him. This young woman had stood in the face of those who make the rules and argued for the life of a murderer, liar, a thief—and won! And for what value to her? None except that of pressing for what seemed right to her. "I owe her my life," Rindar mumbled as he looked over at Tarantor. Tarantor nodded.

They sat for some number of minutes, each engaged in his private thoughts and the marvel of what was happening around them. "What happened next?" Rindar asked.

"Well, Sereline went to get Droga. She convinced him to go, even at the risk of what might happen to him. Rasler brought out some kind of fruit. It was bright orange. She and Vishortan had a heated discussion in the Kor'Alura that I didn't understand before she cut the fruit open and squeezed the juice into your wound and into your mouth. I think that Vishortan thought she should not have the fruit."

"The round orange fruit?" Rindar asked.

"Yes."

"We got them at the Margah in the river. They are very special, but I don't understand it very well. Did she plant the seeds?" Rindar asked.

"I don't know." Tarantor paused before he went back to his story. "So we laid a blanket over Droga's back and laid you on top of that, and then covered you with another blanket. Droga had never been up the dale, of course, so I led. I wasn't sure what I would do when we got here, but I had a lot of time to think about it."

"How long did it take to get here?"

"About three hours. We are very high." He waved up toward the wall of rock on the other side of the pool. "I think that the top of this wall is the rim of the bowl. Anyway, when we got here, I got Droga as close to the water as he dared. He was very afraid, so I uncovered you and slid you off. You were very warm because Droga's heat had warmed your body."

"Then what?" Rindar asked.

"Well, somehow I knew that you would end up down there, where you woke up, so I put our clothes down there, came up and dragged you into the water." He waved toward the pool in front of them. "This thing is incredibly deep. It's hard to see from here, but a couple paces out, it just falls off. I was backing up and slipped off the edge and lost hold of you and you disappeared."

"Disappeared?" Rindar asked. "The water is as clear as glass!"

"You totally disappeared! I couldn't believe it either. I dove down and got caught in some kind of current that pulled me down, and I couldn't get out of it. Down, down, down—I thought I was going to drown. Suddenly I got caught in that upwelling in the middle. I was fairly thrown up and then over that spout, and tumbled down into the pool below."

"I hadn't had time to take a breath and came up gasping for air, and there you were, floating peacefully on the surface, your eyes open and staring up into the sky—and you were breathing."

"No kidding."

"No, not at all. I dragged you up onto the rock in the sun where you would stay warm. I got dressed and went to look after the camp."

"The camp?" Rindar asked.

"It's too late to go down tonight. We're staying at a level spot over there, just around the corner of that rock."

"And Droga?"

"He left as soon as he had dropped you off. I don't think he was comfortable being up here."

"He's a fine horse," Rindar said. "He also saved my life."

Tarantor nodded. They sat still and watched the rolling water in the pool as the sun crept lower. Rindar found it hard to absorb what must have taken place. His thoughts kept drifting back to Sereline. He wondered how she knew, or maybe what she knew, that made her so adamant. Rindar knew he would have to wait another night before he found out.

☩

Drumming, drumming, pounding slow,
Shake the ground and pulse the sky,
Deep and driving, high and throbbing,
Rumbling waves and hissing high...

Evanthalor
The Drums of Halloria

The pounding of the smith's hammer in Rindar's dream faded into reality. He sat up suddenly in the cool mountain air. Tarantor was sitting up and struggling to get his tunic on without exposing too much of his bare skin to the chilly air. "What are you doing?" Rindar asked.

"The drums!" he whispered excitedly. "Did you hear the drums?"

Rindar was about to say "what drums" when he heard them. It must have been their sound that awakened him, blending into his dreams as a hammering smith. A slow, steady beat pounded the air. It was deep and resonant, produced by what must have been enormous drums, and it was coming from above and behind him. "What are they?"

"The drums! The Hallorian Drums!" Tarantor said through his shirt. "The Eladra play them."

They stopped suddenly. Tarantor pulled on his boots. "What are you doing?" Rindar asked again.

"I am going to the rim."

"Now?"

"Of course," he said as he stood up. "I want to see the bowl."

"Right now?" Rindar asked again as he sat up. "It's the middle of the night."

"Yes, and they are playing the drums. I have to see it."

"Wait for me," Rindar said.

"You can't come."

"What?" Rindar's irritation was instantaneous and erupted through the one word.

"There are rules—"

"Rules can be broken," he mocked.

Tarantor was ready to leave, but he paused and looked back. "Only with permission. I was told that only I could go to the rim. It is a privilege for those who have washed in the pool."

"I was washed there too."

The beating started again. Rindar was not sure if it was his imagination, but they seemed to shake the ground. This time, the deep, measured beat of the bass was joined by a more rapid and less booming sound of smaller drums, woven around the sustaining tread. Tarantor looked down. "I don't think it is best," he said softly. "When you have washed in the pool after the seventh spring, you will be able to climb to the rim. I would not risk it now if I were you."

Though Rindar wanted to go, he made no move to extricate himself from the warmth of his blankets, finding the chill on his exposed head sufficient to keep him in his place. The fire had gone out completely, but the fullness of both Tal and Meekar, hovering directly overhead, bathed the landscape in their golden light. As Tarantor vanished around the outcropping of rock to the left, Rindar lay back down. The strange driving rhythm of the drums continued to escalate, as clicks and pops along with high tonal pattering of a multitude of smaller drums joined the rhythmic patterns. Rindar could tell that it was coming from far away, and that knowledge confounded his imagination as to the intensity of the cacophony at the source.

Rindar wondered whether the others at the lodge could hear the drums and what it might sound like. From where he lay, it was clearly drums, but from a longer distance, it could be confused with thunder. The driving, rolling patterns cascaded down the rise of rock behind him and echoed back off the peaks to either side. Somewhere in the midst of all of it, Rindar fell back asleep. He never saw Tarantor return, and he did not remember when the drums stopped.

Minxa had traveled north along the white road with his new companions until they had reached the spur that led them off the road to another huge gateway. There was no hurry. Marhan had not decided what they would actually do, and he remained quiet and irritable. Minxa guessed that it was a combination of the failure to recover the map and his indecision about what to do about it.

None of the group seemed to hold Minxa responsible for any part of the failure, but blamed the mistakes on bad luck and the conniving witchcraft of "that hazen, Rasler." Minxa was not sure what a hazen was, but it was not complimentary, and he did not want to risk any reputation he had with them by asking about it.

The talk in the group was light and competitive: how good they were with a sword, how fast they could run, how many women they knew. Minxa found it amusing and comfortable. He had to admit, when asked, that he had never shot a bow, or hurled a stone with a sling nor had he ever stabbed anyone with a sword or even held one for that matter. When they laughed, he pointed out that they had never held a hazarine. He had to describe what it was, and he was not sure whether they believed him. They dubbed him "future boy" and continually chided him lightly about whether he knew what they were talking about in the most mundane conversations.

Minxa discovered quickly that he could make things up, and there was no way for them to know the difference. "In Vindarill, there are gangs of men that run the streets," he said at one point.

"What do you mean 'run the streets,'?" Parata had asked.

"Vindarill is big—much bigger than any city you can imagine," he said. "It's so big you can get away with almost anything. The gangs make their money by running all the illegal ways there are to make money."

"Such as?"

"Fencing stolen goods, sex for hire, drugs, gambling—"

"What are 'drugs'?" Faranda asked.

"Narcotics, pills—"

Faranda stared at Minxa and shrugged his shoulders.

"In our time, the chemists have figured out ways to make substances that you can eat that change the way you see the world. They make you see things or imagine things, or make you feel better—you know there are some herbs that make you stronger or think better?"

"Like smokeweed or hassemon leaves?" Vormin asked.

"I don't know what they are, but sounds like you know what I'm talking about. Anyway, they take the stuff out of the plants and sell it in pills."

"Sounds convenient." Parata smiled and the others laughed. "So were you ever in one of these 'gangs'?"

Minxa held out his hands. "The best," he said as he showed his wrists. "The Hargas." He made up the name on the spot. "We had to tattoo ourselves to show where we stood."

"You did that yourself?" Tarlin was skeptical.

"Had to. Part of the initiation."

"Ever have to kill someone?"

"Three," Minxa lied. "They were cutting into our part of the city business. We took 'em to an abandoned wharf, tied up their ankles with stones and threw them in the harbor."

After the first day's journey, Minxa had convinced the group that he was as tough as they come. He had been hunted by the marshals and had eluded them by luring them into a cave where they got lost. He had handled millions of drags in the illegal gambling rackets on the waterfront, beaten up countless competitors and led raiding parties into the headquarters of competing gangs, kidnapping and torturing their members to extract details of their organizations. The stories were replete with dizzying details about the cities of the future.

"You may come in handy," Marhan said over his shoulder at one point. Minxa was not sure he liked the sound of that statement.

By the end of the first day they had passed through the gate and were outside the wall around the Crown. Marhan's mood lightened, and they made camp about half a mile beyond the wall, behind a low hill that stood between them and the road. Faranda shot a deer and Vormin found several hess flower roots near the stream that flowed through their camp. It was venison and tubers for dinner, another welcome change for Minxa.

They stayed there three days. Minxa wondered what happened to Rindar. Down inside, Minxa hoped he had survived, but publicly he held that he had most likely died from the wound Marhan had delivered. On the third night, he had a dream that Rindar was still alive.

In the dream, he heard Vishortan pounding in his smithy and went to investigate. Rindar was at the forge, fashioning a sword. He pulled the sword from the fire without saying anything. It glowed red in the dark smithy as Rindar swung it swiftly through the air, back and forth, forth and back, before slamming it onto the anvil to begin his pounding.

Minxa woke up with a start. The pounding continued, but it was not a hammer on an anvil. Far away in the direction of the Crown, he heard drums, or was it thunder? Tal and Meekar were directly overhead, nearly beside one another, and their light lit the landscape with a golden hue. The fire had died and everything else was still like death. No one else was awake.

The drums pounded on. Minxa pulled his blanket over his ears, but the blankets would not keep away the drums. There was something about the drums that scared him, but he could not identify it. He lay still until the distant rumble faded into the background of a restless sleep.

✠

Life that is full, is full of joy.

Vindorian Proverb

Droga was grazing at the trailhead with the other three horses when Rindar and Tarantor arrived. He looked up, tossed his head and whinnied, rolling his eyes as he turned and thundered toward the house, with the others close behind him. Bright sun slanted across the field from behind Rindar, burning off the fine mist into the crystal air. The fragrance of the dew on the newly cut grass overpowered the earthy aroma of the forest trail from which they had emerged.

When Droga reached the bunkhouse, he wheeled around and pushed himself up onto his hind legs striking the air and whinnying again as the other horses trotted around him. Vishortan stepped out of his smithy to see what the fuss was about. His tongs dangled idly in his right hand, and his left, held up over his forehead to shield his eyes from the sun, still held one of his sledges. It was Sereline who captured Rindar's attention.

She burst from the door, her copper hair showering into the sunlight like tongues of fire. "They're here," she shouted as she started running. She ran like the wind, but Droga galloped up beside her, and in a single elegant motion she swung up on his back without breaking stride. In a matter of seconds they were upon the travelers.

As Droga slowed, she slid off, desperately trying to gain her footing as she touched the ground. She had underestimated Droga's speed and she stumbled, losing her balance as she hurtled toward Rindar. As he tried to catch her, she managed to get one foot under herself and came up toward him at full running speed. Her arms wrapped around him, and he tripped as he tried to step back.

Rindar and Sereline rolled head over heels before they came to rest on the wet grass. Sereline was laughing. "You're alive!" she kept saying. "You're alive!" Rindar was flat on his back. She was not quite on top of him, and she had hold of his shirt with both hands in the middle of his chest, shaking him back and forth as she continued shouting.

Rasler entered the comedy next. Rindar had just put his head up when he saw Tarantor trip her as she hurtled past him. Rindar saw him smile. She tried to catch her balance, but stumbled over Rindar's leg, flew over him and landed on Sereline, rolling harmlessly over her, but breaking Sereline's grip on Rindar's shirt.

Tarantor leaned back and smiled as the three of them, sprawled out in the grass and wet to the skin from the dew, laughed joyously.

Rindar sat up. Sereline and Rasler jumped to their feet, grabbed him by the arms and lifted him effortlessly to his feet, brushing off the loose grass from the field before grabbing him tightly in a suffocating embrace.

Sereline started crying. Deep sobs that Rindar could feel before he heard them, rolled up from inside and burst from her eyes and mouth simultaneously. Rasler joined in and for a full two minutes, they hung on him and wept. Rindar looked over at Tarantor as he started to extricate himself gently, but Tarantor shook his head solemnly. Rindar let them cry. Three days of waiting and fasting; three days of pent-up fear, emotion and frustration, coupled with overwhelming and genuine joy, flowed down their faces onto Rindar's already wet shirt. Phonda and Dolar had arrived, but had stopped where Tarantor was standing. They were Rindar's friends, but they were wise enough to let Sereline and Rasler finish washing themselves of their emotions.

Rasler stepped back, gently separating herself and looking up. "I'm glad you're alive," she said simply with a sniff. "We reached for Mah'Eladra, but they gave no reply, not even a whisper these three days."

Something in what she said, her tone, perhaps the words themselves or the tears that still brimmed in her gray eyes, brought down the dam that was restraining Rindar's vorn, and he pulled her back to himself.

Vishortan arrived and waded into their closeness. "Come," he said with a tender firmness that gave them the opening they needed to rise above their embrace, "we must prepare to break the fast." Sereline and Rasler stepped back as he approached. "Long we waited, Mindar Colloden. You are raised up, and now we *must* celebrate." He reached out and pulled back Rindar's shirt to reveal his wound.

The deep purple scar, perhaps the length of Rindar's little finger and almost as wide, ran down the cleft between the round of his shoulder and his chest. As Vishortan touched it, Rindar felt a deep touching, as if Vishortan were reaching down inside him. Rindar must have winced. Vishortan withdrew his hand and gently pulled the shirt over the wound. "It will always be there," he said as he looked into Rindar's eyes. "You must never forget. We will never forget, for as long as I am here, I never see anything like this." He took Rindar by the hand. "Come."

They walked back to the lodge behind Vishortan. Sereline clung close by Rindar's side, and Rasler hovered behind him, with Tarantor, Phonda and Dolar falling in to bring up the rear. No one spoke during the short walk. "I will prepare our breakfast," Vishortan said when they reached the lodge. "Tarantor, take your brothers and get wood for the fire. Copper Hair; Erinshava, we need fresh water from the stream." He looked over his shoulder. "There are clean clothes in your room, Mindar; put them on before you join us in the great hall."

✠

With great ceremony, the old name is deposed and the new name is taken, representing a new beginning; a new person.

Pratoraman
The Middle Way

Vishortan had left Minxa's place at the table, and the strange emptiness of that place caught Rindar off guard. He hesitated as he sat down. "He is gone," said Vishortan as Rindar seated himself awkwardly. "Escorts followed them as far as the northern gate, but escorts do not go outside the wall. They are heading north."

"Will I ever see him again?" The question caused the whole company at the table to pause.

Vishortan sat down deliberately as everyone looked at him. "I am not allowed to say," he said gently as he pulled the heavy chair in behind himself. "Sit down; there is breakfast." He waved his hands slowly over the table.

Four days with no food called for a light meal. Sliced melons and apples, ground berries and a spiced puree of Arden cherries was all that graced the table, save the large goblets of water at each place.

Before they ate, Vishortan rose again at the end of the table. "We are here, celebrating the life of our friend, Mindar, whom Mah'Eladra have given back to us." He looked at Rindar ceremoniously for a moment and then turned to Tarantor. "And the rejuvenation of our friend Tarantor, who today, will choose a new name. He has been made new in the silver pool, looked into the Great Margah and heard the Drums of Halloria." Vishortan raised his arms above his head with his palms upward as if he were holding a large basket of fruit high above his head. He looked up and spoke:

"Var ta vohar I malen var,
O'mantanor do karen vasa li
Hisar van, con dara kar
Missan…missan hata, sora ki."

His voice resonated through the hall as he lowered his hands and opened his eyes and trained them on Tarantor. He sat down. "Tell us your name," he said.

Tarantor stood up slowly. He held up his goblet of water. "To my old friends, Phonda and Dolar, who helped me here when my life was fading, who carried me in my distress and who gave me hope when I had little myself." He turned to face Vishortan with a smile and waved the goblet again. "To Vishortan, who supplied the last strength I needed to make it to the first spring." He smiled as he turned to Rasler and Sereline, who sat beside one another across the table. The goblet swept the air again. "To two brave women who know the value of life and brought my new friend Rindar, and taught me the meaning of passion for life and hope in the face of hopelessness." He looked at Rindar last. "And to Rindar, who has crossed the boundaries of time and distance on Mah'Eladra's journey to become my friend." Tarantor paused as they all stood and raised their goblets, thrusting them forward in the customary salute to the group, and then drank half the contents. The water was laced with some strong, aromatic bitter that made Rindar wince. They sat down, but Tarantor remained standing.

"Today I have chosen my new name. It came to me last night as I listened to the drums. Henceforth, I will be...Lutaka."

Vishortan rose, and as he lifted his goblet high, they all rose again. "To Lutaka," he said, "may Mah'Eladra smile on your life."

As they all swept their goblets high in the salute, a vague, distant glimmer of recognition flitted through Rindar's mind. It was an unusual name, with a strange cadence, not one easily overlooked or forgotten. Some fragment of the glimmer must have shadowed his face. When he sat down, Vishortan stared at him as he spoke to Lutaka. "Where is this name from and what does it mean?"

Lutaka smiled. "It is an old name on Tophan. One of my mother's brothers bore it. He was a man worthy of great honor—a leader of men—a visionary who brought great change to our people. The name means 'High Brother' in our dialect."

Perhaps that was it. There were many sailors from Tophan around the docks of Vindarill. The dialect they spoke was crisp and staccato, with clipped words and strange nonexistent r's, hissy s's and t's that sounded like your tongue was stuck to the back of your front teeth. Maybe that is where Rindar had heard it.

"It is a fine name," said Rasler. "Well chosen and well borne. It has the sound of greatness in it. May you lead in justice, and find favor with all the people."

Sereline raised her goblet. "May it be so!"

Phonda and Dolar stood and bowed to Lutaka, and sat down without words.

Vishortan started passing the bowls that contained breakfast and then stood and poured more bitter water into each of the goblets. They ate slowly between fragments of the conversation, cautiously filling themselves with the foods that would wake their bellies from the fast.

"We will wait here and rest," Lutaka said in response to Sereline's question about the trio's plans, "until the rest of you have completed your cleansings."

"Why?" asked Rasler.

"You are our friends. Besides, it is pleasant here, and we have no hurry. It is still early summer, and perhaps you will join us."

"We will be traveling north," Rasler said, "to Kinvara."

"You know this already?!" Lutaka said. It was as much a statement as a question.

"I am seeking the anthara, who is yet to come. Kinvara is where I will start my search in earnest."

"Why Kinvara?"

"That is where my father found him—and that is where he told me to start seeking."

"Your father?"

"It's a long story."

"Or perhaps a backwards one," suggested Lutaka with a smile. "How will you find him? With the map?"

"Only if Rindar will allow it," she said as she looked over at him.

"We are going back to Kinvara ourselves," said Lutaka. "We passed through the city when we were coming here, and stayed several days. I knew when I entered it that we would come back."

"What do you mean?" asked Sereline.

Lutaka smiled again. "We came to Tessamandria through the Port of Horrinaine. When we arrived, we traveled north to Ordina to see the great Circle of Ordrathan, which I had wanted to see all my life."

"The stone circle?" Rindar asked.

"Yes, Ordrathan," Lutaka continued. "It was on the spring equinox, and we got permission from Metroan, the keeper and stone reader, to spend the night there amid the stones. That night, he came to us and bid me join him on top of the Onarand, in the center of the circle. There he prophesied and told me I had to go to Kinvara and stay there three days; then I was to come here and cleanse myself in the springs. At the springs I would meet three who would accompany me back to Kinvara. I must admit that it was confusing when you arrived and there were four of you, but now this has been cleared up. From there, the prophesy is vague.

"'When you enter Kinvara the second time, you will be lifted up,' the stone reader said. 'Do not refuse those who would do so, for it is yours to reign until the destroyer raises his hand against you and your family.' I asked him if he knew who the destroyer was. 'Mankar,' was all he said. A strange name, by all accounts."

Suddenly Rindar knew where he had heard Lutaka's name. He was the last of the great kings of Tessamandria who was overthrown by the rebellion of Mankar. Rindar's memory of historical details was scanty, but these two were names that any Tessalindrian child would come to know.

Lutaka continued, "Before dawn the next day, I was woken by a strange little man dressed all in white. He told me that in the progeny of the three at the springs, there were three who would finally defeat Mankar and bring an end to his reign of terror."

"Did he give you his name?" asked Vishortan.

"No. He had long black hair—and he was a very odd fellow."

Vishortan remained mystified as he nodded for Lutaka to continue.

"We stayed in Kinvara three nights," said Lutaka. "The busy-ness of people, the lights at night, the buildings, the castle, the soldiers—" His voice trailed off. "On the second night, the taralang sang. I had never heard one, though I had heard of them. As we stopped to listen, I realized he was speaking to me."

"A taralang?" said Rasler. "What did he say?"

"He sang for about half an hour, and much of it I did not understand. Some of it, I did. When he was done, he had confirmed what Metroan had said."

"Do you know why?"

"No," Lutaka said, "but it was very clear." Rindar listened thoughtfully. The taralangs were another piece of ancient history come to life before him. From what he remembered, most people considered them to be prophets of things to come, but others considered them to be harbingers of great change. In either case, they were legendary beings that seemed to have disappeared at some point in Tessalindrian history. Rindar had to remind himself where and when he was.

"I have heard about Kinvara," said Sereline. "I never even hoped I would see it."

"Apparently we will see it together," said Lutaka. "Your company would be welcome for the journey, and it would be safer for us—and you—to travel together."

"That is probably true," mused Rasler as she leaned back comfortably in her chair, cradling her goblet. "We are not sure what has become of Marhan and his minions, but they do not appear to give up easily. They are on a mission. I am guessing that they will not stop until they have achieved it."

Rindar's thoughts suddenly turned to the map. Something in what Rasler had just said opened a pathway in Rindar's head that brought the map into sharp focus. He must have startled. Sereline looked at him and asked. "Are you all right?"

"Yes—"

"Yes what?" she said. Everyone had fallen silent and was staring at Rindar.

"It's nothing, really," he said. "I...I was just thinking about the map."

"You looked scared," said Rasler.

"Scared?"

"Yes, like you were suddenly afraid of your own thoughts," said Lutaka.

"I don't think it was fear," Rindar said. "It just suddenly occurred to me that—maybe I could use the map to find Minxa." Rindar looked around. Rasler's face was grim, and Sereline's bright eyes looked perplexed. Rindar's eyes met Vishortan's stare.

It was almost as if the giant were looking through him. "Be careful with the map, Mindar," he said. "It is a gift, but it is a grave responsibility at the same time."

"I'm not sure I understand."

"You will—in time." He smiled. "Come, let us finish our meal. We have not heard from Lutaka about the silver pool, the drums and the Great Margah." He looked at Lutaka, signaling him to begin.

Lutaka sat up straight and began. It was a beautiful oration, told in the fine oral tradition of ancient Tessalindrian culture; the kind Rindar had heard about, but had never had the pleasure of hearing. It flowed from Lutaka's lips with grace and a clarity that Rindar wished he could have enjoyed, but his mind was somewhere else, wandering north looking for Minxa, wondering about the map and the meaning of Vishortan's warning.

✠

Every journey that is worth starting is worth finishing.

Oratanga
Passages

It was some time after noon on the seventh day after his revival, and Rindar stood on the edge of the silver pool for the second time. Lutaka had not come with him because the final step in the ordeal of the springs was done alone. Rindar was not sure what to expect since the last time he was there, he was unconscious, but he had left his clothing on the rocks below the spout where he had awakened after his rejuvenation.

The black stone formation of the bowl for the pool was ten paces across and set into the side of the mountain. Behind it, an edifice of gray reached skyward. The sun was high enough so that it shone directly into the water. Perhaps it was the blackness of the stone or the rolling surface of the water, but in spite of the crystal clarity of the water, Rindar could not see into the pool beyond a pace or two from the edge. The surface was in constant noiseless motion as the water moved up from somewhere deep below before making its way into the glassy funnel that plunged over the edge to the pool below.

Rindar waded into the water. His feet were visible, but after a couple of paces, he realized that he could not see any detail of the stone on which they were planted. Each step carried him toward the center, as he cautiously tested his footing, waiting for the drop off that Lutaka had described.

The water roiled around him, and it was about halfway up his thighs when he slipped. He tried to reach back, but there was nothing. Down he went, pulled by the force of the water rushing downward, with the sun and the surface dwindling into darkness above him. The water was cool, and as he descended it became cold. The sun disappeared and then the surface as Rindar realized he was running out of air, but the terror that should have been sweeping over him was being held at bay by something much bigger than himself.

The cold blackness surrounded Rindar as he sank deeper. All sense of up or down was erased, and his only awareness was the need for air and the deep chill of the black water.

The words of the voice burst upon the silence: "*Mar 'a tonnar saviin ho kanath managth vor. Lor ina vinda sirren.*" It boomed out of the cold darkness, reverberating through the water and through Rindar's body as well. "*Now is the time to let go of your life. Give it to us.*"

The last thing Rindar remembered was breathing out suddenly and realizing there was nothing to breathe in, and in the next instant he was at the surface again, being thrown over the edge of the cauldron and falling unceremoniously into the pool below. He plunged headfirst into the water, pushed deep by the descending cataract until, desperate for air, he clawed his way to the surface.

As he pulled himself up onto the flat rock where he had found himself earlier, he felt the twinge of stiffness and pain once again in his left shoulder. He rolled over on the rock, trying to get as much as possible of his back in contact with its warmth. The sky above him shone deep blue between the intense green foliage of the trees overhanging the pool. He gasped for air. One deep breath followed another, almost as if he were drinking instead of breathing.

The rock warmed his body, and the gentle aromatic mountain air dried him while he lay looking up, thinking of nothing. It may have been twenty minutes. Maybe it was an hour, but he finally sat up. It was time to get dressed.

✠

The golden stair is by far the greatest legendary hoax of all time.

Ontalar
The Antharan Lie

Rasler and Sereline had each taken their turn at the silver pool that day also. They all met at the small camp where Rindar had spent the night with Lutaka after his reawakening. That night, amidst the thunderous symphony of the Hallorian drummers, they made their way to the rim of the Crown to look into the Margah.

"Look over there!" Sereline pointed east across the deep bowl in the center of the Crown of Tessalindria. "There on the edge of the high peak!" she shouted above the din of the drums. "Do you see it?"

Rasler and Rindar both tried to follow her finger.

Her left hand was cupped around her mouth. "Just to the right of the large snowfield—the gold..."

The Crown was bathed in the light of both Tal and Meekar, like two bright coins suspended directly overhead. They leant their eerie gold-gray light to the landscape of stone peaks and the snowfields that partially covered them, but just where Sereline was pointing was a bright gold-colored thread, curling up off the side of Mount Eliia, the largest of the peaks. It shone like a thin line of the sun against the black star-studded sky.

"What is it?" Rindar yelled.

Sereline shrugged, and Rasler stood with her mouth open. The thin golden thread continued to spiral upward until it had cleared the tip of Mount Eliia, and then it stopped, pointing skyward.

The drums boomed and rumbled beneath them. Rindar, exhilarated by their vantage point on a ridge of rock that spanned the gully between two of the peaks in the Crown, could feel pounding in his chest. The drop into the bowl was nearly vertical for several hundred feet before it swept into steep rockslides down to the floor. The floor was alive with greenery, illuminated from beneath by bluish lights that cast strange pulsing shadows up onto the gray walls of the bowl and under their chins. But it was the strange gold thread that captivated their attention.

Rasler cupped her hands around her mouth and shouted something.

"What?" Rindar yelled.

She pointed toward the golden thread and leaned toward him. "Sessasha's Stair!"

Rindar rubbed his eyes. He must have shaken his head for Rasler nodded vigorously in reply. Another legend, more preposterous than all others, rose before him. He stared in awe.

They stood on the stone ridge bathed in the glow of the twins burning above them and the strange glow from the Margah for perhaps an hour. The drums made any meaningful conversation useless, so Rindar didn't even try. The unreality of the scene captivated him, enthralled him.

Rindar's teeth chattered from the chill as they made the fifteen-minute trek back to their camp in silence. It seemed as if there was nothing to be said. The fire was out, so Rindar pulled his blankets close around himself without taking off his clothing. "See you in the morning," he said.

"Till then," Rasler replied.

Rindar fell asleep listening to the Hallorian Drums for the second time.

✠

May you choose a name that will last a lifetime.

Mythinian Blessing

They stayed two more days in the Verillain Dale. Rindar practiced with Rasler's bow and worked with the sling until his arm ached. "You're quite improved," Rasler said late in the afternoon of the last day. "I certainly would not want to be your target." Rindar would not want to be his own target either. He had learned the basic secret of the sling: timing. There was an undeniable rhythm that one had to acquire, but once he had it, accuracy and power was just a matter of concentration. With practice, a slung stone could easily penetrate the thickest part of a man's forehead.

They spent the last two evenings together at the fire, and the first night everyone took new names. It was odd to Rindar who had grown up in another time when adult names were artifacts that some took out of tradition, but for most, it was considered strange. Now it was a serious matter, and indeed, the entire milieu in which he found himself made the ritual of adult names seem ordinary.

"Erinshava," announced Rasler. "I have known it a long time and was just waiting till the appropriate moment."

"A good choice," said Vishortan. "A fine choice, is it not?" he added, nodding his head and looking around the circle in the firelight. Everyone nodded back. It seemed to Rindar that it was almost a given, having already been used by Vishortan and Visha'andar without objection.

Everyone turned to Rindar next. He was unprepared, and it hadn't occurred to him that there was a choice that had to be made. He looked around. "Mindar," he said. He was more surprised than the others.

"Mindar Colloden," Vishortan echoed. "It has a fine sound, but why did you choose it?"

Mindar was confused. "You've been calling me Mindar since I arrived here!"

"Me?"

Rasler was smiling. Sereline was trying not to laugh. Lutaka did laugh—heartily. Vishortan looked around. "That is rather odd, isn't it?"

"Yes, it is," Mindar said. "But Mindar is a fine name. I do like the sound of it myself. So—Mindar it is!"

"I have been thinking," said Sereline after the laughter died, "that my new name should be the same as the name I have."

Vishortan raised an eyebrow as he looked up at her.

"What?" said Rasler.

"Well, I have always liked my name. It is strong, it is sincere, it flows. I have secretly hoped that I could keep it as my adult name."

Rindar watched her as she spoke; the firelight softened the fine lines of her face, and the flame of her hair glowed in the warmth. It cascaded down over the front of her shoulders and hung in ringlets against her gray tunic.

Vishortan smiled. "It's unusual, is it not? But then—" His eyes sparkled with delight as he paused.

"There are many unusual things in this tiny world," said Sereline, her earnest, steady voice firm in her conviction. "But unusual is not wrong is it?"

"No, it is not wrong," said Lutaka. "I think you should take your adult name as Sereline. The fact that it is the same as your child name does not matter. What is important is that you *chose* your new name."

Everyone laughed. "Sereline it is!" chuckled Vishortan.

The mornings were quiet and private. Mindar took long walks alone, listening to the woods, smelling the rich morning air and seeing details that he had never noticed before. He found himself looking up a lot, as if he expected to see something. The vision of Sessasha's Stair burned in his mind, and each night he forgot to ask about it, but the night before they left, Sereline asked Vishortan.

"It is the stairway to the Deep Sky," he said as he stared into the fire, his forearms draped across his knees and his huge hands dangling.

"Why is it called...Sessasha's Stair," asked Lutaka. "Who's Sessasha?"

"That I cannot tell you," Vishortan replied without moving. "Why do you call it Sessasha's Stair?"

"Well, Rasler—I mean Erinshava—called it that—on the edge of the Margah," Mindar responded.

Vishortan turned to her. "Erinshava?"

"My father told me of Sessasha's Stair, but I never knew what it was. He could not tell me the significance of it."

"You don't know what it is?" Mindar asked.

"My father described it—he told me the name. I don't think he knew what it was about."

"Who is Sessasha?" Lutaka insisted.

Mindar opened his mouth to speak, and Vishortan silenced him with his finger in front of his lips. "You know more than should be told here," he said.

"Why did it only go part way up?—to the Deep Sky, I mean," asked Sereline.

"It is still being built. It will be completed when the time is right," said Vishortan.

"You are speaking in riddles, Vishortan," said Lutaka. "Surely you can explain it more clearly."

"I could—but it is forbidden. Now, have you all settled plans for tomorrow?"

"We will leave early tomorrow—the six of us," said Lutaka. "We plan to travel north to Kinvara. It should not take us more than three days."

Vishortan's face grew serious. "Stick to the main road," he said as he stared into the fire as if he was reading something there. "It is not well used this far south, but it becomes better as you approach Kinvara. Do not linger in the woods where the road turns west; rest before you enter, and do not stop for anything on the way through."

"When you get to Kinvara, go to the road that leads east from the city along the river. There you will find the smith, Valradicca. Stay with him two days before entering the city." Vishortan stopped, as if there were more to say, but he could not or would not say it. They sat for a long moment in utter silence, staring into the fire and assimilating the direction given by their host and struggling to understand its meaning and consequences. It reminded Mindar of the last instructions that Visha'andar gave them about the journey to the Margah in the river: specific, vague and cloaked in trouble.

Vishortan aroused himself from the stupor he was in and spoke again. "Now it is time for bed, for tomorrow approaches quickly, does it not? You are to be away early, so we share breakfast by Asolara's first light. May the peace of Mah'Eladra be with you."

The evening was over, and Mindar walked back to his tiny room in silence. As he lay on his cot, wrapped in the warm blankets against the chilling wind that flowed down from the heights of the dale, his mind would not leave the somber directions of Vishortan, nor his curious refusal to allow Mindar to speak what he knew of Sessasha's Stair.

The clear vision of the golden stairway, rising from the slopes of Mount Eliia into the night sky, was the last conscious thought Mindar had before he plunged into the vast eclipse of sleep.

ᙆ The Inn in the Woods ᙆ

Even the company of evil has its own
psadeq.

Mortag of Horrinaine
Of Beings

Minxa learned quickly that it was not wise to question Marhan. He also discovered that it was not wise to try to figure out exactly what was going on. He felt safe with the six other men he traveled with, but it was the same tenuous safety that he had felt living in Vindarill. They had a code that led to psadeq in the group, but one had to tread carefully around the personalities; and though they shared everything and accepted Minxa, they made it clear that he was the low man on the list. For him to gain their full trust, he would have to demonstrate his loyalty and earn their respect. This is the way it was with men like this, and Minxa felt honored to have a chance to prove himself to them.

They had been at the inn for seven days. Minxa was not sure how Marhan came by the money he needed to sustain such an extended stay, but he thought it had something to do with the two men they met on the road the day they came to the inn. They had appeared out of the forest from nowhere and stood in the road waiting for them. When Marhan saw them, he said, "Let me do the talking; wait here," and went ahead to meet them.

"Who are they?" Minxa asked.

"That is not your concern," Faranda snarled.

"All right, I was just curious!" Minxa said.

"You are not allowed to be curious about some things!" They sat and waited in silence. Minxa could hear Marhan arguing and could see him gesticulating wildly. Finally, he came back. "We have a couple of traveling companions until we get to the inn," he said.

"Inn?" asked Tarlin.

"Apparently there is an inn up ahead," Marhan said. "We're going to stay there until the others leave the Crown." He sounded resigned, as if it was not his own choice to go there.

"Where do we get money to stay at an inn?" Parata asked.

"It's all taken care of," Marhan responded as he looked away and nodded at the two men in the road.

"We don't need to waste—"

The words were barely out of Parata's mouth when Marhan grabbed his shirt and pulled him up close. "I didn't ask your permission—or your opinion," Marhan snapped. "We are staying at the inn!" He pushed Parata away.

When the strangers came nearer, Minxa realized that they were much bigger than he thought. They carried no packs, and they were dressed in an odd armor that looked very old. The larger of the two was the same man who had followed them on the boat from Islag, the one Rasler had called Vashtor, and his face was grave and unsympathetic. They did not speak, but walked along with the group, listening and watching. Several times he felt them watching him specifically.

Vashtor and his companion had disappeared just before they got to the inn. They were there one moment and gone the next, vanished. When Minxa had asked later, no one else had seen them leave either.

The inn was pleasant enough but Minxa shared a room with Parata who snored incessantly. Every day their rooms were cleaned and put in order by the innkeeper's wife and her son. The wife's name was Hannahoruan, a peculiar name for a woman who was equally peculiar in her bearing. She was short and slight, but seemed extraordinarily strong and worked harder than any woman Minxa had ever met. She had reddish blond hair that hung down below her shoulders in kinky waves that made it look like there was much more of it than there was. Minxa guessed that she might have been thirty and a certain mismatch for the innkeeper, who looked as if he were seventy-five, and the young man she claimed as a son, who was at least her age if not older. She had a fine angular face and a pleasant smile, but what stood out most were her eyes. They were as blue as the sky, and when she looked at Minxa, she seemed to be seeing right into his vorn. If it had not been so uncomfortable, Minxa could easily have mistaken it for flirting.

Whenever she caught his eye, he got the strange feeling that he knew her from somewhere. He had only met a few women since coming through the portal, so he was sure it must have been back in Vindarill, but even there, he knew only few women and none of them were like Hannahoruan. Her peculiar habit of addressing everyone as "Master" was an odd, out-of-place courtesy, better suited for a time long forgotten. "Master Minxa," she said whenever she spoke to him.

Banja, the innkeeper's son, was tall and gangly, with unkempt hair the color of wet mud. He hardly spoke, but worked hard and was as strong as a bear. Minxa thought he was a person whom he would like, but for the most part, Banja did his job quietly and did not speak with Minxa or the others, except in the small pleasantries of helping them around the inn.

The days at the inn were a lesson in boredom. Faranda shot a deer on the third day and asked Minxa to help him dress it down. It was a peculiar sensation to see a dead animal stripped and transformed into a piece of meat before his eyes. Tarlin tried to teach him how to use a sling and the short combat sword that he wore strapped to his thigh. The sling was nearly impossible, and they spent hours laughing about Minxa's clumsiness with it. Other than these few diversions, they sat around the table at the inn and ate, drank and competed with one another with outrageous stories about their accomplishments. They went to bed late each night and slept in every day.

This morning was different. Marhan was up early, and Vashtor had returned with the other warrior. They sat at a corner of the main room of the inn and talked with Marhan while Minxa sat with the others for an earlier than usual breakfast. Something was afoot. Vashtor rose suddenly with his companion and left Marhan sitting by the window alone. He sat for several minutes before he rose and walked over to the others and sat down on the chair he had dragged with him. "Today is the day," he said quietly.

"For what?" sneered Faranda.

Marhan ignored the archer. "What I say—you do!" Marhan continued, "Is this clear?" His eyes darted into each face, waiting only briefly for any hint of acknowledgment. Faranda did not respond. "Faranda?"

Faranda put down his spoon and wiped his chin before looking up. His eyes were surly. The two men stared at each other for a long moment before Faranda smiled. "Whatever you say," he relented.

"They have left the Crown and are coming here," Marhan said in a whisper. "Ready your packs and bring them outside, then come back here to join me for one last fine breakfast."

✠ '

They walk before us, and make the way
smooth for our feet,
And turn the shadow bright to chase
away the weight of dread.

The Tessarandin, Book 4
On Mah'Eladra

The northern gate through the wall was larger and more ornate than the Ransom Gate. The thickness of the opening was at least ten paces, as was its width, and the arch of stacked stones soared upward to a slight peak underneath, but was flat on the top. Stairs curled up from either side, but they were wider and grander than the Ransom stairs, and each had a stone balustrade that protected the climbers from falling.

"Last time we did this we spent the day running," Erinshava mused as she let her pack slide off her shoulders. "I'll keep guard on the horses while the rest of you go up."

"We can guard ourselves," said Droga. His voice startled the travelers. He had spoken little since the day he had carried Mindar up the Verillain Dale. In the intervening time, he had become just another horse in their minds. "Go on!" he snorted. "If anything happens, I'll let you know. We're not much for heights, and the grass here is much better."

The view from the top was as breathtaking as from the top of the Ransom Gate. They emerged from the shadow of the Crown as they climbed and stood looking north, the arch casting its shadow far down the slope of trees that steamed as the first rays of light flooded over them. As far as he could see north and west, there was nothing but trees, shadowed by patches of morning fog that lay like a moth-eaten blanket on grass. To the east, a low rim of peaks skirted the horizon, blue and distant.

Lutaka waved his hand to the north and west. "Somewhere out there is the city of Kinvara," he said, "and there is not much in between except trees."

Phonda nodded. "A couple of inns; maybe a settler or two. Some farms near the city." He didn't speak often, and his words were rough and short.

"The place that Vishortan spoke of, 'where the trail turns west into the forest,' what did he mean?" asked Erinshava.

"I was wondering that myself," Lutaka responded. "I don't remember anything peculiar on the way down." He glanced at Phonda and then Dolar. "Do you?" They shook their heads.

"Somehow, I think we will know it when we see it," suggested Sereline. "He seemed emphatic about his knowledge."

"He did not say there was anything remarkable about it, just to be on guard," said Erinshava, "and to go straight through, without stopping."

"Yes, he was quite specific," said Lutaka.

Phonda's voice fractured the conversation. "Look, Sire, over there!" He was pointing to the north toward the horizon. "It looks like a fire!"

"Where?" asked Lutaka as all eyes followed Phonda's finger. "All I see is trees—and the morning mist." Lutaka moved closer to see down the length of Phonda's arm.

"Not quite on the horizon," said Phonda. "The mist is blacker and seems to be billowing rather than flat and lazy."

Everyone seemed to see it at once, except Mindar. Erinshava stood with her hands on her hips, and Sereline shaded her eyes with one hand and moved closer to Mindar pointing in the same direction as Phonda so Mindar could look down her arm. "Just to the left of that little rise— you see the low spot. It's smoke."

Mindar couldn't make out what they were looking at, and the distraction of Sereline's closeness filled the moments before Erinshava interrupted them. "The map, Mindar—maybe we can see what's happening."

Mindar was winded by the time he had retrieved the map from his pack at the bottom of the arch. As he looked up, the smoke was more evident, rising above the mist and curling upward as it might above a large fire. He laid the map out on the flat stone floor. As he expanded its view and moved its vision north to find the location, Lutaka whistled in disbelief. "This is amazing!" he said softly as he peered down on it from one knee. "I have never seen anything like it."

Mindar kept his eyes on the map. Distances were tricky with Lonama's map. Everything became relative, and it was easy to lose the sense of scale in the vast landscape without landmarks. Mindar swept the vision back and forth, searching for clues.

"I can see the flames now," said Dolar. Everyone stood up. Mindar could just see a spark, made tiny by the distance, emerging at the base of the smoke. He bent to the map. "It has to be here somewhere," he muttered.

"There!" Erinshava pointed as Mindar swept the vision east. Mindar backed up. "That spot," she said, her finger hovering above the corner of the map. He magnified the view. "It's near the road, just this side of a small stream," she continued. "Do you remember such a place, Lutaka?"

Mindar looked up. Lutaka was grim. "I don't recall anything there," he said. Phonda and Dolar shrugged in bewilderment as he looked at them.

Erinshava leaned over the map, running her fingers along the ancient border symbols and pausing at each one briefly as if she were guessing what they might mean. "Try this one," she said, looking up into Mindar's eyes. She was pointing at a small hexagon.

"What is it?"

"It's a rune that means 'angle'."

Mindar wasn't sure about the connection, but he touched the rune, and the map shifted suddenly. It showed the same scene, but not directly from above. "Amazing!" interjected Lutaka again. Mindar focused the map onto the structure of a house. He could not see a fire, but he could tell that it was a building and it had no roof. A fire could easily have done it.

"There is only one being," remarked Sereline, pointing to the small bright smudge to the right of the structure.

"You can see people?" asked Lutaka in utter astonishment.

"Right there," Mindar said, "the bright smudge—that's a being of some sort. I would presume it to be a person."

"And there is only one?" Lutaka continued.

Mindar touched the "angle" button again and the map returned to its flat overhead view. "Let's take a look," he said. He widened the vision a little at a time, moving north along the road and keeping the house in view. Suddenly the road took a left turn and became faint.

"There!" said Sereline. "More beings!"

Mindar moved the vision down. "One, two, three—thirteen!" exclaimed Erinshava.

"'Where the road turns west into the woods," muttered Lutaka. "Something is not right."

"Mindar," said Erinshava, "when we were looking at the map the other day, when you found Minxa—how many were there altogether?"

"Ten, I think."

"If this is Marhan's crew, there is trouble," Erinshava continued. "There are thirteen now!"

"Perhaps he set fire to the house. Maybe he has taken hostages," said Sereline.

"There is one still at the house, though." Lutaka stood up as he spoke. "Come, we must go that way anyway. Perhaps by nightfall, we can be there. Then we can find out what happened."

Mindar folded up the map as the others stood up. By the time he joined them, Erinshava had her book open in her hand. They stood in a small circle as she read:

"When the thorn under the skin defies us,
When Asolara's light is dimmed in our hjargs
And shadows are cast backwards,
When fear and treachery eclipse the El
And when the noga flags beneath the burden of presiding evil,
When our breath is short and the road before us long,
And when the vision of the Deep Sky is lost to eyes downcast and heavy,
Then is the power, the magnificence
And the resolution of Mah'Eladra strongest.
They walk before us, and make the way smooth for our feet,
And turn the shadow bright to chase away the weight of dread,
Making our feet light and carrying our burdens,
Lest we despair and fall."

"We cannot fear what is true," Erinshava continued as she closed the book. "Not in the presence of Mah'Eladra. To fear is to doubt—to doubt is to break psadeq. If we break psadeq with Mah'Eladra, our mordage will overwhelm us, and we will be utterly defeated."

"It's time to go then," said Lutaka. He turned and led them down the winding stairs to where the horses grazed contentedly on the dew-laden grass beside the ancient stone arch.

✠

Darkness will chase away light, and the vorn will seek the respite of Oblivion over the immortality of the Infinite.

The Tessarandin, Book 2

Marhan leaned close to Minxa's face. His breath stank of pork sausage and alcohol, a terrible combination for an hour after sunrise. "You have only one job. If you don't do it—" he drew his index finger across his throat. Minxa nodded. Hannahoruan and Banja had their hands tied behind their backs, and they were tied together with a rope that was just long enough so that they could walk beside each other comfortably. Minxa's job was to lead them north on the road while Marhan and the others finished ransacking the inn.

"C'mon," he said gently. He had a job to do, but Marhan had not said that he had to be cruel in its execution.

"Do you know where my husband is?" Hannahoruan asked as they started walking.

"I don't," Minxa said. He looked over and saw that tears were forming in her eyes. He looked up at Banja. His face was grim with anger;
tight-lipped and adamant in refusing to acknowledge Minxa's glance.

"Why are you doing this to us?" Hannahoruan said as she tried to
wipe her tears on her shoulder.

Minxa shook his head. "I don't know," he said. "Marhan doesn't tell
us very much."

"You're a fool to follow a man like that, Master Minxa!" she said
with a sniff.

The response on Minxa's lips was cut short by a shout from behind
them. He turned. Flames leapt from the front windows of the inn.
Marhan held a torch and was carrying it around the side of the building.
When he disappeared from view, Minxa looked back at his captives.
"Keep walking!" he commanded.

They walked about forty paces before Hannahoruan spoke again.
"You let him burn the inn; you do not even know why—and you do
nothing to stop him?"

"I can't stop him!" Minxa protested. He wanted to be angry, but
there was something in Hannahoruan's voice that would not allow it.

"Perhaps not, but you do not have to help him."

"You don't understand! Keep walking and be quiet." When he said
it, Minxa realized he did not know what to do if she refused to cooperate.

"I do not think you belong in this group of men, Master Minxa," she
persisted.

"You know nothing about me!"

"I know little of your history—few of the details—but I have seen
you."

"Shut up!"

They shuffled through the leaves on the narrow trail, which led to
the road. Hannahoruan was quiet. Minxa walked behind them thinking
about what she said. On one level, he did not belong, just as she said.
On the other hand, he knew he could belong if they would just appreciate what he could do for them. He had to prove himself, and making
sure that he did this job well was part of the proof he needed, and there-
fore part of the acceptance he coveted.

When they ascended the rise up to the road level, Hannahoruan
stopped. She turned to Minxa and held up her hands. "Cut my bonds,"
she said.

"I can't," Minxa replied.

"Can't or won't?" she said over her shoulder.

"I *won't!* Keep moving." He shoved her forward.

"We won't run away," she said. "There's nowhere to go."

"I don't trust you."

"But you trust Marhan?"

"Marhan took me in when I was rejected by others."

"He's using you, Master Minxa."

"Keep moving!" Minxa didn't want to talk, but he was not cruel enough to inflict the kind of discipline it would take to make this woman stop. He felt his own weakness, and the only two things that kept him moving were his fear of failure in the simple task he had been given and his fear of Marhan. This kind of fear was not new to Minxa. It was a way of life he had learned on the streets of Vindarill.

"What are the tattoos on your wrists?" Hannahoruan asked.

Minxa knew somehow that were he to lie, she would detect it, and somehow that didn't even matter. "They are a rite of passage into a group of street thieves that I belonged to in Vindarill." It was much more glorious than the truth and gave him a glimpse of some glory in his life, and he glanced over at Hannahoruan to see her reaction.

She stared at him, her eyes burrowing deep into him. "Your mordage is so thick you are beginning to believe your own lies," she said. "Soon, any noble truth you have will be lost altogether in personal truths that are so twisted that they are no longer truths at all."

"Shut up!" It was the most creative thought he had to offer.

"Then the prophecy will be true," she continued. "'Darkness will chase away light, and the vorn will seek the respite of Oblivion over the immortality of the Infinite.'"

Minxa was walking behind them. He stepped around and slapped her hard across the face. "Shut up!"

She stopped walking and looked back at him, slowly turning her head to expose the other cheek to him without breaking eye contact. "Turn back before it is too late."

Minxa raised his hand to slap her again, but he never struck. Some small shred of decency held his hand back, but he could not name it, if it even had a name. He lowered his hand and turned away. "Follow me!" he commanded as he stared at the ground. It wasn't supposed to be this way. He had the same feeling that he always had around Rasler—and Sereline. He felt small. He forced himself to think about Marhan and the hope that he had offered about getting the map and allowing Minxa to get home. A cruel justice flooded over him, and he promised himself that he would not give in to such babbling again.

✠

*You are to respect those whose age proves
they have seen much.*

Sessasha
It Is Said

The roadway north was unkempt and desolate. To Mindar, the woods
even smelled old. The still, heavy air was burdened with the odor of old
mushrooms, rotting leaves and ancient trees, half dead. Fallen branches
littered the road, and living branches arched overhead. Nothing stirred
in the breathless quiet, where the only sound seemed to come from the
travelers, and even that was quickly swallowed by the endless immensity of the forest. An occasional bird darted between the trees and startled
them.

After walking for about two hours in silence, Lutaka held up his
hand suddenly and stopped in the road. He pointed ahead into the verdure. A hundred paces ahead of them, in the middle of the road, were
two deer, their heads turned toward the intruders and ears set forward.
They turned and ambled into the woods without concern.

"Mighty desolate, it is!" mumbled Phonda.

"I don't remember it being this quiet on the way," echoed Dolar.

"Perhaps a little lunch would lift our spirits," Mindar said. "Even
just to sit down for a spell..."

They sat and ate dried verrin fruit and hard crackers on the trunk of
a huge tree that had fallen along the side of the road. "I'm going to miss
the dinners in the Verillain Dale," mused Lutaka. "It's hard to believe
that this came from the same kitchen." He was gnawing on one of the
crackers that looked more like a chunk of dried dough.

"Is it us, or is it the forest?" asked Sereline.

No one answered. Mindar knew what she meant.

"I would guess it's some of both," said Erinshava in the pause
between a swig of water and another cracker.

Lutaka nodded. "I think the Verillain Dale beguiled us into thinking
that all the world is like it. Do you remember when you first came into
the dale; the light, the air, the vigor we felt? Everything seemed new and
fresh. On top of that, we have all washed in the springs, shedding the
mordage that made us think that this was pleasant." He waved his hand
out across the woods and smiled weakly.

"I'm sure we will get used to it again after a time," said Erinshava,
"but it is a shame that we have to. I'm guessing that Lutaka is right, that
the way it was inside the wall is the way that the Eladra built the world
for Mah'Eladra, and what we see here is the result of the accumulated
mordage that claws at our life and darkens our eyes." She stood up,

moved to the middle of the road and beckoned back in the direction from which they had come. "Look at the Crown," she said. "It's full of life and light. Imagine if we were heading toward it, rather than away."

Mindar looked up. What Erinshava had said was true and subtle. When he looked back the other way, the dreariness facing them was undeniable. "Maybe we should go back," he said.

"No," said Lutaka, "we cannot. We need to keep moving, especially if we hope to make it to that house before nightfall."

The realization of the difference between what they faced, and where they had been, lightened the burden of the road ahead somewhat; and the foreboding that had dogged Mindar lifted. Erinshava stood in the road and read another passage from her book:

"We live among the shadows and walk among them.
How will we know the brightness when it comes?
It will flood over us like the tide, like the swift, wide river.
And who will there be to slow its flood?
Can man or beast, or bird or any creature from the depths of the sea,
Can war or famine, plague or storm,
Or vile enemy with murderous intent,
Take from us that which is the province of our vorn?
Nay, that defeat, that which tears and destroys our essence
Cannot come from without, unless it is allowed from within.
And such is allowed, when psadeq fails
And when our mordage betrays the hjarg into the hands of the intruder."

Time fled as they journeyed north along the road. Several times they stopped where small streams crossed their path to refresh themselves with the cool, clear-running water. Twice more they saw deer and once, an elk. They chatted aimlessly, about this and that, oblivious to the passage of the sun as it arched westward toward its rendezvous with the horizon.

Three hours after they had stopped for lunch, they came to a fork in the road. Lutaka stopped and stared. "I don't remember this," he said. He looked at Phonda and Dolar as each shook their head in dismay.

"The map," commanded Erinshava as she dropped her pack.

Mindar spread the map before them. The road to the left swept off in a gentle curve, slowly heading west, and the road to the right went more or less straight north.

"We must not have noticed this on the way down," said Lutaka, "and I don't recall passing any roads this close to the Crown."

Sereline had walked some number of paces down the road leading west. She was looking back. "It's easy to see how you missed it," she called. "From here you cannot even tell a road is joining."

Mindar looked carefully at the way the roads converged. She was right. It would have been easy to miss their juncture coming from the north. "But I thought there was only one road from the Crown to Kinvara," he said.

Erinshava was scratching her head. "Vishortan said nothing of this," she observed, "but the house is on the road to the right. I think we need to go that way."

"I think that's best," Lutaka said.

They shouldered their packs and started down the road to the right. Mindar wondered about the strange confluence. None of them had noticed it on the map until they were upon it. Lutaka and his consorts did not remember it on the way south from Kinvara, and Vishortan had said nothing about it. He shuffled silently along, pondering this strange world and the odd sense of pre-knowledge that seemed to pervade it. The oddity was not so much that various persons knew more than they should, but that their knowledge had gaping holes in it, as if details were given to them, but pieces of knowledge were purposely left out. If this were an unknown force or undercurrent of the world, if it were magic or luck, such omissions would not seem so deliberate.

Sereline had been leading the entourage, but she dropped back beside Mindar as they walked on in silence. He could feel her presence. It was a welcome comfort against the menacing silence of the forest. Her confidence and strength reached out and pulled him in. After they had walked some distance, Mindar looked over at her, and she glanced back and smiled. "Very quiet here," she said softly, "almost as if the birds are forbidden to sing."

"Aside from the deer we saw, and the elk, we have not heard a whisper," Mindar said, "a far cry from Karolil."

"Yes," Sereline sighed. "I miss the ocean."

As if in answer to her thoughts, two seagulls suddenly caught Mindar's eye as they passed lazily overhead, weaving back and forth on some unseen air current above the trail. Sereline looked up, stopped and stiffened. "What is it?" Mindar whispered. Every fiber of her being was focused on something else. Mindar felt Erinshava slip silently in beside him, an arrow nocked in her bow and the string already partially drawn. They stood quietly, listening into the woods, for nearly a minute.

As the gulls drifted to the left and vanished behind the dense canopy of the old forest, Mindar sensed the trouble they left in the wake of their departure. He listened intently, trying to understand the unknown that Sereline tasted. She interrupted his thoughts, "Come out, friend, we mean no harm." Mindar looked at her again. Her eyes were closed, and her face was lifted slightly to the sky. "Come out, friend, we mean you no harm," she said again. They waited.

"Put down your bow. I am unarmed!" cried a voice to the right in the woods. Erinshava spun to face the sound and looked quickly back at Sereline. Sereline nodded and Erinshava lowered her bow, slipping the arrow back into her quiver in a single elegant motion.

"I am unarmed." It was the voice of an old man. Mindar peered into the gloom of the woods.

"Come out, friend, we mean no harm," Sereline said a third time, spreading out her arms, palms up.

"I am unarmed," said the voice.

Sereline motioned for everyone to sit down. "We are having something to eat," she said loudly as she sat down with her back to the voice. "You are welcome to join us."

They sat cross-legged in a circle in the middle of the road and opened their packs for more dried fruit and hard crackers. "Tonight we will have a proper dinner," said Lutaka. He tried to sound casual, but Mindar could tell he was tense.

"If he shows himself," said Sereline in a whisper, "ignore him until he joins us."

"I am unarmed!" called the voice again.

Mindar looked up. "Did you see the gulls?" he asked, trying to keep his voice low as he scanned the sky.

"What gulls?" asked Lutaka.

"I saw them," said Sereline. "That's why I stopped. Gulls have no business this far from the water."

"What were they doing?" asked Erinshava.

"They were shadowing us—or him." Sereline pumped her thumb over her shoulder. A man had emerged and was moving slowly toward them through the woods. Mindar tried to ignore his approach.

He stopped about ten paces from where they sat in the woods. "I come in peace," he said.

"Can I have a sip of water?" asked Sereline as she looked at Lutaka.

Mindar could see the man. He was old, with a long gray beard and a dark brown cloak that hung in tatters nearly to his ankles. He stood still in the shadows of a huge chestnut tree whose trunk was as gnarled and weathered as the man's face, but his eyes shone in the dark under his thick eyebrows. On his head, he wore a cap that held his long hair back from his forehead. However old he was, he showed none of the characteristic stoop that age brings to a man's body.

Lutaka looked up. "Come, have something to eat and drink with us," he called. The man slowly made his way to the edge of the road. "Come on," Lutaka repeated, "we are just resting before we finish our journey for the evening." He slid over to widen the gap between himself and Erinshava.

The man shuffled over and sat down between them. "My name is

Dakan," he said. "Dakan of the woods."

"I am Lutaka. To your right is Erinshava and beside her is Sereline."
The man nodded as Lutaka continued, "Phonda to her right, then Dolar,
and this is Mindar." Lutaka handed Dakan a jug of water. "Drink."

Dakan smelled the water, took a quick sip and handed the jug back
to Lutaka. "Where do you plan to stay tonight?" he asked.

Lutaka smiled. "There is a house a ways ahead, I believe. We were
hoping to make it there before dark." He glanced around the circle.

Dakan's eyes moved slowly from face to face around the circle.

"Do you know of this house, Dakan of the woods?" asked Lutaka as
he handed the guest a cracker and a slice of dried apple.

"Yes," Dakan replied, "thank you." He took a bite of the cracker
while still chewing the apple slice.

"Is it far?"

Dakan chewed his cracker and apple thoughtfully. "About a mile."
He was looking down as he swallowed.

"Have you ever stayed there?" asked Lutaka.

"Yes."

"Is it nice?"

Dakan sat still, looking around the circle again with his eyes as he
chewed slowly.

"Do you know what happened at the house?" Lutaka asked.

"Yes," Dakan said.

Erinshava interrupted the direction of the conversation by holding
up her hand in a gesture for silence. She looked in the old man's eyes
and spoke gently, "We have come a long way, Dakan, and we are tired.
We mean you no harm. We have recently washed in the Jualar Springs,
and we come in peace. We know there is mischief afoot, and we know
that it did not start with you, or the house, but many miles back. We
know its source, but we do not know its reason. Tell us what you know
of the fire, and perhaps we can help."

The old man's eyes widened. "How do you know these things?" he
asked, looking around.

"We saw the smoke this morning from the top of the northern gate
as we left the Crown." Dakan's shoulders dropped and he nodded his
head. "We're going there to see what has happened."

"There is nothing left," Dakan said.

"Where are you headed?" asked Lutaka.

"I am going to—" Dakan stopped short and looked around the circle. "I was going to the Crown."

"Did they tell you that you would meet us on the way?" asked
Erinshava.

"Yes."

"What did they tell you would happen when we met?"

"You would kill me."

Mindar wanted to laugh, but he knew it was not the time for laughter.

"Did they give a reason, I mean, why we would kill you?" asked Sereline.

"They told me that you had killed two of their friends, and one of them showed me a scar on his face where he was almost killed."

Mindar sat stunned. Minxa was the only one with a scar on his face. Mindar did not want to believe that Minxa would tell such a lie.

"Well," said Lutaka at length, "we have no intention of killing you. You are welcome to travel with us, or you may go on to the Crown if you wish." He stood up and slung his pack onto his shoulder. "We intend to make it to the house by nightfall."

The old man looked up. "Why? There is nothing there but ashes."

"We have other reasons," said Lutaka, pushing his other arm through his second pack strap.

Mindar and the others stood up and stretched, and Sereline offered Dakan her hand to help him to his feet. "I would like to go with you," he said. "It would be a great kindness."

"You are welcome," said Lutaka. "Why did they let you go?"

"I was not there when the fire started."

"Yes, but they let you go."

"They took my wife and son," the old man said.

"And you did not go after them to save them?" Mindar could tell Lutaka was suspicious, but he was treading carefully.

"I could not face their numbers alone."

"C'mon," said Lutaka. "We have another mile or so before we are finished with this day."

Mindar felt Sereline nudge him and he looked over. She was pointing skyward. The gulls were back, high above the trees, gliding back and forth in the late afternoon air rising from the still woods. There were three this time. When he looked up, they slid lazily to the side and drifted out of sight above the trees.

⊞

It is a great folly to mock that which you do not understand.

Mythinian Proverb

"If you enter Fazdeen now," Hannahoruan explained, "you will never leave it."

Minxa watched Marhan lean in close to her face as he leered at her.

"Why? Is there some kind of—magic, or will we be beset by an evil spell?"

Hannahoruan did not flinch as she stared back at him. "There is no such thing as magic or spells, Marhan, but there are truths that we all must live by. Fazdeen has laws that cannot be broken. No intruder may spend the night in Fazdeen, and you and your entourage will not make it through before the first starshine. The gates will shut and we will be trapped."

"And what will they do to us?"

"You will have to stay in Fazdeen, be part of the community and work there."

"Ha!" laughed Marhan. "Did you hear the lady?" he asked as he looked about the group.

"Don't mock what you don't understand," Hannahoruan said.

Marhan raised his hand to strike her. She did not move or break eye contact. Her son stood silently beside her; he had not said a word since he had been bound that morning. Marhan turned away with a gesture of disgust.

They stood before an enormous wall of foliage, impenetrable except through the gateway that swallowed the road into it. The gates were open, and two armored guards watched each side of the entrance.

Marhan stepped over to the three warriors who had joined them at the gate. One of them was Vashtor, the second was his companion from before the inn and the third was new. They began speaking in a strange dialect that Minxa could not understand. It seemed that they were arguing. Whenever they talked, Minxa thought they were arguing.

Finally, they stopped and Marhan walked back to them. "We have to go back to the inn," he announced.

"What?" said Parata.

"Vashtor said we have to go back to the inn!" Marhan said through his teeth. "The map is there, and we have the perfect opportunity to reclaim it if we are careful."

Minxa looked up at the name Vashtor, and Vashtor stared at him until he looked down. There was something unsettling in that look.

"It took us an hour and a half to get here!" said Faranda. "Why didn't we just stay there and wait for it?"

Marhan avoided his question. "Who's in charge here?" he asked, roving his eyes around the group. Minxa saw Hannahoruan smile, but she said nothing.

"You are in charge," Faranda said. "I am just wondering why we came all this way simply to turn around and go back. You knew they were coming to the inn. Why didn't we just wait for them?"

"We are going back to the inn," Marhan hissed.

Faranda nodded. Minxa wondered why Faranda didn't answer.

Instead, he leaned over in mock obedience and shouldered his pack, never breaking eye contact with Marhan. "Let's go then," he said.

✠

An ear to the ground, an eye to the sky, my nose to the wind and the El of Mah'Eladra.

An Old Pistisine Saying

"We need to find out where our 'friends' are," Lutaka muttered to Mindar as they collected wood for the fire, "but I do not want Dakan to see the map." He bent over to place another branch against the stone. "There are loose ends to his story that still do not tie together," he said as he stomped down to break the wood under his foot.

"What loose ends?" Mindar asked.

"I think he knows how Marhan knew we had left the Crown. I am not sure he has a wife and son, nor am I convinced that this is, indeed, even his inn."

"Why?"

"He is not emotional enough for someone who has lost everything. He is old. His son would probably be older than he seems to convey. He gave us no indication that his son resisted—I'm not sure, just wary." Lutaka stomped on another stick. "We need to move the horses away from the camp," he continued, his voice low and urgent. "Take them down to the stream for a drink, then lead them to the back side of the knoll on the other side, over there." He nodded in the direction he meant. "Leave Droga in charge and leave them untied. I will keep Dakan distracted. You can check the map then."

They carried several armloads of dry oak branches down from the knoll above the smoking inn. While they waited for the others to return with more wood, Lutaka and Mindar set the fire for the night. The sun was down, but it was light enough to see. Phonda and Dolar arrived with more wood. Dakan was close behind them with kindling branches. "Just what we need," said Lutaka with a smile. "We'll have this roaring in no time." Sereline and Erinshava dropped their bundles of sticks down onto the pile they had started.

As they brushed themselves off, Lutaka looked up. "Mindar, would you and Sereline check on the horses? We'll prepare something for dinner by the time you are back."

Lutaka was as good as his word. Mindar and Sereline returned to a roaring fire. Its warmth welcomed them out of the gathering darkness, and the smell of the stew in the pot heightened their eagerness to join the others. The information gleaned from the map was disturbing, but even more disturbing was what they had found when they led the horses to the stream. Lutaka had not wanted Dakan to know of the map. Mindar and Sereline had agreed that it was best not to let Dakan know about the discovery in the woods either. Mindar remained quiet as he struggled to find a way to tell Lutaka and Erinshava.

Lutaka must have seen the turmoil in Mindar's eyes. "How's everything with the horses?" he asked.

"They're fine. They're set for the night—" Mindar continued staring at Lutaka.

"I'm going to get more water," Lutaka said.

"I'll help," Mindar volunteered without hesitation. He picked up a bucket that Dakan had brought to the fire and started off behind Lutaka. The stream was just over the rise behind the inn, not more than thirty paces, and Mindar followed silently until they got there. "We don't want to get our water here," he said as Lutaka stooped to fill his bucket. Mindar motioned that they move upstream. It was almost dark, but he could still see enough to pick his way along the streambed. The stream made a sharp turn, and as they rounded the bend, Lutaka stopped before he turned suddenly to look at Mindar. "Did you get to look at the map?"

"Yes—"

"What's going on?"

"They're headed back this way. I had to guess at the distance, but it seems that they are about an hour away."

"On the road?"

"So far."

Lutaka turned to face the scene in front of them. "NarEladra," he muttered, "the Sacrifice of Mandareagah." Hanging from a stout limb in front of them by its hind legs over the stream was the boar that Mindar and Sereline had discovered earlier, its head hanging down so that its snout was in the water. Its throat had been cut so that its blood had been emptied into the stream, and scavenger moths covered its carcass.

"Sacrifice of what?" Mindar asked.

"Mandareagah. It is a sacrifice of defilement: a warning, a statement of intimidation; it is the mark of the NarEladra—or those who follow them. Violence and death usually follow soon after. Whatever happened here at the inn was deliberate," Lutaka said, "and it's not over."

"Do you think Marhan is still traveling with NarEladra?" Mindar asked. He was not sure he wanted to know the answer.

"It's hard to tell, but I would rather not have to find out—and neither do you—none of us do."

"What should we do?"

"We need to be careful. Right now we need to get back to the fire with some water."

Mindar nodded. They walked around the boar's carcass and filled their buckets with water upstream from its fouling presence. "Nothing should be said of this at the fire," said Lutaka as he stood up from the stream. Mindar nodded, and they trudged back, carrying the full buckets.

It seemed very dark. The only light was the firelight on the bottom of the leafy canopy beyond the rise that separated them from the others. As Mindar picked his way along the stream, he felt the intimidation and defilement of the sacrificial beast flowing in the black gurgling water, and the vast empty forest that had seemed so friendly closed in around him. Mindar felt small, and it made the group around the fire seem small, threatened and vulnerable.

Mindar looked at Erinshava as he took his place in the circle. She was laughing at something Sereline had just said, and her laughter seemed to drive back the darkness if only slightly. Phonda and Dolar were smiling, but Dakan sat still, staring into the fire.

"We are glad you are back," said Erinshava, smiling. "We were thinking you got lost, and we would have had to eat all this ourselves."

"It's a long walk to the stream, and this water is very heavy," Lutaka answered. "But now we're here, there is no need to wait any longer." No hint of the darkness appeared in his words or his voice. It was as if he had seen and felt nothing.

Sereline began serving the stew as Phonda handed out the hard crackers. It was not much. Beans in some sort of spiced gravy with some reconstituted meat. The savory aroma was significantly more appealing than the actual taste, but no one seemed to care; after a long day walking and the lunch of dried fruit and crackers, it was a feast. They all sat preoccupied with their own thoughts, chewing slowly and mesmerized by the fire, pondering their smallness in the vast, dark forest.

Lutaka broke the silence. "We will have to leave early tomorrow if we want to make it through the forest as Vishortan instructed us," he said as he ran his finger around the rim of his plate.

"I have been wondering," said Sereline, "why he said nothing about this inn or what we would find here."

"Me too," Mindar echoed. "It seems odd that he could be so specific about so many things and then—" He did not know what else to say.

"I think he could only tell us what Mah'Eladra revealed to him. Nothing more," said Erinshava.

"One would think that Mah'Eladra would have known about this," Mindar said.

"They know, but choose not to reveal it to us," Erinshava continued.

"That's probably true," said Lutaka, "but why? Why one thing and not the other?"

Erinshava stirred the fire with a stick, and sparks leapt skyward into the darkness. "Perhaps we would have had no way of knowing the things we were told without being told."

"But this?" Mindar prodded.

"Well this is something we have to figure out ourselves. What do you think, Dakan?"

The old man stirred. He had been silent the entire meal. "I don't know much about these things."

"Well, do you think it is safe to stay here tonight, for example?" Erinshava's voice was gentle, but keen.

"They may come back here if that is what you mean, but there is nothing here for them, unless you have something they want." He looked around the fire before he looked down.

Erinshava pressed on. "Do you think we should hide somewhere in case they come back?"

"Why are you asking me?" Dakan said with a shrug. "I don't know what they want. They took my wife and son—"

"And you made a deal with them that you would lead us to them, or was it that you would keep us here for them to find us?" Lutaka asked.

The old man sat like a statue. It was hard to tell if it was fear or stubbornness.

Erinshava bent toward the fire. She held her small book in her hand. "Listen, Dakan, I will read you something from my book."

"There is but one thread of noble truth.
It does not waver in the wind of our thoughts."

The old man stiffened and sat up straight as the words flowed from Erinshava's lips.

"Its flame does not flicker or dim, though surrounded by darkness,
Nor is it tangled by our ignorance or deceit.
It is truth and remains so, untainted, unmoved, resolute,
A line, stretching from one eternity to the other.
When we lie, we twist ourselves, not the truth,
Because noble truth stands outside the province of our effect—"

Dakan interrupted,

"But when we speak the truth, we align ourselves with that singular
thread,
And it guides us toward the Infinite."

His hands shook on his knees. His eyes were closed, and his face turned upward as if he were drawing a deep breath through his nose. He spoke slowly. "You read from the Tessarandin, and yet you accuse *me* of lying."

"We do not accuse you of lying. We seek truth," said Erinshava.

"You doubt that what I have told you is true, yet you deceive me."

"In what way?"

Dakan opened his eyes and lowered his face to look straight into Erinshava's eyes. "Your friends are plotting to leave me here to face my enemies again while you escape. They have moved the horses to the other side of the knoll because the enemy is close by, and they know that you are here." He turned to look at Lutaka. "You have seen the defilement in the stream, so you know they are bent on destruction. I must stay, for the sake of my wife and son. When they find you are gone, they will try to kill us. You know this." Lutaka looked down, unwilling to face the old man's stare.

"What defilement in the stream?" Erinshava demanded as she looked at Lutaka.

"Mandareagah," Lutaka muttered as he tossed a stick into the fire.

"A sacrifice?" Erinshava's voice hissed as she leapt to her feet. "Here?"

"Upstream." Lutaka tossed his thumb over his shoulder.

Erinshava turned to the old man. "How do you know all this, Dakan?"

He looked up slowly. *"An ear to the ground, an eye to the sky, my nose to the wind and the El of Mah'Eladra."*

Erinshava dropped to one knee in front of him and took his left hand and touched her forehead with it, then rose quickly. "Come, we have little time."

"No," Dakan replied, "I must stay here and wait for them. Erinshava, stay with me." He looked at her and spoke several rapid phrases in some ancient dialect before turning to Lutaka. "Take your two men with you and go to the horses," he said. "Lead them west behind the knoll. There you will find an old trail leading northeast. Follow it until it turns suddenly to the northwest and wait there. When Tal is descending, head west until you find the road. We will meet you where the road turns west into the gate at Fazdeen."

Lutaka was staring into the fire. There was a sense of embarrassment and defiance in his eyes. "Do as he says," Erinshava said. "You may not live until tomorrow if you do not."

Lutaka stood up. "Let's go," he said to Phonda and Dolar as he looked Dakan in the eyes.

"When you get to the horses, send Droga back to me—leave your dinnerware where it is," said Dakan. "I need proof that you were here and left in a hurry."

Lutaka hesitated.

"Go!" said Erinshava. "You don't have time to think about this."

Lutaka stood and pulled his pack onto his shoulders and turned into the darkness toward where the horses were hidden. Phonda and Dolar followed silently.

Dakan turned to Sereline. "Take Mindar and go straight that way into the wood," he said as he raised his arm and pointed. "Go a hundred and thirty paces; and turn down the hill to the road; then head back toward the Crown until you see a large boulder on the right." Mindar remembered seeing the boulder. It seemed distinctly out of place when they passed it earlier. "On the back side of the stone, you can climb to the top," he continued. "Stay there until Meekar is directly overhead. It will be safe then. Follow the road north until you meet the others. Is this clear?"

Mindar nodded as he stood up and pulled on his pack. All words seemed suddenly out of place, as if the time for silence had descended to cover him like a thick blanket. Sereline waved, and he followed her into the threatening darkness of the woods.

⚜

Who said waiting in the darkness was supposed to be comfortable?

Erengnira
The Tiger in the Tree

From the road, Mindar would never have guessed what the boulder was. On the back, a set of hand and footholds had been carved into the stone forming a stairway to the top. The top itself was relatively flat, but had a depression carved into it so that if one lay down, a person standing on the ground would have no indication that anyone was there. To one side, a small basin had been carved into the depression that captured the rainwater.

When they got to the top, Sereline whispered, "We need sleep. I will wake you when it is time to go."

"I don't think I can sleep right now," Mindar whispered back. Tal's glow was just appearing on the horizon through the trees. There was little light, but he could see Sereline staring at him in the dark. "There are too many questions."

She pulled her blanket around her and leaned back against the wall of the depression.

"I mean, who is Dakan, for instance?" Mindar asked. "And how did he know so much about what was happening?"

"I think he is a Pistisine," Sereline said softly.

"A Pistisine guardian?"

"It makes sense, doesn't it? You heard what he said to Erinshava, and then her response to it?"

Mindar nodded. "Do you suppose they are safe?"

"If he is a Pistisine, we should not worry; about them—or us."

"I suppose—" Mindar said. "Then I find it curious that he sent us in different directions. Not just separate ways, but direct opposites."

"He must know something we don't."

"They have all our horses—"

"Except Droga."

"Right." Mindar shook his head. "That didn't make any sense either."

"Perhaps we will find out tomorrow," she offered.

Mindar looked over at her. Tal's light was just beginning to filter through the canopy above them, and he could see her well. It gave the whole scene a sense of unreality. Her face was lit from the side, accentuating her profile, and her hair shone in the darkness. "And why here? And why just you and me?" His irritation surfaced in his voice.

Mindar saw her shrug under the blanket wrapped around her. "We will have to wait—and we should be quiet," she said.

A slight breeze had sprung up, and the cool air chilled Mindar. He pulled his blanket around him and slid down, working his body to find a comfortable position on the cold stone. Sereline lay still. It was as if she took no notice of the discomfort of the rock, or perhaps she had found a comfortable spot. Mindar finally found a place he could sleep and tried to settle in.

He was exhausted but unable to sleep. The stars were barely visible through the leaves that shifted nervously with each breath of wind, and he could not identify a single constellation. He may have dozed, but did not remember. He did remember watching Sereline, sound asleep, or seemingly so, unmoving, with only her face and the top of her head visible in the pale light. She seemed achingly close and far away at the same time, unafraid and at peace. So he waited as Tal crept up higher and higher, in the utter silence of the woods, perched atop this strange stone.

Sleep had always amazed Mindar. One can sleep through thunderstorms and hurricanes, yet be wakened by the slightest sound. He sat up suddenly. Sereline was already awake and crouching beside him. She held her fingers to her lips as he sat up. Voices filtered up to them from somewhere below. Guessing from Tal's position, they were about two hours from the time appointed to leave their perch on the rock. Mindar strained to hear what was being said.

"Why are you always complaining?"

"It just seems like we get to do all the weird things—look at this. He wants us to climb this thing and keep watch on the road."

"It is a good place to see the road."

"That's not the point."

"What *is* the point?"

"Do you really think anyone will escape?"

"No."

"That's what I mean—what are we doing here?"

The voices were coming closer. Mindar heard a twig snap and the rustling of lazy feet dragging through the leaves on their way to the stone as every sound thundered in his ears. Sereline leaned close and whispered, "Let them come up." She held her hand over his mouth and pretended to hit him on the head.

"Hey, look at this," one of the voices said. "There are handholds cut into it."

"They go to the top?"

"Looks like it."

"I don't feel like climbing."

"Look, Marhan told us to wait on top. I think we'd better do it."

"He'll never know."

"I dunno. He has a strange sense about him and with Vashtor around—besides, you got anything better to do?"

"Take a nap?"

"You're pathetic. I'm going up. C'mon, this is even easier than it looks."

Sereline had moved to the left side of the depression where the climber would enter from the steps, and Mindar had moved to the other side. She signaled again and waited. It did not take long. The climber's surprise at their presence was comical.

Mindar lay quietly as the first climber came over the edge of the rim, and as he stood up, Mindar lunged up from his right side. He managed to yell, "Hey—" before Mindar got his hand over his mouth. Sereline was quick. Mindar didn't actually see what she did, but the intruder sank like a stone into his arms.

"Hey, what?" came the voice from below. Sereline made a motion to Mindar to speak.

"This is unbelievable!" Mindar called.

"What?"

"Get up here, ya gotta see this!"

"What?"

"Just c'mon!" Mindar yelled, trying to imitate the first speaker's irritation in his earlier conversation.

"Okay, okay—I'm coming." He muttered something else, but Mindar could not hear him. Sereline dragged the first climber away from the stairs and then joined Mindar for their assault on the second. She pointed that Mindar should stand. He faced away from the entrance. The second man was puffing when he reached the top.

"All right," he said as he came over the rim, "just what is it I gotta see?"

"This!" Mindar said as he turned. The surprise on the man's face disappeared as Sereline struck him from behind, and Mindar stepped forward to catch him. It was all too easy.

Sereline moved fast. "C'mon, we have to tie them up before they wake."

"What did you do?"

"Quick, tear strips out of their cloaks," she said. "Tie their hands first—" She worked feverishly and Mindar followed. When they had them bound, they propped them up against the side of the depression and covered them with the blankets. "They will be very cold when they wake up."

Sereline had taken the knives from their belts. "We will leave these at the bottom. They will eventually be able to free themselves, but we will be long gone."

They sat down opposite their captives to wait. The night chill took over, and Sereline sat close beside him. "Our friend the archer—I can't remember his name," she said, "and Drofan!"

"Do you suppose that Dakan knew they would be sent here?"

"I don't know."

"How could he possibly have known?" Mindar muttered.

"If he is a Pistisine—well, they have a way."

"You know much about the Pistisines?"

"Only stories. What was it he said to Erinshava?"

"'An ear to the ground,'—'an eye to the sky'—"

"'A nose in the wind,' I think," she added as Mindar paused, "and what was the last phrase?"

"Something about the El of Mah'Eladra," he said.

"Yes, that's it. The El. The Pistisines claim their power through the El. They seem to know things that they can't possibly know—"

"Like—that these two would be here?"

"Yes, or maybe not that they would be here, but that we needed to be here. Either way would have worked, right?"

Mindar nodded. "It sure seemed like Dakan was lying to us, didn't it? I mean, when he met us on the road."

"I was thinking that too," she said, "but looking back, I realize he did not actually lie."

"But he did let us get drawn into our own suspicions; especially Lutaka."

Sereline moved closer to Mindar. "What was Erinshava thinking?"

"I don't know. She stayed quiet the whole time. I think she must have suspected something, and maybe she was waiting for an answer. She does that a lot."

"She sure came on strong at the fire."

"Maybe she had figured it out and wanted to press the issue," Mindar mused.

"Maybe—"

It was chilly on the stone. "I don't feel obligated to freeze while these two stay warm," Mindar said. He got up and took his blanket and handed it to Sereline, using her blanket to cover both unconscious men. When he sat back down, he pulled it over both of them. Sleep was not an option, so they sat quietly waiting for the next turn of the conversation.

"Mindar—" Sereline was sitting close beside him, staring straight ahead. He looked at her, but she did not look back.

"Do you like me?" she asked.

In that brief instant, Mindar thought he understood the archer's surprise when Mindar had risen up to clap his hand on his mouth. "Like you?!" Mindar stammered. She looked at him. It was his turn to look away, but he could feel her staring.

There was a long pause. "Never mind," she said as she turned her eyes back toward Drofan. Her voice was quiet and deflated.

"No, Sereline...I...I think you are beautiful." It sounded stupid even as he said it.

She rocked forward, wrapping her arms tightly around her knees. "But you don't like me."

Mindar was desperate. "No, that's not what I said. Sereline—I—" He stared at Drofan. Every phrase that rattled through his head, that he so desperately wanted to say, would have sounded as stupid as the last one.

"It's fine," she said. "I'm not sure why I asked."

The door was closing slowly. Mindar's words froze somewhere in his throat and, of all the ridiculous things he could have said, he chose the worst. "Do you like me?" He could not look at her. They sat for a long time, staring into nothing, each caught in a whirl of thoughts.

Sereline was close enough for him to feel the warmth of her body. She seemed like a walking paradox. Not ten minutes before, she had hit two grown men so hard that they were still unconscious, and then she had let down all her defenses and opened herself to him. It was ten minutes before she spoke again. "I like you Mindar Colloden," she said. She was still staring away and rocking very slowly. "I don't know why, but I liked you the day we met—at the Margah in the river. Do you remember?"

"Yes. That was a painful day."

"I have seen many painful days." She sniffed and Mindar looked over to see her wiping her eyes with the back of her hand. He had to say something, but didn't know what. His heart beat wildly. He knew what he wanted to say....

"I like you Sereline," he said, "and I have liked you since we met also." Mindar knew she was listening. "I have watched you, and you seem so strong, so purposeful, and I am just a street viddik from a far-away time and place." Mindar wasn't sure he should say his next thought. "I could not tell if you cared at all—until I heard what you did for me in the Verillain Dale."

"I couldn't let you die—it would have been one senseless thing too many."

"I will remember it forever, Sereline."

She leaned against Mindar and put her head on his shoulder. "Thank you," she whispered.

Drofan stirred, groaned, then lay still for a moment. Neither of them moved. Mindar was savoring the quiet moment of acceptance that Sereline had given him and did not want to lose the gentle closeness he felt. Perhaps she felt the same. They sat like that until Drofan moved his head and tried to sit up. His efforts to move awakened the archer who unleashed a string of profanity almost before he took a full waking breath. Sereline sat up straight, but made no effort to move.

"What's going on?" mumbled Drofan.

The archer swore again, rolled over and sat up. "Sit up," he growled to Drofan, who struggled to do what he was told. Even in the dark, Mindar could see the anger in his face. Sereline sat still and watched them. They were completely helpless in their bindings.

As Drofan sat up, he looked at Mindar and his jaw dropped. "Wha—?" he said as a scowl clamped down over his face. "How did they get here?" he said as he turned to the archer, who shook his head and looked down. Drofan looked from Sereline to Mindar then back to Sereline. "Why did you tie us up?"

Sereline stood up and stretched. "Why did you come here, Drofan?"

"Don't tell her anything," muttered the archer.

"It's none of your business," echoed Drofan.

"Didn't Marhan tell you that you would find us here?"

"He told us—"

"Shut up, Drofan," snapped the archer. "She is trying to trick you!"

"You've already been tricked," Mindar said. The archer spit at Mindar's feet. Mindar felt Sereline's restraining hand on his arm as Mindar moved to slap him.

"Maybe we should explain what is going to happen here," she said, "since it's almost time for us to leave. We're going to leave your packs at the bottom of the rock—" She bent over and grabbed Drofan's pack and tossed it over the edge. "We're not thieves."

Mindar heaved the archer's pack. It hit the ground with a thud.

"Are you leaving us here to die?" Drofan's voice showed his fear.

"We should, but that would make us murderers, wouldn't it?" Mindar said.

"How will we get down?"

"Shut up! We will figure it out," growled the archer.

"Won't Marhan come looking for you in the morning?" Mindar asked.

Neither of them spoke. Drofan looked as doubtful as a man can in the pale light of the moons and the stars. The archer looked down so Mindar could not see his face.

"Let's go," said Sereline.

Mindar and Sereline climbed down the rock to the sound of the captives arguing above. Drofan was whining; epithets and profanity peppered the archer's sentences.

They walked out onto the road. "How will they get free if Marhan doesn't come to save them?" Mindar asked.

"There are two of them," Sereline said with a smile, "and they both have teeth." She took Mindar's hand and squeezed it. "The question is how long it will take for them to figure it out. C'mon; we need to hurry."

✠

A good horse makes a man out of a boy.

Old Mythinian Saying

They had been walking about five minutes when Sereline stopped and grabbed Mindar's arm. "Quick," she whispered, "horses—coming fast." As he dropped over the edge of the road into the shallow ditch, he heard them for the first time. Two were galloping towards them. In the shifting patterns of light from the moons through the canopy, they emerged from the shadows like ghosts, tossing their heads back and forth as they approached. One was dark and the other white. The dark one on the right looked like Droga, but Mindar could not be sure in the shadow world of the road.

As they sped past, Sereline whistled. Both horses stopped abruptly in the road, wheeled around and walked toward them as Mindar and Sereline climbed up onto the road. Droga tossed his head, and Mindar knew he wanted him to get on. Sereline mounted the white mare. They were barely on their backs when Droga snorted and started back toward where they had come from. Mindar held on for his life. Shadows sped past them, and the cool night air, thick with the scent of hemlock, spruce and Droga's sweat, filled his senses as it raced through his hair and whistled in his ears. He looked over at Sereline, her copper hair streaming out behind her, her dark silhouette straddling the white horse. It was like a dream.

They slowed down as they approached the short road that led to Dakan's inn; the horses became almost silent. There was still a faint glow in the trees from the fire. Mindar wondered what had happened there, but it wasn't the time to ask. When they were out of earshot of the inn, they picked up the pace again, racing into the darkness down the road. They rode for more than a half hour before the horses slowed again, this time to a slow walk.

In front of them the forest thickened into a dense wall that towered above them. In the shadows Mindar could see what looked like a hole in the wall where the road disappeared into deep blackness. The horses stopped. Mindar did not know what to do. Sereline looked at him and shrugged.

The arrow startled Mindar as it hissed over their heads and clove to the trunk of a huge tree to his left. Droga jumped, and Mindar felt the panic flood through him as Droga started toward the darkness with Sereline close behind. "Whoa," Sereline called. Droga slowed. Sereline turned her horse back to the tree where the arrow was lodged. "These are Erinshava's fletchings," she whispered as she worked it gently out of the wood. Then she turned and peered up into the woods in the direction from which the arrow had come, holding it high above her head.

A low whistle, like an early morning bird, filtered down from the darkness of the rise. Sereline slid to the ground. "It's safe now," she said. Mindar followed her as she led him carefully up through the trees. "That was an old tracker's trick," she said quietly. "If it had been anyone else on the horses, they would have been spooked and fled. It was Erinshava's way of making sure it was us."

As they came to the top of the rise, Erinshava stepped out from behind a large stone and threw her arms around Sereline. "Let's go," she said smiling. "You need to sleep before the journey tomorrow."

"Where are the others?" Mindar asked as they picked their way along in the near darkness.

"A bit higher up," she said. "They're all asleep except Dakan. He would not sleep until you were here."

They came around a huge boulder into a clearing where the group lay sleeping around a fire. Dakan was sitting cross-legged in front of the fire, with his hands on his knees, his back straight and his eyes closed. "We're all safe," said Erinshava.

Dakan opened his eyes and turned to them. "Good. We must sleep now and sleep fast. The gate opens when the last star disappears from the sky. It's just a few hours."

"It'll be a long day," said Erinshava. Mindar saw her bow slightly as she spoke.

"It will, indeed, Erinshava." Dakan smiled. "Sleep where you like, but stay close." He stood up, took several steps away from the fire, and laid out his blanket. There were two others beside him when he lay down. Lutaka, Phonda and Dolar lay on the other side of the fire. Mindar felt awkward.

"Mindar, why don't you sleep with Lutaka," Erinshava said. "Sereline and I will take care of the horses and sleep over there." She pointed to an open space close to the face of the boulder.

Sereline smiled at Mindar and turned her attention to the two horses, following Erinshava the few yards to where the other horses stood. Mindar lay down and pulled his blanket over him, losing consciousness to the gentle currying strokes of Sereline and Erinshava as they brushed down the two horses in the dark.

⋁ The Road to Kinvara ⋁

Fazdeen is a place like no other, where men have preserved the heritage of what Mah'Eladra had given them through the Eladra.

Mindar Colloden
The Great Fathers

The small group stood shivering in the chill morning air beside the opening in the wall of greenery. What Mindar had seen the night before was a carefully cultivated wall of trees and vines, nearly impenetrable and reaching upward twenty paces. A sturdy iron gate that opened at the middle into the interior barred the dark entrance.

"We must not stop on our way through Fazdeen," Dakan said as they waited in the early dawn for the gates to open. "We need to make sure that we are through before the gates close for the evening."

"When is that?" asked Lutaka.

"When the first star appears in the sky."

"Vishortan never told us about Fazdeen," said Erinshava.

"Nothing?"

"He told us to go straight through the forest without stopping, but he said nothing about gates or anything special about it."

"We cannot leave the road. It is forbidden. Does everyone have water?" Dakan continued.

Mindar checked his bottle. It was full. Everyone nodded.

"We will take turns riding the horses. If you are tired, be sure to let me know. Do not take—don't even touch—any of the fruit along the road. It is considered thievery."

"Is there anything we can do?" asked Lutaka.

"You may look; you may talk; you may walk. You may eat food that you bring. The horses may drink from the streams, but not us."

"Will we see anyone else?" asked Erinshava.

"You will see many, but it is forbidden to talk to them."

"What exactly is Fazdeen?" Mindar asked when the conversation lagged.

"Perhaps my wife can answer that best," said Dakan. He looked at his wife who stood close beside him, and she looked up briefly before she looked at Mindar. Even in the half-light before dawn, he felt her eyes probing him. "Fazdeen is a country within a country; it is a region, and it is a separate and ancient people." Her melodic voice was soft and strong, and her accent was not at all like her husband's.

"Is it big? I mean, couldn't we just walk around it, instead of having to go through it?" Mindar asked.

Hannahoruan smiled. "Fazdeen is a square, twenty miles on a side. Two roads run through it. This one goes from southeast to northwest and the other goes southwest to northeast. We could walk around it, but I think it will be best to go through it." Mindar barely heard the words. He was searching deep in his memory, racing through the myriad pathways in search of clues about where he had seen this woman before.

"So we have no choice," said Lutaka, interrupting Mindar's thoughts.

"We do have a choice," Dakan declared. "We have been through Fazdeen before. There is no danger unless we violate their codes."

"It was one of the first civilizations to flourish on Tessalindria," continued Hannahoruan, "and it was the first to be attacked when Vishtoenvar and the NarEladra fled from Mah'Eladra and the Crown. The NarEladra were eventually expelled, but at a huge cost to the people of Fazdeen. The Elder council of Fazdeen closed the doors, built the wall and refused to allow any interference from outsiders. It took years of negotiations with the kings of Tessamandria to even allow the roads to be opened through it. They guard it carefully, and you will see why as we travel through."

"What happens if we do something they consider a violation?" asked Sereline.

"The stories vary," said Dakan. "Some are imprisoned, others disappear altogether. The only consistency is that the arrest is swift and ruthless. You do not want—"

A sudden movement inside the gate captured Mindar's attention. Two guards in polished armor worked to unlock the massive gate. It took both of them, working on either side of the lock for several seconds before the gate began to swing back. Mindar looked up quickly. He could see no stars.

"Sereline, Erinshava, Horuan and Banja: onto the horses!" commanded Dakan urgently. "Remember the laws; there may be no second chance." Mindar watched them swing up onto the horses. "Stay close. Look, but don't touch," Dakan reminded them.

They walked through the gate and into mysterious Fazdeen. In the thick shade, it was still quite dark. Dakan led. Lutaka, Phonda, Dolar and Mindar walked close behind him, and the horses followed two abreast. The smooth, clean road was comfortably wide for the journey. It seemed to be of the same white stone as the Harhazian Road around the Crown, and it stretched in front of them like a white arrow into the gloomy mist of early morning. On either side, Mindar could make out a low hedge, which neatly defined the road's edge. The trees grew over it such that a tall person on a horse could just touch their leaves if he stretched. Everything was cultivated perfectly, pruned as though each tree, branch and leaf had been carefully placed. The air was warmer than outside the gate and very still, redolent of spices, fruit blossoms and the thick overpowering fragrances of a flower shop. A strange otherworldly feeling of perfection pervaded the near silence, disturbed only by the cadence of hoofbeats on the white stone roadway.

Dakan moved fast. All the oldness of the man whom they had met the day before seemed to be gone, and his stamina seemed a match for all of them put together. Mindar's mind raced. There were so many questions. Other than the brief encounter at the gate, Hannahoruan and Banja were still mysteries. She seemed very young. Mindar would have placed her age in her mid–twenties, and Banja he would have guessed to be fifty. He seemed quiet, strong and detached, while she had an aura of bursting, penetrating energy. It seemed impossible that Banja was Hannahoruan's son, but there were strange things in this world, and as the darkness gave way to the brightness of morning, the strangeness of Fazdeen eclipsed Mindar's thoughts of Dakan and his family.

Through the trees, he could see small dwellings. They were low and cleverly built into the woods, so that they seemed to be part of the woods itself. On either side of the road, there were breaks in the hedge where narrow paths led off into the orchards and clearings where they could see the inhabitants. Occasionally, they would look toward the travelers and smile in acknowledgment. Children would stare and point, giggling to one another, then turn and run away.

Lutaka was the first to speak. "They seem friendly enough," he said.

"They are a kind people, and generous," responded Dakan.

"How do you know if you have never been able to talk to them?" Mindar asked.

"Horuan lived among them for a while, many years ago," he said. "Ask her."

His wife was riding in the back with Banja. Sereline on the white mare and Erinshava on Droga were directly behind Mindar and Dolar. It would have been difficult for Mindar to ask. He looked back. Hannahoruan was staring at him, her eyes reaching deep into his vorn. Mindar turned hurriedly forward again.

"What is that sound?" asked Erinshava.

"I was wondering the same," said Lutaka.

Dakan turned his head back toward them and smiled. "Fazdeen has developed many things that we don't understand. They guard them jealously. I believe that one is a tool they have for cutting wood."

Mindar listened carefully. Many other strange sounds began to appear as they moved deeper into the heart of this strange world. He could hear the hammers and the strange buzzing they had heard earlier. There were whistles, hissing sounds and metallic screeches that reminded Mindar of things he heard in Vindarill when they were building the massive skybuildings in the center of the city. He strained his eyes to catch a glimpse, but the sound was filtered through the thick perfection of neatly trimmed fruit trees and the impenetrable verdure that lined the road.

They had been walking for about an hour when the road widened suddenly to the left. Straight ahead, it crossed a flat bridge over a gurgling stream, and a spur dipped at the left to allow travelers access to the stream. "Let the horses drink," instructed Dakan. "We must stay on the bridge."

"How do you know all these rules?" Mindar asked Dakan as they leaned on the bridge's railing and watched the horses drink.

"They are ancient, passed on by word of mouth and experience," he said.

"Do you suppose Marhan or any of his friends would know them?"

Dakan smiled. "It's hard to tell. My guess is that he doesn't. I doubt he has ever been through Fazdeen. I think he's from the south; perhaps he's Mooriman—"

"Do you think he will try to follow us through?"

"I am hoping he does," Dakan said with a smile. "Right now he and his followers are waking up with bad headaches and the even more painful realization that they have been tricked. If he starts through Fazdeen today on foot, he will never make it, and it's likely that we will never see him again."

"What did—what happened last night?"

"Well, Hannahoruan is an herbalist—a good one. Their water had a little too much something-or-other in it."

Mindar heard Erinshava laugh behind him, and when he turned to look, she smiled. "What happened?" he asked her.

"I'll tell you later," she said.

"C'mon," Mindar begged. "Tell me!"

"I want to know, too," said Sereline.

"Do you know what satarin root is?" asked Hannahoruan. She was leaning over the railing on the other side of Sereline, who stood beside Mindar. He shook his head.

"Isn't satarin root poisonous? Even deadly?" asked Erinshava in surprise.

"Yes, it is," said Hannahoruan, "but when steeped in the right proportion with child bane, it produces a potent sleeping toxin. The only side effect is a nasty headache when you wake up."

Mindar watched Hannahoruan as she spoke. She had long kinky hair that flowed down and out in a thick mass behind her shoulders, a luminous orange color that Mindar had previously seen only in sunsets. She was graced with a thin nose, fine thin lips and cheekbones that were slightly on the high side. All of her features drew inward to her penetrating blue eyes that seemed to define who she was. "How did you get them to drink it?" he asked.

"Well, we all drank—" she said. "Banja and I had taken an antidote. My husband is one of the rare individuals that is unaffected."

"And Erinshava?"

"She was up in a tree, watching. Lutaka and his friends had gone to take the horses."

Erinshava laughed and shrugged as Mindar looked at her. "Someone had to be up the tree watching."

The horses had drunk their fill from the stream. "We will all walk and give the horses a rest for now," announced Dakan. "We still have a long way to go." Mindar had not noticed any markers to indicate distance, and the straightness of the road and the uniformity of the land on either side of the trail made it difficult to mark progress.

Mindar looked up to see that they were nearly surrounded by quiet soldiers, each dressed in polished plated armor, and each carrying an odd weapon under his arm, almost like a long-gun that the polls in

Vindarill carried on their night patrols. They just watched. Dakan saw Mindar staring. "They appeared when we stopped," he said with a low voice. "When we start walking they will disappear."

Sereline took Mindar's hand. "Walk with me," she said. They fell in behind Erinshava and Hannahoruan. Dakan was leading beside Lutaka, with Phonda and Dolar close behind and Banja walking quietly behind them in front of the horses. Mindar felt uncomfortable at first, holding Sereline's hand as they walked, but no one else noticed or seemed to care. "Thank you," she whispered.

Erinshava and Hannahoruan engaged themselves in an animated discussion about Fazdeen. "I was only here for two years," Hannahoruan was saying, "and most of what I saw, I am forbidden to tell."

"How did you come here?" Erinshava asked.

"It was many years ago. I was making my way east along the river, collecting herbs and medicinal plants that grow only on the riverbanks. I came to the edge of Fazdeen, where the river runs out of it on the western side; and I was forbidden passage up the river, so I worked my way around until I found the gate. I had heard the lore; I knew the rules, so I waited overnight outside the gate. Several highwaymen, who thought I might be carrying something of value to them attacked me and left me for dead outside the gate. The gatekeepers of Fazdeen found me in the morning and brought me in. They were severely punished for doing it, and I was forced to stay."

"Forced?"

"They have very strict codes about intruders. The way I came in constituted an intrusion, even though I had not done so deliberately. They could have held me forever, but they chose not to do so. It was a decision of the Elders to let me leave; I think partly because of the way it happened."

"So if Marhan and the others get trapped here, it might be for good?" Mindar asked.

Hannahoruan turned her head. "It depends—"

"On what?"

"It depends on the Elders. They would decide."

"And when did you meet Dakan?" he asked.

"I left Fazdeen by the southeast gate, the one we came through, traveling toward the Crown and the Jualar Springs. I stayed at the inn. After my trip to the springs, I came back this way and stayed there again. Dakan was so gentle and strong. He was young then, but well guided." Sereline squeezed Mindar's hand. "We married that summer and lived there until today. Banja grew up there, but now it is time to move on."

"Where will you go?"

"We have often talked about Kinvara. There is room for another herbalist there, and Dakan is getting old. We know many people who have come through Fazdeen on their way to the Crown. We have always welcomed travelers, and we will find a welcome home in Kinvara for us and our son."

As they walked deeper into the heart of this strange place, the surroundings grew more and more intense. Almost every tree had some sort of fruit on it, much of it within reach of the road. They came to another low bridge, this one entirely of stone, with a rushing cataract spilling under it. From the height of the sun, Mindar knew it was almost noon. Dakan stopped the group. "We will eat lunch here. Remember, do not touch the fruit." He led the horses down to the water to drink.

"I'm glad he said that," whispered Sereline as she sat beside Mindar on the wide stone railing. "There is so much of it and it is so close." She was right. He could have picked an entire lunch without leaving the rail of the bridge. The delicious odors of the ripe fruit perfumed the air and made Mindar's dried meat and crackers seem all the more tasteless and salty. The water from Mindar's bottle was warm and tasted old compared to the fresh smell of the stream rushing beneath his feet.

"It's hard to believe that they would be so touchy about a few pieces of fruit," Mindar said absently. The words were barely out of his mouth when he was pulled ferociously backward off the railing and thrown down onto the stone pavement. Dakan was standing over him.

"You must not allow such thoughts into your head!" he said angrily.

Mindar swallowed. "I wasn't going to touch anything," he said, blinking in the sun that was directly over Dakan's shoulder.

"You're right; you're not going to touch anything. I will not allow you to jeopardize our passage." He reached down and grabbed Mindar's tunic and lifted him to his feet with one hand. "You will stand here in the middle of the bridge until we are ready to move on."

His voice carried the force of a man who would not be disobeyed. Mindar glanced over at Sereline, who looked away when their eyes met. Mindar felt himself flushing. Even the thought of breaking the rules appeared to be unacceptable. They moved on, the scent of the trees and the fruit growing stronger and more tempting with each passing moment. Sereline had taken Mindar's hand again, which was comforting in the face of the embarrassment he had suffered. He consoled himself by arguing that it could have been anyone.

In less than fifteen minutes, the road opened suddenly into a large circle. "Halfway through," announced Dakan as he led them across the opening. The circular plaza was about thirty paces in diameter, and there were eight roads leading from it, each marked with one of the signs of the Kirrinath embedded in the white pavement in brass plates. In the very center was a mammoth sundial. It was a statue of a huge archer on one knee, carved in white stone with his drawn arrow pointing up at an angle toward the sky.

The archer was heavily sculpted, with angular muscles that spoke of strength and determination. His face looked up the shaft of the arrow, forged of iron with a polished brass arrowhead. His bow was also of iron, as black as the night sky. Mindar had never seen anything like it. They stopped in front of it for a moment to stare at the archer's awesome visage, and when they looked down, they found themselves surrounded again by Fazdeen soldiers.

"We need to keep moving," Dakan said as he pointed across the circle, "to make sure that we are out of Fazdeen before the gates are closed." His voice was elevated slightly so that the soldiers that blocked their way heard what he said. As he started to walk, the soldiers parted and the travelers moved past them. They neither smiled nor acknowledged their passage.

✠

There is a time to leave legends behind...

Arafinda
Irhandarin (The Journey)

When Mindar and his companions arrived at the northern gate on the road out of Fazdeen, Asolara was barely two diameters above the horizon. The afternoon walk had been comfortable and uneventful. As they approached the open, unguarded gate, it suddenly occurred to Mindar that for some distance before it, all the noises and subtle hints of surrounding activity that characterized the road through Fazdeen had been stilled as if no one were allowed near the outer wall.

"We have an hour, perhaps a bit less, before the first star shines," said Dakan as he led them out through the gate without slowing down. As soon as they came out into the sun on the open road, he stopped. "We've made good time," he said, "but we should rest here and have something to eat." They stood on a low bridge over the rushing stream that ran along the northwestern wall of Fazdeen.

In front of them lay a patchwork of low hills, with broad sweeping fields, burnt by the sun and dotted with clumps of thick forest. They were not very high, and the road wound into them toward the northwest and disappeared not five hundred paces from the bridge. They glowed in the late afternoon light. The word "barren" came to Mindar's mind, but that would have been an overstatement. Mindar looked back. The high wall of thick green that surrounded Fazdeen and the yawning green darkness where the road disappeared into it marked a stark contrast to what lay before them. It left Mindar with a sense of empty sadness that he could not place.

"Drink well and fill your water jugs," said Dakan. "Water is scarce along the road."

"We should have a look at the map," said Lutaka. Mindar pulled the box from his pack. As he unfolded the map onto the flat stone top of the bridge railing, he wondered whether they would see their pursuers and how far behind they might be.

Mindar glanced at Erinshava. She sat on the railing with her feet hanging over the water surveying the countryside. She seemed at ease, and this lent an air of comfort to his vorn. Mindar trusted Erinshava's awareness of danger. Sereline had walked a few paces up the road and was studying the roadbed. Droga had led the other horses to a place where they could drink and then graze on the green grass that lined the stream.

Mindar's first look at the map perplexed him. He could see the stream, and the landscape before him looked more or less as expected, with the sepia color of the map in the sunlight showing the ghostly images of the hills and the road moving out in front of them. If he leaned forward so his head cast a shadow on the map, he could see each of the travelers, huddled near the bridge.

Lutaka whistled under his breath. "By the lightning of the Crown," he muttered.

"What?" said Erinshava, swinging her legs over the rail and dropping down to join them.

Behind Mindar, the map was blank. Where Fazdeen stood, there was complete emptiness, as if it had been wiped from the surface of Tessalindria. Mindar turned around to look. The green wall stood as before with its still, cavernous entrance. He looked back at the map. There was nothing there.

Mindar peered back into the opening at the gate. Everything was quiet and serene.

Dakan smiled. "Fazdeen, with its mystery and legend, is behind us, so we must look forward; we must move forward." He waved his hand, beckoning to the map. Mindar leaned down to the task of trying to see the road before them.

"It's not showing us anything," Erinshava observed.

"Or perhaps it's showing us that there is nothing to see," observed Lutaka.

Sereline sidled up beside him. "There were horses here yesterday, as many as ten, perhaps a few more."

"Yesterday?" asked Lutaka.

"I believe so. They came in on the road and left it here, traveling north along the streambed." Sereline waved her hand in the direction she meant. "And there were several big people on foot with them."

"Were they leading the horses?" asked Lutaka.

"No, the horses had riders."

"How do you know?" asked Erinshava.

Sereline smiled. Mindar reeled the map back in time and worked backward slowly on the day before. "There!" said Erinshava. Mindar stopped. "But there are only two." The two faint smudges lingered for a while on the road, then headed north.

"I know there were more than two," Sereline said as her brow furrowed into a frown. Mindar continued to work backward. "Look, three—right there!" She was pointing to three smudges that also lingered and then began to move northeast.

A few touches sent the map scurrying back farther. "Another one," Erinshava pointed out. All in all, they counted fourteen, in pairs, ones and threes, spaced out from dawn to nearly dusk on the day before. They could not tell from the details who they were or which were on horseback and which were on foot. Mindar moved back to the first smudge and followed it east. It kept to the streambed, even when the stream moved away from the wall of Fazdeen. They followed it until the map showed late in the day. The others were spaced out behind, moving about the same speed with no apparent convergence.

"Strange," muttered Lutaka. "Were there any earlier today?"

Mindar's fingers danced and the map moved under them. "There!" said Sereline. Not an hour before they had emerged, a pair of smudges paused at the gate, before departing to the east.

Erinshava touched Mindar's shoulder, "Sssshhhh." It was very soft, and then in an instant, she vaulted over the bridge rail and onto the bank below. He saw her run down the bank and disappear into the bushes where the stream turned to the right. As she vanished, Mindar looked back. The others were staring at the road.

Lutaka moved in front of the map. "Put it away," he whispered urgently. When Mindar folded the map, it fairly leapt into his hands and folded itself as it slipped into the box and then into his pack.

"Hallo!" Mindar finally looked up. Two men were approaching on the road, one on horseback and the other leading the horse by its bridle. They must have just come over the small rise. The tall footman made the horse seem small. His clothing was that of a soldier, with leather and steel armor covering most of his body and heavy sandals that were laced up around his calves. A long sword hung from his belt. On his right side, Mindar could see the rim of a shield that was slung over his shoulder onto his back.

The man on the horse was shorter, but gaunt. The long brown robe that hid most of his body was fastened about the waist with a gray sash. Its hood covered his head, and the hem and sleeves were long, so that only his hands and face showed. His dark eyebrows crowded together over his eyes, and his lips were pursed into a scowl.

They walked toward the travelers without hurrying and came to a stop about five paces from the bridge on which they stood. Mindar glanced around anxiously. Sereline had vanished and so had Banja. The man on the horse spoke with a raspy voice and a heavy accent. "Greetings." He almost smiled.

Dakan nodded to the rider, "Greetings to you, stranger," and then to the soldier, "What is your destination?"

"We are seeking friends who were to come through Fazdeen." The rider raised his right hand as he spoke and moved his hand in a peculiar flourish, which ended with his palm facing them and fingers closed.

Dakan mimicked his gesture. "We are traveling north to Kinvara. Do you know how far it is?"

"It is two days, perhaps three—there are six in your party?"

"Yes, but we move quickly."

The rider looked puzzled. He glanced down and spoke to the soldier, who had remained motionless, holding the bridle. "We'll wait here, for our friends."

"We were just leaving," suggested Lutaka, "but you may travel with us."

The rider hesitated, and the soldier looked up and spoke for the first time. "No, we need to rest, but perhaps we will catch up to you this evening." Mindar had heard that voice before, but he was not sure where. He found himself staring at the soldier as he tried to untangle his memory.

As Mindar shouldered his pack, Lutaka whistled for the horses. Mindar could feel the soldier staring at him, or perhaps at his pack. The strangers remained motionless as Mindar walked past them. Something was wrong, but Dakan walked away casually, and the others followed without looking back as the horses fell in behind them. Mindar wondered where Erinshava, Sereline and Banja had gone. He had seen Erinshava run, but not the other two.

Mindar looked back over his shoulder as they came to the top of the rise. The strange pair had turned so they were facing them, but otherwise nothing had changed. As the companions descended the back of the rise, Dakan spoke. "Quick, follow me," he said as he moved quickly off the road. "Stay low."

They snaked down into a dry streambed that followed the valley between the two low hills. They were almost jogging. The horses pranced along behind them in the packed sand. "Where are Erinshava...and the others?" Mindar asked in a whisper.

"They'll find us," said Dakan without emotion. "Keep moving."

They came to a place where another streambed merged with the one they were following. Dakan ducked under the low branches of the bushes that hung over it and headed up the bed, moving quickly. They had gone about two hundred paces up the new streambed when Dakan stopped. "Quick, the map!"

Mindar slung his pack down and pulled it out, opening the case in a single motion. The map spilled onto the sand. He moved as quickly as he could, scanning back to the entrance into Fazdeen. "Just what I thought," muttered Dakan. "NarEladra!" There were seven dark smudges near the gate.

"How do you know?" asked Lutaka.

"Too stiff," said Dakan, "and too dark. We'll have to move faster!" He started off before Mindar had the map put away. Mindar stuffed the case into his pack and started running before he had the pack fully on his shoulders. Dakan was leading, and Lutaka and the others fell in behind. The streambed twisted and turned, becoming less distinct as they moved farther up. Mindar sensed that they were getting farther from the road but had no way of knowing for sure, having lost all sense of direction in their haste under the canopy of the scrubby trees that surrounded them.

It occurred to him as they were running that they had not seen any trace of the other three friends on the the map, unless they were still at the bridge and he was confusing them with the NarEladra. A curve in the streambed ended in a small clearing strewn with large rocks. It looked like a dry pool, perhaps a spring at one time, the source of the stream. Dakan stopped.

"Quick, Mindar," he said, "the map."

Mindar was breathing hard. The pack fell off his shoulder, and he had the box out before his pack hit the ground. He folded the map out onto the sand. They could see in an instant the trouble they faced. Four smudges were close behind them in the streambed below, and seven others surrounded them in all directions at varying distances, but none more than several hundred paces.

"Close it up, Mindar, and give it to me." Dakan's eyes flashed as Mindar's eyes flicked from Dakan's outstretched hand up to his face. Mindar hesitated. "There is no time; you must give the map to me," Dakan said. Mindar folded the map, slipped it into the box and handed it to Dakan slowly. From what Mindar knew of the map, *he* was the bearer and it was useless to Dakan; but the old man took it reverently and lifted it high above his head, looking up to the sky as if he were offering it to Mah'Eladra.

He stood for a long moment as the others watched in silence, unwilling to break into his reverie. When he looked down and lowered the map, he spoke quickly. "Droga, take the horses and flee. Go to Kinvara, to the house of Valradicca the smith, west of the city. We will meet you there. Go!"

Droga snorted and reared, thrashing the air with his hooves. When he came back down, he whinnied and bolted. The horses thundered away, disappearing into the woods.

Mindar held out his hands for the map. "No, Mindar, I must keep it for a short while."

"But it is mine," he protested. "You know that."

"I know, and all this is true. You will bear the map, but now you must trust. They want this map, even though they probably know that they cannot possess it, that it is anathema to try. Yet they try."

Mindar heard the coarse guttural growlings of the approaching NarEladra. As they drew nearer Dakan explained. "They do not know who the map bearer is. They must believe it is me."

"No," said Hannahoruan. There were tears in her eyes.

"It is the only way. When they have the map, and they have the map bearer, they are likely to leave you alone." He pushed the box into his pack.

Hannahoruan stepped forward and wrapped her arms around him.

"Can't we fight?" asked Lutaka, his face twisted with frustration and anger.

"You know the NarEladra, Lutaka," he said. "Your only chance is to deceive them. They are deceivers, so deceit is the only gambit possible."

Hannahoruan was still holding her arms around her husband when the first warrior arrived. He stopped about five paces from them, eyeing them thoughtfully as he waited for the others. They arrived quickly, forming a quiet, threatening circle around the group. They were all on foot, except the rider they had met at the gate. He arrived last, his horse still led by the same stiff soldier.

The rider's face remained wooden as he spoke, as if his vorn were empty. "So we meet again. Do you know what happened to our friends?" He looked from each of them to another as if he were trying to ascertain who the leader was.

"We think that there was another party following us," Mindar said, "but we never saw them." He hoped that the rider would think he was the leader.

Lutaka spoke next. "We know nothing else about them. What do you want with us?"

A faint smile stole across the man's scowl. "We were told—by our friends—that there was another party coming through Fazdeen...but there were supposed to be eleven."

Lutaka looked around and counted. "Only six, as you saw at the bridge."

The rider's eyes narrowed. "We believe you bear a certain...article that we seek. We have been instructed to acquire it from you."

"What is it that you seek, stranger? We are traveling to Kinvara and have little of value with us," said Lutaka.

"Do you value your lives?"

Lutaka hesitated. "Yes, we value our lives. It is not our lives that you seek, is it?"

"No. Unless you do not give us what we do seek."

"You have not told us what you seek, stranger," said Dakan.

"Ahhh. We seek Lonama's map. We were told that the map was being carried by a young man, in the company of two young women."

Dakan stood unmoving as he spoke. "There are no young women with us, only my wife of fifty years, who is here." He waved to Hannahoruan who nodded.

"So, who is the map bearer? I will not play games any longer." The rider raised his hand, pointed at Mindar, and two soldiers leapt forward and grabbed Mindar's arms. Their hands were as cold and as strong as iron bands. Mindar couldn't move. "If you do not want to pay with your life, then tell me who the map bearer is."

Dakan bent slowly, pulled the map case out of his pack and held it before him. "I bear the map," he said.

The rider waved his hand, and the two soldiers released Mindar and stepped backward. "Open it and show me that you are the map bearer."

Dakan knelt down and laid the case carefully on a flat stone. He lifted the cover as if he had done this before. The soldiers crowded in to see better as he lifted the map and unfolded it onto the sand, then sat down cross-legged before it and put his hands on his knees.

"Show me that you can work it," demanded the rider.

"No." Dakan looked up. His face was serene and defiant. "I do not serve the NarEladra, nor do I obey their voice. Tell Vishtoenvar, if he wants the map, to come and get it himself."

A storm swept over the rider's face. He swung off the horse and landed heavily on the ground, and with two steps, stood looking down on Dakan. "Show us that you are the map bearer!" he growled.

"I am the bearer, but I will not show you or anyone else what I know of it."

The rider hesitated again, unsure what to say to such defiance. "Fold the map and put it in this sack." He pulled a sack out of one of the saddlebags.

"I will not." Dakan's back was straight, and his face showed no expression or emotion. "If you want that done, you will have to do it yourself—you or one of your helpers—what is your name?"

"I am Mardacha." The rider turned to face the soldier who had been holding his horse, and they spoke to one another in the same guttural tongue. When he turned back to Dakan, he motioned towards the others and said, "Vashtor! Take them away!"

Before anyone could move, the NarEladrim soldiers overpowered them and started to drag them away. Mindar could see Dakan sitting still like a statue with Mardacha leaning over him threatening him with a drawn sword. Lutaka, Phonda and Dolar were shouting and struggling with the soldiers who held them. Hannahoruan was silent, and Mindar could not see her. She was in front of him as the soldiers dragged them off into the woods. Mindar knew it was futile to fight the strength of the soldiers who held him, so he resisted by doing nothing, allowing his entire weight to slump toward the ground.

"Over here," Vashtor grunted.

"In the cave?" asked another.

"It will be easier to guard them," said Vashtor as he waved into the cave.

The warriors shoved them into the shallow cave one at a time. Lutaka was all fight. Mindar could hear him, the last one into the cave, grunting and muttering as he tried valiantly to disengage himself from the two warriors who held him. They threw him through the low opening. When he lunged back up, the point of a spear met him at the entrance. "The stone—the big one!" said Vashtor. "Roll it over the entrance."

Mindar stood helplessly with the others at spear-point while the stone was rolled up against the entrance. It fell with a thud. It seemed impossibly large for the three warriors who moved it into place, and more than impossibly large for the five captives to ever hope to move away. It did not seal the entrance entirely. Mindar could see light and heard sounds faintly from the outside. "That will hold them," sneered a voice, followed by a conversation in the ugly foreign tongue that Mardacha and Vashtor had used.

Lutaka sat down heavily beside Mindar. He was breathing hard. Mindar could see Phonda's silhouette against the faint light that filtered past the stone. "Some fix," said Dolar.

"Perhaps...there is another entrance..." said Lutaka between breaths.

Hannahoruan spoke next. "We should rest a few minutes. We have no light, save what is given us past the stone." Her voice was calm.

"Aren't you worried about your husband?" Mindar asked.

"Dakan knows what he's doing. He will be fine."

"There is something I don't understand," Mindar said. "If all they wanted was the map, why didn't they just take it?"

"The NarEladra, in fact the Eladra, are forbidden to touch Lonama's map." Hannahoruan's voice was calm. "It was given to us. If they touch it they will be thrown into Oblivion."

Mindar thought back. "That is why Vishortan and Visha'andar would not go near it."

"Yes," continued Hannahoruan, "Mardacha and Vashtor were to meet Marhan and his followers when they came through Fazdeen, and *they* would have been able to take the map. But none of the NarEladra here can touch it. They may believe that only the map bearer can touch it, since they are forbidden."

"So what will happen?" asked Lutaka.

"As long as Dakan refuses to touch it, they are helpless. Our hope is that Erinshava, Sereline or my son can find help."

"Where will they find help out here?" Mindar asked.

"Erinshava has a guardian—"

"Visha'andar?" Mindar had forgotten about his strange appearance in the NarEl Waste.

"She did not tell me his name."

"Will she be able to call him?"

"That is our hope." The rich melodic tone of Hannahoruan's voice was especially noticeable in the dark. There was no fear, no anger or resentment, just an energy that filled the cave with warmth when she spoke. Mindar thought he could feel her eyes, even in the dark of the cave. Forms were emerging as vague shadows, as their eyes became accustomed to the dark cave and the sliver of light that edged past the stone.

"Shhhhh!" Dolar was trying to listen to what was going on outside. "I think the warriors have left," he whispered. The rest waited silently as he continued to listen. "We should at least try to move this thing."

"Wait until dark," suggested Lutaka.

"Dark may be too late," Mindar said. "If Dakan needs our help, he may need it now."

They moved up against the huge stone, laying their shoulders against it and struggling to get their footing on the loose floor of the cave that sloped away from the entrance. As far as Mindar knew, they never moved the stone, even a fraction of an inch; and after half an hour, they gave up, exhausted, and sat down to think.

✠

Should it surprise us that the fruit of arguing is another argument?

Pratoraman
The Middle Way

Minxa sat with his head in his hands. He had tired of the arguing.

"I told you this was the wrong road," Marhan said. He was berating Faranda.

Faranda stood his ground. "You told me no such thing. You were as confused as the rest of us."

"I don't understand how you could not have noticed which road we came in on," Marhan continued.

"Might I point out that you didn't notice either?" asked Faranda.

"And you even had the sun to give some hint of which direction to go!"

"So did you," Faranda pointed out.

"Shut up!"

Minxa wished they would all shut up and actually think for a moment without arguing, but he dared not speak, lest the abuse leveled at the others be turned on him. They sat at the end of the second road they had taken from the great archer. It ended the same way as the first, abruptly dividing into numerous small paths that disappeared into the thick vegetation somewhere in Fazdeen.

"What did they say would happen if we did not make it out by nightfall?" Drofan asked.

"They weren't all that clear, as I recall," said Tarlin, "but they did make it clear that we had to be out."

"That's what Vashtor told us," said Vormin.

Tarlin looked at Marhan. "Did Vashtor tell you what would happen if we did not make it out?"

Marhan was irritated. "No," he said, "he just warned us not to fail."

"And you didn't bother to ask?" Faranda said, goading Marhan with his tone.

Marhan lunged at Faranda, but Faranda's fist caught his chin before Marhan laid a hand on him. Marhan fell to the ground, and Faranda pounced on him. Before Marhan could move, Faranda had a knife at Marhan's throat. "I am sick of you. Give me a good reason not to kill you now!"

"I'll give you several reasons, stranger," said a voice behind Minxa.

Minxa whirled around. Eight soldiers stood behind them, their swords drawn in readiness. "Any man who spills another's blood in Fazdeen will die in the manner that he kills. The law is immutable, even for outsiders."

Faranda put the knife slowly into its sheath without looking up. He stood and pulled Marhan to his feet before he turned to face the leader of the soldiers. He said nothing.

The soldier stared at him thoughtfully for a moment before looking up through the trees. "The first star of evening has appeared below the Deep Sky," he said. "The gates are shut, and you and your party are still within the walls of Fazdeen."

Marhan was brushing himself off. "We got lost," he said. "We fully intended to be out of here."

"You have violated the trust of Fazdeen and her people."

"Look," said Marhan, the irritation rising in his voice, "show us the way out and we will gladly go."

"No! You will remain here in Fazdeen."

"Overnight?"

"Forever." The captain waved his hand, and the soldiers surrounded the group. Minxa felt his stomach sink. Something about the way he said it made Minxa believe that he meant it.

Faranda swore and reached for his knife.

✠

Can we judge in the moment whether hardship or imprisonment is for our discipline or for our protection?

Hispattea
The Essences of Corritanean Wisdom

The water was gone, as was all the food from their packs. Lutaka and Mindar had explored the cave, finding that it ended about thirty paces from the entrance. Phonda had kept his ear to the gap between the stone and the cave wall, but heard nothing from outside as they watched the subtle shifting of the daylight move twice through its cycle and as their hope slowly sank.

Hannahoruan lifted their hope with songs about life, love, passion, heroes and heroines. She seemed to know everything, and explained it as if she had lived during every moment of it. It was there, in the deep grayness of that cave, that Mindar first realized his love for the history of Tessalindria, the depth of its legends and the richness of all that had happened even before this time.

Hannahoruan seemed also to know about things that were yet to come, and she spoke of things that had not yet happened as if they already had. She talked about the anthara, and how he would live and die. It rekindled memories of Mindar's meager education in Vindarill; but as he pieced it together, he concluded that although her facts were right, her chronology made no sense whatsoever and she often contradicted herself.

Hope slipped another notch as Asolara took the last flickers of light from around the stone for the third time. They sat in darkness and the absolute silence of the cave, doomed to a slow death of thirst, losing hope and losing their minds with it. Phonda sat at his place by the largest crack around the stone, and the rest were sprawled on the cold, uneven floor, trying to find comfort for another delirious night in the netherworld of half sleep.

Mindar had always wondered about his death, but had never imagined it would come like this or at this age. Perhaps in a street fight, or in the crush of a subterranean collapse in the caves of Vindarill, or maybe in the gutter on some frozen night with nowhere to go, but dying of thirst had never crossed his thoughts.

"Something's happening," said Phonda in a hoarse whisper.

"What?" Mindar asked.

"Shhhhh!"

Mindar could not see or hear anything.

"There are voices!"

"What kind?" asked Lutaka.

"Shhhhh!"

They waited in silence. Mindar sat up and opened his eyes wide, struggling to get a glimpse of even a glimmer of light. He could hear each of the others breathing.

Minutes passed. "Anything else?" he whispered.

"No—" said Phonda.

"Are you sure you really heard voices?" Mindar asked.

"Yes. They were unmistakable, but very brief."

"Any words?"

"Not that I could—"

Bright bolts of white light, stabbing through the cracks around the stone, interrupted Phonda's sentence. Mindar covered his eyes in pain. Then he heard yelling, chaotic, shrill voices of surprise and anger. An explosion shook the ground, and the white penetrating rays turned yellow and red, flickering like fire. There was more screaming and snarling, mingled with the clanging and crash of weapons.

Wisps of acrid smoke began to drift into the cave. It smelled of burnt things that did not belong to the woods, and it burned Mindar's eyes. Phonda began coughing, and he reeled back from the boulder. "Move back into the cave!" ordered Lutaka. They heard horses thundering past the entrance as they started back, and more flashes and explosions shook the floor of the cave. Small pieces of debris fell from the ceiling above them.

Then, almost as suddenly as it had started, the light disappeared, and all the sounds stopped. All Mindar could hear was Hannahoruan breathing beside him.

"Now what?" said Lutaka.

"Quick—back to the entrance," Hannahoruan urged. "This may be our last chance! Shout!" She started shouting. Everyone fell in, the deafening cacophony resonating off the stone walls of the cave. The smoke outside had cleared, so they pushed up to the entrance, each seeking to be as close to one of the small openings as possible. When their breath ran low they stopped, nearly in unison. "Again," she urged, and again they yelled for all they were worth. Their lives depended on it.

In the hopeful silence after the fourth outburst, a voice said, "Hello? Hello?"

It took a moment for Mindar to recognize who it was. "Vakandar?" he yelled.

"Small voice—big stone. Hello?"

"Vakandar! Is there anyone to help us?" he yelled again. Everyone held their breaths.

"Very big stone. Very big indeed! Must go."

"Vakandar!" No sound came from outside. Mindar spoke. "If Vakandar is here, either Erinshava or Visha'andar is near. It won't be long now." No one answered, and they sat in silence until the first flicker of light danced through one of the small cracks around the stone. It was a moving flame. "Over here, behind the boulder! Here! This way!" they shouted.

The torch danced close, so they yelled again and stopped, waiting breathlessly. "Lutaka? Mindar?" It was Erinshava.

"Yes!" they all yelled.

"Stand back from the stone!"

They tripped over one another in their hurry to comply with the faint voice of their friend. More of the white light filtered in around the boulder, mingled with hurried voices in the Kor'Alura, and the grinding noise of the stone being pulled from the entrance.

Erinshava was the first through the opening. The brightness of the torch was painful on eyes that had hardly seen light in three days. She looked around and uttered an angry oath. "Get in here and help us! Get water!" she yelled as she pushed the butt of her torch into a crack between two rocks and knelt down beside Hannahoruan. "Are you all right?"

Hannahoruan smiled. "Thank you for coming," she said as she tried to stand. "Is Dakan safe?"

Erinshava caught her as Hannahoruan lost her balance trying to stand. "You need water; then we will talk," she said as she helped Hannahoruan to the entrance. Two huge warriors reached in and lifted her out.

"What happened?" Mindar asked as Erinshava bent over him.

"Later," she said. "We need to get out of here first."

As he came up out of the cave, Mindar saw where the white light came from. Eladrim warriors surrounded the entrance to the cave. There were about fifteen in all, and two of them glowed like the stars, their features barely discernible in their brilliance. Mindar could not look at them, so he sat on the ground looking down until everyone was out of the cave. Erinshava approached the two shimmering giants and knelt before them. She said something Mindar did not understand, and they saluted and turned, vanishing with a slight hiss after taking two steps.

All that was left for light was Erinshava's torch, which seemed but a candle compared to the luminance of the glowing Eladra. Two warriors came running with water skins, bringing them into the circle and handing one to each of them. "Do not drink too much," one of them said as he handed Mindar the skin. Mindar took a drink. It hurt when he swallowed, and he could feel the cool water running all the way down into his belly.

Vakandar strutted around among them. "Dirty cave," he kept saying as he cocked his head toward Mindar. "Very dirty cave, indeed."

"Where is Sereline?" Mindar asked hoarsely.

"She is safe," said Erinshava, "but she is needed somewhere else right now."

They sat for five minutes sipping water, surrounded by the quiet sentinel Eladra. It was a great comfort. Erinshava sat on the ground with them, but said nothing until they all were refreshed. "Come," she said as she stood up. She helped Hannahoruan to her feet and wrapped her arm around her waist to support her. Mindar followed, and the Eladra fell in beside them, walking silently toward the place where they had left Dakan with the map.

It wasn't far, and as they approached the spot, Mindar could see the annihilation that had taken place. The ground was charred, and in the small circle of illumination cast by Erinshava's torch, he could see burned stumps of trees and rocks. Their surfaces were blistered and glazed by an intense heat which still radiated from them, giving the air a close, burned feeling. The pungent odor of sulfur blended with the wisps of wood smoke that rose from the stumps and drifted into the surrounding woods.

From behind Erinshava, Mindar could see the low area where Dakan had been sitting. Several more Eladrim warriors guarded its perimeter, and in the middle were three figures. The streambed, which had been dry when they had left, flowed with water, splashing over the stones through the intense, hot deadness. Sereline was kneeling over one of two prone figures, her unmistakable hair glowing in the orange light of a second torch that was stuck in the sand beside her. She looked up as the group approached and then glanced quickly down again. Hannahoruan broke free of Erinshava's support and bolted to Sereline's side.

As the Eladrim guards formed a circle around them, Hannahoruan began giving orders. "Erinshava, we need faganwort—a handful; we need bowls of water." Erinshava moved like a cat, with two warriors falling in behind her as she leapt out of the circle into the darkness with her torch. One of the guards broke rank and moved to the stream, filling two bowls with fresh water.

It took a moment for Mindar to comprehend what he saw. Banja lay on his back, his face contorted in the strange stillness of death, a large gaping wound torn through his chest as if something had reached in and torn his vorn from him. Mindar looked away as a wave of sickness swept over him.

Sereline and Hannahoruan knelt over the body of Dakan, mostly covered with a blanket, and from what he could see, Mindar was sure he did not want to see the rest of it. Dakan's head was tipped back to help him breathe, and the breaths were short and agonized. His face was disfigured to the point that Mindar would not have recognized him except for his hair and what was left of the beard that had been burned off.

Sereline was gently cleaning the deep wounds of his face and neck. She looked up as Mindar approached. Her eyes glistened with tears, and the fine features of her mouth twisted in anger as she looked back to her task. Hannahoruan worked quickly on a wound in Dakan's side that Mindar could not see. The blanket mostly covered her healing hands. Mindar knelt down opposite Sereline and silently offered his help. She handed him a small piece of soft cloth that had been torn from her tunic, and they worked together without speaking, gently cleaning his hideous wounds as their friend gasped the last breaths of his life.

Hannahoruan rose to meet Erinshava as she returned with a handful of the small purple flowers. "Hold them in his face," said Hannahoruan. Erinshava knelt beside Dakan's head, holding the flowers directly under his nose. He gasped twice and then coughed, and his eyes opened for a moment, then rolled back and closed. As her hands worked feverishly on his wound, Hannahoruan began singing. It was soft at first, some sort of poem in the Kor'Alura. Dakan coughed again. When she brought her hands out from under the blanket, they were sheathed in blood. She jumped up and stepped to the stream, washed them rapidly in the flowing water, then turned back to her husband. Erinshava stepped aside and handed her the faganwort.

Dakan opened his eyes. Hannahoruan was still singing, softer now, directly in his ear. Mindar could not understand most of it; but Dakan smiled weakly, his eyes rolled back, and his body slumped visibly. His wife stopped singing and sat up. Tears flowed down her face freely for several seconds before she buried her face in her hands and began sobbing. Mindar looked up at Sereline. She, too, was crying and shaking as she tried to suppress her tears with the heels of her hands. Lutaka sat on a stone behind Sereline. Phonda and Dolar stood behind him. Mindar could see Lutaka's lip quivering.

They waited and wept together for the death of Dakan and his son, the husband and the only child of Hannahoruan, who sat before them and cried without shame for her loss. For half an hour no one moved. Mindar listened and watched, helpless and overwhelmed with the grief of the others around him. He wondered about death. He wondered about the senselessness of what had happened. He wondered why it had taken so long to get help, and he wondered about Dakan, and his suffering and what it meant. He searched in his vorn for answers, but there were none. It made him angry; it made him sad—sad for their loss and angry at the way it happened.

Visha'andar was the first to speak. "It is time to go," he said. "Mindar, get the map."

In all the turmoil of their imprisonment in the cave and the drama of their release, Mindar had forgotten the map. It lay where Dakan had put it three days before, covered with blood, sand and ashes. The box lay upside down at the edge of the stream, half in the water. Mindar picked it up and shook the water off.

He was not sure what to do with the map, so he took it to the stream and dipped the corner of it in the water. The filth washed away, yet the map did not even seem wet, so he plunged it in the stream to wash away the blood and grit. The remarkable substance of the map was unaffected by the abuse it had endured, and he didn't even have to dry it as he folded it into its box.

"Shouldn't we build cremation fires?" Erinshava asked.

"We cannot do that here," said Visha'andar. "We carry the bodies with us until we are safe." The gentle urgency of his voice refused disobedience. He waved his huge hand and spoke in the original language, and two of the warriors broke from the circle. "I need four blankets," he continued.

Mindar pulled his blanket from his pack, and Lutaka, Phonda and Dolar followed suit. When the warriors returned, they carried four saplings, stripped down to make stretcher poles. They quickly swaddled each body in a blanket, then wrapped it with another. Thus bound and secured between two saplings, each body could be easily lifted and carried by two people using the pole ends.

Visha'andar faced the group. "We travel in the dark, for it is several hours until daylight. The road is behind me, four hundred paces over the hill," he said, waving his hand toward it. "When we get to the road, the warriors will spread out." He looked at the others. "You remain close. The enemy will regroup and return. We must be ready, and we must not fear. Come, let us go."

Four warriors stepped forward, lifted the poles effortlessly to their shoulders, and started off first, with Dakan, then Banja, flanked by torch bearers. Erinshava, her arm around Hannahoruan's waist, walked with her right behind the body of her son. Lutaka followed with Phonda and Dolar close behind him, and Sereline and Mindar walked at the rear. They had gone about twenty paces when Sereline took Mindar's hand and moved in close beside him.

Mindar looked down at her eyes. They still shone with moisture in the flickering torchlight. The tears continued to flow, silently washing her vorn of fear and anger.

"What happened?" Mindar whispered after they had ascended the low shoulder of the road.

She looked up into his eyes and shook her head. They walked in silence in the eerie light of the four torches, without the sounds of the horses to which they had grown accustomed. The quiet tread of many feet murmured as they moved steadily through the dark woods. The Eladrim warriors surrounded the group, each a match for ten men, yet they remained vigilant and stern, aware of some threat that Mindar could barely comprehend.

No one spoke. Whether it was respect, fear, sadness or anger didn't matter, for each bore the tragedy in a different way. Sereline walked close beside Mindar, her right hand in his left and her left hand on his forearm, as if she would not let go. Occasionally Mindar could feel her hands trembling as if some unseen foe shook her vorn and the shaking rose to the surface unexpectedly. She did not let go until they stopped to rest at a stream that crossed the road.

Visha'andar unrolled a sack of thin wafers. He laid them out on the cloth they had been rolled in, and raised his hands and eyes to the sky before passing them out. Each got two. Mindar was famished after two days without food, and as Visha'andar handed them to him, his hunger surged. "Eat them slowly," the giant warned. "They are sufficient to the greatest hunger. They are the gift of Mah'Eladra."

Mindar took his advice and nibbled at the first piece. It had an odd texture, with layers that flaked off and crumbled at the slightest touch.

It tasted of honey with a hint of some elusive spice that reminded him of cinnamon.

"Eat slowly, friends," Visha'andar said again, "and drink freely from the stream."

Mindar nibbled and drank and drank and nibbled. "What is it?" he asked.

"It has no name," Visha'andar responded.

"No name. No name at all," echoed Vakandar from his perch on Visha'andar's shoulder where he was preening his feathers.

Mindar continued nibbling. "Thanks for finding us in the cave," he said to Vakandar at length.

Vakandar stopped preening and cocked his head so he could see Mindar. "Dirty cave," he said. "Nasty cave!" Mindar was thankful for Vakandar's presence. The raven seemed immune to the sadness and fear that surrounded them, living his life by rules that Mindar would never understand, simple rules that had no relation to the vorns of men.

Mindar continued watching the raven as he ate his wafers. By the time he had finished the first one, he felt he had eaten almost enough. By the time he was halfway through the second, he was quite satisfied. He looked around. Everyone else had stopped eating also.

"Whatever you have not eaten, I must collect," Visha'andar said as he stooped in front of Erinshava. She hesitated, then dropped what was left into the cloth bag from which it had come. Everyone did the same. "Drink one more time, and we must go," he said when he had finished collecting the pieces. The strange bread strengthened Mindar and satisfied his hunger, and the warmth and brilliance of the morning sun brought a fresh awakening of his vorn.

As they traveled north, the land became more open, and they began to see signs of cultivation. Small houses, nestled into the remaining clumps of trees between the fields, were a welcome sight to travelers who, with the exception of Fazdeen, had seen nothing but wilderness for nearly a month.

Sereline stayed close by him as they marched along, still surrounded by the Eladrim guard, ever silent and vigilant. It was midmorning before she spoke. Her hushed voice was timid, and her eyes focused somewhere over the edge of the world. "I followed Erinshava—not sure why," she started. "Banja found us later." She paused and Mindar waited. "I don't know how Erinshava knew, but she was right. We saw you leave, and we saw the NarEladra come—materializing one by one, as if summoned by something. We saw them go after you."

"Where were you?"

"Erinshava led us to a small hill overlooking the road. We could see everything—almost…when they disappeared, we headed east, along the wall of Fazdeen. I begged her to go back. She said we needed help...we were no match for the NarEladra.

"By nightfall we had come to a high hill, the top of which was bare rock. She built a fire on the highest point. For two days, she sat by the fire and kept it burning. She would not leave. She pleaded with the Deep Sky.

"Finally, in the late afternoon of the third day—before we came to find you, Visha'andar appeared." She looked over at Mindar for the first time. "I had never seen how the Eladra come and go, that strange hiss, the faint light. They talked, but I could not understand what they said.

"Visha'andar disappeared and when he returned, all these came with him, along with the other two."

"Who were they?" Mindar asked.

"I am not sure. I think they are Eladrim princes. They are far more powerful...we walked all the rest of the afternoon and into the night to find you. We walked right past the cave where you were hidden. Then—" Sereline paused. Mindar could feel her trembling, and he squeezed her hand.

"Erinshava and I stayed behind. Banja went with the warriors..."

"What were the explosions and the white lights?" he asked.

"I don't know," she said in a whisper as she stared to the horizon. "The princes did something...then there was a lot of fighting—Banja was killed. There were seagulls everywhere...screaming, swirling. The Eladra—and the NarEladra—fight with swords. When they die, they vanish." She stopped talking and they walked on. She was holding Mindar's hand tightly.

"What happened to Dakan, do you know?" He tried to keep his voice low enough so the others would not hear.

Sereline stared straight ahead, her lips contorted in an effort to hold back her tears. She nodded but said nothing. They walked on, her entire vorn bound to the pain of what she had seen. "He was...the gulls were...they were eating him." Tears rolled down her cheeks. "His stomach." She wiped the tears with the sleeve of her tunic. "It's...it's a ritual...a torture invented by the NarEladra." She shuddered, and her grip on his hand tightened further as she sniffed and wiped her eyes again.

"We are safe now," Mindar said with as much hope as he could.

Sereline continued as if she had not heard. "I don't understand why it took so long for help to come..." She looked at Mindar suddenly. "Why were you in the cave?"

Mindar explained what had happened.

"Dakan was alone with the NarEladra for three days?!" Her eyes flashed from sadness to anger.

"Nearly. We were helpless...and he seemed to know what he was doing, as if he were protecting us with his own life."

Sereline was silent. Mindar looked up from their conversation. A farmer, not a hundred paces from the road, had stopped plowing and was watching their progress. Mindar wondered what he thought. It was a glorious day. The sun warmed the earth and surrounded them with the odors of the hay and mustard flowers from the patches of yellow carpet on either side. High above them, in the blue vastness of the cloudless sky, Vakandar circled slowly. He stayed with them until nightfall, carving his invisible spiral into the door to the Deep Sky.

☩

There is no way to hide a smithy.

Timmaneaus

Valradicca had built his smithy outside the walls of Kinvara, on the rim of the circle of dwellings that surrounded the city. Visha'andar seemed to know exactly where it was, and by the late afternoon on the second day of traveling, Mindar heard the ring of his anvil before they came around the bend in the road, allowing him to see the shop.

Visha'andar hailed him from the road when the hammer stopped, and he appeared at the door for a moment, then vanished. He emerged from the smithy running as he wiped his hands on his apron. He was tall and thin with broad shoulders and arms that looked disproportionately long. A shock of gray hair made him look considerably older than the twenty-five years he claimed for his age, and his black eyes made Mindar think of Vakandar. They were deep set and penetrating and gave Mindar the sense that he seldom blinked.

Hannahoruan ran to meet him, throwing her arms around him as they met. They embraced for a moment before she broke away and led him by the hand to meet the rest of the group. "This is Valradicca," she said. "He is a fine blacksmith and an old friend." She introduced each of them briefly. Valradicca bowed as each name was spoken, his intense gaze penetrating each in turn. "And this is Visha'andar, Erinshava's guardian, who saved our lives from the NarEladra."

"NarEladra? Where?" he asked.

"They were waiting for us at the northern gate of Fazdeen," said Lutaka. "We barely escaped. Two of our number were killed."

Glancing at the two bodies, he said, "I see that. Do I know them?" His voice was inflected with a soft accent that was new to Mindar.

Lutaka glanced at Hannahoruan before he spoke. "It's Dakan—and his son, Banja."

Valradicca buried his face in his huge hands for a moment, took a deep breath and looked up at Hannahoruan. The strength that she possessed to restrain her grief at that moment was something that Mindar could not understand at the time. She looked the smith in the eyes. "We would not dishonor them by cremating them in the wilds," she said without breaking, "and we were in danger of another attack by the NarEladra, so we brought them here to see if you will help."

Valradicca bowed again. "It brings honor to me to cremate two from the stem of Rizarand. We will cremate them tonight in the orchard by the river. Let me tend to my fire, then I will help." He looked at Lutaka. "There is a clearing by the river down this path." He swung around and motioned to the right of the smithy. "Take the bodies of our friends there. There is plenty of wood for the fires there also. I will join you presently."

Valradicca turned back toward his smithy. The procession filed onto the path to the river, their grief and the burden of death lightened by the efficient hospitality of their new friend, the blacksmith Valradicca.

✠

Death is inevitable, but the consequences of death are not.

Pratoraman
The Middle Way

"What are you thinking?" Sereline asked as she and Mindar gathered wood for the fires.

"I was wondering about death," Mindar answered. He carried an armload of branches gathered from the bank of the river, and they were headed back to where Lutaka and Valradicca were building the pyres for the cremations.

Sereline nodded but said nothing.

"It's different here," Mindar continued.

"Where?"

"Here! This place—this time. Death is different." Many thoughts flooded through his mind, and he was not sure where to start. They dropped their loads of wood on the ground near the pyres that Lutaka and Valradicca were building.

As they walked back toward the river, Mindar tried to start again. "I have never seen a cremation," he confessed. "In Vindarill, cremation is something that everyone is aware of, but few people ever get to see."

"What do they do?" Sereline was genuinely surprised.

"Well, when someone dies, their body is taken away and incinerated—for health reasons, I think. It's considered a distasteful and morbid task, given to thugs and ruffians who know nothing of and care little about the deceased. So cremation is reduced to a vulgar formality." Mindar paused to see if Sereline had anything to say. She was listening, her eyes looking far away across the river where the deepening blue sky of twilight crept toward them.

"In the higher ranks of society it's a little different," Mindar continued. "There is some sort of ceremony, but I think that's because they have the money to do it, and it's more a display of wealth than anything else. Among the Sessashians, as far as I know, cremation has a special significance, but it might just be another one of the rituals they keep.

"But it's different here," he said, "because it is held in high honor. Here, death seems to have a purpose—it is accepted as part of life—people know they will die; and the inevitability of death gives them reason to find purpose in their life, and even in their death." Another armload of wood was ready for the pile, and they headed back to unload their burden.

"Where you come from—people don't have a reason to live?" Sereline was staring at Mindar.

"I don't think they think about it that way," he responded, "but in Vindarill, the culture, the way we lived, reduced death to some sort of thing that everyone feared and no one wanted to face. We were taught to sweep death aside in our minds in the hope that, if we did not face it, it might go away."

"They teach that?"

"No, not exactly, but..." Mindar realized that he did not know why it was that way; it just was. It was possible that not everyone was like this, but he could not remember ever meeting anyone who had the purpose and direction of the people who surrounded him now. "I think it's more that the things they do teach offer very little worth really living for. That leaves people with nothing worth dying for," he said. "Life is reduced to making sure you have enough money to live on and trying to improve your position in society. This haunts the shadows of their vorns, giving them a false sense that by continuing to do so, they will escape death and live forever."

"I don't think I would like Vindarill," said Sereline.

Mindar looked over at her, expecting more, but there was no more. Mindar wondered if he could like Vindarill again. He wondered whether he ever really liked Vindarill or whether, having known nothing different, he had just accepted his place in it and, for the same reasons he had just given Sereline, had never lifted his eyes to look beyond it.

"What did Valradicca mean, 'the stem of Rizarand'?" Mindar asked.

"I'm not sure," Sereline confessed, "but apparently, Dakan was in the Rizarand Chain; and that would mean that Banja, as his son, was also from Rizarand."

"But what is Rizarand?"

Sereline looked up, puzzled. She opened her mouth and then hesitated before she spoke. "There is an ancient legend that the anthara, who is to come, will come through the lineage of the great prophet Rizarand. No one knows why that I know of, nor do most people take stock in it or know who is in the chain. It is unusual to find someone who claims this heritage. If it is true, then this stem is broken with the death of Banja."

They continued gathering wood. Behind them, the sun dipped low over the orchard as the armloads of wood were slowly transformed into the shoulder-high pyres needed for the cremations. They continued to talk about the meaning of life and the purpose of death. When the last armload of wood had been gathered and the sun slipped below the rim of the horizon behind them, Sereline took Mindar's hand. They stood staring out over the river toward the east.

"What is that star called?" Mindar asked, pointing to the first star that had appeared in the sky.

"That is Arathan," Sereline said. "It is the eastern star."

"Eastern star?"

"At this time of year, it rises in the east. It is the brightest blue star in the sky, and there is one day each year when it rises directly east at the same instant that Asolara sets."

"The day of Arathandar?"

"Yes."

"I have heard the name, but never knew why it was called that," Mindar confessed. They stood still for a long time, watching the sky darken as other stars began to appear. "I think that should be my star," Mindar said at length.

"It is a good choice," Sereline said as she squeezed his hand. "I think we had better get back to the smithy."

Mindar nodded and turned to lead the way. Sereline followed, her hand resting gently in his as she walked beside him.

✠

Should we grieve or should we shout for joy when a noble man dies?

Mirradach
The Tiger in the Tree

Mindar faced the slow, wide river, surrounded by the orchard that decorated its bank, redolent of the sweet scent of apple trees midway through fruiting. He stood before the two huge stacks of wood, ceremonially laid with the bodies flat on their backs on the top, their faces and feet uncovered and facing skyward, the rest wrapped neatly in white linen. The contrast of the white, supine figures, nearly at the height of Mindar's eyes, and the dark wood, stacked vertically in a steep pyramid, lent a sense of awe to the setting.

The sun had set several hours before, and the sky above them shone with the brilliant summer constellations. Neither Tal nor Meekar were up to dim their majesty. Miseratta, kneeling to draw her water somehow reminded him of Hannahoruan, and straight ahead over the river, the twin horses of Elgatora galloped side by side, speeding toward them to carry the vorns of Dakan and Banja into the Infinite. The only other illumination came from the ring of torches held by the Eladrim warriors who had stayed with them and formed the greater part of the ring of beings surrounding the fires.

His eyes filled with tears. He thought about Dakan and what had happened: his torture at the hands of his NarEladrim captors, and his stubborn insistence to yield his own life to save Mindar and the others; then fighting for his life in those last moments when help was available, and finally yielding to death in the arms of his wife.

Mindar looked over at Hannahoruan, who held a single torch. As next of kin to the deceased, it was her honor to light the fires that would send them to the Deep Sky. The entire party waited for her to initiate. While they waited, Mindar thought about Banja, the last in that line of Rizarand, the ancient and honored lineage through whom would come the anthara. In the bold effort to save his father, he had cared less about his own life. Mindar struggled to remember fragments of history from school in Vindarill about the Rizarand Chain, unbroken from the prophet Rizarand to the anthara. Mindar's tears flowed again as he looked at the broken stem of the Rizarand branch lying on two biers before him.

Somewhere in these thoughts, he suddenly remembered the old man. He must have twitched involuntarily, for Sereline squeezed his hand. He wondered if the old man's death at his hand had been as senseless as Dakan's death among the NarEladra. Something gnawed Mindar deep inside. Had the man been cremated with honor in a Sessashian ritual or thrown on the truck and namelessly incinerated in the death furnaces of Vindarill? Maybe he had died nobly, sitting in his chair with the map in front of him as Dakan had died, with a great purpose to which Mindar would have been blind at the time. Perhaps his death had saved the lives of other unseen people as Dakan's had just saved his.

Here in the orchard as Mindar faced the pyres where two men that

he barely knew lay dead, he was suddenly overwhelmed with the pres-
ence and the realness of death and the incredible brevity of his own life.
The only movement was the flickering of the torches in the still night air.
It was as if the world had stopped and everything was dead except for
fire; the fire that would carry the bodies of death high into the Deep Sky.
The tears continued to flow down his cheeks as he waited in the stillness.

He looked back to the pyres in front of him as Hannahoruan bent
to light the fires. A single torch, set to the base of each pyre, ignited the
twin inferno that engulfed the bodies and forced everyone to move back
from the intense heat. Sereline squeezed his hand again. It was a simple
and gentle gesture, affirming that life was real and worthwhile amid the
grief and that grief was part of life.

As they stood together and watched the roaring fire shoot into the
dark Tessalindrian sky, he wondered about Minxa. Where was he
tonight? Was he rejoicing in newfound friendships or despairing in fear
and self-pity? Mindar shuddered as he thought about it, and then he
wept again. The hot tears drew a fine line between the deep grief and
loss of friends and the profound joy of understanding life in a way he
would never have understood it without their deaths. It was the same as
the fine lines between the fantasy of legends, the truth made alive by
death, and the prophetic promise of life in the face of inevitable death.

PART II

1° Descending Darkness 1°

Imagine any blade you can,
But not a blade to harm a man...

Timanneaus

The odor of the smoldering smithy filled Mindar's senses as he stood beside the forge that Valradicca had built fifty years before, now exposed to the full sun for the first time. There was nothing left, except the standing posts of the wooden structure and the iron, most of which was buried in ashes. He was facing east toward the old orchard. Its gnarly trunks and fresh leaves dripped with dew that sparkled like diamonds in the newly risen sun. Mindar could almost see the clearing where they had cremated the old Pistisine, Dakan, and his son, Banja, when he first arrived in Kinvara nearly thirty-seven years earlier. Above him, three seagulls wheeled and called to one another in the otherwise empty sky.

He had never seen gulls in Kinvara, and they reminded him of the distant prophecy from the keeper at Ordrathan that Lutaka had told them years before at the Crown. Mindar had pondered it often in recent years. Lutaka had been king now for nearly forty years, and in all those years Mindar's research as court historian to the king had never uncovered even a mention of the name "Mankar." With many glorious years of leadership behind him, Lutaka did not seem eager to be concerned with the final words of the prophecy.

"What do you suppose happened?" asked Kalarra, Mindar's personal assistant and liaison to the king. Mindar was not ready to answer. He did not know the answer, so he looked up into Kalarra's eyes. The fear there was real, and if Mindar's suspicions were correct, there was a good reason. He had pulled a dagger from the ashes and held it in his hand, and as he thought through an answer, he flipped it over. It was made completely of steel, and though blackened by the fire, it was intact.

"This is not something Valradicca would have made," Mindar said, "or even had in his shop."

"And?"

"I am guessing it was dropped by someone," Mindar said as he stared at the dagger. He could not place its familiar image in his memory, from somewhere long ago, crowding the edge of his consciousness.

"You think someone was here?" Kalarra asked. He was a heavy young man, strong as a bull with broad shoulders and arms as thick as Mindar's legs. His brown moustache hung down over his upper lip in such a way that it wiggled curiously when he spoke, and his coal black eyes always seemed to be moving, even when he was looking directly at something.

"I do not think this was an accident," Mindar said as he kicked at the heap of tongs that lay strewn on the floor. A cloud of ashes billowed into the air and floated lazily toward the river. "For one, we have not seen Val or his son, and his wife was found dead in their house this morning."

Three soldiers had picked their way through the ashes of the collapsed building, and the lieutenant saluted as he stopped in front of Mindar. He was one of Lutaka's messengers, but Mindar did not know his name. "Lutaka requests your presence in the great hall," he said smartly. "Please come with us."

Mindar nodded and weighed the dagger in his hand. As he debated whether to take it or leave it behind where he found it, that haunting sense of the familiar flooded over him again, so he carefully tucked it into one of the folds of his tunic. The soldier saluted again and turned to lead Mindar away from the smoldering remains of his friend's smithy.

It was about a mile from the smithy to the fortress where he would meet with Lutaka in the great hall. The road was familiar enough so that Mindar hardly remembered any details along the way. He had been to Val's smithy so many times; and the discussions, the thoughts, the friendship with the smith were so keen that memories of the road consisted of details of their relationship rather than the rows of low houses that lined its turns. This time was no different.

It seemed impossible to Mindar that Val could have died in the inferno, but if he had not, then he would not have gone anywhere else. The death of his wife was equally disturbing. It had been simple and quick, a single sword thrust through her heart with no apparent resistance. There had been much talk lately of a growing evil, but from his inquiries into the stories, all seemed to be hearsay and nothing had been substantiated. Alaavar and his generals had been put in charge of the investigations and reported that nothing of substance had happened.

Alaavar was an odd selection. Mindar had never liked the man, but could find no reason for Lutaka to dismiss him from his service. Alaavar had risen through the ranks in Lutaka's army, showing himself unsurpassed in his loyalty, courage and ambition; and Mindar had to confess that he did not understand Alaavar very well. The whole mindset of a man who carried a sword and was willing to use it on other men was something that revolted him. He was thankful on many occasions that such persons existed, but he did not feel much in common with them.

There were other differences between Alaavar and other soldiers. He had a focus and drive that showed in his eyes and surfaced in language that was a step beyond Mindar's comfort. The generals he had collected around him were equally unsettling—dark men, who were willing to follow him without question, having on numerous occasions proven themselves ruthless and clever, and unswerving in their allegiance to Lutaka.

Lutaka had confided to Mindar that he was uncomfortable with Alaavar's choices for his generals, but they did their work so efficiently and thoroughly that Lutaka did not challenge Alaavar about them. Erinshava had once told Mindar that Alaavar's men's ambition would never allow them time to know peace. Mindar never would have thought of it that way, but she was probably right.

An old rhyme, that Mindar believed was Mooriman in origin, kept rising to the surface of his consciousness:

"A short sword for the soldier boy,
A long sword for the king,
A wrong sword in an idle hand
Is quite a fearsome thing."

Mindar could not remember the context, but somewhere in the next few lines he thought there was something about a dagger. It played in and out of his thoughts, lurking somewhere in the shadows of his awareness.

✠

The best decisions are made in the counsel of many advisors.

Old Mythinian Saying

The gates of the fortress were shut when Mindar and the soldiers arrived. "I have never seen them closed during the day," Mindar commented, as they swung open slowly before them.

"There is something afoot, Your Honor," said the lieutenant.

"What is it?" Mindar asked.

"I do not know, Sir, I was just sent to find you and bring you here."

Mindar heard the gates close behind him as they moved up the great central avenue of the fortress, passing the guardhouses and soldiers' barracks that lined the corridor leading to the great hall in the center of the fortress. There was activity everywhere. The thoroughfare was buzzing. Soldiers milled about in full battle dress save their helmets, and the army of attendants to the various commanders swarmed back and forth, carrying messages, weapons and armor.

"Are we going to war?" Mindar wondered aloud to Kalarra.

"I do not know, Sir."

A line of soldiers stood at attention on either side of the stairs ascending to the great hall. They watched carefully as the entourage walked between them. Had he not been escorted by soldiers, Mindar was sure he would have been stopped. The massive brass doors to the hall were open, and the inside was filled with the many officials of Lutaka's court. It would have seemed like a grand occasion but for the pall of the events of the day, and Mindar felt the anxiety of the restless crowd. Certainly, the single event at Val's forge could not account for this gathering.

As chief historian for Lutaka's court, Mindar was well known, and a ripple of chatter flowed through the crowd at his entrance. He was used to this kind of attention, but the gnawing in his stomach made it uncomfortable today. The lieutenant escorted him to his seat in the semicircle of chairs surrounding Lutaka. The third chair to Lutaka's right had been his place for the nearly twenty years since Lutaka had appointed him to his position. Between Mindar and the king sat Alaavar, the general of the armies of Tessamandria, and Eulavaan, the court clerk and personal secretary to the king.

Alaavar nodded as Mindar sat down to his right, and his dark eyes flashed with peculiar intensity. He was an intense man in everything he did, and he was large in every way a person could be large. It struck

Mindar how much Alaavar reminded him of the NarEladra that had captured them as they left Fazdeen so many years before, and once Mindar noticed the similarity, he wondered why he had never seen it before. He also knew in that instant that he would never be able to rid himself of that impression.

To Mindar's right was Mazantara, the emissary from Immerland, and to her right sat the copper-skinned ambassador from Mythinia, whose name Mindar did not know. He looked across the semicircle. Erinshava's seat, the third to the left of Lutaka, was empty. When Lutaka became king, he had appointed her his chief advisor, and she was publicly positioned to be his personal attaché on matters concerning the unseen world of Mah'Eladra and related things. In reality, she was more of a personal intelligence officer. Her job was to keep him informed about the comings and goings of suspicious persons and known enemies of Tessamandria. The two areas were intimately connected in Lutaka's mind. His experience in the Crown, and the events that had followed on the way to Kinvara had given him ample insight into the connection between evil and vornal depravity.

Amidst the general hubbub of the untamed gathering, Lutaka looked over at Mindar. After nodding toward Erinshava's seat, Lutaka raised his eyebrows in a question. Mindar shrugged. He hadn't seen her for several days. Lutaka nodded back before he stood up. Two men on either side of the circle raised their long brass horns to their lips and quieted the gathering with a short fanfare.

"Residents of Kinvara," Lutaka began, "last night we experienced a vicious attack against our people by an unseen enemy. Thirty-three persons were killed in fires that erupted around the city in what we believe is a concerted effort to strike terror into the hearts of our people."

Mindar nearly gagged as a ripple of whispers swept through the crowd. Lutaka held up his hand for silence. "We do not know the perpetrators of this evil, but we will find them, and justice will be administered appropriately." He had just finished his sentence when Erinshava appeared at the edge of the semicircle, quietly making her way to her seat. Lutaka continued, "I have, gathered here, the best of my court. Together we will take measures to assure your safety and to protect this kingdom from further attack. Already, I have authorized General Alaavar to mobilize the army and provide protection for anyone needing it." Lutaka held out his hand to the general, and all eyes turned to Alaavar, who rose beside Mindar and smiled, nodding to the assembly. A roar of applause erupted from the crowd.

Lutaka held up his hand again for silence, and the applause abated. As Alaavar swept back his tunic to sit down, a dagger, tucked into the silver scabbard on his right side flashed into Mindar's view for a moment.

It seemed to be identical to the one he had found in the ashes of the smithy, and he felt for it involuntarily in the folds of his own tunic. It was still there. Whether there was any connection, Mindar did not know. At least he knew that it was not Alaavar's dagger that he had found, but the similarity was striking.

"We will hold council this very noon," Lutaka was saying as he looked around at those seated in front of the crowd, "and we will put other safeguards in place. Kinvara and its people will be made safe again. Tessamandria will stand against all such evil!" The crowd applauded, and all in the circle stood up to acknowledge the trust of the people in their king. Mindar glanced over at Erinshava. Her face was dark with foreboding and anger as if she knew something the rest of them did not.

Lutaka turned and led the procession of his court away from the crowd toward the smaller hall behind him. They walked in two rows. Erinshava was beside Mindar, but she didn't look at him or speak. He sensed that what she had to say required privacy. Alaavar was in front of Mindar, his huge frame swaying back and forth like a man with great purpose. Mindar could not imagine him as an enemy. Beneath that tunic lay the dagger, not necessarily out of place for the general of the army, but it burned Mindar's thoughts: *"A short sword for the soldier boy, A long sword for the king..."*

Mindar wondered what he should do with the dagger he had found. Something inside him convinced him that he should use great caution in revealing it. Another nagging thought was slowly convincing him that the haunting memories of the dagger were not satisfied by having seen its twin on Alaavar's belt. Perhaps he had seen it before, on Alaavar or one of the other generals, but he had seen it somewhere else; perhaps on Islag or in Karolil.

"Stations, everyone," said Lutaka. He was standing at the head of the broad oval table. Each of them had an assigned seat, which they stood behind. When all were stationed appropriately, Lutaka sat down; and each followed his lead, waiting respectfully until everyone was comfortable and quiet.

"Reports," commanded Lutaka.

Eulavaan stood and addressed the table. "It is confirmed, Sire. Thirty-three are dead—or unaccounted for, every one of them or a member of their family loyal to your throne. Kandar, retired admiral of the Vorsian fleet, his wife, his two sons, his daughter and her husband. Phonda, your friend, his wife and twin daughters. Vinarhan, the map-maker and her husband—her son cannot be found. Valradicca the bladesmith, and his wife. Their son is missing..."

Mindar had to wonder whether it was his imagination or coincidence that Alaavar shifted in his chair at the mention of Val's son. He shuddered as the list was read. Erinshava remained grim. Each on the list was someone Mindar either knew personally or had met at one time or another. The pattern was frightening. The best and the brightest, the most loyal and the most highly educated: all eliminated in a single night. Whoever was behind the murders had been very thorough.

When Eulavaan sat down in the profound stillness of the hall, no one moved for many seconds until Lutaka broke the silence. "Hardaga?"

The man to Lutaka's left stood slowly. He was the mayor of Kinvara, charged with the task of making sure the city was well run. He ran the courts as well and was appointed to administer justice and settle disputes within the city. "We are overwhelmed by what has happened, Sire. There is much fear, and there is little we can do unless we are able to find those responsible. The courts are ready. We have sought out everyone who is capable of helping, and they stand ready to do so. The resources of the city are ample for a time, and we are hoping that these events will not affect our supply lines. We stand ready." He sat down, a blank stare settling over his face as he did so.

Alaavar rose. He seemed to tower above Mindar. He brought his fist down on the table with such force that it rattled the goblets at the far end. "Never have we seen such villainy in this fair city," he growled. "We will find those whose treachery violates our trust and ruins our lives. They will be brought to justice. With your permission, Sire, my generals and I will scour this city and the outlying villages and deal with these as they deserve. The army is at my command, and we will act as soon as your word is given." He sat down, a jealous fire flickering in his eyes.

"When we have heard everyone," said Lutaka, "we will decide on a course of action. I will remind you, General, that it is the place of the courts to administer justice, but your help in finding the offenders will be appreciated." Alaavar nodded. Mindar sensed that he wanted to say more, but held his tongue. Lutaka looked to his left and nodded to Visara, the man between Hardaga and Erinshava. Visara stood, his hands resting on the table and his head down as he composed himself. He was the captain of the royal bodyguard.

"I am afraid," Visara started. "I fear that, although these events occurred outside the city wall, the perpetrators may be within the city."

Lutaka's eyes narrowed, but he held his tongue.

Visara continued, "If that is the case, then we do not have sufficient protection for the king and his family. Whoever did this is more than just one person, or even a small group. The distances between the...the fires last night and the timing of them mean that it is a concerted effort of several groups, carefully planned. Such planning speaks loudly that this is just the beginning of a larger effort."

Visara paused, as if exhausted by the weight of what he was saying. He looked down again at his hands as they still rested on the table. He was an older man, with thick graying hair and hands that looked as if they had been through a war all by themselves. A single scar ran from his right ear nearly to the tip of his chin; and his thick eyebrows, furrowed with concern, shadowed his eyes. "That all the targets of these atrocities were supporters of the king and key leaders of various disciplines essential to our strength as a nation, indicates that this is, in fact, a coup against the king—but just the beginning of it."

As Visara sat down, Alaavar shifted heavily and turned to look at Mindar. Mindar rose. He was unsure what he would say until he started. Lutaka turned his eyes to him as his hand went to his chin. He sat back in his chair, eyes narrowed in thought, listening wisely to his most trusted court members. Mindar felt the burden to be positive and truthful, more urgently than ever before.

"I visited the site of Valradicca's burned smithy this morning," Mindar said. "It is a tragedy beyond belief. Val was a friend of mine and was known to be a man of peace. The service he rendered to this kingdom was unparalleled. He had no equal in ability to make the tools that we use. He was a smith tutored by Vishortan himself, the teacher of Timmanaeus.

"These atrocities rival any that I am aware of in the history of our world, except perhaps those perpetrated by the NarEladra when they were driven from the Crown and fled to Mooriman. My fear is that what we see here is a shadow of what is to come. It is not rooted in the common pettiness, jealousies and failings of our people, but comes from an evil beyond our own natural weakness. It's driven by envy and hatred, kindled in the earliest histories of our world, and from places and times before that. It is not about this kingdom or even Tessamandria. It is about Tessalindria and who shall own her and shape the vorns and determine the destinies of her inhabitants.

"If history tells us anything, it tells us to watch carefully and to seek the larger view. We must open our eyes wide to that which is unseen, and listen intently to that which is unspoken. I do not have any answers, King Lutaka, but I know this is true, and being aware of it is the first step to knowing the answers."

When Mindar sat down, Lutaka sat forward and asked, "Are you saying that we are under attack by NarEladrim forces?"

Erinshava stood. The sudden movement and her stern countenance commanded the attention of the entire court. "I will answer that," she said. Her voice was firm and determined. "We have not seen our attackers so we do not know how they came or how they went. We only know that no one was seen, that no clue has been found at any of the sites that tie the attacks to any known enemy of the king." Mindar wondered about the blade in his tunic. It was a single clue. He found it difficult to believe it was the only one. "What Mindar Colloden has said should be considered carefully. Such villainy is not arbitrary. I have faced NarEladra before. They set their course; they stay their course, and they are relentless in pursuit of their goal. Since the rebellion of Vishtoenvar, since the desolation of the NarEl Waste, since the genocide of Mooriman, their goal is destruction of all that is good; and they have been a continual plague in our world."

When she paused, Alaavar interrupted her. "When have you faced the NarEladra?" He looked around the room with mocking eyes. "From what I know of them, no one could stand against them, particularly a woman."

Erinshava ignored the taunt. "Before the anthara comes, it is said that the world will be plunged to near destruction at their hand. One will arise from their number who will lead others, even to the point of rebellion against Vishtoenvar himself. He will nearly succeed, but will be vanquished. Out of the desolation, the anthara will rise to lead Tessamandria to new understandings and wisdom.

"The preparation necessary to fight this enemy is beyond our resources, and we must seek the help of Mah'Eladra and the Eladrim princes. They will only help us if we are united in our plea to them." Erinshava sat down. Alaavar laughed.

"Silence!" ordered Lutaka as he stood up. "We are not through hearing from the court. Mikkalt?"

Mikkalt was the magistrate for the lands immediately surrounding the city of Kinvara. His responsibilities ranged from helping manage the agricultural needs of the farmers to the development of the network of transportation that fed the city with goods from all over Tessamandria. His son, who worked for him, had died the night before in one of the attacks with his wife and two daughters. He rose slowly beside Mindar, looking from face to face around the circle with keen eyes that had seen long years of service to Lutaka. He was known for his brevity.

"If this enemy is as swift to destruction as we have seen from only one night, it will take many hands and much vigilance to know who it is. If it is as Erinshava has proposed, then there is but one hope, and that is to do as she has suggested." Mikkalt sat down and buried his face in his tired-looking hands.

The figure beside Erinshava was that of Cornavis, consult to the foreign diplomats that Lutaka had gathered from every country on Tessalindria. He wore a purple robe with gold trim that complemented his long white beard and piercing blue eyes. His gravelly voice was unmistakable in the court.

"The ambassadors from Mythinia, Tophan, Vann, Vindor, Hartana, Otalla, Werenvar and Immerland have unanimously decried this terror. They have pledged their help. Envoys are already on their way to inform the Fathers of these nations of our grief and our need for help. Fazdeen has shut its gates. No one may pass through; no one may enter. Mooriman, with whom we have, shall we say, a somewhat strained relationship, has denied any complicity in these events. The ambassadors from Dorfrand and Northstrand are not here.

"We have asked the envoys if anyone in their countries has Lonama's map and would be willing to come and help us, but we do not hold a lot of hope. Map bearers are secretive and unknown, a hard lot to track."

At the mention of the map, Mindar glanced over to Lutaka. Lutaka did not flinch. Erinshava looked his way but remained expressionless, looking back at Cornavis as he sat down. Mindar had not looked at the map in years. When he first arrived in Kinvara, he had made a habit of studying it regularly, and he learned more each time until he became proficient in its use. Over time, finding himself tied to the affairs of Kinvara, the map seemed less and less useful; he finally laid it aside. It had faded so much in his memory that it had not even occurred to him to use it in this situation until Cornavis mentioned it, but Lutaka's non-reaction and Erinshava's only slight acknowledgment warned him of their own suspicions. Much caution was in order.

All eyes turned to Lutaka as he rose to speak. His words confirmed Mindar's need for caution. "We will wait for an answer from each of the envoys, but this will take time, perhaps more than we have. I am not sure what value Lonama's map would be. Even if it is more than mere legend, the ability to gain knowledge from it is undoubtedly exaggerated.

"We have heard and seen much today. Each of you has contributed well to what we must do, but facts are scarce and emotion is high. Each of us must take what we have learned, what we have heard and sleep on it for one night. We will convene tomorrow at noon, here in this chamber.

"Alaavar. You and the generals are to gather as many facts as you can about the attacks. Try to find witnesses. Go over the sites again, and see if there is any evidence we have overlooked. Post a double guard at each gate to the city.

"Hardaga. Set the storehouses in order and have them inventoried. Any available surplus of goods in the city is to be stored. Set guards at each storehouse, but make them discrete. We do not want the people panicking. Mikkalt, if there is a surplus in the fields, bring it in. We may need it. Do your best to keep it quiet."

Lutaka paused, as if he were assessing the weight of his next state-ment. "I know that not all of you share the profound allegiance to Mah'Eladra as the esteemed Erinshava, but heed her words well. Each of you must weigh your conviction against the need of the hour, for every legend has a basis in some fact, and some undoubtedly more than oth-ers. If ever there was a time to believe your beliefs and doubt your doubts, now would be that time. We must each go to his task. Tomorrow, at noon, we will convene again; so until then, be alert, be aware, and be wise."

Leaving Lutaka's court was always less formal than entering. They filed out through the huge double doors of the halls, each preoccupied with his own thoughts. Without speaking to one another, they diverged into the square, heading to their various destinations. Mindar wanted to go home. Sereline would want to know what had happened, and he needed to speak with her.

The streets of Kinvara were narrow once one left the main roads run-ning from the gates to the central plaza, and Mindar walked quickly, dodging other people and horses and the multiplied soldiers that now populated them. He had gone several blocks when Erinshava stepped from a doorway he was passing. "Keep walking." Her voice was low. They took several paces before she spoke again. Her eyes darted about the streets, and she did not look at him. "You are in great danger," she said, tossing the words from the side of her mouth. "Meet me at the apothecary in one hour. Bring the map." Mindar had looked away, dis-tracted by some commotion down one of the side alleys to the street on which they were walking; and when he turned back, his mouth open to respond, she had vanished. He stopped and turned around, but she was nowhere to be seen.

A sinking feeling washed over Mindar, and her words seemed to echo off the pavement. *You are in great danger!* He quickened his pace, but the few blocks to his house seemed like an eternity. Everything that he encountered threatened him: the dog chewing a bone that had been thrown him from a local butcher; the children that passed him in the street, playing soldier with their wooden swords; the two soldiers that walked side by side, their swords and sataliins swinging from their belts, their shields slung across their back.

What did he have to fear? Mindar had walked these streets for almost forty years and had never had reason to fear, yet Erinshava was not an idle worrier or one given to alarms without purpose. On the sur-face, little had changed, but in the eyes of the people there was much fear.

Sereline met him at the street-gate as he swung it open. "I am glad you are here," she said as she led the way up the narrow steps to the door into their house. "I was worried that you might not come back."

"Why?" he asked. Mindar felt her agitation, so uncharacteristic of Sereline, who usually remained composed in the most desperate of situations. She sensed that he had stopped when he asked the question, and she turned at the door.

"Two soldiers came looking for you this morning; here, at the house." She pushed the door open, and he entered into the dim interior from the bright sun of the street. As Mindar pulled the door shut, she wrapped her arms around his shoulders, kissed him and laid her head on his shoulder. "Something is not right and I feel it." He felt her trembling. "I wanted to run this morning—run away—but I could not leave the girls." She looked up. "I had the same feeling I had that day when we left Fazdeen—at the gate, do you remember?"

"Awareness of danger?" Mindar looked into her eyes. They were moving back and forth rapidly. "I never had that feeling," he said, "but then, I was the one who got trapped. Listen, I have to go to Hannahoruan's. Erinshava wants me to meet her there with the map. It's urgent."

"Why the apothecary?"

"I'm not sure, but I think it's safe there."

"You haven't touched the map in years—" Her voice trailed off into a thought she did not speak.

"I know," Mindar said. She relaxed her arms on his shoulders, and he slipped past her into the main room of the house. The map was hidden under one corner of the floormat and covered by a pillow that lay on top of it. Mindar felt Sereline watching from behind him as he tossed the pillow aside and drew back the mat. When he had retrieved the ancient box and replaced the pillow, he stood up.

"What should we do while you are gone?" his wife asked. She stepped close in front of him again, laying her right hand on his forearm. Mindar opened his mouth to speak, but was interrupted by the twins as they erupted into the room. "Daddy," they yelled in unison, "have you seen all the soldiers?" Mindar knelt down as they plowed into him, nearly knocking him over.

"Yes, Serinda," he said smiling, "I have seen many soldiers today."

"We've never seen so many," Therall said, the excitement nearly choking her own words. "Come. You can see them from our window." She grabbed his hand and started pulling him toward the door to the back room where they had their beds. Serinda grabbed the other hand, and Mindar was helpless.

The girls' window faced to the east and overlooked an enormous field just inside the wall of the city. The knots of soldiers that filled the normally empty space surprised him. They stood about talking or sitting on the grass, waiting for orders. Each was fully dressed for war with his war belt and leather armor, shield, sword, lance and his sataliin on his right hip. The city did not need war, but perhaps it was inevitable. *"A short sword for the soldier boy..."* Mindar shivered.

"Look at all the soldiers, Daddy," Therall said.

"I see them," he responded.

Serinda looked up at Mindar. A wave of disappointment swept across her face. "You don't like the soldiers?"

Mindar knelt down. "No," he said, "I like the soldiers, but I do not like what it means to have so many of them."

"Why?" Therall was still holding his hand. She looked into his eyes. At ten years old, she was just old enough to have thoughtful discussions with her father.

"Do you see the swords on their belts?" he asked. "And the lances they are carrying?"

Both girls peered out the window. "Yes," they said in unison as they looked back at him.

"If they have to, the soldiers use them to hurt or even kill other people."

They stared at him blankly.

"Serinda, do you remember when you cut your finger last winter on the knife in the kitchen?"

"It hurt," she grimaced

"I remember," he said, "and there was a lot of blood, right?"

Serinda looked down at her hand and turned it over to see the scar across her right index finger.

"When soldiers cut with their swords, they cut people very badly, and they do it on purpose—to make people hurt and then die." He looked over his shoulder. Sereline was leaning against the doorframe to the bedroom with her arms folded. Fear was evident in her eyes.

"Why?" asked Therall, tugging on his hand to get his attention.

"We don't always know why," Mindar said, "but it is not right. Sometimes you fight with each other, right?"

They both nodded.

"You fight about silly things that seem very important when you are fighting, right?"

They nodded again, but with more skepticism.

"When adults fight, it seems very important and it is very dangerous. Many people get hurt, and many of them do not know why. Sometimes many men die before it is over." He stood up and looked out the window. "I hope that does not happen now," he added.

"Come, girls," said Sereline, "we have to go to the market, and your father has to run an important errand."

✠

The map only shows that which is, which includes the past.

Colloran
The Outworlds

The half-mile walk through the streets of Kinvara to Hannahoruan's apothecary was routine. Except for the abundance of armed soldiers that wandered about, ready but not yet called up, there was nothing noteworthy. The twisting canyons between the two-story dwellings had been warmed by the late morning sun. The familiar odors of the city swirled around Mindar and shifted with the light breeze that changed direction at each intersection. Long shafts of light angled past the tops of the buildings, leaving deep shadows under the awnings of the shops and in the inset doorways that lined his path.

Hannahoruan's shop was on the northeastern side of the city, not far from the eastern gate. She had opened there shortly after they had arrived in the city, and after thirty-seven years had made the reputation of running the finest shop in the city. It was small, but organized in such a way that any sense of its smallness disappeared when one entered. She had never named it, and the carved sign that hung over the street on an iron bracket read simply, "Fine Herbs." The door was open, but as Mindar crossed the threshold, he paused to let his eyes adjust to the dark interior. The familiar potpourri of the apothecary filled his nose.

"Uncle Mindar!" Gayan's distinctly lyrical voice greeted Mindar from the shadows as the young man emerged from the doorway at the back of the shop. "Welcome to our shop."

"It's always good to be here," said Mindar as he smiled up at the tall man before him. "Is your mother in?"

"She is upstairs," he said waving his hand and pointing toward the ceiling. "And the Honorable Erinshava is with her. I think they are expecting you."

"Yes, I believe so. May I?" Mindar said as he pointed toward the stairs at the back of the shop.

"Of course." Gayan smiled. He had the kind of grace and fluidity in manner that was rare in a man. When he spoke, his arms and face moved so that one had the sense that he did not need to speak at all, and the penetrating blue-gray eyes he had inherited from his mother left Mindar feeling that he knew what Mindar was about to say before he himself did.

Mindar turned as he reached the doorway at the foot of the stairs.

"Gayan?" Gayan looked up from the chair he had seated himself in.

"Do you remember an old rhyme—Mooriman, I think—that starts with 'A short sword for the soldier boy'?"

Gayan looked up, as if thinking. "...A long sword for the king, A wrong sword in an idle hand is quite a fearsome thing."

"Do you remember any other lines—something about a dagger?"

Gayan's hand went to his chin and he pursed his lips. "Vaguely," he said. "I am sure that I can find it."

"That would be helpful," Mindar said as he turned to the stairs again. "By the way," he said over his shoulder, "I think it would be best if no one knows we are here."

"I know."

Mindar started up the stairs. Hannahoruan had raised this young man single-handedly, and his bearing was a testimony to her strength and goodness. He was the son of Dakan, born seven months after his father's death outside the gates of Fazdeen, and he bore the strength and clarity of his father. His mother had taught him everything he knew, which was considerable; and now he ran the shop while Hannahoruan traveled, searching for her wares. She had been away for some time, and only recently had returned to Kinvara. Mindar hadn't seen her in months.

She rose as Mindar entered the small kitchen, hugged him and kissed his neck as she always did. "It is good to see you well, Master Mindar," she said. Erinshava was right behind her. When the greetings were done, Hannahoruan beckoned him to the table. When she did so he noticed, as he always did at some point in her presence, that she had not seemed to age since the day they met at the southern gate to Fazdeen. Asking her about this had never seemed appropriate, so Mindar simply marveled and sat down.

"Drink this." Hannahoruan shoved a mug of hot tea in front of him. "You will need it."

Mindar looked up at Erinshava who was sitting across the table from him. She sipped from a similar mug. She was dressed the way she had been when he first met her in the woods on Islag: dressed for action. He had not seen her that way for years, and she stared back at him over the rim of her mug. Erinshava had aged, but it was hard for Mindar to believe she was nearly sixty years old. Fine gray hair graced her temples, and her face was set with age in such a way that one knew she was not young, but she did not look old either. Her eyes sparkled keenly, and her body did not show any of the stoop that age often brought to people much younger than she.

"Did you bring the map, Mindar?" asked Hannahoruan.

Mindar reached into his tunic and slid the thin box out of its hiding place. "I have not looked at it in years," he confided as he cautiously lifted the lid and set it aside on the tabletop. "It did not even occur to me to look at it until it was mentioned this morning in court." The map unfolded easily onto the flat table between them.

"Can we find out what happened last night?" Erinshava asked.

Mindar found himself staring at the map in wonder, its infinite detail spread before him in sepia tones, the warm brown lines and shadows that carried the information for the entire planet buried somewhere, waiting to be revealed. His eyes scanned the border. It was familiar but remote. He tried to think back to the last time he had used it, but he could not remember. He looked up.

Hannahoruan was staring down at the map, her hands and forearms shoved uncomfortably under the table, and a peculiar wariness shaded her eyes. She looked up at him. "Go ahead," she said.

"Is everything all right?" Mindar asked.

"Yes—go ahead and try to find out what happened."

Something was wrong, but Mindar reasoned that he would not find out without addressing the map. He dropped his eyes back to the border and moved his hand, touching the circles that allowed him to control the map. He spread the view until it encompassed all the area around Kinvara and included Val's smithy, then drew the smithy to the center of the map. Then almost as quickly, he drew it down so that the area around the smithy filled the map. Everything came back to him quickly, and within a minute, he had scrolled back the time to the night before.

"What time did the attacks start?" asked Hannahoruan.

"I heard that the fire started a couple hours after dark," said Erinshava. "Can you get to that time?"

"I think so," he said as he pointed to the small sundial in the upper right corner. It showed the location of the sun relative to the current map time. He worked backward to sunset and then started moving slowly forward in time, watching for the appearance of any visitors to the smithy. Mindar looked up at Hannahoruan. She wore the same odd expression. "You're sure everything is all right?"

"I have never seen the map this close."

"You've seen it before?" Mindar asked in surprise.

"I saw it a couple of times before Dakan died, remember?"

"Right." he nodded and turned his attention back to the map.

"I have seen other copies, but not this close." Her tone of voice carried a strange awe, a reverence that made Mindar uncomfortable.

"Have you ever used one?" he asked absently as he moved the map's view slightly to include the road approaching the smithy from the fortress gate.

"I cannot touch it, but I can watch."

Mindar was about to ask why when Erinshava gasped. "Look!" She was pointing excitedly at the road west of the smithy. He had scrolled forward to the appearance of eleven dark smudges. One of the discoveries he had made about the map in the years of studying was the ability of it to track time actively. He reached over and touched the circle that held a small glyph of an hourglass. The map sprang into motion, almost as if it was alive.

"They are moving too fast for foot soldiers," he said.

"Horsemen?" Hannahoruan had spoken their thoughts.

Mindar nodded. "Seems so."

Erinshava pointed to the smithy. "Must be Val and Narahu."

"Working late?"

"Or there to meet someone," he mused.

"Can we tell who it is?" asked Erinshava.

"If the map can tell us, I have not figured it out," he said as they watched the figures file into the smithy together. Five entered, the other four remained outside.

"He must have been expecting them," said Hannahoruan, "or at least he knew them…"

The conversation dropped as they sat, eyes fixed on the map. There were no details about what was actually happening. At one point the four figures outside the smithy moved quickly inside, and several of those inside went out the back door. Then all but one went out the front again. One of the figures in back moved hurriedly to the river, and others from the front of the smithy moved in pursuit. "It's like watching ants," he said. "Something is happening, but I could not tell you what."

"When do you suppose that the fire starts?" asked Erinshava.

"Maybe it is already burning," said Hannahoruan. "I wonder if we could even tell."

Mindar thought back to when they had watched the inn burning from the top of the northern gate of the Harhazian wall. He was about to move the map when Erinshava spoke. "Look," she said, "in the middle of the river. He must be swimming. There are three now…"

"And the others. On the bridge," Hannahoruan remarked. "And look, the smithy…"

Mindar moved the map in close. Pieces of the smithy's rectangle were disappearing. "The fire," said Erinshava.

The small smudge of the being in the smithy faded with the last vestiges of the smithy. They sat dumbfounded. "It must have been…Valradicca," whispered Erinshava.

Mindar nodded in disbelief at what he was seeing, his eyes transfixed on the spot where a life had been removed before him. An eerie chill swept over his shoulders and down his spine. He looked back toward the bridge, over to the road, and then down the river. "They're all gone," he said in disbelief. "Where did they go; what happened?"

"Look, there. There is one left." Erinshava put her finger down on the map. Downstream and nearly off the map, a lone smudge was moving east from the riverbank.

Hannahoruan muttered something.

"What?" Mindar asked.

"It's Narahu," she said.

"The boy?" asked Erinshava. "How do you know?"

Mindar looked up at Hannahoruan. There were tears in her eyes, and she was staring up at the ceiling of the small kitchen. "I know it is him. He has a hard road ahead of him, but he will find his way. Mah'Eladra will lead him now."

"Can't we help?" asked Erinshava.

"No, we have much to do here." Hannahoruan's eyes were bright, the vestige of tears remaining only in the corners. "We have to look at the other sites that were attacked last night; but before we do, can you back up and see where these marauders came from?"

Mindar moved the map back in time, watching the small sundial in the corner, and positioning the time so that it was earlier. He started the map moving forward. No one spoke. They did not have to wait long. The small smudges of the approaching riders appeared on the road, fading into view in a matter of seconds.

"NarEladra!" said Hannahoruan.

Mindar looked up at Erinshava. Her face was grim. "You were right."

She nodded at his acknowledgment.

"And that would explain what happened after the fire—when they all disappeared again."

"We need to see what happened to Kandar and the map maker," said Erinshava.

"Do you know where he lived?" Mindar asked.

"Kandar lived in West Barren, on the left of the road leading to the sea."

"How far out?" He was already moving the map.

"Two miles from the Westgate. Perhaps a bit more."

Hannahoruan sat still, her hands shoved under the table, her bright eyes mesmerized by the shifting landscape of the map. Mindar wondered what she was thinking, but dared not ask. He focused on the map, moving it along as Erinshava guided him along the road until they came to the junction where Kandar's house had stood. The map moved back in time at the touch of his fingertips. "Same time?" he asked.

"I am not sure," said Erinshava. "It was after dark, but we do not know how long after."

"After dark," Mindar murmured as he watched the sundial inching back the time increments on the map. "There, about an hour after." Four small blurs of light appeared in the large house.

Erinshava bent low over the map. "No sign of trouble yet, can you move it forward."

He touched the map, working it forward in time. It was sometime after midnight that they suddenly appeared. Seven smudges approaching and encircling the house. He worked it back. It was nearly the same: the sudden appearance of the beings, apparent panic in the house, and then the fracturing of the house and the disappearance of the smudges that were inside. This was followed by the flight of the terrorists and their sudden fading.

It was the same for Phonda and his wife and twin daughters, and for Vinarhan and her husband. One at a time they traced them all down. Several of them seemed to happen simultaneously. Erinshava sat back against the chair, her arms folded across her chest and her blank stare leveled at the map.

Mindar felt equally perplexed. "How does one fight something like this?" he ventured.

"We need a lot of help," Erinshava murmured without moving her eyes from the map, "and we need a clue about what we need to do."

"I have one clue," Mindar said.

Erinshava raised her eyes to meet Mindar's. He felt Hannahoruan looking at him. He reached into his tunic and drew the dagger from its hiding place, laying it on the table beside the map. Erinshava leapt from her chair. "Where did you get it?" Her eyes were wide with astonishment.

"From the ashes at Val's smithy."

"May I touch it?" she asked. Mindar shrugged and waved his hand to let her know she could. "Val never made blades like this—he never made weapons."

"I think that's true, but perhaps it's just an assumption we have made," Mindar said.

"No I am quite sure he didn't," she answered. "He told me that is why he stayed outside the fortress—he wanted nothing to do with the weaponry they make in the smithies here."

"I saw its twin on Alaavar's belt this morning at court," Mindar said.

"What?" Erinshava looked up from the weapon in her hand. She stopped turning it over.

"When Alaavar stood up to speak this morning, I noticed that he had a similar dagger in a sheath on his armor belt. That is why I did not show it in court." Mindar looked up to see Gayan staring at the dagger.

He had finished his chores downstairs, and he had come to join them around the table. He spoke without taking his eyes off the weapon:

"A boot knife for the footman,
To guard him in the fall,
A dagger for the general's belt,
To terrorize them all."

Mindar started. The missing verse was more real than he wished to think.

"I remembered it after you came upstairs," Gayan said.

"Mooriman!" said Erinshava.

"Does anyone else know you have it?" asked Hannahoruan.

"No, I don't think…no, wait! There were two guards with me at the smithy when I found it."

Erinshava started pacing, moving from the window to the door of the kitchen and back. "Fortress guards?"

"Soldiers. At Lutaka's command, they escorted me to see the ruins. Is there something wrong?"

"Not necessarily. I am just trying to put all the pieces in place," said Erinshava. "We are probably not going to learn anything more from the map," she continued, "but it is not safe for you to keep it, Mindar. Put it back in its box, and leave it here with Hannahoruan."

"Why here?" he asked.

"There are still people alive who know you have it."

"Lutaka…Dolar…" Mindar was counting on his fingers, "both of you…"

"We don't know for sure what happened to Marhan and his men."

"They were trapped in Fazdeen!" he said.

"Are you sure?"

Mindar pursed his lips. He had to admit he was not sure. He had never seen any of them again, but that was scanty proof. "Any one of them might know about Hannahoruan."

Hannahoruan stirred from her fixation on the map. "Mindar, the map will be safe here. No one suspects me. I am not and have never been associated with Lutaka and his court. Marhan's band does not know that I joined you."

"What about the NarEladra who killed your husband?"

"They do not remember." Hannahoruan was staring at Mindar, her penetrating eyes burrowing down into his vorn.

"How do you know that?" he shot back.

"Mindar, I know who I am, and I know Mah'Eladra, and I know that the map is safe here. I also know you can come here whenever you want and use it safely, but there is no other place where you can do that."

Mindar knew that what she was saying was true. Somehow, he knew that Hannahoruan, the slight, sparkling, never-aging herbalist spoke truth at a level that he did not understand and made the hardest of truths seem palatable. He folded the map into the case. As he replaced the lid and looked up, Erinshava spoke, "I do not think it wise for Lutaka to know where the map is."

"Lutaka?" he said in disbelief.

"Mindar, we do not know what is going on here. I trust Lutaka, but he does not need the burden of knowing where the map is. It is enough for him to know that you have it."

✠

Our past is part of who we are. We can learn to ignore it, live with it, live around it or live beyond it, but it does not ever go away.

Pratoraman
The Middle Way

Somewhere in the next room, the shoemaker was tapping his tack hammer rapidly against the sole of one of a pair of shoes for the king. Mindar wanted him to stop, but he just kept tapping. Mindar wanted to shout at him, but thought he might disturb the twins. Tap, tap, tap, tap...Why won't he stop? Why doesn't he realize how annoying it is? And the twins, if they wake up, there will be all sorts of trouble.

"Answer the door, Mindar," said Sereline.

The old man in the rocking chair in the corner smiled at Mindar's annoyance. What else would he be smiling at?

"Someone is knocking on the door," said Sereline.

Mindar sat up suddenly. The cool darkness of their bedroom swirled in and covered the scene. The shoemaker stopped tapping. "What time is it?" he asked.

"I don't know," whispered Sereline, "but someone is knocking on the door."

The front door to their house was on a narrow alley that ran from the street to the fields behind. From their bedroom, he could see the entryway but could not see the door because it was set into the wall several feet in the typical Kinvaran style.

Mindar was wide awake and suddenly aware again of the dangers that surrounded them. He moved to the window and looked up at the stars. Katarin, the night rider was reared back and facing up. It was only a few hours before dawn. "Go into the room with the twins," he whispered to

Sereline, "but don't wake them. I will see if I can find out who it is."

Sereline was standing beside him at the window as he pulled on his tunic and belt. "Be careful," she said as she moved toward the hall.

"I will," he answered.

Kinvaran houses were built with formidably strong doors with latches that could only be opened from the inside. To the side of the door was the talking hole, a u-shaped hole that went around the door-frame so that those outside and those inside could talk without the door being open. As Mindar descended the stairs, another series of seven knocks landed on the door.

"Who's there?" Mindar said into the talking hole after a moment's hesitation and a deep breath.

No sound came from outside.

"Who's there?" he said a little louder.

There was another pause. "Rindar?" He had not heard that name in many years, and the voice was thick and low.

"Who is it?" he demanded.

"Billy Billy, bub'n scrump, champy's in the cataroup..."

"Minxa!?"

"Coppa Coppa attabump an' paaddi's got the misselsoup."

There was no one else on Tessalindria who could have known those lines. They had made them up in the tunnels under Vindarill, and when he realized who it was, he could hear Minxa's voice behind the nearly forty years of separation. Caution held sway as Mindar hesitated.

"Rindar," said the voice hole, "it is not safe for me to stand on the street too long."

Mindar took a deep breath. Erinshava had taught him that there were times that he had to trust, and there were times when the better part of wisdom was caution. "Are you alone?"

"Yes, let me in!" The urgency in his voice was pleading.

Mindar drew the bolt on the door and stood back as he pulled it toward him. It was dark, but he could see Minxa's soldier silhouette as he ambled through the door into the black interior of the house. "No lights?" he asked as Mindar shut the door behind him.

"I thought I would let you in first." The bolt knocked the bottom of the hole in the door casing as Mindar threw it shut. "Wait here a moment."

When Mindar returned with the candle, Minxa was standing where he had left him. His face was grim and weathered with age and hard-ship. The scar on his cheek was unmistakable, and his long, gray hair fell over his shoulders under the shallow Tessamandrian war helmet. "Come and sit down," Mindar said, indicating the chairs pushed neatly against the wall where Sereline kept them. He pulled two to the table.

"Would you like something to drink?"

"Water." He was curt, but gentle.

"Last I saw you was in the Crown," Mindar said as he returned with a mug of water. It was awkward, but the shock of seeing Minxa again under such circumstances left no option for anything less than awkward.

Minxa took a long drink, bringing the mug down gently on the table. "Don't remind me," he grumbled. "I came here, Rindar, to warn you. I don't know why I should."

"Warn me? About what?"

"What happened yesterday...last night—was only the beginning. You and your family are on the list."

"There's a list?!" Mindar asked.

"A big list." He took another drink, emptying the mug as water seeped out the corners of his mouth and ran down into his gray beard.

"How big?"

Minxa's eyes got cold. "I came here to warn you, but I will tell you no more."

"Why are you warning me?"

Minxa looked down at the floor. "I don't know."

Mindar felt the emotion that Minxa bore. He knew Minxa wanted to talk, but Mindar was not sure how to let him start. He sat and waited while Minxa opened and closed his hands in front of him, his elbows resting on his knees and his eyes glued to the floor.

"How long were you in Fazdeen?" Mindar asked at length.

"Twenty years." His fingertips were pressed together, and even in the dim light of a single candle, they were white with the pressure.

"How did you get out—I mean..."

Minxa was still looking down. "They forced me to leave." Anger filled his voice. "I—after twenty years—I hated it there at first. They made me work and wouldn't let me go. They took care of me but I hated it." He looked up and shook his head. "When I finally realized that I was never going to get out—then I started to like it. When that happened, they drove me out!"

"And then?"

Minxa looked up. "I came here and joined the army."

"Why?" Mindar knew that Minxa hated discipline. The two of them had considered running from Vindarill at one time. Mindar had suggested joining the Morlan army. He remembered Minxa's disgust and his adamant hatred of soldiers.

"Marhan wanted me to do it."

"Marhan?"

Minxa looked up. "He said it was the best way to be useful. I hate it!"

"Is Marhan still alive?" Mindar asked.

Minxa raised his eyebrows and nodded as a hint of a smile curled his lip momentarily.

"Is he in the army also?"

"I can't say any more, Rindar." Minxa's voice was resolved but wrapped in sadness. He looked down at the floor again as he asked the next question. "You still got the map, Rindar?"

A wave of cold fear swept over Mindar's vorn. "No," he answered, "why do you ask?"

Minxa paused and twisted his hands together. "Where is it?"

"I can't tell you."

"Is it in Kinvara?"

"I won't say. Why do you want to know?"

Minxa looked up with dull, hopeless eyes. "I want to get out of here. Away from this place, this time. I know Vindarill was not perfect, but that is where I belong." His voice was pleading.

"Then why don't you leave?" asked Mindar.

"They would hunt me down. I can't just leave right now."

"Who is 'they'?"

"I can't tell you that."

Mindar waved at Minxa's mug. "Do you want some more water?"

"Yes—more water," Minxa said.

Mindar went into the kitchen and ladled water from the bucket that hung beside the sink. "I have never helped someone through a portal, or done it myself, except that one time," he said as he returned, speaking to the empty chair on the other side of the table.

Mindar looked around. Minxa had vanished. He set the mug onto the table, took the candle and moved to the door. It was bolted from the inside. There were few places to go, so Mindar moved swiftly up the steps two at a time. At the landing, he turned into the girls' room. Sereline's face was white in the candle flame. "He went into our room," she whispered, pointing across the landing at the nearly closed door.

"Stay with the girls," Mindar whispered. The door yielded silently to his touch. All he could hear was his heart beating loudly as he peeked into the room. To his relief, the window on the far side was open. It led out onto a small roof overhanging the street. From there, one could climb to the roof and then move across the rooftops for some distance in either direction. Mindar blew out the candle and leaned out the window. The cool night air opened his lungs from the stiffness of fear, but Minxa was nowhere in sight.

"Who was it?" Sereline asked from behind him.

"Minxa," he said as he pulled in the bars on the window and secured them from inside.

"Minxa?" she said, letting the thought roll around in her mind for a moment. "What did he want?"

"I'm not sure," Mindar said. "He seemed to be afraid—and desperate. He wanted to know if I had the map and would help him get back to Vindarill."

Sereline sat down on the bed deep in thought. Mindar sat down beside her and put his arm around her shoulders. "What are you thinking?" he asked.

She shook her head. "There are far too many questions."

In the pause that followed her statement, Mindar was suddenly aware of a new danger. He jumped up and leapt through the bedroom door and threw open the door to the girls room. The bars on their window were swung back and the window itself was open. They were not in their beds. He heard Sereline gasp. "No!" Mindar turned to look, and she had disappeared out through the door. He rolled over the windowsill onto the gently sloping roof tiles that inclined toward the drill field where they had watched the soldiers earlier that day. Meekar was nearly full and Tal was on the half, but the landscape was bright with their light. There was no sound until Sereline catapulted through the window.

Her graying hair was tied back tightly, and she wore black trousers and a black shirt. She stood up beside him as she tied a black kerchief around her neck, hiding her throat. She had black gloves. "I am going after them," she said, her voice resonating with a deep anger.

"You can't," Mindar protested.

Either she did not hear him or refused to acknowledge his statement. She knelt under the window momentarily and then straightened. In three steps she had reached the edge of the tiles and leapt across the gap to the neighboring roof.

"Wait!" Mindar called.

She paused again, running her hands over the tiles where she was kneeling. "Find Erinshava," she called over her shoulder before she moved again. Three steps to the roof drain, scrambling up to the next level like a cat up a tree. "Meet me at Gayan's at sunrise," she said before she disappeared.

Mindar stood on the roof, stunned into inaction by the crushing awareness of what was happening. A faint but unmistakable hissing sound made him turn back to the window: an Eladra, engaging his time space. He was sitting on the roof with his arms around his knees and his back against the wall of the house. "Sit down, Mindar Colloden," he said as he pointed to the roof beside him. It was Visha'andar.

Mindar moved up the roof to sit down. "Be still," Visha'andar said with a low voice.

"My daughters... " Mindar started.

Visha'andar nodded his head. "I know," he said, then held his finger to his mouth. "*Stay very still,*" he said in telepathy.

They waited for several minutes. Mindar began to feel cold in the night air as his thoughts raced over the recent events, trying to find refuge in waiting on the roof. He wanted to speak, but did not dare to do so. Sereline could take care of herself, but there was little else to be sure of. He was not even sure that Minxa had taken the girls. It could have been someone else, and Minxa was just the decoy. Perhaps it was someone else, and Minxa was not involved at all; a frame, a setup. And why was Visha'andar suddenly here? Had Erinshava sent him? Why were they just sitting when it seemed like a time to take action?

A flicker of light on the wall of his neighbor's house caught Mindar's eye, and he felt Visha'andar's grip on his upper arm, warning him not to move. Low voices, muffled in the darkness, accompanied light. More light followed; orange light that moved and wavered as it progressed toward them along the wall. "*Hold steady...*" Visha'andar warned.

The crash of the first window shook Mindar like an earthquake. Visha'andar's grip grew tighter. The voices shouted now, and more windows caved inward from the thrust of the torches. The curses and jeers, mingled with cruel laughter, curled upward through the wisps of smoke. In a matter of minutes, the house would be an inferno. If any of them had been inside, they would never have escaped.

Mindar looked over at Visha'andar. He had his finger to his lips, but his eyes told Mindar he was listening and waiting for just the right instant. It came sooner than Mindar expected. With a swift motion he stood up and in a single bound, leapt through the hot acrid smoke that billowed from the window below them, onto the next roof, dragging Mindar with him. No one on the ground could have possibly seen them through that foul black curtain that seared his eyes as it blasted skyward.

Visha'andar wasted no time. They traveled from roof to roof as the shouts and screaming faded behind them. Mindar had never traveled the rooftops of Kinvara, and it was not long before he was lost among the endless sea of buildings. Visha'andar still held his arm, giving wings to his feet and strength to his legs as they leapt over dark chasms and skipped across the tiled roofs. He seemed to know where he was going, so Mindar made no protest.

Then, as suddenly as they had started, Visha'andar stopped short on a long sloping roof with a huge chimney jutting up from the middle of the slope. He pulled Mindar down into a sitting position against the chimney. From the position of Tal in the sky, Mindar reasoned that they faced south. Far away in front of them and to the left, Mindar could see the slopes of the Crown of Tessalindria, milky white against the star-studded sky. He was breathing hard. Visha'andar seemed at rest as if he had not moved in hours.

"We have to wait here now," Visha'andar said out loud.

"How long?"

"Until Asolara gilds the sky in the east."

"Then what?" Mindar gasped.

"We go to Hannahoruan's, to Gayan's. There is safety there—and your wife."

"And my girls?" he asked.

Visha'andar cocked his head, as if he was listening. "I do not know."

Mindar felt the anger flaring in his throat. "You don't know, or you won't tell me?"

"Both."

"How do you know my wife is safe?"

"I am told to tell you that. I do not know."

Mindar sat down and looked up to let the air flow freely into the tightness of his throat. Arathan shone steadily halfway between the horizon and the twins, and he stared at it as he tried to slow his breathing and calm his hjarg. It was his star; constant, quiet and never dimmed by man's wretched hatred and lust. Mindar watched to see if it would twinkle. It didn't, but it gave him hope that amidst all the ferocious ambition of men, there was a place of respite and peace.

✠

> Can any weight of silver or gold ever tip the scales against the life of any single man?
>
> Sessasha
> It Is Said

Somewhere deep inside his vorn, if there really was such a thing, Minxa had convinced himself that deceiving Rindar was the only way he was going to get what he wanted. Maybe he had not convinced himself, but had let Marhan do it for him. Either way, it did not matter. He consoled himself with Marhan's words: "Look at it this way, you'll be saving his life, won't you?—and the lives of his wife and girls! That ought to convince him to help you out."

Minxa trudged through the narrow alley that led back to his quarters on the west side of Kinvara. He had spent nearly an hour walking through the deserted streets of the city trying to make sense of the decisions he had made that brought him to this place. Though he could rationalize each of them, the sum effect was not very satisfying. He was not sure, in fact, that Rindar and his wife had actually escaped. Marhan had convinced him that they would. "He's escaped every attempt on his life so far, hasn't he?"

This was true, but it seemed like a shallow argument. Rindar had been lucky many times. Even Marhan had said that, but everyone knows that luck can be very fickle; and at any given time, it can turn on the lucky one in treacherous betrayal. Minxa had seen it happen in his own life and had slowly learned not to trust in it. Luck was a dangerous thing to trust in, almost as dangerous and tricky as trusting other men.

Minxa was also not sure where the money had come from that Marhan had given him. Panic drove his hand to make sure he had not lost his purse in his flight across the rooftops. It was still tied to his belt under his tunic where he had secured it, and the silver coins made a dull clanking as he jostled it. Fifty twenty-drag silvers was a lot of money for a soldier in the army, even a Dojan commander like Marhan.

It had occurred to Minxa to give the money back to Marhan and call the whole thing off. It probably would have been a safer course if he had acted on it before he had gone to Rindar's, but he had given in to his cowardice and pride. Now the money felt heavy in his purse. With what Minxa knew was about to happen, he wondered whether the coins would be worth anything tomorrow in Kinvara, so he consoled himself with thinking that if he made it to Vindarill, they would be worth a fortune to collectors of old coins.

It was still dark when Marhan woke Minxa from a bad dream. "C'mon," he whispered, "we need to get going."

Minxa followed him out into the courtyard in front of the bunkhouse. No one else was around. "I've hardly slept," Minxa muttered.

"Shut up," Marhan hissed.

Minxa followed him until they got far enough away from the bunkhouse that they would not be heard. When they stepped onto the main street leading east into the heart of Kinvara, Marhan turned to him, talking as they walked rapidly. "You did a good job," he said. Minxa could not see his expression in the darkness. "The girls are hidden, and Rindar and Sereline did escape. You still have the money?"

"Yes," Minxa answered, "but why do you care?"

"Just curious," Marhan said. Minxa knew it was more than curiosity, but he did not want to anger Marhan by challenging him. "Vashtor located Rindar on the other side of town early this morning after he fled the fire. I think I know where he is going, and we want to be there before him."

"I don't understand why Vashtor would help you find him," Minxa grumbled. The plan to get the map from Rindar was completely outside the orders of General Omberon, who was Marhan's commander in the army, and Omberon reported directly to Alaavar, as did Vashtor. It was unimaginable that Vashtor would be acting on his own, and even more ridiculous that Marhan thought he could get away with what he was doing right under Omberon's nose.

"I don't ask questions about such stuff," Marhan answered, "but I think that if we can help Vashtor get that map, his position among Alaavar's generals will be strengthened."

"And if he fails?"

Marhan smiled. "Then no one need know. We're doing this on our own time, remember?"

"And what about us?" Minxa asked.

"Well, I will gain Vashtor's favor, right? And you will be in—"

"Vindarill?"

"That's the plan, isn't it?" Marhan said.

Yes, that was the plan, at least as far as Minxa knew. But it all seemed too simple. Nothing was that simple, and he was never sure whether Marhan was being honest with him. Marhan helped him get into the army after they were driven out of Fazdeen, and Marhan had covered for him numerous times in the intervening years, but that just made Minxa suspicious. The only reason Minxa could find for Marhan's interest in helping him was related to the map. Marhan spoke of it often, and Marhan was the one who had finally put the plan together to get it.

So far, the plan had worked, but Minxa could not figure out how. He was convinced that there was more going on behind the scenes than he knew. It made him nervous because he did not know whether Marhan might be committed to others in ways he did not know or how much of a gamble he was taking by trusting him. He could not distinguish whether he was over his head in a deadly game between enormous powers he did not understand or whether his luck had returned.

"When we get to the apothecary," Marhan was saying, "you go inside and wait. When—"

"Hold on," Minxa said, "what apothecary?"

"Remember the wife of the innkeeper...south of Fazdeen?"

Minxa knew the exact shop. "Why would Rindar go there?"

"His wife is there. You must convince him that it is in his best interest at this point to help you with the map. Use whatever arguments you need to persuade him."

"He claims he does not have the map."

"That may be true, but he has to know where it is!"

"What about—you know, Lutaka?"

"It's already done, Minxa." Marhan smiled in the gray morning light. "The streets will be chaos before Rindar arrives. It will be a perfect cover for the rest of the plan."

They trudged on toward Hannahoruan's herb shop. Marhan fell silent, and Minxa kept his anxieties at bay by going over details of how they planned to escape from Kinvara after they procured the map. The gray, morning-shadowed streets seemed to advance and recede, emerging from the shadows in front of them and falling into shadows behind as they walked. The streets were quiet for now, but Minxa knew they would soon be awakened to an infamy that Tessalindrians would never forget.

✠

Much trouble and grief line the path of the one who trades psadeq for self.

Oratanga
Passages

Mindar must have fallen asleep against Visha'andar's shoulder. Visha'andar nudged him awake as the first glow of the sun was turning the low clouds to salmon and the last stars overhead faded into the deep purple of the morning sky. The chilled stiffness from sleeping on the tile against the chimney made his legs ache when he tried to straighten them. Mindar groaned as Visha'andar extended his hand to help him up. "Come," he said. "We must hurry."

As Mindar stood up, Visha'andar slipped his cape around him and pulled the hood up over his head. "Hold this closed and follow me."

He moved down the sloping roof, and Mindar stumbled along behind him, with each step a little more aware as his legs warmed from the movement. "Is there anything more you can tell me?" Mindar grumbled.

"No."

"I thought as much."

"There is much danger in the street," Visha'andar said when they had almost reached the bottom of the roof. He barely paused as he leapt over the edge and floated to the cobblestones, fifteen feet below. Mindar looked down and hesitated. Visha'andar gestured vigorously for him to follow, holding out his arms. Mindar jumped. Visha'andar caught him, and in a simple motion, Mindar was on his feet and walking beside him as if nothing had changed. *"Pull up your hood."* Mindar did as he was told, and Visha'andar picked up the pace, turning this way and that through the maze of narrow streets in a part of the city where Mindar had seldom been.

It was dirty. The air was thick with the odors of the garbage that clogged the gutters. In the gray dawn shadows of the canyon streets of the deep city, there was no color, and no living thing stirred to remind him that anything could live there. No tree or potted plant was to be seen. Mindar walked close beside Visha'andar as he continued to move north through the desolation.

They had been walking about half an hour when Visha'andar stopped and faced Mindar. "Do you know where you are now?" he asked.

Mindar looked around and shook his head. Visha'andar moved ahead a few steps and beckoned to him, pointing toward what Mindar thought might be east. "Go to the end of this street and turn left. Go two blocks, and you will then know where you are. Do not go through the great court. Make your way to Hannahoruan's, and when you get there, tell Erinshava that I am coming." He stepped to one side and vanished with a hiss in the darkness of a doorway.

Visha'andar's disappearance left Mindar alone in the cold, empty streets of a hostile city. In the same instant, he was aware of the city awakening. A rat ran across the flagstones in front of him, and a window creaked open on its tired hinges somewhere above him. Mindar moved forward in the direction that Visha'andar had indicated. It was east, as could now be ascertained from the sunbeams that cut obliquely across the tops of the buildings, finding their way between the chimneys and roof corners. With their light, the colors brightened from grays to dirty browns. Mindar pulled Visha'andar's dirt-colored cloak close in to protect him from something he could neither see nor feel.

At the end of the two blocks, according to Visha'andar's directions, Mindar found himself looking down a narrow alley that led directly into the great court in the center of the city. Hannahoruan's apothecary lay just on the other side and two streets over. To his left lay the castle, and to the right was the promenade that led to it. He could see soldiers hurrying back and forth, and the shouts of their commanders and captains ricocheted down the stone walls. He started to the east, skirting the court. He planned to make his way back along the other side. More soldiers appeared in the street, all of them in a hurry and each dressed for battle. They stopped talking as Mindar approached, peering at him suspiciously as he swept by, and resumed their conversations after he was safely past.

Until he approached the street where he felt he could turn north, Mindar had not smelled the smoke. Suddenly, it was everywhere; first just wafts of its odor in warm puffs as he passed alleys or doorways, then visible wisps, tumbling over themselves as they crossed in front of him. It began to collect into a haze, and Mindar could taste the acrid burning in his mouth. He pulled the cloak up around him.

Then everyone started running, all at once, the soldiers toward the great court and everyone else in the opposite direction. The silent streets erupted into yelling and cursing as the wisps of smoke rolled into billows. "They're burning the city!" someone yelled. Mindar started running himself.

The street where the apothecary stood sandwiched between two taller buildings was unfamiliar with smoke and frenetic desperation. The shouting and crying mingled to make an unholy wail punctuated by profanity and the crashing of carts and debris falling from burning buildings. Mindar kept Visha'andar's cloak wrapped close over his face so that only his eyes were exposed, though they were nearly useless in the hot acrid smoke. His steps were guided by instinct, counting doorways in the gloom until he thought he should be in front of the right door.

Mindar paused and looked up at the sign. A man swept by him with his arm raised, pointing toward where he had come from. "Run!" he shouted. "The soldiers are right behind me!" He disappeared into the smoke, and Mindar heard the tread of the approaching horde. He backed into the shallow doorway.

As he did so, the door behind him opened, and he was pulled backward into the gloomy interior of the shop. Mindar tripped over the threshold as he tried to step back and sprawled into the darkness on his back.

"Rindar! Are you all right?" Minxa's face appeared out of the gloom above him. He tried to sit up and simultaneously bring his fist into a fierce collision with the scar on Minxa's cheek, but someone else caught his hand and pressed him back onto the floor.

"You are safe here, Uncle Mindar," Gayan exclaimed as he cupped his hand behind Mindar's neck and helped him sit up.

Mindar looked at Minxa. "Where are my daughters?" he demanded.

Minxa extended his hand to Mindar. "They are safe for now, but we do not have much time." As Mindar stood up to face Minxa, he saw the great sadness in his eyes. "Come upstairs," Minxa said, "we have much to discuss."

Gayan was brushing the dirt from the back of the cloak. Mindar looked at him and Gayan nodded. Minxa turned and Mindar followed him through the back door and up the stairs, with Gayan close on his heels.

The usually bright kitchen was dark because of the smoke rolling past the windows. Hannahoruan and Sereline were seated at the table, and Erinshava stood at one of the windows, her bow in hand, peering into the smoke. They all turned as Mindar entered, and Hannahoruan motioned to one of the empty chairs. Sereline rose, her face stained with tears. She put her arms around Mindar's shoulders and buried her head in his neck.

He could feel her sobbing as he wrapped his arms around her. Hannahoruan stood and watched them as she waited patiently, knowing Sereline's need in the moment. "We have to trust," he murmured into the graying cascade of his wife's hair. "Now is not the time to fear." Even as the words came out of his mouth, he was not sure he could do that himself. They held their embrace for several moments before Mindar had the courage to talk. "What is going on here?" he asked.

Minxa moved to the table, pulled out the chair at the end, and sat down heavily. In the gloom, it was hard to read his face, but Mindar thought he saw a flicker of a gloat sweep across it.

"Where are they?" Mindar asked again.

"They are safe—for now."

Sereline stepped back from their embrace. "He's blackmailing us, Mindar," she said as she wiped her tears with her fingers.

"With what?" Mindar was appalled and confused. "Everything we have is gone," he snarled. "You want this cloak? Is that it?" He was staring at Minxa, once his friend, now hard at work becoming his worst nightmare. Mindar knew Minxa had the upper hand.

Minxa stared back, unmoving. "I want to go back to Vindarill."

Mindar pursed his lips and nodded as Sereline turned to sit down in the chair. Hannahoruan sat down beside her, and Gayan stood silently in the corner like a sentinel. "What makes you think I can do that for you?"

"The map, Rindar, the map!"

"I've never navigated a portal—I told you that. I don't even know how to do it."

"You're a fast learner," Minxa sneered.

"I also told you I didn't have the map."

"And I believed you. You didn't have the map when you told me that." He was playing with a bit of string he had pulled from his pocket, and he smiled as he watched his busy hand. His amusement lit the lower fires of anger in Mindar's belly. Minxa continued, "But you know where it is, and you won't see your daughters until you put me through a portal to Vindarill."

The idea of submitting to blackmail galled Mindar, especially from Minxa, but it gave him confidence that Hannahoruan and Erinshava, who both knew where the map was, had respected him enough not to let Minxa know where it was.

Sereline sniffed and wiped both eyes with the heel of her hands. "For all we are, Mindar, give him what he wants," she said. "Send him away."

The sight of his wife's tears brought Mindar back to the reality before him. "How can I trust a man who has kidnapped my daughters—"

Minxa interrupted him. "I *saved* your daughters," he growled. "You would never have gotten them out of that fire, and you would not have escaped yourself. As it is, you have your life, the life of your wife and your daughters, and those who came to destroy you think they have. Isn't that enough?"

Mindar looked at Hannahoruan. She was staring back at him, her bright penetrating eyes boring into his vorn as they always did. Erinshava still stood by the window, an arrow nocked in the string of her bow, and Mindar knew she could put an arrow through Minxa's heart before he had time to stand. Gayan stood like a statue, watching his mother.

"If I am able to send you through the portal, how would you release my daughters?" Mindar asked.

Minxa smiled. "Marhan and Drofan will see to that."

Mindar felt the anger rise into his chest, but he knew he had to tread lightly. "They have Therall and Serinda? What makes you think they can be trusted? And what makes you think that I will ever think they can be trusted?"

Minxa remained calm and in charge. "First, you have no choice. Second, they owe me a favor."

"What kind of twisted psadeq is this?" Mindar growled. "You blackmail them; you blackmail me—and you escape it all by running through a portal?"

"That's about it."

"You can't run from yourself, Minxa," Mindar said. "Psadeq doesn't work that way. You break psadeq with me; you break psadeq with Marhan—you break psadeq with Mah'Eladra."

"You speak as if that matters," he sneered.

"Of course it matters! In the end that's all there is, and that applies in Vindarill as much as it does here. When you run, the Minxa you have created runs with you, even through a portal."

"I don't buy your self-serving rhetoric, Rindar. You broke psadeq with me when you dragged me through that portal into this wasteland. If there is any hope for you, you can restore it by sending me back. Psadeq, baah." He turned and spat on the floor. "Get the map, Rindar. You can't win. All I want to do is leave this place. You and your daughters, your wife—you can all stay. Just let me go!"

Over his shoulder, Mindar saw Erinshava move and he looked up. She nodded. It was the first indication from anyone in the room that he should cooperate with his enemy. He kept his eyes on Minxa. "Bring me the map," he said as he sat. Gayan disappeared through the door. Ten seconds later he returned carrying the map box. He laid it gently on the table in front of Mindar and returned to his place.

Minxa smiled and leaned forward. As he reached out his hand to touch the map box, Erinshava leapt forward, the bow drawn and the tip of the arrow pressing lightly into the back of his shoulder. "Don't touch it!" she commanded.

Minxa withdrew his hand and laughed. "Ah, yes," he sighed with a mocking sneer, "Lonama's map. Only Mindar Colloden, historian to the late King Lutaka, is allowed to handle it."

Mindar felt himself pale.

Minxa laughed and continued, "Lutaka was first on the list, wouldn't you know? Don't you see, Rindar?" He swept his hand around the room to the others in a grand gesture. "Don't you see there is nothing left here for you either? Mankar is in charge now, and you are still on his list."

"Mankar!?" The name sent shivers down Mindar's spine.

"Alaavar has declared himself king under a new name," Minxa smiled. "He is now *Mankar, King of Tessamandria.* But he thinks you're dead—so he won't care if you escape through the portal with me." For all the things that Mindar was unable to remember from history prior to coming through the portal, the name of Mankar was one that no one on Tessalindria would forget. Suddenly, everything began to make sense.

Mindar looked around the room. Sereline had her head in her hands, and Hannahoruan was staring at him with her bright eyes. No one except he and Minxa knew what was happening to Tessalindria. Minxa hoped that the portal would help him escape into a world that was safe from the savagery of what was about to descend on them. Even in his twisted thinking, Minxa knew that he wasn't safe in Tessamandria, even as a servant of Mankar.

Erinshava's telepathy broke through the standoff: *"Don't give in to his taunts. You must have much armatan in this."* She was standing behind Minxa where he could not see her face. She was smiling. Mindar knew she understood something that Minxa did not, and her smile gave Mindar confidence to move ahead. He leaned forward and opened the map box slowly, folding the map out onto the table in the dim surreal protection of Hannahoruan's kitchen while the world raged in the streets below, the smoke of its burning blotting Asolara's warmth with its darkness.

✠

Wisdom is a gift so profound that Mah'Eladra do not deny it to anyone who asks and who does not lack armatan about it.

The Tessarandin, Book 4

"You have until nightfall," Minxa had said when he left. "I will be back then. I can't protect your girls any longer than that."

The echo of the words haunted Mindar's efforts to stay focused on the map. Sereline slept on a mat that Gayan had brought for her, and Mindar could see her face as she lay peacefully with both hands tucked under her cheek. A single lock of her hair drooped down where every breath moved it gently.

Gayan sat across the table from Mindar, quiet and alert, but unmoving as he gazed at the map. Hannahoruan sat to his left and Erinshava to his right. It was midafternoon. Much of the smoke had died down, and the noise from the street was sporadic.

They had made little progress in the quest to find a portal and had no clue at all about how they would use the map to navigate it. Mindar was exhausted, having had no sleep at all since Visha'andar had woken him twelve hours before. Staying awake was a matter of desperation. As he stared at the map, it swam before his eyes, eyes that he held open with his fingers, his chin resting in his palms and his elbows pressing heavily into the wood tabletop.

Every symbol on the map had been touched. Mindar had tried expanding it to see if they could see a portal. They had gone back to Islag and focused in where Mindar remembered the portal being at the northern end of the island, but there was nothing.

"We need a revelation," Erinshava said.

Mindar looked up and shook his head as the sleep that crouched in his eyelids made another effort to consume him. "A revelation?"

"It's obvious that everything we have tried hasn't given us the answer."

"Perhaps the answer isn't in the map," Mindar suggested.

"No," she said, "the map has the answer. You saw the portal when it was open to you when you left Vindarill, didn't you?"

"Yes."

"Then we know it is here. We just don't understand how it works."

Mindar shook his head again. "Brilliant!"

Hannahoruan touched Mindar's arm. "Get some sleep, Master Mindar."

"There is no time," he protested.

"Perhaps time is the answer," she said. "We are to know where the portal is and do not need it yet. When we do, we will know."

"But Therall and Serinda—"

"They are safe for now."

Mindar opened his mouth to protest, but his words were interrupted by the hissing appearance of Visha'andar and another Eladra by the window. The second warrior was larger and had a luminance that lit the dim room. Visha'andar had brought an Eladrim prince.

Visha'andar spoke directly to Erinshava. "Vistar and I must speak with you, princess," he said as he nodded toward the back room. Erinshava stood and bowed slightly before she led Visha'andar and the Eladrim prince out of the kitchen. Visha'andar shut the door behind him.

Hannahoruan smiled and shrugged. "It has to be good," she said. "Gayan, make some faganwort and caabris tea for our guest." Gayan moved to his task. "Master Mindar!"

Mindar looked up at Hannahoruan's word. She was staring at him intently, and she took his hand when he made eye contact. "Your armatan is weak about this, but there is an answer in the map."

"Maybe the Eladra know," he said, nodding toward the back room.

"No, they know little about the map."

"But we've tried everything."

Hannahoruan smiled. "Perhaps trying is not the answer."

He looked up. He was sure she could read the doubt in his mind, probably through his eyes.

"Perhaps it is just time to wait and listen."

"Just wait and listen?" he echoed, intoning a question into the statement.

"You have been asking many questions, but like a child who asks and does not stop to see if there is an answer."

He put his head between his hands and shook it again. "I—I'll try," he said.

"The faganwort will help," Hannahoruan said. Mindar could feel her gentle, comforting hand on his shoulder, and he closed his eyes to allow his mind to stop for a moment. He was not sure who he was listening to or what he listened for. The caabris-scented steam awakened him, so he bent down to the smoking mug and inhaled the aroma. It made his nose tingle.

"We will all listen together," Gayan said as he sat down.

Gayan's voice rang in Mindar's ears. The melody of his speech was otherworldly, more like a song. Mindar never tired of listening to him, though he seldom spoke. He was a man who knew how to listen. His statement held sway over Mindar's desire to verbally agree with him, and Mindar remained silent, inhaling the calming steam and sipping the invigorating infusion that Gayan had made.

They sat for many minutes. Mindar could hear the muffled conversation from the back room and the occasional ruckus from outside. He had not been to the window since he arrived, but he knew from the sounds that there had been much destruction. The warm mug in his hands brought a certain comfort. The tea pulled back the veil that shrouded his thoughts, and the silence gave him respite. Sereline slept unmoving, the same wisp of hair swaying gently in front of her mouth.

Thoughts swirled through his mind like leaves in the wind, twisting around one another as they scurried by. Suddenly, one thought, vague but sustained, landed in front of him, commanding him to look at it. He set his mug down. The swirling faded away slowly, and that one thought was all that was left.

Mindar opened his eyes and reached out toward the map, and as he did, the sleeve of his tunic caught the brim of his mug. The wave of tea splashed across the map, running in little beads on its surface. Gayan saw it coming and grabbed the edge of the map, to keep the tea from rolling off the other side. Mindar grabbed the edge nearest him and did the same, pooling the water in the center of the map.

"Pour it into here," said Hannahoruan. She righted his mug and moved it under one edge of the map. They lifted and poured so the steaming liquid slid off the map into the mug. As Mindar raised his two corners, he noticed the large Kirrinath medallion that adorned the back of the map, and when the last drops had fallen into the mug, he held up the map to see the back better. He was facing the windows where the midafternoon sun broke through the haze of destruction outside. Mindar noticed he could see through the map, and from each of the points of the Kirrinath a thin line ran through the map that was not visible from either side.

"What is it, Master Mindar?" asked Hannahoruan.

"I think I found the answer."

She moved around the table and stood staring at the back of the map. Gayan swung around on the other side. "The lines," Mindar said, "the ones in the map—one of them points directly to Islag!"

Gayan bent down, peering at the map and pointing with long, delicate fingers. "Here," he said, as he moved his finger up the river from Kinvara, stopping where it bent northeast toward the mountains. "It looks like there is a portal just to the east and south of the river."

Mindar looked closely and saw that Gayan was right. "Hold the map up for me, Gayan," he said.

Gayan took the corners of the map, leaving Mindar's hands free. He traced his finger along the line inside the map from the Kinvara Portal to the point on the Kirrinath where it connected.

"Karva," said Hannahoruan. "The Karva Portal."

Mindar touched the Karva symbol. Gayan gasped. He dropped the map, and it fell face-up onto the table. He was shaking both hands. "What happened?" Mindar asked.

"I don't know," he responded. "It felt hot—" He was looking carefully at his finger tips. "No, maybe it just slipped—I don't know."

"Are you all right?"

"Yes, it just felt odd."

Mindar turned back to the map, quickly expanding its range and moving the image east along the river as fast as he could. In a matter of moments, the small black smudge of the portal appeared. It was close to the river. "I know this area," Gayan said. "It is the Vanjar Escarpment."

"The caves?" asked Mindar

Gayan nodded. "Many of them—a vast network leading everywhere and nowhere. No one knows how far south or how deep they go."

Mindar leaned back and folded his arms as he stretched out his legs under the table. Exhaustion settled over him as he relaxed. "At least we know where it is, and we have the map to help find it," he said.

"Getting there might be a challenge," Gayan continued. "There is no known entrance from the surface; all the openings are in the face of the escarpment, some of them submerged in the river."

"So we will need a boat." Mindar said. "I have heard that the Vanjar Escarpment is the domain of river pirates."

Gayan nodded. "The opposite side of the river is fortified with a garrison of the king's best archers and slingers. Their job is to protect the supply boats that come down the river. The trade barges always stay close to the north bank when they pass the escarpment because the currents are tricky there where the river turns. Only the king's best navigators are allowed to pilot the boats through."

They were interrupted by the return of Erinshava and the Eladra. Her face was grim. "It's true. Lutaka has been killed," she said as she sat down. "Nearly all of the council has been eliminated, and the city is on fire everywhere except the citadel in the center, which is occupied by Alaavar—*Mankar* and his generals. Most of the army has been corrupted, and the part that refused to join Mankar is being hunted down. We are safe here for now, but we cannot remain inside forever." She continued, "So we must find a way to escape after we have freed Mindar's girls."

"Why do you think we are safe here?" Mindar asked.

"No one may touch this building," she said. "No one will even think to touch this building until we leave."

Mindar was going to ask for specifics when Gayan changed the direction of the conversation. "We must find a boat."

Erinshava turned to face him. "A boat?"

"Mindar has found the portal," Gayan explained. "It is in the Vanjar Escarpment. We will need a boat to get into the caves there."

"That's going to be difficult," Mindar said. "If Ala—Mankar is in control, it will be difficult to use the river without arousing suspicion."

"Perhaps Minxa can get a boat for us," said Hannahoruan.

"How would he?" Mindar asked.

Hannahoruan smiled. "He is well connected in Alaavar's regime. He follows close to Marhan, who is a direct liaison to Omberon, one of—Mankar's generals."

"How do you know this?"

"I know many things, Master Mindar," she said as she looked over at Sereline who was still sleeping on the mat.

"And why would he help us escape—how could he?"

"Mankar seems to be in charge, but he is a rebellious vorn. Rebellion breeds rebellion, and though there are many who follow him, they are also rebellious. He rules them with fear, and in the end, fear cannot build an empire. And Master Minxa has his own plan. He has served Marhan and Mankar in turn, only to position himself to execute his own plan." She looked up again, her bright eyes burning with passion. "Now, in the chaos, he can move. You must be careful, Master Mindar. Your affection for him may cloud your judgment."

"I have no affection for him," Mindar protested. "He kidnapped my daughters and is holding them for his own selfish end!"

"Be careful, Master Mindar," she repeated.

✠

The biggest enemy of hope is resentment of the past.

Karendo Marha
Journey to the Infinite

"I don't know if I convinced him or not," Minxa said to Marhan. The way Marhan ate had always disgusted Minxa. He tried to ignore it, but the finger licking and the way he wiped his hands on his shirt was something Minxa had never gotten used to.

"What was there to convince him about?" Marhan asked through a mouthful of crackers. "He has no choice! Did you point that out?"

"Yeah, but I don't think he knows how to find the portal—or how to set the time on the map when he finds it."

"He'll figure it out."

"What makes you so sure?"

"This is blackmail!" Marhan countered. "If he doesn't figure it out, his daughters will die." He licked another sliver of oiled fish into his mouth from between his fingers, then wiped them on his shirt under his arms.

Minxa looked away. He was trying to figure out what Marhan really wanted. Drofan had been quiet the entire time, and Soldar was much more interested in his food than what the others were talking about. It did occur to Minxa that he had not really told Marhan *his* part of the plan. He had decided he couldn't take that chance. In the end, Marhan would get what he wanted, and that was the map. For a fleeting instant, Minxa pondered the effect of his deceit, but it quickly led to the realization that they were doing very little that was based on anything but deceit.

Minxa had his own piece of the plan that he had told no one else. Omberon did not know what Marhan was up to. Vashtor was undoubtedly using Marhan for his own devices against Omberon, devices that Marhan probably did not understand thoroughly. Alaavar and all the generals under him had spent years building a web of falsehoods that had erupted today in unspeakable violence. Minxa shuddered and forced himself to stop trying to understand it. He could not see into the darkness that lay beyond his thoughts, and even though he could not see it, he knew that facing the truth would be too painful to bear and cost far too much. None of his plan would be fulfilled if it were discovered.

Marhan provided a welcomed diversion for Minxa's thoughts. "Don't forget the pain of the last forty years, Minxa," he said. "Today you will have an opportunity to escape. Finish what you started."

Minxa was still looking away. Finish what he started? Is that what this was all about? He shook his head and looked back at Marhan who was busy licking his tin plate. Marhan did not look back at him. "Don't forget Fazdeen," Marhan continued between licks.

Minxa thought back. He had hated Fazdeen, but did not know why. For all the time he was there, he was fed and clothed. Everything was taken care of. He had to work every day, but he had to do that in the Tessamandrian army. It had galled him that they would not let him leave. It still galled him, but he did not understand it. He could not leave the army either, and the food and other provisions of the army were far inferior to those in Fazdeen. He had often wondered if loathing his situation had been all in his head, a self-feeding anger that was fueled by resentment at how he had come to be there. At least in the army, he had volunteered for service, no matter how bad it was.

Minxa couldn't shake the sense of injustice of an imprisonment that could end so ingloriously. The situation was so inexplicable that he could do nothing but resent it, and the resentment ran deep enough that he lied to himself and others about what had happened in a vain attempt to justify his own bewilderment at it.

"Time to get back to the shop, Minxa," Drofan said as he stood up and finished wiping his hands on his tunic.

Minxa stirred from his thoughts. He hated himself and everything he had become at the hands of other people, but he stood up dutifully and shoved his thoughts down deep in his vorn where they would not get in the way of the plan. "All right," he said, "let's go."

The door to the shop slammed downstairs. Sereline sat up suddenly, and Visha'andar and the prince moved toward the window together, vanishing into the wall with a hiss.

Several sets of boots made their way up the stairs toward the small kitchen, but the heavy tramping footsteps were lost in the cacophony of angry voices that accompanied them.

11 The Vanjar Caves 11

Any place can be made into a prison.

Hispattea
The Essences of Corritanean Wisdom

M indar never found out where Minxa secured a boat on such short notice. The river transport was designed for shallow passage and for carrying bales of hay and coal down the river into Kinvara from the mountains. Wide floor planks kept any cargo out of the water that seeped through the bottom or collected in the bilge from rain. This particular vessel had been outfitted for smuggling, for several of the planks could be lifted to provide a way into the bilge and then replaced without any evidence that they could be moved.

"Down you go," Minxa said. When Mindar hesitated, he smiled. We gotta get you out of the city; then we'll let you out."

When Mindar looked at Sereline, he saw the terror in her eyes. He was still trying to understand why she had insisted on coming, and now, he was sure she was wondering the same thing as she stared down into the hole. Sereline was afraid of small places. "This will take the worst kind of courage," said Erinshava as she laid her hand on Sereline's arm, "but there is no choice. Minxa is right."

"I'll go first," Mindar said as he stooped down by the hole. Mindar heard Minxa snap his fingers, so he looked up.

He held out his hand as if Mindar was supposed to put something into it. "The map!" he snapped.

Mindar shook his head. "The map stays with me."

"Give me the map!" Minxa growled.

Mindar stood his ground. "It's useless to you without me," he said. "You know that. It stays with me."

Minxa reached out to grab Mindar's shirt collar, but Marhan caught his hand. "Let him keep his map, Minxa," he said. "You just make sure this stinking little barge trap doesn't sink with him in the bilge. Besides, you will never be able to explain how you got it if we get caught."

Minxa glowered at Mindar for a second before shaking free of Marhan's hand. "Get in the hole," he growled.

Drofan laughed and Minxa swore at him, but Mindar's mind was already in the hole in the floorboards. He wriggled down between the thick planks. The bilge was only about a foot deep under the boards, so he lay down on his back. The water that was already there soaked him to the skin with a cold, foul stench of slime accumulated in countless years of inattention. Mindar wriggled to the side so that Erinshava could get through the opening. She lay down and then inched her way over to the other side of the boat, so there was just enough room for Sereline to work down between them.

Mindar could feel Sereline's fear as she lowered herself into the close prison, and he heard her gasp as Drofan's sneering face spouted out, "Have a nice trip," before he dropped the heavy timber floorboard over her face. Perhaps worst of all was the heavy thump of hay bales being dropped onto the floor, sealing out the light and driving puffs of dust down between the cracks into their faces. Sereline's hand gripped Mindar's with ferocious fear. He shut his eyes to keep out the dust, which caused him to sneeze and bang his head against the solid flooring above his face.

The voices of the four men who held their lives in their hands faded, giving Mindar the confidence that they would hear nothing of his conversation with Erinshava and his wife. "I wasn't expecting it to be quite like this," he confided. Sereline cleared her throat but said nothing.

Erinshava's voice came softly out of the darkness after a brief pause. "I think Mah'Eladra are teaching us that we must not fear."

Sereline was shaking. "There is a lot to—be afraid of, isn't there?" she said through clenched teeth.

"There is indeed," said Erinshava, "but we are being guarded."

"By whom?" Mindar asked.

"Didn't you see the Eladra who followed us to the boat? There must have been a dozen of them."

Mindar laughed to himself. "No," he said.

"I don't think Minxa or the others saw them either," Erinshava continued, "but several of them are on the boat with us." There was a long pause. "Besides, you have the map, Mindar, and there is a great purpose in you bearing it. Whatever that purpose is, it will not be thwarted by the small, selfish plans of these four men."

Mindar thought back instantly to the Margah by the river. He had the map then, yet both Sereline and Minxa had almost lost their lives because he had the map, and three of the same men who had sought it then, were seeking it now. He opened his mouth to say something, then decided that it would not be best to remind Sereline of those times. "Why did you want to come with us?" he asked, his own breath hot and damp against the boards a few inches above his face.

There was a pause before Erinshava answered. "When they forced you to leave your daughters and Sereline decided to come, I knew I needed to be with you."

"But they wouldn't let you bring your bow or...anything."

"Another opportunity to trust," was her answer. "And I knew it would help you to trust."

Mindar squeezed Sereline's hand. "Are you all right?" he asked.

"I am very...afraid," she said, her teeth still clenched. "You know how much...I hate small spaces—and I am afraid for Therall and Serinda." Minxa had brought the girls with him when he returned to the apothecary, but had insisted that they remain there while he and Mindar came in search of the portal.

"They are safer there than here with us," said Erinshava as if she read Mindar's thoughts. "Hannahoruan's home is the safest place in Tessamandria right now, and Prince Vistar and Visha'andar will remain there until we return."

They were out in the river now. The oars creaked against the thole pins, and the sound reached them through the thick walls of their wet, wooden prison. The boat swayed in the free water, and they traveled on in silence for many minutes, each lost in private thoughts and fears. Mindar was getting used to the damp filth of the bilge, but he had the sense that they were taking on more water. The water was slowly creeping up through their clothes, so it was difficult to know whether it was actually getting deeper.

"How far is it to the escarpment?" he asked.

"I think it's about five miles east of the city walls," said Erinshava.

"Seven," said Sereline. "At the rate the river flows, and with only two rowers, it might take about three hours."

The conversation was interrupted suddenly by a series of shouts from the deck. The boat started rocking, and they listed suddenly to one side. Bilge water spilled over toward Erinshava, and Mindar heard her gasp as a violent thud shuddered the boat to a stop. More shouts and angry indistinguishable words flew about the deck as the boat rocked back and forth. Mindar could hear Sereline crying in the dark. "What's happening?" he asked.

"Don't know," said Erinshava through her teeth.

There was another thump against the boat, and it listed the other way. The bilge water flowed past Sereline and surged around Mindar, cold and putrid, up around his ears, soaking his hair and drenching his clothes. He bit his tongue to keep from yelling in panic. More muffled yells filtered down from the deck as the boat suddenly pitched forward and then stopped again with another thud.

Feet were running above them on the deck. The oars stopped suddenly, and so did everything else except the angry yelling; then the boat lurched forward again as the creaking of one set of oars resumed.

"How long do you suppose we have been out?" Mindar asked.

"I can't tell," said Erinshava.

They lay in the dark, filthy bilge and waited. The boat seemed to be bobbing a bit more now, and the sound of the water sloshing and slapping the sides was more urgent. "I think…we are outside the city," ventured Sereline. She was trying to quell her fear. Her hand still gripped Mindar's. "There is a section of the river that narrows and rises…as it rounds the bend about a mile…outside the city walls."

"That means we are about halfway there," said Erinshava.

"What will we do when we get there?" Mindar asked. "I think we can find the portal, but I have yet to figure out how to make sure that when we send Minxa through, he ends up in the right place…and time."

"Does it matter?" asked Erinshava.

Mindar hadn't even thought about that. "I am sure it will matter to Minxa," he said. "I doubt he will just jump in without that confidence."

"Mindar is right," said Sereline. "So Minxa will just have to wait until you—we—figure it out."

"Perhaps there is nothing to figure out," said Erinshava.

"What do you mean?" Mindar asked.

"You never figured out where the portal went when you came through the first time," she mused.

"But the legends about the map tell of people who went to specific places and times," he said.

"Maybe it just seems that way, but it's all in the hand of Mah'Eladra or the Eladra," Erinshava countered.

"Perhaps. On the other hand, we have no evidence to show we can't know. There is still a lot about the map that I do not understand."

"Still, we will have to keep our wits about us. There is something about Marhan's presence that does not make sense."

"What do you mean?" asked Sereline.

Erinshava paused before continuing. "He is so selfish, ambitious— and such an opportunist. Why would he help Minxa escape at the risk of his own future; at the risk of his own life?"

They fell silent, each pondering the complexities of their situation.

✠

When all life seems lost and confused, there is always the river.

Erengnira
The Tiger in the Tree

Minxa stayed as close to the bank as possible to keep out of the main current of the river. His job was to steer the craft, and he had already allowed the boat to run up on two of the rocks that peppered the shallow water that he was navigating. Marhan, who was perched in the bow watching for them, had expressed his anger about it both times with a string of profanity. Minxa could not see the rocks from where he sat with the steering oar in his hand because of the bales of hay piled in front of him, and the erratic rowing of Drofan and Soldar made control of the boat difficult even when he could see them.

"How much farther do we have to go?" Minxa asked after he had successfully piloted the boat past several obstacles.

"Just keep rowing!" Marhan's irritation was evident.

"I was just wondering," Minxa muttered. What he was really wondering was why Marhan had to make such an issue over a simple question. Besides, Minxa was not rowing.

"Rock to the right!" Marhan called.

Minxa pulled on the steering oar, and the boat glided past the boulder.

"I think it's just around the bend—up there," Marhan said as he waved his hand up river. The land on the right side of the river rose sharply, and where it met the water, it began to take the form of low cliffs. "It shouldn't take more than an hour."

"It would be quicker," Drofan said between strokes on his oar, "if you would help row."

Marhan ignored him. "Better yet," Drofan persisted, "you could toss—these bales and make—our friends row."

Marhan turned to Drofan. "We barely escaped from the city," he growled. "We aren't going to let them out until we are near the caves." He turned back to watching the river. Drofan pulled on his oar again and made a face that mocked Marhan.

"What about the pirates?" Minxa ventured.

"Do you believe that stuff?" Marhan said. "I've been up and down both sides of this river. Never seen any pirates."

"Then why did the king post his garrison up on the heights?" Minxa asked as he nodded toward the bluff to their left. A simple battlement crowned the cliff. From this vantage, an observer could see the whole river, upstream and down for miles, as well as the vast escarpment that rose above the river on the far side. The escarpment was just coming into view as Minxa spoke.

"It isn't for pirates," Marhan said. "It's just an outer defense for the city—in case anyone decided to attack the city from the water."

"So the pirates are just legend? Those caves look like an awful good place to hide."

"There aren't any pirates, ashtemba!" Marhan swore.

"All right, take it easy." Minxa had seen a lot of legend-turned-fact in his internment in this time. He also knew that Marhan was frequently wrong, but Marhan had perfected the art of self-deceit. What carried him through it was an arrogant confidence that somehow sustained him despite many obvious failures. Minxa wondered about himself, whether he might be living under the same delusion as Marhan.

If he were deceived, how could he possibly know it? It occurred to him that he could ask someone else. If Marhan were to ask him and if he could muster the courage to answer him honestly, then Marhan could find out how deceived he was. Minxa knew two things that would preclude this: first, Marhan's pride would never let him ask, and second, Minxa would never have the courage to be honest. Being honest would probably require that he be honest with himself first, and he was too proud to do that.

Minxa could break out of the cycle of deceit and ask first. He had never seen anyone that he respected do this, so the thought of him doing it was unimaginable. It would be worse than the confused circular paths of reason that tangled themselves in his head, so he consoled himself with rationalizing that he had never had to do this before and saw no reason to start now, especially when he was so close to closing the door on this portion of his life.

"How come Vashtor did not come along?" Minxa asked.

"He was busy with some other business for Mankar."

"Does he even know what we are doing?"

"Shut up, and make sure we don't hit any more rocks, ashtemba!"

Minxa knew he had stumbled on the truth. He was not sure how Marhan thought he would escape with the map, even after he acquired it, but that did not matter to him anymore. If he made it through the portal, it would no longer be his concern.

"I think he still wants the map himself," said Sereline. "He wants to see it work, then take it from us."

"If that is true, then I am surprised he let you come along, Erinshava," Mindar said.

"Odd, isn't it?" she responded. "But we do have the map, and you are the only one who can use it. We do still hold the upper hand in the bargaining."

"Until Minxa is gone," said Sereline. "As soon as Marhan fulfills his promise to Minxa, he can do as he likes with us."

"Not with the Eladra to protect us," said Erinshava.

"He may not know they are there," Mindar added.

Agitated shouting on the deck interrupted their conversation. The boat lurched to the side suddenly and then crunched into something. The boat's frame shuddered, and they heard timbers groan and crack. Sereline gasped. "No!"

The boat nosed down and then suddenly up again. As bilge slime rushed forward and aft, it would have swept them with it, had they not been packed so tightly together. "Rapids!" shouted Erinshava. "We must be passing under the fort on the north bank. We should be on the other side."

As she spoke the boat turned. The urgency of the rowing increased, and the second set of oars joined in the creaking. They were moving sideways and rolling more as the crew headed the boat across the river toward the escarpment. Bilge water sloshed back and forth as the boat bobbed in the water, and Mindar could hear Sereline gasp each time the water rolled over her. The creaking of the oars stopped suddenly, and they heard them being dropped into the bottom of the boat.

More shouting followed from the crew and splashes over the side of the boat, then a glimmer of daylight as the hay bales were pulled off the decking. The shaft of light that entered the bilge when the center floorboard was removed forced Mindar to close his eyes. He felt Sereline move up and away. "All right, sister," said Marhan, "up you go."

"Ugh!" said Minxa. "The stench!"

Erinshava was next. Mindar saw her being pulled out, and within seconds he had wriggled over and was yanked roughly to his feet as he squinted in the bright sunlight.

"I'll take that," said Minxa, as he snatched the map from underneath Mindar's arm. "Into the water, the lot o' ya, an' wash off that filth."

✠

The being who does not trust, cannot see the fullness of life.

Pratoraman
The Middle Way

The escarpment towered above them. Mindar guessed that two hundred feet of rock face separated them from the ribbon of green vines cascading over its rim. Deep holes pocked the edifice as if bubbles had been frozen in the pale yellow stone, then sliced by a large knife. Where the rock face plunged into the river, the holes were filled with water. Some were large enough for the boat to enter them.

Mindar shivered as they approached the wall. He was still dripping from the bath they had taken in the river, and they were deep in the shadow of the cliff where the sun could not warm them.

"I thought we might see some pirates," Mindar said to Minxa.

Minxa scowled as he steered the boat carefully across the current. It was more sluggish near the wall, but there were still boulders in the water where shards of rock had fallen into the river from the massive escarpment wall.

"Make for that one there." Marhan pointed to one of the larger openings where the water was quieter. His voice was guarded. Everyone else was rowing except Minxa, who steered. Even with the heavy oars, Mindar was thankful for the movement after the cramped quarters of the bilge. "When we get into the cave, keep yer voices low," Marhan drawled. "We don't need any more attention than we need." Mindar smiled at his odd choice of words.

It was then that Mindar first noticed Vakandar. He was flying low over the water, barely visible against the dark rocks of the other side of the river below the battlements. He was moving fast, sweeping back and forth as if he were watching. It gave Mindar a sense of comfort, knowing that every time he had appeared, deliverance was at hand.

They were less than ten feet from the cave mouth, and Mindar was staring over his shoulder into its meandering depths when his oar, which was idling in the water, was jerked down. The handle shot up. He turned his head just enough so that it grazed his right ear as it swept past. Drofan was not so lucky. Mindar heard Drofan's oar hit his chin. Minxa swore. In the next second the water erupted around the boat as a dozen bodies shot up. Wet hands grasped the gunwales as they pulled themselves into the boat. Marhan was yelling, but Mindar didn't understand a word he said.

In an instant they were overwhelmed. Two overly muscled men held Mindar pinned to the floor of the barge. They wore only ragged black shorts, and their bodies were painted the color of the river bottom. One of their attackers held his hand firmly over Mindar's mouth. "Take it easy, fann, we godja now," said the one who held him. "Evything be alright, don' ya see. Take it easy, fann." They all laughed and babbled to one another.

The boat moved rapidly into the mouth of the cave, powered by some unseen force. As they passed into the dark mouth, Mindar could feel the chill wind that flowed out of it, like the wind that flowed from the caves behind the forge in the Verillain Dale. He could only see up, and he assumed that his companions were similarly pinned on the deck.

Mindar's captor looked down. "Donja see deery," he smiled. "Dju bring hus goodjy, goodjy boat an' seven peeps." His hand came off Mindar's mouth, and with a single tug on his tunic with his left hand Mindar was sitting upright again. "Set still, vi donna wan' no trouble, see?"

Mindar shook his head, acknowledging that he was not about to give anyone any trouble. He looked behind at Sereline. Her eyes were wide. It was not exactly fear, but something else. *"Don't move."* Erinshava's telepathy was like a fresh wind. *"Not our trouble."*

The gibberish dialect heightened as they wound into the cave, and torches flared to provide light they needed to navigate the winding corridors. After about ten minutes, Mindar felt the boat lurch then grind against a small beach of fine stone. "Out! Out! All dju out da boat." The speaker wore a red bandana on his shaved head and bands of red cloth on each wrist. "Come quick, quick now. All dju, jessa folla usn."

They walked single file up a winding passage through the solid stone, led by the man in the bandana. In front of Mindar and behind him, two huge men blocked his view of anything else. No one spoke as they walked. Mindar lost all sense of direction as they twisted and turned into passages that led to the left and to the right, and he lost any hope of finding his way back after the third branch.

It took fifteen minutes to reach their destination: a sudden opening of the passage that led them into a huge hall in the stone. From somewhere high above, daylight filtered down in several places, giving the place an eerie sense of dusk, with the primary light still coming from the multitude of torches that hung in sconces on the wall of the huge chamber. A large, bright fire burned in the center, contained in a carefully built fire pit that had various hooks and cranes of fine ironwork built into it.

The smoke curled upward toward the source of the daylight, but filled the hall with its smell, mingled with that of roasting meat and other food that Mindar could not see.

Many more men, as well as women and children, filled the hall. This was not a band of roguish men, but a community living in the caves of the escarpment.

Their escorts lined them up in front of the fire with a row of men behind them, standing ready in case of trouble. The one with the bandana walked slowly in front of them, looking each in the eye and inspecting them carefully. Hundreds of dark eyes watched them from the circle around the fire. When the leader was done with his inspection, he walked to a small pedestal in front of the fire and turned to face them.

"Welcome," he thundered. The crowd cheered. "I em Da*jaan.*" He drew out the last syllable of his name with great enthusiasm. "We are Piraste! We eat together, yes? Then talk, no?" The crowd cheered again and broke into a series of hurried tasks as low tables and cushions were brought out onto the rough stone floor. The tables had three legs so that they sat firmly on the uneven stone, and the thin cushions were strewn around the tables so that ten to twelve persons could sit at each of them.

"Ya seet with me family, yes!" Dajaan said as he nodded over his left shoulder to a larger table that was being set for the dinner. He turned back to Mindar unexpectedly. Why he spoke to him and not the others Mindar could not tell. "Yes?" he asked again. Mindar looked at Erinshava.

"Yes, with your family," Mindar responded.

Dajaan raised his hands above his head and clapped twice. The entire hall fell to a dead hush in an instant. He raised his hands straight up, and staring toward the filtered light at the top of the hall, he uttered two sentences in his native tongue. The crowd echoed his sentences with a unified rumble, "Halla!"

As the rest of the people in the hall moved to their seats, Dajaan took Mindar by the hand and led him to the table. Sereline was close behind him with Erinshava behind her, followed by Drofan, Minxa, Marhan and Soldar. They sat at the table in the same order, but between each of them was another member of Dajaan's family, including several children. Dajaan was to Mindar's left, and a young girl of about seven sat between Mindar and his wife with another girl, perhaps twelve, between Sereline and Erinshava.

Mindar looked at Sereline as they sat down. There were tears in her eyes. There was no way Dajaan could have known about their daughters, but there was an uncanny trust he seemed to put in them. Between Erinshava and Drofan was a huge young Piraste and similarly between Drofan and Minxa, Minxa and Marhan, Marhan and Soldar, and then again between Soldar and Dajaan's wife who sat to Dajaan's left.

Dajaan raised his hands and clapped again as they sat down. From where Mindar sat, he could see the huge central fire and its strange construction. Several men around the structure started working feverishly, opening doors and pulling on various chains and ropes. Hot food poured from the ovens and from on top of the fire pit, dropping onto platters that were carried rapidly to the various tables around the hall. The people rumbled again, "Halla!"

Mindar looked across at Minxa. He met Mindar's eyes and scowled as Dajaan touched Mindar on the shoulder. "Bread?" he ventured as he looked into Mindar's eyes and handed him the first platter. The bread was so hot Mindar could hardly handle it. There were no plates, so he placed the huge slab onto the table as Dajaan had and handed the platter to Dajaan's daughter. "Bread?" he asked.

She giggled and took the platter, handing it to Sereline after sliding a slab onto the table. Platter after platter arrived at the table: roasted meat, which was laid on the bread, fresh fruit and raw vegetables, followed by several bowls that contained hot liquids, spiced with flavors that Mindar could not place. Everyone waited until the platters had stopped. Dajaan looked up and nodded, and the meal began.

Everyone watched Dajaan and the other Pirastes, to follow their lead. After several mouthfuls, Dajaan paused and looked up. "It is good, yes?"

"Very good," Mindar said after swallowing the bread he was chewing.

"Et much now," he laughed. He was dipping a piece of bread in one of the bowls, and his face suddenly sobered. "Why ya come here, taday?" he asked. Mindar hesitated, and Dajaan looked from him to Marhan. "Why ya come here, taday?" he repeated looking directly into Marhan's eyes.

Marhan stopped chewing, looked back at Dajaan without expression and said, "There is much trouble in the city."

"Ha!" Dajaan smiled. "Allus much trouble in de city, but taday, taday and yesday, dey be much-much trouble. No? Ba you come taday, and ya ha nuffin in de boat, ceppin dees people." He waved his hand toward the side of the table with Mindar and Sereline without breaking eye contact with Marhan. Mindar could feel the edge in his voice. "An ya come ta da caves, taday. Why?"

Marhan looked down and took another bite of a carrot-like root from the table. Dajaan waited patiently for a reply as he also put another piece of bread in the bowl and then to his mouth. A sudden flurry of activity behind him diverted the conversation. There was a lot of laughter and squawking, and a young Piraste entered holding onto the feet of Vakandar. "Let go, let go, you must, you must!" insisted the bird as he flapped his wings and squawked repeatedly.

The young man stopped until Dajaan beckoned for him to approach. He marched up to the table, speaking rapidly in Piraste. Dajaan laughed. "Dees bird, he says da he knows ya alla, is true?"

"It's true," Erinshava said. "You can let him go. He won't be any trouble."

Dajaan snapped his fingers, and the young man let go of the tethers that held the raven's legs. Vakandar fluttered to the floor. "Nasty, nasty," he squawked as he began picking at the tethers with his beak. "Nasty cave."

Dajaan laughed again, then spoke to one of his daughters. She jumped up and ran off. When she returned she had a small plate with fresh fruit on it. She laid it on the floor in front of the bird before she took her place at the table again. "Thank you! Thanks to you!" Vakandar said.

Dajaan turned his attention back to Marhan. "Ya come ta da caves, taday. Why?" he repeated as if nothing else had happened.

"We wanted to escape the city," Marhan lied. "King Lutaka has been killed, and the city is on fire. It is not safe there."

"Ya, ya, is not safe. Ba ya dinna come faw t'ascape," Dajaan continued, looking up after shoving another soggy piece of bread into his mouth. "Ya come ta bring dees people. Ba dees people, dey don' wan be here." He leaned over to his wife and said something rapidly in his own language. She stood up and left the table immediately. Dajaan looked up again. "Name," he said. "Wa's ya name?"

"Marhan."

"An dju?" Dajaan asked as he waved at Minxa.

"Minxa."

Dajaan nodded toward Drofan as he leaned over the bowl and took a bite out of an over-ripened pear.

"Drofan."

"Soldar."

"Erinshava." Dajaan's eyebrows shot up when she said her name, and he stopped chewing.

"Erinshava…Erinshava. Hmmm. I know dat name. Long go me thinks, long go." He paused before turning his eyes to Mindar's wife.

"Sereline." Dajaan nodded and looked at Mindar.

"Mindar," he said.

"Mindar," Dajaan echoed as if committing it firmly into his memory. He waved to Sereline and Erinshava. "Dees you wife?"

"Sereline is my wife," Mindar said with a smile.

Dajaan nodded. "Chidren?" he asked.

Mindar looked at Sereline before answering. "We have two girls."

"They old?"

"No, they are ten," he said. "Both ten."

"Ha! Tveelings. Ba dey don' come wid ya?"

"We had to leave them in the city. They are safe there."

Dajaan shook his head in disgust. "Beeg trouble in da city."

Dajaan's wife returned carrying a canvas sack. Dajaan stood. "Me wife, Arisan, me dawdas, Klimna an Virana," he said bowing to his wife and then waving to the two girls to Mindar's left and right. "An dees ma boy cousins, Vasat, Kafan, Saj, Dwagga an' Fawn." Each nodded as Dajaan spoke his name. "An now we see wa's in da bag, no?"

He swung the bag up so that it landed with a thunk on the table beyond his food. It sounded like a bag full of weapons. He opened the mouth and pulled out Marhan's sword, and laid it on the table, out of reach of its owner. Next came Drofan's then Minxa's and then the dagger. Mindar saw Marhan's eyes widen briefly as he laid it between the swords. "Where did that come from?" Marhan asked.

"Da dagga? Hit be carried ba Mindar, no?" he asked as he looked over at Mindar. Mindar nodded. Marhan's eyes bore into him with a coldness that he could feel. Dajaan continued, "But dees ting," he said putting his hand back into the bag, "who hadda dis one?" He pulled out the map box and laid it on top of the bag, sweeping his eyes around the table. Arisan put her hand to her throat, and Vasat's eyes grew wide.

Mindar was not sure whether it was good to be the owner of the map or not. "It's mine," he said. All the eyes at the table converged on him at once.

"How lon' ya had Lonama's map?" asked Dajaan. His voice was soft and warm.

"Thirty-seven years," said Mindar.

"Ya use it? Ya know how?"

"I know some about it," Mindar said, "but I do not know how much I don't know."

Dajaan raised his eyebrows.

"Every time I use it I learn more. I don't know what else it can do."

Dajaan was still standing. He leaned forward on his fingertips. "Why dja bring da map in da boat?" He was staring at Mindar. Erinshava must have done something to catch his attention because he suddenly looked up at her and nodded.

"We came here to find one of the portals," she said. "We know it is somewhere in these caves."

Dajaan sat down with a smile. He nodded with the satisfaction of having discovered a significant piece of truth. Erinshava continued, "Do you know where the portal is?"

Dajaan looked around the circle. Before he answered her in his strange pidgin, he said something in his native tongue that made the family laugh; then, looking back at Erinshava, he answered her, "Ha! Ya, we know where da port be hidden. Deep in da caves; way deep, ya? Ba why dja wan' find dees port?"

Erinshava stood and leaned on the table. "Our friends, Minxa and Mindar, came through the portal on Islag many years ago, from another time and another place." She nodded to each of them. "Mindar has made his home here, but Minxa wants to go back to his time and place. Mindar owns the map and has the knowledge to help Minxa go to his home. Marhan and Drofan are Minxa's friends, and they brought us here so we could send Minxa home."

Dajaan nodded and smiled. "Ba why ya hide in da boat? Why da dees *friends* ha alla da weapons?" He swept his hands over the swords.

Erinshava did not hesitate. "We hid because of the danger in the city. Marhan, Drofan, Minxa and Soldar have...connections, so that the city is not as dangerous for them." She was being honest with a slanted caution. Dajaan seemed to sense the delicate line she walked.

"Ba ya didna bring da chidren, no?"

"No, we were not allowed, and they are safe where they are."

"If da city be'n big trouble, how da chidren be safe, hmmm?"

"We left them with a friend who will protect them until we get back."

"Den we muss hope, no?"

"We know they are safe," said Erinshava with a hint of a smile. "The bigger question is whether *we* will be able to get back there safely."

Dajaan stood and clapped his hands above his head. Servants swarmed around the table picking up the various bits of food and the bowls until the table was clear. Mindar watched the other people in the hall clearing their tables and disappearing into various corridors. Dajaan waited until they had mostly gone before he spoke again. "I don'a unnerstan'. Ya say Lutaka be killed?" He was looking at Mindar again.

Mindar nodded.

"Ya say da dees men ha' connections so dey be safe, ya?"

Mindar nodded again.

"Dey connected wi' dey da' killed da king in Kinvara?"

"*Careful!*" Erinshava's telepathy shot into the conversation.

"I don't know the connections exactly," Mindar answered, "but they are not under suspicion by the usurpers as we are. Our names," Mindar swept his arm toward his wife and Erinshava, "are on a list to be killed by the usurper."

"Usurper?"

"It seems that General Alaavar has taken over the city," Mindar said. "He has taken a new name: Mankar. There is much evil afoot and much greater evil to come."

Dajaan rose from his seat. "Alaavar?" he thundered. "Dees one be evil, evil down deep. Evil from where evil come." He turned to Marhan. "Dju be friend a' Alaavar?"

"No," said Marhan. Mindar could not tell if he was lying. "I serve in the army. That is all."

"Do you know Alaavar, Dajaan?" asked Erinshava.

Dajaan leaned on his hands, his eyes roving about the table, filled with fire. "He come here, mebby' one mon' ago. He wan' talk. He wan' my help. He wan' me an' alla dees Piraste people a help him."

"With what?" Mindar asked.

"With I dunno. I dinna ask. I tol'a Alaavar a go way, 'at Piraste people na gonna help. He waz evil, an Piraste people, we na help da evil."

Erinshava changed the direction of the conversation. "Will you help us find the portal?"

Dajaan looked at her thoughtfully. "Dunno. We gonna sleep. Denna we tink if we help da evil or da good. Ba dju nah fear, ya? Yous much safe wid Piraste people."

He called loudly in Piraste, and a number of men surrounded the table. Dajaan picked up the swords, the dagger and the map and put them carefully back into the bag and handed it to his wife with a smile and a few strange words. She nodded and smiled back. It was clear that no one would find them without his permission. "Yous folla dees Pirastes. Getta you sleep an' we talk in da mawning." He turned and strode off without another word.

They were separated into two groups. Sereline, Erinshava and Mindar were led off in one direction. Vakandar flutterhopped along behind them. "Dirty cave. Nasty cave," he said repeatedly as he struggled to keep up with them. Marhan, Minxa, Drofan and Soldar were taken somewhere else. It was all very cordial, yet it was clear they had no choice.

✠

No being knows so much that he cannot learn more.

Old Mythinian Saying

The cold hand on Mindar's shoulder called him gently out of his shallow sleep. In the pitch black cavern, he could see nothing. The hand across his mouth kept him from calling out. "Yous follow. Come?" The voice was old and soft. When the hand was removed, Mindar sat up and rubbed his eyes as if doing so would enable him to see.

He didn't know why he should trust the complete stranger, but in this dark underworld he had little choice. The old man's hand was bony but strong, and as he pulled Mindar to a standing position a faint light glowed from under his cloak. He lifted his right hand to reveal a green glowing lump about the size of Mindar's fist. The faint aura illuminated a wrinkled face almost hidden behind a long white beard, a thick mustache and eyebrows that nearly covered his eyes.

The man bent over and whispered, "You fella, musta ha more map knowing, come?" Mindar could feel the man's breath on his ear, and his beard brushed Mindar's face. Mindar looked around. Sereline was sleeping soundly, and even Erinshava seemed unaware of this stranger's intrusion into the small chamber. Vakandar stood near the wall, his head tucked under one wing. "Come. Quick!" the man whispered urgently.

Mindar grabbed his damp shoes and followed him out. After the old man had closed the door silently behind him, he took Mindar's hand and smiled into the lump of green. "Yous muss learn." He turned. The soldiers who guarded the room looked as if they were asleep on their feet. Mindar followed the man about ten paces before he stepped to the side and waved Mindar into a room off the main corridor. "Sit," he said, pointing to a chair beside a table.

"Me? I em Klaria…Klaria," said the old man as he started circling the room, lighting candles in the sconces that hung on the walls at regular intervals. When he was finished, the room glowed with yellow, smoky candlelight. "Now, yous learn, yes, Maza Mindar?"

Klaria seated himself in the chair opposite Mindar, reached under the table, pulled the map from what must have been a shelf in the table, and laid it carefully on the table top. "What do I need to learn?" Mindar asked.

"Ha! Ya needs'a learn more de map. Ya needs'a learn portals om ya gonna send Maza Minxa fru, yah?"

"I know about the portals!" Mindar protested.

"Wha dju know?" Klaria shot back as he leaned forward and pushed the map box closer. "Yous show Maza Klaria den."

Mindar's trust moved to suspicion, and suddenly, this odd stranger across the table from him seemed to change into an enemy. Mindar wondered whether he meant harm or good. There was no way to know whether his purposes were noble or whether he was on some selfish mission. Mindar wondered why he had come alone and why in the middle of the night.

Mindar opened the map box slowly and lifted the map onto the table, unfolding it with a deliberation intended to make Klaria feel it. The old Piraste seemed nonplussed. "Where is Dajaan?" Mindar asked.

"Dajaan? Ha! He'sa sleep. Ba me come an teach ya bout de map."

Mindar spread the map out on the table. "If you are supposed to teach me, then teach me!"

"I's gotta know wha ya know, yes?"

Mindar looked at the old Piraste thoughtfully for a moment, reflecting on all the other encounters he had had with strangers about the map. The map belonged to Mindar. It seemed that no one could take it from him until his ownership ended, but because of the way he had inherited the map, he had no idea how tenuous his possession might be. "All right," he said looking down, "this is what I know."

Mindar moved quickly on purpose, flying through various motions by rote, using the symbols and figures and showing Klaria what the map did when he manipulated them. Each time he looked up or paused, Klaria would nod and smile stupidly. Mindar couldn't tell whether he was lost or simply waiting for him to get through his demonstration.

Mindar saved what they had just learned about the portals until the end. When he turned the map over to show Klaria the face of the Kirrinath, its points and its connection to the portals, Klaria leaned closer, and the hooded eyebrows seemed to rise so Mindar could see his eyes sparkling under them. This seemed new to him. "De Kirrinat!" he interjected.

Mindar nodded.

Klaria shrugged and smiled. "Show me wha'else ya know, yes?"

Mindar set to his task again, shaken by the upside down method of the old man's teaching. He showed Klaria how to find the portals by touching one of them and then turning over the map to reveal it on the other side.

"So dees how ya fin'da portal in dees caves, yes?"

Mindar looked up. Klaria wore the same expression, but his arms were crossed and he was leaning back in the chair. "Yes, that is why we came here."

"An, ya know how Maza Minxa go in diss portal?"

"We think so."

"An' where Maza Minxa comes out, ya? 'E go in here an' wassa portal he come out?"

"I haven't figured that out."

Klaria put his hands to the sides of his head and laughed. "Yous think Maza Minxa no wan know der end? Where he's goin?"

Mindar flushed with anger. "Of course he does. I just don't know how to send him there."

"An' where? Das eeasy! Ba do ya gon know when, no?" Mindar looked into his wrinkled smiling face. In that instant he realized that being angry because of his own ignorance wouldn't be productive.

"You're right. I don't know how to determine either where or when the person would end up."

"Ya, ba now ya ken learn, cuz ya know sumpin ya don' know, ya?"

Minxa nodded humbly.

"Klaria ken show yous how diss map happen, but ken no' toucha da map, ya?"

"You can't touch the map?"

"No, no, nooooo! Maza Mindar only." He wagged his bony index finger. "Dju know 'bou' da Cirag an' Danag el'ments?"

"Some, but only a little."

"Ha! Dissa portal is Karva!"

"I know that."

"Karva! Is da' Danag?"

"No, it's Cirag," Mindar said.

Klaria smiled, pursed his lips and nodded. "So, Maza Mindar, ya know da Cirag Portals, yes?"

"The portals are Cirag and Danag?"

Klaria tapped his head. "Tink, Maza Mindar! Alla portals ha' da Kirrinat names…"

"And Cirag Portals only move to Cirag Portals?"

"Wheres Maza Minxa wan' go?"

"Vindarill."

Klaria furrowed his brow and put his hand in front of his mouth in a thoughtful frown. "Han heard," he said shaking his head.

"In Morlan," Mindar continued, "on the eastern coast."

"Show me."

Mindar lifted the map into the light and traced the faint line from where Vindarill would be to the Kirrinath star. It led to the Vin Portal. Part of the Cirag cluster. He touched the star and laid the map down, pointing to where Vindarill should have been on the map. He put his other index finger on the Harvan River near Kinvara.

Klaria shook his head again, looked up and scratched his chin deep under his beard. "Wha' time?"

"Ahead, far ahead."

"Yous know how make de time on de map, no?"

"Do you?" Mindar snapped back.

"Ha! Ya," was all he said as he sat back in the chair as if he were going to watch Mindar figure it out.

Mindar watched him for a moment before he spoke with a hint of deference. "Will you show me?"

"Yous ask nice."

"I need your help. Will you please show me how to set the time?"

Klaria leaned forward with a chuckle and muttered something to himself in Piraste that he thought was very funny, then laughed out loud at himself before sobering instantly. "Dees rrrrrings," he said pointing at the carefully drawn concentric rings of symbols that surrounded the

Kirrinath star on the back of the map. "Deys de time rings. Yous turn de rings, I tink."

Mindar eyed the six rings carefully. The four inner rings had the eight faces of the Kirrinath neatly scribed into them with a ninth position that contained a small, black, six-pointed star. The fifth ring out had thirteen symbols around. The only recognizable one was the little star, which was lined up perfectly with the inner rings. The last ring was crowded with twenty-five or thirty symbols, and the same little star lined up with the others.

"Yous turn de rrrrings, I tink," Klaria said again. Mindar looked up. Klaria was staring at him intently.

Mindar put his finger on the outer ring and tried to drag it around the paper. Nothing happened, so he moved to the inner ring. Nothing moved. The same effort on the middle rings produced the same result. Mindar looked up. "Tink, Maza Mindar!" Klaria's voice resonated with urgency.

Mindar shook his head and stared back at the map. Klaria reached across and took Mindar's index finger firmly between his thumb and index finger. "Tink!" He moved Mindar's finger to the ninth symbol on the inner ring then let go, settling back in his chair with a smile on his face.

Mindar pulled and the ring slid. He moved to the outer ring and did the same, and the ring obeyed his touch. He could see the map flicking faintly as the rings moved, so he stopped and turned it over. It looked the same, but Mindar had to confess that he had not observed it very carefully before. He hit the little symbol that set the map to now and turned it back over. All the stars were lined up again. Klaria smiled. "Now you make'n progress, ya?"

"So the rings set the time, but by how much? Why the six rings?"

"Ha! Maza Mindar. Yous gotsa figger dat. I canna' help." He sat back in his chair and folded his arms. Mindar stared at the map. He turned it face up and moved it forward in time as he had learned before. He thought perhaps half a day would be sufficient. When he turned it over, none of the rings had moved. Klaria nodded, but said nothing.

Mindar continued to play with the map, but had no sure way to know exactly what values to attach to the rotation of each of the rings so he could tell exactly how far in the future he was supposed to send Minxa. Klaria sat and watched with an amused smile on his face, his legs stretched out in front of him and his arms crossed over his chest.

After about ten minutes Klaria took a deep breath and sat up. "Nows time ta go," he said. "Yous needin sleep, ba' der esa one mo' ting." He reached behind his back and pulled out the dagger and stood up. "Diss dagga, yous, no?"

"Yes, that's mine."

"Good. Donna eva' le' no one hava det, yousa unnastan'?" He flipped the blade in the air, caught it deftly at the end of the tip and shoved the handle toward Mindar. "Neba' eba.'"

Mindar took the dagger. "Thank you," he said.

Klaria moved to the nearest sconce and blew out the candle. "Yous folda da map—muss hurry." By the time Mindar had the map back in its case all the lights were out, and Klaria had pulled the green lump from his cloak again and picked up the map box.

"Ha'va much sleepin'," he said outside the door to the chamber. "An' don' worry bou da map." He patted the box softly and turned away down the corridor. "Yous gon get it in da mawning." Mindar slipped into the room in the dark and carefully made his way to his bed. His thoughts dissolved into a deep sleep as soon as he lay down.

✠

There is no artifice capable of removing mordage save that of true metnoga alone.

Tristaron Harrista
The Kirrinath

Minxa lay awake. He did not know why he woke up, and the pitch-blackness of the cave made it impossible to know what time it was or where he was, or even how to find light. He lay wondering whether he should even try to get up, knowing that he would undoubtedly wake others if he did, so he remained quiet, unable to sleep and unwilling to move.

His plans were fading. His luck seemed to have abandoned him again, and now the map had been taken from them and so had their weapons. They were hopelessly lost. The labyrinth of the caves was beyond his ability to absorb, and without light there was no hope of finding his way out or of finding the portal. Trying to escape from the Pirastes would be an exercise in futility because of their knowledge of the caves.

For now Minxa just wanted to sleep: a dreamless sleep that would shut off even the emptiness of the darkness, but sleep was as elusive as light. He lay still. Time crawled by as he counted the measured breaths of Soldar who was snoring gently to his right.

Somewhere in the quiet darkness, Minxa became aware that some-one else in the room was not asleep. He did not know how he knew, but he could feel it as he listened intently. He could hear the breathing of three men lying on the floor near him. Whoever it was, it wasn't one of his companions. He lay frozen in quiet helpless fear, knowing that there was nothing he could do. He could not even tell exactly where the being was.

Minxa did not know how long he waited, his tired eyes hopelessly scanning the darkness and his ears straining until they buzzed with the silence. He still felt the presence of the other awake being, but where it was, he could not tell. A slight puff of air by his cheek startled him. He would have cried out, but a firm hand clamped down over his mouth as a voice hissed in his ear, "Don'a speak."

Minxa froze again.

"Yous comin wif me, Maza Minxa, no?" whispered the voice.

Minxa nodded, and in the next moment he was lifted to his feet with a hand behind his head, leaving his blanket behind on the floor. The being was in front of him. A green rock, perhaps the size of Minxa's fist, emerged out of his cape, and the pale light illuminated an old man with a long white beard and bald head that looked perfectly round. His ears stuck out from the corners of his beard, and his eyes were buried beneath overgrown white eyebrows. "Yous follow, come?" The man turned and headed for the door.

Minxa followed, stepping over Marhan carefully. They passed the two Piraste guards, fast asleep on their feet at the door. They went about twenty paces down the corridor, and the old man turned down a side passage that opened into a small room with a table and two chairs. "Sit, sit," he said with a smile, pointing to one of the chairs.

"Me? I em Klaria...Klaria," the man said as he laid the glowing rock on the table in front of Minxa and started walking around the room, lighting candles in the sconces on the wall. Each one flared to life as he brought his fingers in close. When Klaria was done, he turned and sat down opposite Minxa, pulling the map box from his cloak as he did so. He set it on the table between them.

"Dess map. Is yous?" Klaria asked.

Minxa wanted to lie, but he chose a more cautious route. "It belongs to a friend."

"Ahha." Klaria nodded. "Ba you'sa know ha ta use dissa map?"

Minxa shook his head.

Klaria frowned. "You gon try?" he said as he pushed the map across the table until it sat in front of Minxa. "Open da box, no?"

Minxa lifted the lid off the box and unfolded the precious map onto the table. The yearning of many years descended on his vorn. Here it was, the treasure of the ages, spread out before him and him alone. Years of waiting, thinking and scheming flooded before him. Lonama's map was at his fingertips with no one to keep him from owning it except the frail old man across the table.

Klaria stared at him. "Why you wan' da map, Maza Minxa?" he

asked without blinking, his small round nose poking out between his moustache and his drooping eyebrows.

"I want to go home," he said as he looked down to the map again. "That's all." The last phrase was little more than a hoarse whisper.

"Yous don' know how ta use da map! Yous know *where* you wan go? *When* you wan go?"

Minxa sighed and shook his head again. "I know both, but I don't know how to get there."

"Whos know?"

"My friend, Mindar."

"Ah! Ba he be lockt'a up too!" Klaria grinned. As Minxa looked him in the eye he sobered suddenly. "Ba why ya wanna go der, Maza Minxa?" he asked.

Minxa looked down at the map and ran his fingers over its surface. Nothing moved. Nothing changed. "Vindarill is where I was born, and it's where I want to die."

"Ya, ha. How long ya been in diss place? When ya come?"

"Nearly forty years—forty years ago."

"An ya still donna like it?"

"I never liked it here," Minxa said. The anger rose in his voice as the he spoke the words.

"Ba if'n ya go back, mebe det citee be diffent. All diffent."

"Not if I go back to the same time!"

"Ya, Ha! Ba den *you* be all diffent, no?" Klaria smirked. "An alla ya friends be young, yes?"

"It's not the people; it's the city," Minxa retorted.

"I ken help'a ya get back."

The sudden turn caught Minxa by surprise. "How? Why?" he stammered.

"Yous gonna hav'ta trust."

"Trust who?"

"Maza Mindar."

"What?!"

"I tink ya donna trust nobuddy," Klaria responded. His eyes were fixed on Minxa with a peculiar intensity. "If'n yous wanna go in da port—if'n yous wanna find de citee, den ya must'a trust Mindar."

Minxa sat still and stared back at the old Piraste who remained unmoving opposite him.

Klaria raised his hands. "You'sa vorn iss all *skretch*!" he said, wringing his hands together in a motion that complemented the emphasis of his words. "Ya donna trust nobuddy. Ya hate. Ya lie—even ta dem dat tell ya true. Yous psadeq—iss all skretch! Der be nuffin good!"

Minxa looked down, his pride stinging from the accusations. "You know nothing about me!" he said.

"Ya be greedy! Dem coin, dey hang yer belt berry hebby. Ya hurt yous friends cuz ya be greedy. Ya steal people. Dat be berry ebil."

The words pounded Minxa with a ferocity he had never felt in his life. Even Marhan hadn't berated him like this. He wanted to look up from the map where his eyes were fixed, but he couldn't. Its sepia color turned red as he stared at it in anger. "I could take this map and get there myself!" he said as he looked up, but even as he said the words, they sounded ridiculous.

"Ya, yous gonna take da map," Klaria said with a smile, "ba if'n ya donna gib it ta Maza Mindar, an if'n ya donna trust 'im, den yous will see da citee, ba dat won' be da same!"

"What do you want from me?!"

"Metnoga."

Minxa's anger rose when the word was spoken. He had come to hate any words associated with the whole idea of kirrin. He didn't believe in all that superstitious jargon, and the idea that he might be expected to participate in it, or apply it to his life, that it might be required to achieve his plan dove deep into his vorn.

"If'n ya don change, den life be close t'blivion in ya citee."

"This is blackmail!" Minxa blurted out.

Klaria was undaunted. His eyes remained steady and his face firm. "Yous gotta choose."

Minxa looked up. "Do I have time to think about it?"

Klaria rose and opened his hands face up on either side of him. "Maza Minxa. Ya take de map. T'night ya gotsa decide: metnoga—" he looked at his left hand, "or Oblivion," he said as he looked at his right hand. "Ya gotsa choose. In da mawning, we see yous decision." With these last words, Klaria turned and started extinguishing the candles around the room, one by one.

As the light in the room slowly dimmed, Minxa sat and stared at the map, his emotions boiling inside. Resentment, anger, hatred and fear swirled around him. His pride fought back, arguing that it was unthinkable to yield to such blackmail, but the taste of hope, the slight chance that he might make it through the portal to Vindarill, a forty-year passion that was now within reach, argued back ferociously. Minxa picked up the map and folded it slowly. By the time he had put it back into the case and replaced the cover, the only light in the room was Klaria's strange green lump.

"Yous folla me," the old man said. There was no detectable resentment in his voice or demeanor.

Minxa followed Klaria the twenty paces to the room where the others were still sleeping. The guards stood sound asleep by the door. Klaria pushed it open and waved, and Minxa slipped past him holding the map under his arm. Klaria waited until he had lain down and covered himself before he pulled the door shut. The last vestige of the green light vanished with a slight click; and Minxa found himself utterly alone, burdened by the weight of a decision that he alone, in the profound darkness found only in deep caves, had to make.

✠

The words we use to express our thoughts, betray the intentions of our vorn.

Sessasha
It Is Said

Mindar's slumber was interrupted by an entourage of Pirastes who paraded into the chamber to wake them up. All the usual signs of morning did not exist in the cave so there was no warning. "Up, uppa alla yous! Iss time fr' t'eat!" one of them shouted as he lifted each of them out of their blankets while the other Pirastes stood around holding torches. He shoved a bottle under Mindar's nose. "Drinka dis! Uppa you wake, yes?"

Mindar took a swig. He nearly choked on the harsh bitter liquid, but its effect was instantaneous, and he needed no other inducement to alertness. Sereline and Erinshava both choked down a swallow before they were led out to breakfast without even the opportunity to wash their faces. Vakandar squawked, shuddered his feathers and stretched his right wing before fluttering up onto Erinshava's shoulder. "Nasty cave, very nasty," he said. Mindar smiled as he felt for the dagger that he had tucked into his tunic before he had lain down following his encounter with Klaria. It was still there.

They walked in silence to the great hall. The journey seemed shorter than the night before, and Mindar pondered the odd encounter with the strange old Piraste, Klaria. He was quite sure that it had not been a dream. The dagger attested to that, but the map baffled him: how Klaria had gotten it and why he had kept it.

They sat at the breakfast table spread with fruit and bowls of soupy sweet porridge for dipping slices of fruit from the trays. Dajaan was in a foul mood. He had not spoken to any of them, and his warm confidence from the night before seemed to have vanished. Mindar smiled and nodded as he mimicked the way their hosts slathered the porridge onto their food and seemed to almost swallow it whole in their hurry to eat, belching and stretching frequently between mouthfuls. No one spoke.

"Sumbuddy tooka da map inna night!" Dajaan announced as he sat back and wiped his hands on a napkin in his lap. "An wenna we fin' diss one..." He drew his finger across his throat and frowned. Mindar looked over at Minxa who had a long sliver of fruit hanging out of his mouth, caught frozen in the revelation of the missing map. "Dis wassa a' locked up. Der no Piraste da' coulda take it." He looked over at Mindar. "I's sorry."

Mindar was surprised. "For what?" he asked.

"Da' werna ours map ta' take, no. Lonama's map, is alus belong a' sumbuddy. Diss one belong ta you."

Marhan broke the silence that followed. "You let someone steal the map?"

Dajaan looked up. "We donna let no wan a' take it. Ba' issa jes gone!"

Marhan started to stand, but the two burly brothers on each side of him put their hands on his shoulders and pulled him down into his seat.

"Don't you know where the portal is without the map?" asked Erinshava.

"Ha! Ba' dess is na da pro'lem..."

"Then what is the problem?" asked Minxa.

"Well, we fin'a da port, ba' ifs yousa goes inna dat, poof, yousa gon' an we don'na know where. An' der ain'a noway a cum back, no." Dajaan caught the flicker of Minxa's amusement. He stared at him curiously as a smile slipped across Minxa's lips. "Wa's funny?" Dajaan asked. Marhan's eyes narrowed.

"I know where the map is," Minxa said as he looked down into the slush bowl in front of him and shoved another finger of melon into his mouth. The table was silent. Mindar looked around at all the silly faces that were waiting for Minxa to stop chewing.

"Where issa det?" asked Dajaan without moving.

Minxa picked up a piece of orange fruit with his left hand, eyed it deliberately and while he pushed it into the porridge, he reached into his tunic with his right hand and pulled out the map box. He laid it carefully on the table in front of him before he stuffed the fruit into his mouth and smiled.

Dajaan scratched his bald head with both hands, and Erinshava started laughing. Sereline shook her head.

"Ba' how dju get wif it?" Dajaan asked.

The table waited until Minxa stopped chewing. "An old Piraste visited me last night and gave it to me," he said. Mindar saw the other Pirastes around the table move and exchange glances with one another.

"Old Piraste, no?" Dajaan's eyes narrowed as he spoke. "Wa' wassa 'is name?"

"He said his name was Klaria," Minxa answered.

Dajaan jumped up. *"Klaria?"*

Minxa nodded. Mindar was surprised by Dajaan's animated excitement at the name and equally surprised by Minxa's revelation.

Dajaan burst into a string of commands to the Pirastes at the table. Two of the young men jumped up and ran in different directions. Dajaan raised his hands above his head and clapped twice, then stood staring at Minxa while he waited for two armed guards who hurried up beside him. He flashed off two more commands without breaking eye contact with Minxa, and the guards sprinted away.

"Hows yu know 'bou' Klaria?" Dajaan said. His expression was full of storm as he sat down heavily.

"He visited me last night," Minxa repeated.

"When?"

"I don't know—it was dark. He carried a lump of green...something. We went to a small room near where we were sleeping, and he showed me the map. Then he gave it to me and told me to give it to Rindar because he is the owner." Minxa leaned across the table and shoved the map so it slid toward Mindar, who caught it before it fell off the table.

Dajaan stood again and barked a sharp order in Piraste, then sat down again, and turned to Marhan. "Is dissa tru?" he asked him.

Marhan shrugged, a helpless look of ignorance gilding his face.

"No one else woke up," Minxa interjected, "either when I came or when I went—even the guards."

Two guards ran up to Dajaan and saluted. He stood to meet them. The rapid exchange was unintelligible to Mindar, but he guessed that they had been guarding Minxa's room. Both guards shrugged and shook their heads as they spoke.

"Da' gards. Dey say da' nobuddy, wazza come in da' room!" Dajaan said looking at Minxa.

Minxa pointed to the map and shrugged. Dajaan dismissed the guards and sat down with his head in his hands and his elbows on the table.

"Who is Klaria?" Mindar asked.

"Was, *was*," said Dajaan shaking his head. "He was da' one dat made da' Piraste. When he com'sa back, dersa allus bigs trouble."

"He's dead?" Mindar asked.

Dajaan nodded.

"How long?"

Dajaan looked up. "Mebe hunert yea's. Mebe longa more."

"He came to my chambers last night too," Mindar said.

Dajaan shook his head and looked down. "Talked to you?"

"Yes," Mindar said, "it was almost the same as what Minxa said, except he did not give me the map. While we were in the room together, he taught me a few things that I need to know in order to get someone through the portal." Mindar glanced at Minxa who was staring back. "But he did not leave me the map," he said. "He must have visited Minxa after me."

"And no one'a else waked up?" Dajaan's eyes moved rapidly to Sereline, who shrugged, and then to Erinshava, who slowly shook her head. "An' da guards?"

"They were like dead men, standing at the door," Mindar said.

Dajaan rose and clapped his hands again. Several Pirastes whisked away the platters and bowls that had been breakfast. He looked into Mindar's eyes again, with renewed confidence and energy. "Sos yous tink ya know whata yous need a' use da' map now?"

"I think so."

"Good!" He stood again and barked several orders, then spoke to his family around the table. Several guards hurried in, and as they approached the table, the family stood and bowed to them before leaving quickly and silently.

"Wes gonna go t'da portal an's send Maza Minxa home. Den yous alla gonna go."

"What about our weapons?" asked Marhan, a residual anger gurgling around the edges of his voice.

"Yor'sa swords in da' riva. You'sa don'na need dem here!"

Marhan swore.

Dajaan jumped up and circled the table. Marhan rose to meet him, but Dajaan was too quick. His right hand grabbed Marhan's throat, and his left fist plowed into Marhan's face with the force of a blacksmith's maul. Marhan sank like a stone. Dajaan shook out his fist and looked around the circle at the stunned audience. "No ons usa words lika dis in dess caves, no?" Everyone nodded gravely.

"Now wees goin'," he said.

✠

The one who knows kirrin does not have to argue with himself.

Tristaron Harrista
The Kirrinath

They trudged through the seemingly endless corridors in near silence. Minxa knew that others were wrestling with the events of the night before. He figured Mindar was wondering why Klaria had not given the map to him, but chose rather to give it to Minxa to give to him, and maybe he was wondering why, after so many years of desperately seeking the map, he had given it back at all. Dajaan's alarm at the appearance of Klaria was evident, and he seemed in a hurry to be done with the series of events that apparently led to his re-appearance.

Marhan was unconscious from Dajaan's punch. Drofan and Soldar had little to say, and any attempt to contribute their thoughts to the situation would have been trivial and unappreciated. Minxa guessed that Erinshava and Sereline were most likely just hoping that the whole desperate situation would be over soon.

Minxa had his own troubles to worry over. He was still not sure exactly what it was that Klaria had said to him. The Piraste had implied that he would make it through the portal to Vindarill, but how he made it through would somehow make a difference in the outcome of it. He had to trust Rindar. He had been required to give Rindar the map: that part of it made sense because Rindar was the only one who could work it. But was there something else? What he could remember of the conversation rattled through his head:

"What do you want from me?!"

"Metnoga—If'n ya don change, den life be close t'oblivion in ya citee."

Minxa remembered saying something about blackmail.

"Yous gotta choose."

"Do I have time to think about it?"

"T'night ya gotsa decide: metnoga—or Oblivion. Ya got'sa choose. In da mawning, we see yous decision."

The vivid image of Klaria looking from his left hand to his right would not go away, but now instead of just once, Klaria was looking back and forth, forth and back. *"Metnoga—or Oblivion. Oblivion—or metnoga."* What was he supposed to change? His attitude? His plan? Klaria could not possibly have known what he was going to do. No one knew his plan. It would have been unreasonable for Klaria to expect him to change his feelings toward Rindar in such a short time. Almost forty years of accumulated frustration, anger and hurt was not something that could be resolved before they went through the portal.

For a fleeting moment, Minxa realized that they might have all the time in the world, that there was no rush to get through the portal. It had been there, according to legend, since the beginning of Tessalindria and would be there long after he was gone. In one view of life, Minxa had all the time in the world to change—but the portal was so close and he had waited so long.... He pushed the thought out of harm's way into one of the dark corners of his mind where he hid unthinkable thoughts. He was close now, and he would have to take his chances with Oblivion. His luck had returned, and the words of the old man were not going to rob him of it now.

✠

Sometimes the doors of this life shut behind us and cannot be reopened.

Oratanga
Passages

Somewhere on the way to the portal, Marhan revived, and the guards that were carrying him called out to Dajaan. The entourage stopped while they poured water on his face and waited for him to be awake enough to walk. Two guards helped him as they started out once more.

They traveled up, winding back and forth and following Dajaan as he moved down corridors without hesitation. Multiple passages branched off, leading through the rock in all directions. Mindar had spent many hours in caves, but nothing like this: the tubes through which they passed were smooth and the walking was easy; but sometimes they had to crawl, and there were numerous holes in the floor that dropped down into black darkness.

"How far is it to the portal?" Mindar asked when they stopped for a drink.

Dajaan laughed. "Mebe seve'na holes more, mebe eight."

"Holes?"

"Da, hols in da' bottom," he said pointing to the floor.

Mindar nodded. He counted as they traipsed off. After seven floor holes, they stopped. Dajaan smiled. "Da' portal! Iss jus der." He pointed to a corridor leading off to the left. "When yous ready, Maza Mindar, we alla go der."

Mindar pulled the map from his tunic and opened the box carefully onto the stone floor. Dajaan was right. The black smudge of the portal was just around the corner at the back of a large chamber. Mindar looked up. "Shouldn't we go into the chamber and set the dates there."

"No, da' woulda be na' good. Da' portal iss bery dangous unaless yous hav'a da map."

"I have the map," Mindar said.

Dajaan eyed him carefully, then looked up and spoke Piraste with several of the guards. The guards looked nervous as they answered their leader. "We willa go, ba' we stay 'way from da' portal, ya?"

"If you wish."

"Yous be first!" said Dajaan.

Mindar led the procession into the chamber, and the Pirastes set the torches they were carrying into cracks in the wall so they would not have

Lonama's Map

to hold them. Mindar looked around. In the dim light, he could tell that they were nervous. Sereline and Erinshava stared across the room at the blackness of the portal. "It's incredible," said Erinshava.

"Looks good to me," growled Minxa. "I wanna see you set the date, map man!"

Mindar looked up. A cruel smile curled on Minxa's lips. As much as he regretted it, it was going to be nice to be rid of him. Mindar glanced at Marhan. His face bore no expression over the black circles that were forming under his eyes. Drofan's eyes were wide with terror at the sight of the portal.

Mindar moved to the center of the chamber to spread the map on the floor, and as he turned it over, it became obvious what the rings meant. Perhaps it was the sleep. Perhaps it was the ghost of Klaria or the hand of the nearly unseen Eladra that had accompanied them into the chamber, but it suddenly made sense.

Sereline was by his left side with her hand on his shoulder. It was trembling. Minxa was opposite him, and Erinshava was crouched between Sereline and Minxa. To his right, not ten feet away, was the inky nothingness of the portal. Vakandar strutted back and forth, cocking his eye to the blackness. "Nasty, nasty, nasty darkness!" he said

As Mindar touched the first ring, the darkness shifted. There was no way to describe it, since there was nothing to see, but something in the nothingness changed. "What year is it?" Mindar asked. He knew the answer, but he needed to let Minxa know what he was doing.

Minxa looked at Mindar stupidly. "1240 by the Markarhan Calendar," he muttered.

"And what year are you wanting to go to?" Mindar asked.

"2255, same calendar."

"'55? Are you sure?" Mindar asked. "That's a year before we left."

"Look," Minxa snarled, "I have been thinking about this for almost forty years. I know when I want to go back."

The look in his face and the deadness of his eyes gave Mindar no room for mirth. Mindar looked down to the map and did the calculations in his head. "One thousand and fifteen years, right?" he said without looking up.

"Can't you just set the date?"

"It works on the differential," Mindar said. "The inner ring is in thousand year increments." Mindar moved the ring one notch into the future. "So that's a thousand, leaving fifteen years. The next one out is in one hundred year increments, so we can ignore that—then the eight-year ring and there are...let's see..."

"One," said Erinshava with a smile.

Minxa looked up and scowled. Mindar laughed. "Right, one—

leaving…"

"Seven," Erinshava was smiling when Mindar looked up.

"Right," he said. Mindar slid the eight-year ring one notch, moved his finger to the next ring and counted off to seven slowly. He could see Minxa's head bobbing with each count. To his right he could feel the portal shifting as he inched it along.

"The next ring is in months," Mindar said as he looked up. "Which month do you want?"

"Oratar!" Minxa was emphatic. "I want it to be warm—and getting warmer."

Erinshava smiled. Mindar moved the fifth ring into place by selecting the number for the month of Oratar which always preceded the spring equinox.

Mindar set his finger on the last ring and pulled it around to the middle of the month. "There," he said as he held the map up to the light and traced the invisible line from Vindarill to the point on the Kirrinath. "You are fortunate, Minxa," Mindar muttered as he turned it over. "Not all the portals lead to all the other portals. But you *can* get to Vindarill from here."

"Good," he grunted, "that's where I want to go."

As rapidly as Mindar could, he focused the map in on Vindarill and swept in close. "Look familiar?" he asked as he looked up at Minxa. Minxa almost smiled. Mindar looked around at the Pirastes hugging the walls of the chamber opposite the portal. They were stern and silent, and he could tell they would rather leave and do it quickly.

"So you think the portal is set?" Minxa asked.

"I think so," Mindar said as he stood up. "Are you ready to leave?"

Minxa rose and stood facing Mindar. "Are you?" he asked smiling.

"You know I am not going," Mindar said. "You seem to think there is something there for you, but I know there is nothing there for me. I belong here now, with my family."

"Your *family*," Minxa sneered. "I was your family once, you know that."

"We have gone down different paths now, Minxa," Mindar said. "I guess it is time to finally part forever. I am hoping you find a place for yourself in Vindarill, but my place is here."

Minxa's face softened for a moment, and he took a step toward Mindar and hesitated. Mindar stared into his eyes. He could see the struggle, or what he thought was a struggle. Then Minxa stepped forward and wrapped his arms around Mindar in a tight embrace, whispering in his ear, "Billy Billy, bub'n scrump, champy's in the cataroup…"

Mindar sensed Erinshava stepping toward him, but as she started to speak, Minxa, his arms still tightly wrapped around Mindar, lurched toward the blackness. After years of military training, Minxa was much stronger than Mindar. In two swift steps, Minxa had dragged him near to the dark vaporous wall of the portal. "Sereline!" Mindar yelled, struggling to free himself from Minxa's grasp. Erinshava had caught up to them and had grabbed hold of Minxa's ears. He howled in pain and kicked at her, losing his balance. Sereline screamed, and the cavern echoed from all sides. Mindar felt the fluff of Vakandar's wings as the black bird landed on Minxa's head.

Minxa heaved again. Mindar saw Erinshava's fingers closing around Minxa's eyes, but nothing was going to deter him from dragging Mindar into the portal. Mindar tried to drop, but Minxa's arms were under his. Mindar pitched his forehead into Minxa's nose as hard as he could, and Minxa swore an oath in pain. They were half in the darkness when, with a mighty tug, Minxa threw them both into the inky nothingness. Erinshava's hands disappeared. Vakandar's wings fluffed again, and Minxa bellowed in pain, his hot breath swirling around Mindar's face.

All the sound vanished. They were still on solid ground, but Mindar knew that would not last long. "Please!" Mindar begged into the darkness. "Let me go."

"You dragged me...into this once," Minxa breathed heavily in his ear as Mindar struggled against him, "I'm...just...returning...the favor." With a surge of strength, Minxa threw Mindar over the edge of nothing. Mindar felt Minxa falling with him. Vakandar screeched, and Mindar heard his wings beating against the darkness as they fell together.

18 Vindarill 18

Every being needs a companion for the dark hours of life when he cannot find his own way.

Oratanga
Passages

For the first time in years, Mindar found himself afraid of his own anger. He sat still on the cold stone floor in the darkness of the cave while vague recollections of Vindarill floated through his mind. They were from so long ago that they contained little reality. He was also not sure how much of all of it was distorted by two trips through the portals. Three great fears reached beyond his anger:

First, if the portal was in the same place as when he and Minxa left Vindarill, and he had indeed returned sometime before the time they left, then the path to the portal by which they entered was not yet open, leaving him at a complete loss about which direction to go.

His second fear was that if he moved, he would fall back through the portal into another time and place altogether.

The third was that if Minxa had come with him, he was likely to be nearby, and Mindar did not want to have any more to do with him. All the teachings about selkah, kariis and love for the unlovable shouted into the irrational vacuum of fear in his noga. Perhaps in time, he could do this, but right now Mindar wanted to be as far from Minxa as possible.

He listened carefully for any hint of Minxa's presence. After several minutes, he noticed the slow dripping of water off to his right and reasoned that it was safe to move in that direction because no sound would come out of the portal.

He stood cautiously, not knowing how low the ceiling of the cavern was. As he stood, Minxa spoke. "Rindar." The blood froze in Mindar's veins at the sound. "Are you there?"

Mindar stooped slowly and slipped off his left shoe and stuffed it in his tunic.

"I can hear you, Rindar." Minxa's voice was full of anger. Mindar's right shoe came off in his hand.

"I am here, Minxa," Mindar said. As he did so he moved quickly away from where he had been standing. Minxa shuffled madly to the spot Mindar had left.

"Don't leave me, Rindar," he pleaded. "Rasler gouged my eyes before we got to the portal. I can't see!"

Mindar inched away from his voice, moving his hands slowly in front of him and above his head to make sure he did not hit his head on stone. He stubbed his toe and stifled a gasp.

"Why do you hate me, Rindar?" Minxa pleaded.

Mindar had run into a large boulder. He felt his way around it, and when he was standing safely behind it, he spoke again. "I...I don't want to hate you," he said.

"Liar!" Minxa yelled as he launched toward Mindar again. Mindar heard his head hit the boulder. Minxa swore a vile oath in Mooriman, and Mindar used the diversion and Minxa's subsequent bellowing to distance himself further. "You have always hated me!" Minxa yelled. "But I need your help. I can't see anything!" His voice was shaking, somewhere between anger and fear, alternating abruptly between oaths and pleading for mercy. Mindar crept away without daring to speak again.

Mindar was on his knees and crawling slowly when he felt the huff of wings near him. Vakandar had found him and was nearby. He had not said anything, probably out of fear, the same reason that Mindar was reluctant to speak.

"I'll find you," Minxa growled. "I'll get out of this cave. You know I will. You won't be able to hide from me, Rindar Colloden!" Mindar had crept about twenty feet during Minxa's tirade, a safe enough distance to sit down and think.

He sat for a long time. Every once in a while he could hear Minxa shuffling around and talking to himself, but he seemed to be making no effort to go anywhere. At some point, Vakandar had approached Mindar and pecked lightly at his leg. Mindar extended his hand and gently stroked the bird's back. Vakandar didn't move. Mindar touched him several times. It was comforting to have another being with him, even if it was only a bird.

Mindar thought about what had happened back at the other side of the portal. Tears filled his eyes in the darkness. He could still hear Sereline screaming as Minxa dragged him into the darkness. She would now be dead nearly a thousand years.

He wondered if Erinshava had ever found her way to the anthara and about what must have happened to the map. It had been open on the floor when Minxa grabbed him. The emotions ebbed and flowed. He fought the urge to blame Mah'Eladra for allowing this to happen to him. He had devoted himself to them, and they had let him down, and now he struggled to find meaning in this tragic turn of events.

The unmistakable hiss of an Eladra engaging nearby interrupted Mindar's thoughts. He froze. For about ten seconds nothing happened. "Ssshhhh." He felt a cold hand on his shoulder and a whisper in his ear. "*Awann avar.*" The original language, but he knew what it meant: "Follow now."

"I hear you again, Rindar!" Minxa raved, "I am begging you, don't leave me to die here!"

A strong hand lifted Mindar by his upper arm. It guided him rapidly at right angles to the direction from which Minxa's voice offered up a new string of epithets and curses. They had gone about ten feet in utter darkness, his feet stumbling along the rough floor of the cave when suddenly, a faint green glow filled the corridor in front of Mindar. It was not much, but his light-starved eyes leapt to its glimmer. They hurried on in silence. Mindar's guide had let go of his arm and was two steps in front of him, as Minxa's echoing rants faded behind. He heard an occasional huff of Vakandar's wings behind him, but he dared not look back.

When they were safely out of reach of Minxa's ears, his savior turned and spoke. "Yous wanna sum wata?" He held out a bottle with a cork in it.

"Klaria?"

The little Piraste held the green lump he was carrying up in front of his face. "Yous look lika you seena ghost."

Mindar shook his head.

"Yous donna wanna wata?"

"No, no," Mindar said, "I *do* want water, thank you."

"Sitza youself, Maza Mindar. You'sa safe hea."

Mindar sat down on a ledge of rock that jutted out into the cave as Vakandar strutted into the corridor in front of him, cocking his head to watch but saying nothing. Mindar took the bottle gratefully from Klaria's hand and worked the cork out of its neck. Klaria laughed as Mindar took his first gulp. It was the same bitter liquid they had given him that morning in the Vanjar caves. Mindar nearly choked. "This isn't water," he said angrily.

Klaria snatched the bottle from his hand and waved it in front of his nose. "Ha! I's maida beeg mistake, ha!" He started laughing again.

"What is it?" Mindar asked.

"A deesa here, det be kaffa! Da Piraste usa det fur a waka dem up, no?"

"I know."

"Ba' you na like it?"

"Why would anyone like it?"

Klaria made a corkscrew pattern with his finger near his ear. "Dosa Piraste, deysa lita…"

"You aren't Piraste?" Mindar asked.

"Ho no! Me? I em Eladra. Ba' ya knows dis, no?"

"You look and talk like a Piraste," Mindar observed.

"Ha! I's gotta talks lika sumbuddy when I stops here, no?"

Mindar shook his head. "Do you have any real water?" he asked.

"Come. We's finda sum real wata."

The trail through the fissures and cracks that led upward to the surface grew tortuous and rough, unlike the Vanjar caves whose passageways had been carved by water. Large shards of rock lay piled on one another in the chaos in which they had fallen from the ceiling of the cave. Each had to be navigated respectfully, sometimes over the top, sometimes under or between. They spoke little as Klaria led them on. Vakandar did not speak. He alternately strutted and fluttered along the floor between Mindar and Klaria, obviously eager not to be left behind. Mindar wondered how Minxa would ever make it out, and he wondered in the same instant whether he even cared. In his vorn, he knew that Minxa would escape and that he had not seen the last of him.

"Dajaan said that you were the first Piraste, and that when you show up, there is always trouble," Mindar observed as they sat and rested by a small stream coming from a fissure in the rock.

"Ha! I allus come when da Piraste ha' de trouble. Dey jussa tink I's da cause. Yous gonna drink?"

Mindar knelt by the stream and slurped water into his dry mouth. It was clean and cold and refreshed him. "How far is it to the surface?"

"Deta iss na' far. Ba' det take sum time."

It took them nearly an hour to get to the surface from that point, and their emergence from the cleft in the side of the hill overlooking Vindarill was anticlimactic. It was night, it was cold, and a thick fog lay over the city. Clouds covered the night sky. Mindar felt like he had never left the cave except for the light chilly wind that flowed down the hill from behind him.

☩

Water is the basis of physical life, and pure water offered in genuine concern was an icon of his love for others.

Terrasinden Varr
Sessasha's Way

Vindarill was a foreign city to Mindar now. He did not remember it being as dirty and as hostile as it seemed. He tried to think back and remember, but his memories were all of his youth and were jaded with years of separation.

Klaria had left him at the exit from the cave, and Vakandar had vanished with the little Eladra without a word. Klaria had given Mindar the bottle of kaffa, a lump of dry bread, an apple and some unsolicited advice: "Yous gotsa be much careful in diss city," he said sternly. "Ders much piple in diss city, an' sum a' dem be berry ebil. Sum a' dem is yourz kind, an' yous gotsa fin' *dem*."

"How will I do that?" he had asked. "How will I know them?"

"Deyz don' wan' nothin' fum you. Deyz jus offa ya' wata."

"Water?"

"Jus' wata, no kaffa, ha!" He laughed at his own joke with a simple mirth.

"Will I see you again?" Mindar asked.

"No, no, Maza Mindar. I's gottsa keepa me eyes fur doz'a Pirastes." He smiled again and laid his hand on Mindar's shoulder. "Ba' derz be udders who keepa der eye fur you. Drink'a de kaffa slow, ya?"

He nodded. Klaria turned and disappeared with a hiss, and Mindar never saw him again.

He had plenty of time to think about what Klaria had said. He had no idea what time it was, but the streets of Vindarill were empty. So Mindar made his way toward the waterfront, hunting for some place he could escape from the rain. He had no money, and his tunic was nearly soaked through.

"*Deyz jus offa ya' wata.*'" The words rang in his head as he tried to remember ever being offered water on the streets of Vindarill. He could

not think of a single instance when this had happened. Perhaps, in his
youth, as hostile and aggressive as he was, he would not have been the
kind of kid that anyone would have offered water. He was not sure what
"yourz kind" would be. Older people? People with no money and little
hope? People who had bathed in the Jualar Springs or those who had
seen Eladra? People who had no place to live? Maybe it was people who
had been through a portal or whose best friend had betrayed them.

Mindar knew that the waterfront would be the most likely place to
find shelter. The warehouses and dockyards were filled with awnings
and doorways that the street people used at night. As he drew near, he
could smell the water, mingled with rotting fish, creosote and seaweed.
It was similar to the smell of the ocean on Islag or Karolil, but vile and
corrupted by its distance from the open sea.

He walked down an empty dock until he found an unoccupied
doorway to one of the fishmonger's shops. It was wide enough so he
could stretch his legs across it, and it had an awning that kept the upper
step and threshold to the door dry. Mindar sat down in the leeward side
and pulled his tunic around himself. It was wet, but the wool kept him
warm in spite of the dampness.

He pulled his lump of bread out of his tunic and gnawed on it slowly. It was stale, but sweet; and after eating about a third of it, he was satisfied. He stuffed it back into his tunic and leaned back, stretching his
legs out across the stoop.

"Get up, ya bum." Someone was kicking him. "Get outa here. The
market opens in fifteen minutes," the voice shouted again. Mindar
shook his head and opened his eyes. The angry shopkeeper was so close
that Mindar could smell his breath. He slapped Mindar's face. "Get up!"
he shouted again as he grabbed Mindar's tunic, and rolled him down
the two steps to the pavement.

"This ain't no hotel, viddik!" he growled as he turned his back to
open the door. Mindar involuntarily looked at the back of his hands. He
was a marked man in this culture, but he had forgotten what it meant.
For so many years, the tattoos were simple curiosities to people. Here
they meant persecution and rejection.

Mindar got to his knees. Gray streaks of dawn showed themselves
across the harbor. He was dizzy from the fall and still not fully awake,
so he fetched the bottle of kaffa from his tunic, pulled the cork with his
teeth and heaved a slug of it into his mouth past the cork. He recoiled
from the taste, but it woke him up. He stood up. "Don't sleep here
again, ya wino," the merchant called. "Next time I'll get the polls first."
The door to the shop rattled as the man slammed it shut behind him.

The waterfront was waking up with the dawn. It had been years since Mindar had seen a petrotruck, and as one passed him on its way to one of the markets, the warm suffocating swirl of exhaust in its wake reminded him once again where he really was. He stuffed the bottle of kaffa back in his tunic.

The gray dawn gave way to the sun, which rose like a red ball over the harbor as Mindar watched the gulls alternately strutting around on the dock and arguing over filthy scraps of fish. He still hated the gulls, now even more because of their association with the NarEladra. He wondered whether it was the same here in Vindarill, a thousand years later, but even if it were not, he did not trust them. Their bickering brought back thoughts about the old man. Somewhere in this city, in a small kitchen that he could probably not find, an old man would soon die. Mindar thought Minxa's calculations had been off and that they had returned closer to the time of the event that had started him on his journey.

Tears welled up in Mindar's eyes. He felt the choking tightness in his throat of a cry that could not escape. He breathed deeply and tried to relax, looking up into the clouds that were retreating from the wind coming in across the harbor. For a brief moment, he wondered whether he could have prevented what happened and what would have been different if he had. He sighed and looked back down to the harbor as he wiped his eyes on his sleeve.

The wind was chilly, but the comfort of daylight shining on the wet streets made the city seem tolerably clean. Mindar had no agenda, no schedule, nowhere to go and no one to see. Those whom he really wanted were unreachable. He tried not to think of Sereline and the girls, but he wondered if or how he would ever know what happened to them. He still was not sure he understood what took place in Kinvara, but figured that if he could ever get into a library, he could find that in the history books, or at least in the stories. A thousand years is enough to make a legend out of any truth. It felt odd to be on the other side of all the legends that he ignored as a youth.

Mindar sat on the edge of the dock watching and listening, feeling largely anonymous in the busy morning fish market. Boats came and went, unloading their cargo before the critical eyes of the buyers. Money changed hands, flowing from person to person, but none of it available to him. He knew he needed money and had none. It would be dangerous to have a lot of money in Vindarill, he knew that, but he was equally aware of how dangerous it was to have none at all. People were suspicious of those who had no money. It was a petty crime to be caught without money, because what would one be doing anywhere in the city unless he were intending to transact some sort of business; and no business deals happened without money, unless they were illegal.

Mindar took stock of what he did have: an apple, which he fully intended to eat, the dried lump of sweetbread that would meet the same fate, about four more days of kaffa in the bottle and the dagger, still tucked into the folds in his tunic. Being caught with the dagger would be dangerous without a good explanation for it, but he dared not discard it because of Klaria's urgency about keeping it with him.

When the sun finally broke through the clouds in earnest, he stood and stretched. He was mostly dry, though still chilled. Mindar filled his lungs with air and his noga with a more positive attitude, and then he set out to find a job—any job that would put bread in his hands.

He stopped at the first boat that pulled into the dock. "You need help unloading this thing?" he yelled as the crew sidled the boat to the wharf. The captain eyed him carefully between barked orders to the crew as they secured the boat.

As the captain jumped off the boat he said, "Sure, old man; if ya gotta back that can take it."

"I'll do my best," Mindar assured him.

The fish were hauled out of the hold in large baskets by a winch. Mindar's job was to empty the basket into the petrotruck that had pulled up to the boat as soon as it docked. He stood on the back of the truck. When the basket swung in, he had to catch it, grab the handle on the bottom and upend it into the truck. Twice he got knocked over by the swinging basket, slipping on the fishy truck deck and falling into the pile of fish, much to the amusement of the boat crew. Both times, he laughed and got up quickly to continue the work.

When the truck was full, another took its place. He loaded three of them before the hold of the boat was empty. When the last truck pulled away, he stood and waited on the edge of the dock, covered with fish slime from head to foot, but thankful for the work. The crew of the boat stowed the tackle and began washing down the boat. The captain ignored him from the cabin, making notes in a book and adding and re-adding numbers. He looked up when he was finished and poked his head out the door. "There's nothing else to do here," he said.

"I'd like to be paid for my work," Mindar answered.

"I don't pay viddiks," he said with a grin, nodding toward his hands.

"I worked for nearly an hour and a half," Mindar observed desperately.

"Yes, you did, and it was a fine show," he said, "but I don't pay viddiks. Now get outta here before I call the polls."

Vindarill! As a kid he had put up with this kind of treatment because he had never known anything else, but now, having experienced being accepted and valued, he was angry. He was angry, not only at this particular captain, but also at the entire wayward society where people were held in contempt because of their birth heritage and nothing more.

Mindar leapt onto the deck of the boat and moved toward the captain. The captain put his fingers to his mouth and whistled. Three crewmen grabbed Mindar before he could reach the captain. They hauled him to the end of the boat and threw him over the rail like a sack of grain. He came to the surface sputtering in the oil slick leaking out of the back of the boat, his apple and his bottle of kaffa floating beside him.

The fishermen laughed. Mindar took the sweet bread from his tunic and shook off the sticky mass in the water. Somewhere between insult and outrage, he collected his apple and his bottle and swam to the ladder. He left to the jeers of the crew without looking back.

After walking a few hundred yards down the dock, he sat down and wrung out his clothes as well as he could without taking them off—he knew *that* would mean trouble. Then he sat down to think.

"What you got in that bottle, friend?" He turned to see another man making his way to sit beside him. He was about Mindar's age, and his clothes looked as if he had worn them for years. He smelled like he hadn't bathed in months. Mindar saw the tattoos on the man's wrists as he extended a small bottle to Mindar. "I'll trade what I got for a taste a' what you got," he said with smile. He was missing two teeth.

"What you got?" Mindar asked.

"Just a bit a' water," he said with a wink as he passed the uncorked bottle under Mindar's nose. It was not water.

"Swig for a swig?" Mindar asked, figuring the amusement would be worth the chance.

The stranger nodded.

Mindar handed him the bottle of kaffa, and he took the little bottle, wiping its rim with the corner of his sleeve. They swigged together, but Mindar barely let it into his mouth. Whatever it was burned Mindar's tongue. The man gulped the kaffa and then spit it all over the dock in a burst of profanity. He shoved the bottle back to Mindar and grabbed his own, upending it into his mouth to wash out the taste of the kaffa.

Mindar laughed and the man swore again. "What you do that to another viddik for?" he gasped.

"You wanted to trade," Mindar observed.

"What is it?"

"Kaffa."

"Never heard of it?"

Mindar nodded.

"You *like* that stuff?"

Mindar shook his head. "No."

The man stood up. "You're strange," he said and turned to leave.

"Wait," Mindar said.

The man turned back to Mindar.

"You offered me water," he said, "but it wasn't water."

The man eyed him suspiciously. "You didn't see m'wink?"

Mindar wasn't sure what to say. "Is there any place around here that a viddik can get a job?" he asked.

"*What?*"

"I need a job—no, I need a little money. How can I get some?"

The man looked at his hands. "Steal it!"

"No—without stealing," Mindar insisted.

The man shook his head at him and turned away. "You gotta steal—ain't no one gonna give a viddik no money."

Mindar spent most of that day trying to find someone who would hire him for even the most vile jobs, but each time, when they saw his hands, they would say no. Some were polite, even sympathetic, but none would help. He ate his apple for a late lunch and got some water from a bucket he found under a drain spout sitting by the road. Mostly, he just pondered his situation as he wandered around the waterfront.

Mindar knew that hunger and fear were his greatest enemies. The hunger he could mitigate by fasting, a discipline he had cultivated during his years in Kinvara. He also knew that the fasting would produce a mental and emotional clarity in his vorn that could be had no other way, and he needed that at this time also. Fear was a greater enemy. Erinshava had taught him not to fear, or at least the discipline of focusing on the right things and laying out his fears verbally before Mah'Eladra. He talked out loud, imagining and then believing that they heard and would do something about his needs.

In an odd way, he could never prove he was being heard, but in the usual depths of paradox, the fear would subside and the path was made straight before him. Mindar's only explanation for what happened was that they did hear him. Life became simple again, and he always found a path through it that did not force him to leave the paths of the Kirrinath.

Mindar walked the waterfront for the rest of the afternoon, alternately muttering to himself and listening for an answer. It wasn't exactly listening, but more of a waiting until something happened that was clear enough to act on. Most people stared at him and gave him plenty of room. He was sure they thought he was just a crazy old viddik, down on life and thoroughly deserving of it, but his vorn was refreshed and he grew bold again.

Late in the afternoon, he walked past a shop at the north end of the docks that he had passed twice already in his journey up and down the docks. A man stepped from the shadows of the shop. "What're you doin'?" he asked.

"I am learning, listening and looking for a job," Mindar said simply as he looked the man in the eye.

The shopkeeper looked down at his hands. "Unfortunately, you won't find one here," he said. There was a note of genuine sympathy in his voice as he continued, "But I have a friend who may be able to help. Can you read?"

Mindar's anger flared inside, but he realized that it was a fair question on the docks of Vindarill. "I can," he said.

"Can you do physical work—I mean lifting and loading?"

"Yes."

"Wait here."

He disappeared into the back of his shop. Mindar stood in the orange sun and waited, hoping against hope that the ray of light would become a beacon. The man returned with a bottle in his hand. "Would you like some water?" he asked, looking into Mindar's eyes with an earnestness and politeness of a man whose vorn had been tempered by kariis and was truly interested in his welfare.

"Yes, thank you," Mindar answered.

The man handed him the bottle with a piece of paper wrapped around it. The man never broke eye contact as he spoke. "Go three blocks south to Varhaven Street, and head west until you come to a small park. Drink your water there and read the note on the bottle." He did not smile, but he did ask a question that stirred Mindar's vorn. "What is your name?"

"I am Mindar Colloden."

The man's eyebrows shot up, but he regained his composure quickly. "Mindar Colloden," he said without emotion, "my name is Takada. I hope we meet again."

Mindar nodded. It was clear that it was time to move on. Takada's kindness was genuine, but it was also guarded, as if what he had just done was a dangerous thing. Mindar stuffed the green bottle of water into his tunic with the bottle of kaffa and headed south along the hostile docks of Vindarill.

✠

Acceptance and kindness, born out of true kariis, should always be seen as a far greater gift than money or food.

Tristaron Harrista
The Kirrinath

Mindar stood in front of the large door to the warehouse that the note had indicated, waiting for a response to his knock. It seemed like a long time, as petrocars and pedestrians swarmed past him on the way home after their busy day driving the economy of the city. People gave him plenty of space. His clothing smelled, and the tunic was an oddity that he could not hide, but his wrists were the most offensive of all. He breathed a sigh of relief when he heard the bolt being drawn from the inside.

The door creaked open and a diminutive man in a gray uniform peered out at him. Mindar held out the green bottle and asked for water. "Takada sent me," he said.

The man peered through his thick eyeplates, and a faint smile flickered on his lips. "I think I can get you some," he said, "but you will have to come inside." He stepped back to allow Mindar to enter.

"Wait here for a moment, please," he said after he had closed the door.

Mindar stood in a small anteroom. The far side had a large window in it that looked over a warehouse stacked high with boxes, crates and bales of every shape and size. Mindar watched the little man wend his way across the floor, disappearing occasionally behind stacks of boxes. There were other people in the warehouse, moving its contents about and cleaning.

The man found the person he was looking for and handed him the water bottle. The tall, thin man looked up toward the glass cage. Mindar looked back and knew that the thin man saw him. The two men exchanged words, and the short man made his way back as the tall one disappeared into an aisle between the cartons.

The short man had barely made it back when the tall one sauntered up behind him, with the bottle still in his hand. They entered the room together. "Would you like some water?" the tall one said as he handed Mindar the bottle.

"Yes, thank you," Mindar responded. The thin man handed him the water and made a little motion that he should drink. Mindar put the bottle to his lips and drank. It was cold and refreshing.

When he was done, the tall man extended his hand to shake Mindar's. He was a viddik. "I am Glordan," he said with a smile. "This is Mirad, my bookkeeper."

Mindar shook his hand. "I am Mindar Colloden," he said. "Thank you for the water."

Glordan smiled. "That is a famous name, but odd for a viddik." There was no offense or resentment in the way he used the word viddik. It was just a word to him. "Do you need work, Mindar?"

"My need is for a small amount of money, and if my work will earn me that, I will work well for it."

"We cannot pay a lot here, but we will pay you fairly. We have many people we are trying to help, and we share what we have, but you are safe here as long as you do not break psadeq with us."

It was refreshing to hear a man speak who used words that reflected a knowledge of the Kirrinath and a vorn shaped by them.

"Do you have a place to sleep tonight?" Glordan asked.

"I slept in a doorway on the waterfront last night," Mindar said.

"And the night before?"

"In a cave in the Vanjar Escarpment on the river north of Kinvara—in Tessamandria."

Glordan's eyebrows rose perceptibly. "You have come a long way to be with us, Mindar. You may sleep here tonight." There was no scorn or doubt in his voice. "Mirad will show you to a bunk. It is not much, but it is dry and clean. Dinner will be served in one hour. I would like to talk to you after that."

He turned to Mirad. "Find Mindar some suitable clothes," he said gently. "Show him where the bathing rooms are and burn these," he said pointing at Mindar's clothing before he turned back to Mindar. "Will you sit with me at dinner?"

Mindar nodded. "Thank you," he said. "Could you wash the tunic?" he added. "It was a special gift from a friend."

Glordan smiled. "Of course. Until then," Glordan said as he strode through the door into the warehouse, closing it noiselessly behind him.

"Come along," Mirad said, "you must be tired."

"I am," Mindar said as he walked along behind Mirad down a corridor that skirted the edge of the warehouse floor where natural light filtered down through numerous windows in the ceiling. Workers paused to look at them as they passed. Most nodded and smiled as if they knew him.

The bunkroom was at the back of the warehouse. It consisted of two large rooms, one for the women and one for the men, and was filled with rows of bunks, two high, each made up with clean blue and green blankets. Mirad made his way to a closet and pulled out a pillow. "You may pick any bed that does not have a pillow," Mirad said. "When you put this on it, it becomes yours. The box at the foot of the bottom bed, belongs to it. The box at the head belongs to the top bed. You can put anything personal in the box, but when your box is full, it will be time to find another place to sleep."

Mindar's questioning look triggered an answer: "We live simply, Mindar. If a person begins to collect things that exceed the volume of the box, it is fine, but it is also a time to make room for others who have less."

Mindar nodded.

"I will get you some clothing," Mirad said as he turned away, leaving him to select his place among the beds.

At the far end from the door were large windows that faced north, and most of the beds near the window were unoccupied. Mindar thought this was curious, but made his way there. Light was important to him; any light, even the light of the night sky. He chose the bed on the very end, under the window, placing his pillow ceremoniously in its place, claiming a small piece of space to call his own in the huge, hostile city of Vindarill.

✠

Do not allow yourself to tire in the pursuit of truth.

Vindorian Proverb

Dinner was a simple affair. The large room where they were to eat was filled with small tables and chairs, all efficiently placed so that there was barely room to walk between them. Each table held eight, three on each side and one at each end. Mindar guessed that the dining room could hold seventy to a hundred persons.

Mirad had given him clean clothing. It wasn't new, but it fit reasonably and comfortably. The loose shirt and trousers were all gray, with a hint of blue, suitable but nondescript. He had two shirts, two pairs of pants and several pairs of underclothing. "Tomorrow we will get you some shoes," Mirad had said. He had given Mindar a comb when he came out of the shower, so for the first time in nearly forty years, he was able to comb his hair properly. He felt new and he felt clean; those were the best words he had for it.

People laughed and chatted as they filed into the hall in pairs or groups of three and four. Most of them were Vindarillians, many of them viddiks, but there were many others: Otallans and Dorfranders, Vindorians, several who looked like they could be Immerlanders and several Mythinians with their copper skin and deep reddish hair. They reminded him of Sereline, and he had to look away. A number of the diners were not dressed in the warehouse grays and appeared to be from outside, and there were several children of varying ages who sat at the tables with the adults.

Mindar sat with Mirad at a table off to one side. As people noticed him they would break off from their groups and approach him, look him in the eye, introduce themselves and welcome him to the warehouse. There was no presumption, no uneasiness, and no fear or reluctance. Each said their name and that they were appreciative of his presence and that they hoped he would be comfortable at the warehouse.

Glordan entered with his wife and looked around. When he saw

Mindar and Mirad, he pointed and moved to join them. "This is my wife, Marall, and my son Jeshwa," he said as he gently touched his wife's shoulder and gestured to his son. Both nodded.

Marall held out her hand. "Glordan tells me you have traveled far to be with us." Her eyes were as black as coal and her hair a deep chestnut color that shone in the lights suspended above the tables. She was simply dressed in a faded blue smock with a thin necklace of shells. She wore no other jewelry except the ring on her middle finger, and conveyed a quiet, startling beauty without pretense.

"It has been a long road, but I am glad to be here," Mindar answered.

"Please sit down," said Glordan. "Dinner will be ready shortly."

Mirad was on Mindar's right and Jeshwa sat to his left. Across the table, Glordan sat in the middle with Marall to his left. Mindar guessed that Jeshwa was about eighteen, with dark hair and dark eyes like his mother, but with his father's long thin nose and angled chin. They had barely sat down when Jeshwa picked up the pitcher of water that sat in the middle of the table. "Mr. Colloden, would you like some water?" he asked. His eyes were filled with an earnest willingness to serve.

"Yes," he said as he picked up the tumbler on the table before him, "I would like some water."

Jeshwa poured Mindar's glass full then watched him expectantly while he drank from it and set it down on the table. Then Jeshwa handed him the pitcher. Mindar took it in his hands, a little embarrassed about what he was supposed to do with it. Glordan smiled. "It is your turn to offer water to Mirad," he said.

Mindar felt a little foolish as he turned to Mirad. "Mirad, would you like some water?" he asked.

"Yes, thank you, I would like some water." He waited patiently while Mindar poured his tumbler full. After Mirad drank, Mindar handed him the pitcher, and Mirad asked the same of Marall, who thanked him graciously. Mindar stole a glance at the other tables around him. Each was engaged in the custom of circling the table to the right, pouring water for each other. Klaria's words rang loudly: *"Deyz will offa ya' wata!"*

It was simple and beautiful. When the pitcher was back in the middle of the table, Glordan raised his hands, looked up and said, "Water: by his example." Everyone nodded and said, "Yes," in unison. Glordan looked at Mindar. "Now we eat. Come." He rose and helped his wife up from the table and led Mindar to the line that was forming outside the kitchen that adjoined the hall. "Are you hungry?" he asked Mindar as they stood and waited.

"May I speak with you?" Mindar asked.

"Speak freely," Glordan said as they stepped back from the line a couple paces.

"I am very hungry," Mindar said, "and I am very thankful for your hospitality, but I have taken a vow not to eat anything until I have earned money with which I can pay for food." He felt a little foolish, but somehow he knew Glordan would understand.

"The food here is given without pay, and you are free to eat," he said, "but we honor your fast, and we honor your discipline and example. Please stay with us while we eat."

"I will do that if it will not offend you," Mindar said.

"It would offend us if you left." Glordan smiled as he put his hand on Mindar's shoulder and pushed him back into the line.

The fare was simple: fresh bread and a thick stew that smelled of savory spices with some kind of meat. Fresh carrots, slices of raw potato, uncooked green beans and a bowl of fruit waited at the end of the line. No one served the meal. Mindar guessed that whoever had prepared it was standing in line with the others. He waited until everyone at their table had taken their portions, and they walked back to the table together.

No one seemed to notice that he had taken no food. As they sat down, the conversation began. "It was a good day today, I believe," said Glordan. "We secured an account with Dargon's for all their paper goods and made all our deadlines for deliveries."

Mirad nodded. "Three new people were sent to us today, and no one left."

"We have much to be thankful for in these troubled times," said Marall. She was looking at Mindar as she spoke. He got the feeling that he was the object of her thanks, but it was Jeshwa who opened the issue wide.

"Where are you from, Mr. Colloden?" he asked simply as if he were a peer in the conversation.

Mindar looked at Glordan, knowing that he knew more than he had let on. He nodded, so Mindar looked back at Jeshwa. "I come from Vindarill. I was born here, but I have traveled far on my journey to here today."

"Where?" Jeshwa asked as he took a mouthful of bread.

"I have been to Islag, to Tessamandria—"

"Mooriman?" he asked.

"No, but I did cross the NarEl Waste and visited the Crown."

Jeshwa nodded as he swallowed his bread. "Is it as deep as they say?"

"I don't know how deep they say it is," Mindar said. Glordan laughed.

"Well," continued Jeshwa, "I have heard that you can't see the bottom from the top of the rim."

"I don't know about that." Mindar smiled.

"Was it really as black and empty as they say?"

Mindar hesitated. "No," he said slowly, "it was full of life and light, like a paradise."

Jeshwa stopped chewing and stared at Mindar. "When did you visit there?"

"It was a long time ago," Mindar said. He looked up at Marall. He could feel her watching him.

"Must have been very long ago," Jeshwa continued undaunted as he carefully cut his next mouthful of meat. "The legends say it hasn't been like you described since the NarEladra invasion of Tessamandria, when the NarEladra overran Fazdeen and invaded the Crown again."

The legends! Mindar's life, most of it anyway, was now just part of the great legends of Tessalindria. "How do you know all this?" Mindar asked. "Have you ever been to Tessamandria?"

Jeshwa looked up at his father. "Not yet," he said with a smile. "Someday I want to go to Kinvara and study the history of that area. Right now I get most of my information from the books in the library. They never teach us much at school." He filled his mouth again as only a young man his age could.

"Is the library far from here?" Mindar asked. Jeshwa looked at him curiously as he chewed his food. "I mean, I have not been here in a long time. I don't remember where it is."

"It's two blocks west of here, right on the city commons," said Glordan.

"Is it open to everyone?" he asked.

"Yes, by law, but if you are a viddik, they may try to prevent you from entering—but that is illegal. Since you know this, you can insist, and they will allow you in."

"Is it open in the evenings?"

"Yes, but only so late." As Glordan finished speaking he looked up over his shoulder and smiled as he rose from the table. Mindar turned to look. The man who offered him the water on the dock, Takada, was wending his way toward their table, followed by a young woman whom he could not see well. When Takada arrived at the table he embraced Glordan, then pulled out the chair at the end of the table to seat his friend.

She was young, with long kinky orange hair and penetrating blue eyes that seemed to see inside Mindar when she looked at him. "Hannahoruan?" he croaked.

The woman smiled. "Hanara," she said as she held out her hand. Her voice was unmistakable.

"You know Takada?" Glordan's voice broke into his surprise.

Mindar looked up and rose hurriedly. "Why, yes. The bottle on the wharf."

Takada nodded then gestured to Hanara. "This is Hanara. She owns the local apothecary. If you have any medical needs, she is the one to see." Hanara smiled.

Glordan took the pitcher from the table. "Would you like some water?"

Takada smiled. "Yes, thank you." Then Takada did the same for Hanara.

Mindar's mind and heart were racing. There were subtle differences, but there was no doubt that this was the same person as the Hannahoruan from Kinvara. The way she looked at him and the penetrating eyes—but how could this be? If it was, then she may know what happened to Sereline, Therall, Serinda and Erinshava. Had she also come through the portal? Mindar had many questions, but he knew they would have to wait.

"Takada's shop on the waterfront sells our goods to the dockyards," continued Glordan. "He is a trusted friend and a fine man. You may get a chance to visit him with some of your deliveries."

"That would be a pleasure," Mindar said. "Thanks for the water today."

Takada raised his glass, "Water: by his example."

Mindar smiled. There was more to this than he understood. He had many questions, and they were not questions the answers to which he feared to know. Somehow it all seemed right and good. The conversation shifted to the easy and mundane pleasantries of daily life: the weather, economics, surprising events in the city and in the world. Mindar listened and watched, overwhelmed with the genuine affection and closeness of the relationships. He felt like he had with Sereline, Erinshava and Lutaka in the early days in Kinvara, and he was beginning to understand Klaria's words: "*Sum a' dem is yourz kind, an' ya gotsa fin' dem.*" He knew he had.

Mindar went to bed hungry and satisfied. It wasn't late, but it was dark. Neither of the twins was up, so he watched the stars through the window by his bed as he sat quietly thinking. Arathan was high and just barely visible near the top of the window from where his head lay on the pillow. It had not moved in a thousand years, but in Vindarill it was not as bright as it had been in Tessamandria.

The sounds of the bunkhouse shifted slowly from quiet conversations to squeaking springs under turning bodies to the gentle hush of deep slumber. Mindar remained wide awake, pondering the series of events that had led to this strange place and all the gentle people who inhabited it. Hanara was on his mind. He was sure it was Hannahoruan, but he had not had enough of a conversation to confirm it. In his vorn, he held onto the hope that she would know answers to his questions about what happened after he left. And how had she gotten here? If not through the portal, then how? Some vague recollection that he should know the answer to his own questions haunted him. He took comfort knowing that the library was close, and he would avail himself of its resources as soon as possible.

After about half an hour, Mindar turned from the window to lie down. He knew that he needed sleep in spite of his wakefulness. As he did so, he caught a faint glimmer in the corner of the room out of the corner of his eye. He looked back but it was gone. When he glanced about, he noticed several others: two by the door and three others, barely visible, standing beside beds in the hall.

He lay down on his bunk. The presence of the Eladra was a good sign, but odd. Why were they here? What was this place that warranted the attention of so many guardians? Mindar fell asleep without answers, but content in the safety of his newfound home.

✠

Fair pay for hard work is like water on dry lips.

Old Mythinian Saying

"Your job will be to help unload the petrotrucks at our clients' businesses," said Mirad as he showed him around the warehouse. "Glordan wanted you to be out in the city."

"Did he say why?" Mindar asked.

"He thought that you would probably like to see the city after so many years."

"That was very kind," he answered.

"Here is a pair of gloves for unloading the goods; they will cover your hands."

"I am not ashamed of my hands," Mindar answered.

"Neither am I—and neither is Glordan, or any us for that matter; but this city is hostile toward viddiks, and it is better if you don't advertise it."

Mindar took the gloves from his hand. "Thanks."

They had stopped by the line of trucks at the backside of the warehouse. "You will ride in truck seven with Misarda," continued Mirad. "He is one of our best, and he knows Vindarill like no one I know. If you have any questions, you can ask him."

"I have many questions," Mindar said as he walked down the length of the truck.

Mirad raised his eyebrows.

Mindar smiled. "Good questions," he reassured him. "But I will ask Misarda."

"Ask me what?" came a voice from behind. Misarda was a huge man, built like a bull with light hair that was so short one could not tell if it was gray or not. His gray eyes and dark skin spoke of his Mooriman descent, and his long moustache twitched rapidly when he spoke. He was a head taller than Mindar with hands that dwarfed anything they touched. He smiled as he held out his right hand to Mindar.

"I am Mindar Colloden," Mindar said as he shook Misarda's hand.

"I have heard much about you already, and you may have to compete with me for questions," Misarda said, raising the back door of the truck as if it were made of paper. "Right now, we have to load this thing."

They spent an hour stacking bales of paper and cloth into the truck. Each was marked with its destination, and as Mindar carried them onto the truck, Misarda packed them carefully based on his knowledge of the city and where each would be unloaded. Mindar was tired before they finished.

"C'mon," Misarda said when they finally pulled the door shut. "Get a drink, and let's get on the route." Mindar drank from the fountain at the back of the warehouse and hoisted himself up into the truck. "Got your gloves?" Misarda asked. Mindar held them up for him to see. Misarda smiled and pulled the truck slowly out of the warehouse yard.

They spent the day delivering the goods, stopping only for lunch in the truck, which Misarda had brought. Mindar did not eat because of his vow. "When I get paid, I will eat," he said, "to fulfill a vow I made." Misarda nodded and ate Mindar's portion without even asking if Mindar cared.

"Glordan says you are a portal walker," he said between mouthfuls.

"I am," Mindar affirmed. "Twice."

"Are you the famous historian, Mindar Colloden, from way back—whenever?"

"I am Mindar Colloden, and I wrote a book once. I think it was about a thousand years ago, but I don't know if it has made me famous."

"It has," Misarda answered, "*History of the Great Fathers*—everyone knows about it. Is that yours?"

"That sounds right."

"Does Jeshwa know who you are?"

"If he does, he did not say anything," Mindar said, "but perhaps he was just being polite."

"Jeshwa is like that—and he is a fanatic about history. Knows all kinds a' stuff. Don't have any idea where he finds it all."

"The library?" Mindar asked.

"Probably. He goes there often and stays late. Sometimes I have to go get him."

Mindar nodded and stared out the window. The view of the city from the front seat of the truck was very different from the view of a pedestrian. They were high up and looking through glass, isolated by it yet right in the middle of everything. Mindar had lowered his window, and that gave him a little more sense of belonging to the crowds that moved about on the sidewalks and crossed in front of them.

"Lived here all your life?" Mindar asked Misarda.

"Most of it. Born in Mooriman. Moved here when my father came to find work. I was about six."

"Never been anywhere else?"

"Had to work all my life." He smiled. "And you?"

Mindar laughed. "Well, I feel like I've been everywhere and yet nowhere at all. I was thrown back in time so far that nowhere I have been has anything to do with where you might go anymore."

"How did you find the portal in the first place?"

Mindar spent the rest of the afternoon delivering goods to shop-keepers and answering Misarda's numerous questions about his journeys through the portals, the places he had been, the people he knew, all about his wife and the girls. Misarda seemed so enthralled that Mindar didn't stop answering in order to ask questions of his own.

When the truck was empty, they headed back to the warehouse, arriving just in time to clean up for dinner. When Mindar sat down, there were seven small silver coins piled beside his plate. Mirad smiled. "No, we are not paying you to eat," he said. "Misarda told us you worked well and hard. Put it in your pocket so you can join us for dinner."

As it had been the night before, and as it was for several days after, dinner was simple but satisfying. Mindar went to sleep each night with a profound gratefulness for what he had found and was comforted by the return presence of the Eladrim guardians. There were six. Mindar slept well.

Mindar did not get paid a lot at the warehouse, but all his needs were met, so the coins began to collect in his chest at the end of his bed. Coins, the now empty kaffa bottle and his dagger were all that was there besides his clothes. It was a simple life and complete in every way: growing friendships, warm consideration, clean and safe accommodations, and good work.

Misarda entertained him with stories of growing up in Vindarill and the various troubles and antics that he had gotten into as a child on the streets. His father had died when he was twenty-two and his mother

died two years later. He found himself with no place to live. At one point
he had been invited to the warehouse, and he had come. But the envi-
ronment overwhelmed him; and three days later, he left, preferring life
on the street to the protected safety of the warehouse. A year later he was
assaulted by thieves, and in spite of his strength, sustained a knife
wound that nearly killed him. In the hospital, after a long fight for his
life, he finally regained his strength. "Somewhere in the midst of that
time, I promised myself that I would change," he said, "but I did not
know how. It never occurred to me that the answer was here at the warehouse."

"What do you mean?" Mindar asked.

"Three months out of the hospital, I had still not been able to find
work. One of the men I had asked for a job, offered me a bottle of water
instead. I was angry, but I was also thirsty. There was a note wrapped
around the bottle when he gave it to me."

"And it sent you to the warehouse."

"I was even more angry. I spent one more night on the street. That
night it occurred to me that perhaps I was my own worst enemy."
Misarda laughed. "I went back. There was complete acceptance here. I
have never left."

Each night Mindar sat with a different group at dinner. It seemed to
be the way in the warehouse; but on the third night, after an unusually
light day on the truck, Jeshwa made it a point to sit beside him again. "I
am going to the library tonight after dinner. Would you like to come?"

"That would be the greatest of pleasures," Mindar said.

✠

*Knowledge is one pillar of wisdom, but
knowledge by itself will not make a man
wise.*

*Pratoraman
The Middle Way*

"I hope that I am not being rude by asking," Jeshwa said after they left
the warehouse some distance behind on their way to the library, "but do
you realize that your name is the same as a very famous historian?"

"Misarda told me that," Mindar answered. "What did he do?"

"He lived about a thousand years ago," Jeshwa said as they walked
up the long flight of stairs to the entrance of the city library. "He wrote
a book called *The History of the Great Fathers*, which is considered to be
the authoritative work on that period of history. It's a miracle it survived."

"Really?"

"We think he finished the book shortly before the Mankar Rebellion. It had not been copied that we know of, and the miracle is that it survived Mankar's attempt to rewrite history during his reign of terror."

"Who is 'we'?" he asked.

"I belong to the city's historical society." Jeshwa looked at Mindar with a sense of pride.

"How old are you?"

"Eighteen."

Mindar smiled. They walked through the oversized brass doors of the huge library entrance. "You seem young for a scholar."

"I am not sure I am a scholar, but I am good at what I do. I am the youngest in the society."

"I would say," Mindar said.

"Excuse me!" announced the woman behind the large wooden desk by the door. "Viddiks are not allowed in the library."

Jeshwa did not flinch. "He's with me," he announced.

"It doesn't matter, Jeshwa, he is not allowed in the library."

"Excuse me," Mindar said as politely as he could. "The law of Vindarill specifically allows me to be in all public buildings, including the library."

The woman would not look at him. "He's right," said Jeshwa. "C'mon, Mindar."

The woman grabbed a small bell that sat on the desk and started ringing it vigorously. Two guards, armed with hazarines appeared in the doorway behind the desk. She pointed at Mindar. "This viddik is trying to get into the library," she crooned.

Jeshwa stepped in front of Mindar as the guards approached. They stopped. "The laws of Vindarill do not allow you to reject this man," he said sternly. "You should not lay a hand on him until you have confirmed or denied this truth." The guards looked nervously back at the woman.

Another man appeared in the door behind the desk. "Is there a problem here?" he asked. The woman conferred with him privately, gesturing toward Jeshwa and Mindar as they stood with the guards. The man disappeared briefly and then returned with a large volume in his hands. "So, young Jeshwa," he said handing the book to him, "will you find this law that you are invoking?"

Jeshwa took the book to the desk and laid it down. He turned to the index and scanned it briefly, flipping back and forth in the pages, looking up and down its columns and checking back in the index. The guards had begun chatting with each other when Jeshwa looked up with his finger pressed into the text. "Brief 17, article 34, section 8, paragraph 3," he announced.

The man in the suit pulled a pair of eyeplates from his vest pocket and slipped them on as he bent over the book. He read the lines that Jeshwa had pointed out, then stood up, bowed to Mindar and said, "You may enter the library, but we will be watching you. If there is any trouble, we will throw you out." He turned to Jeshwa and glared as he picked up the book, slammed it shut, and stuffed it under his arm. "You must register at the desk."

Jeshwa stepped out again. "Why?"

"Everyone is required to register at the desk on entering the library. There is no law against that!"

"I have never registered here in my life!" insisted Jeshwa.

"You," said the man in the suit, "are not a viddik!"

"I will register," Mindar said.

"Can you write?" asked the woman.

"Quite adequately," Mindar said as pleasantly as he could. She handed him a pen. He bent over the nearly empty book and penned "Mindar Colloden" into the space for his name. In the column asking for his occupation, he wrote "Historian."

The woman glared at him. "Your impudence does not go unnoticed," she said.

"I have no other name," Mindar replied.

"C'mon, Mindar, we have work to do." Jeshwa tugged at his sleeve, and they walked up the sweeping marble steps into the interior of the library.

Mindar's burning question could not wait. "How is it that your father is a viddik and you are not?"

Jeshwa smiled. "My mother is not a viddik," he said. "By law—another law one usually has to fight for—if the mother is not viddik, then the child does not have to be marked as such."

"Only the mother?"

"If you think about it, the mother can argue that there is no proof that the father was a viddik." Jeshwa chuckled. "There is no way to prove—or disprove—such an argument, so the law allows it."

Jeshwa led the way through the stacks to the historical research area where he took Mindar down a side aisle off from the main table. "Look here," he exclaimed as he pulled a large volume off the shelf and laid it in Mindar's hands.

Mindar was speechless. There in his hands lay an ancient and worn copy of a book he had never dreamed would end up here, in the library of his hometown. He opened the cover carefully and read the title page, then thumbed through the first few pages. The words were almost his. It had been heavily edited, but most of the thoughts seemed intact. Mindar looked up to see Jeshwa staring at him.

"That's you, isn't it?" Jeshwa asked. There was a fire in his eyes.

"Yes," Mindar said in a hoarse whisper, "that's me!"

Jeshwa smiled. "I won't tell anyone—and you shouldn't either. There are people here that would go crazy if they knew, and I have a thousand questions," he added, "maybe a million."

Mindar found himself cradling the book in his arms against his chest, breathing heavily. "And I have about that many for you."

Jeshwa looked at him with a question mark in his eyes.

"I know nothing of what happened after I left, except what I learned as a viddik on the streets of this city when I never knew that I cared about history. Now I know what the questions are," he said, "and I have to know the answers."

Jeshwa stepped past him. "Come," he said. "I will introduce you to those who will know, if the answer is known." He stopped suddenly and turned. "Is there something I can call you while you are here so no one will know who you really are?"

"Rindar."

Jeshwa stared at him for a moment, thinking.

"It is my childname, but it will do for this purpose."

Jeshwa nodded and turned to lead him back to the huge round research table. Mindar brought the book with him, thinking that he should browse through it, to see what the editors had done and to refresh his memory.

They sat at the large table beside one another. "What do you want to know?" Jeshwa asked.

"About Mankar and what happened; how he came to power, how he took over and what happened afterward." He paused struggling to formulate the next question. "I want to know what happened to my wife and my twin daughters." He could feel the tears in his eyes. "I want to know what happened to my friend and teacher, Erinshava, and to another friend Hannahoruan, and her son."

Jeshwa listened attentively, carefully penning the names into his small bound notebook that served as his history diary and journal. When Mindar mentioned Erinshava's name, Jeshwa raised his eyebrows slightly but said nothing. He smiled when Mindar stopped. "There is a lot about Mankar," Jeshwa said, "but we don't know how much of it is legend or truth. A lot is conjecture mixed with fact that makes a wonderful tale."

"You seemed to recognize Erinshava."

"Yes, that is a curious name. There was an Erinshava who served in Sessasha's circle, but I know of no other."

"I would like to find out more about her. I have other questions too," he said, "but let's start with these."

"Wait here," Jeshwa said.

Mindar sat and waited. Jeshwa disappeared into the corridors of bookshelves that surrounded the table. Several other older men and one woman worked diligently around another table, and Mindar caught them stealing glances at him as he surveyed the room, but no one spoke.

When Jeshwa returned he had a stack of books. He dropped them with a thump on the table: *The Rise of the Mankar Rebellion, Mankarian Legends: Fact and Fiction, Empire of Evil, The Fall of Fazdeen, The Mooriman Invasion of Tessamandria, Annihilation of Greatness* and several others. "These are classic resources on the time period you are looking for. The indexes leave a lot to be desired, but the information in them is very good." He handed him the thickest. "This is probably the most accurate—and the most difficult." Jeshwa smiled.

Annihilation of Greatness was written by Gwendar Hladrian. It was a monstrous tome, perhaps two and a half inches thick and bound in real leather, as if it had been done in the library in Kinvara. Mindar opened it carefully. It had been printed nearly one hundred and fifty years before, and the endless stream of long, unbroken paragraphs in small, handset type was dizzying. There were chapters, but they were simply numbered with no titles, and there *was* no index. Mindar looked up at Jeshwa who sat staring back at him. Jeshwa laughed as their eyes met. "I told you it was a tough one, but it is the best."

"Sssshhhhh!" The small bald man from the other table expressed his annoyance at their conversation.

"Oops," whispered Jeshwa. The man returned his focus to the task in front of him. "That's Garva," Jeshwa whispered. "If it's here, he knows it."

"Why don't we just ask him?" Mindar whispered back.

"You can only ask Garva if he asks you. He is very odd about that."

"How do we get him to ask?" Mindar pressed.

"Look like you are studying hard, and he will notice and—"

"Sssssshhhhhhh!" Garva hissed again.

Jeshwa waved his hands over the books, indicating that Mindar should start his studying.

✠

The truths of Tessalindria are often more bizarre than our fantasies of the outworlds.

Colloran
The Outworlds

They had stayed till the library closed, and when they left, Tal was up high enough to look down into the street canyons to give them light on the way home. Mindar had found nothing pertinent in his search for answers. What he had found was fascinating and overwhelming at the same time. He was sure that he had been exposed to it in school as a child, but most of it seemed new to him now.

Another question burned in him, begging an answer. "Is there anything in the legends about a being—a person—who lives forever?" he asked.

"Forever?"

"Well, yes, forever—as in, they never get old?"

"Not that I recall," Jeshwa said as he looked at him curiously. Mindar could see his eyes, even in the shadow of his eyebrows in the dim light. "What are you really asking?"

"The woman Hanara, the one who joined us for dinner the first night I came to the warehouse—" He paused not knowing what he was trying to say. Jeshwa waited as they walked. "There was a woman in Kinvara, the owner of an apothecary, a healer. She had a son Gayan...I mentioned her name back at the library, Hannahoruan."

Jeshwa knew Mindar was not finished. He said nothing as he waited patiently for Mindar's real question.

"I knew Hannahoruan well. We met on the journey to Kinvara from the Crown, so we were acquainted for nearly forty years." He looked up. Jeshwa nodded. "During that whole time, she never seemed to get older. Her son Gayan grew and was nearly that age when I last saw him, but not Hannahoruan—"

"—and Hanara reminds you of her," Jeshwa said in the pause as Mindar searched for words.

"Remind is not the right word."

Jeshwa looked at him quizzically.

"She is identical: same eyes that seem to look into your vorn when you look at her; same coloring of hair; same height—she even dresses the same, I mean, given the time difference—and she runs the local apothecary." Mindar looked up again. Jeshwa was smiling.

"When your father introduced her the other night," Mindar continued, "I knew it was her, but she did not give even the slightest hint that she recognized me. Hannahoruan would have thrown her arms around me, then stood back, looked inside me and then made some comment about something she had no way of knowing."

Jeshwa stopped. "That's odd," he said, "she does that to me all the time."

Mindar turned to face him as he stood still on the sidewalk. "So that's my question," he said. "Is there anything in the literature about a being that might be able to do that?"

"Do what? Maybe she came through the portal. You did leave the map behind, right?"

"But she didn't arrive yesterday if she did," Mindar continued. "I mean she has been around a while, right?"

"Yes, but she could have come here at a time earlier than you, even though she left Kinvara later."

"I suppose," Mindar muttered, "but she would have aged more on both ends."

They started walking toward the light above the warehouse door. "Do you know how long she has had the apothecary?" Mindar asked.

"I don't remember a time when she did not," Jeshwa said before he fell into deep thought. "There is one legend," he said at length, "but it is so vague and implausible that I have never pursued it."

"What?" Mindar asked.

"It's the legend of the Melendars," Jeshwa said, "but I do not know that I know the details."

"Tell me what you know."

"In The Beginnings, when Mah'Eladra divided the waters and they set the man kind into nations, the legends teach that we were made to be immortal, to live forever in the world as the Eladra had built it for us. But when the spirit of Vestin came and corrupted the vorns of our world, this immortality was taken—from most of us. Mah'Eladra left a few, to walk among us—Melendars they were called. They were those whom the spirit of Vestin could not corrupt. There has been much conjecture but no proof. The legends also say that the Melendars were not only immortal but multi-lived."

"What do you mean?" Mindar asked.

"They can be alive in several places at once."

"Like the Eladra?"

"No. As we understand it, the Eladra can only be in one place at a time, but they can move through time to be other time-places. The Melendars are credited with actually living physically and simultaneously in different places. It seems odd and defies all notion of reality, but we do not understand the depths of Mah'Eladra, and I suppose that if they wanted to create such beings, it's possible."

"Do you have any idea how many there are?"

"No. As far as I know they don't really exist, though this may be the first tangible evidence for them. If they live as ordinary people, how would one ever know who they are?"

"Is there any conjecture about why Mah'Eladra would create such a being?" Mindar asked.

"As I said, I have not given it much thought—it's a rather quaint and elusive legend." Jeshwa smiled. "That's all I can remember, but we do have the library, and we can learn more about the Melendars there."

"If Hanara is a Melendar," Mindar mused, "it would explain many things, but have little consequence, in some ways, I suppose."

Jeshwa looked at him, "What do you mean?"

"Well, she did not seem to recognize me, which means that even though they are multi-lived, those lives may be separated enough so that each life is lived separately, completely in the present of where they are."

"Perhaps," Jeshwa said, with a shrug, "but all the same, they must be very special beings and have a special role to play in the plan of Mah'Eladra. Your encounter with both makes you a special person."

"I don't feel that way," Mindar said. "I feel like a misfit, twice displaced in time, who because of my birth will never be accepted in my own culture."

"You wrote one of the most important history texts of all time!" Jeshwa exclaimed.

"I lost my wife and never got to see my children grow up," Mindar countered. "All that is of greater value has been taken away from me. All I have are memories that are a thousand years old."

"Perhaps it is the way of Mah'Eladra," said Jeshwa.

"Why did you say that?" Mindar asked.

"I believe it. I see it!"

"Do you believe it in general, or is there something specific that you know?"

"Look," said Jeshwa, his hands moving to emphasize his words, "you carried Lonama's map for almost forty years! You don't guess that during all that time, Mah'Eladra were not using you to shape history, to create a path of psadeq for many?"

"If I did, I would like to have a clue how. I saw several people die because of the map, and I lost my best friend to the jealousy created by it. Even my possession of it could not help what happened in Kinvara with the onset of Mankar's Rebellion and the horrific evil that was unleashed."

Jeshwa waited patiently as Mindar spoke. "You don't suppose," he said when Mindar was done, "that if Mah'Eladra had wanted you to use the map to discover what was happening, that they could have done that?"

"I suppose—"

"And you don't even know what might have happened if you had. Perhaps it would have been worse. Perhaps it would have started later and not ended the way it did. Perhaps it would have changed something that would have prevented the anthara from coming."

"What do you mean?" Mindar asked.

Jeshwa looked at him blankly and then laughed. "When the twins of Huravag stole the swords, Mankar vanished. Some say he was killed, and others say he just went into hiding, but no one knows for sure exactly what happened. His power was broken, but his influence continued. Mooriman invaded Tessamandria and used that as a base to rule the Vorsian Sea under Admiral Vaktrata. That's when Vindarill and Farhantra were established by the Mooriman invaders. We call it The Grayness in history. No one was sure what was happening or how it was all going to work. You have no idea whether something you did may have affected any of this."

Vague flickers of memory were returning from years past. "The Grayness," Mindar mumbled, "was followed by the Long Night, right?"

"Yes. The dividing line was the Genocide of Otalla by the Mooriman invaders. Dark times! But that darkness spawned the arrival of the anthara in Kinvara."

"Sessasha?" he asked. "You believe Sessasha was the anthara!?" More memories were returning.

Jeshwa nodded gravely.

"You're Sessashian?!!"

"I am," Jeshwa said.

"You seem to be some sort of expert on Sessasha," Mindar confided.

"I try to know as much truth as I can about him—historical truth. There is a lot of controversy about his teaching and the meaning of what he did—not for me, you understand, but this historical search is for what actually happened—beyond the myths and legends."

Mindar fell silent. Sessashians were not popular in Vindarill, though the law protected them against abuse. They were like the viddiks—second-class citizens, looked upon as superstitious at best, and as a threat to society by their more aggressive antagonists. "Is your father Sessashian?" he asked.

Jeshwa did not look at him as he answered, "You should ask him that."

"And Mirad—and Misarda?"

"You have to ask them," Jeshwa said as he turned to look at Mindar. "They must answer for themselves, just as you have to answer to what you believe."

"I don't know what I believe," Mindar said. "I don't think I know enough to know what I believe." It sounded stupid as he said it. "Erinshava showed me the way of kirrin—but that was before Sessasha." He looked up to see Jeshwa's reaction, expecting to be reproached.

"Yes," Jeshwa responded, "that is true, and it is your responsibility to remedy that. I believe that Sessasha refined our understanding of kirrin. He simply made the paths of the Kirrinath clearer. Many believe he was a charlatan who twisted and bent the Kirrinath to his own purposes, and of course there are those who don't believe in kirrin at all."

They were standing at the door to the warehouse. A cloud of new thoughts formed a fog around Mindar's head, and Klaria's words returned to him as they stood silently in the near darkness of the street. *"Sum a' dem is yourz kind, an' yous gotsa fin' dem."* From what he remembered, he would never have guessed that perhaps his kind were the Sessashians, but he had to admit he had no real basis for that judgment. Mindar felt himself staring at the young man waiting patiently, his hand on the heavy door handle, seeing in Jeshwa's youth a stark contrast to his deep understanding of the world he lived in.

"C'mon," Jeshwa said, "I need to be up early, and you have another big day on the truck."

Inside the door, Jeshwa disappeared, and Mindar made his way to the bunkhouse. It was mostly quiet, save the gentle snoring of several of its denizens. Six Eladra hovered in the corners and by the door. Mindar wondered as he passed each bunk if the person sleeping there might also be Sessashian. Tal and Meekar were both high overhead before he finally faded into the true darkness of sleep.

✠

He held that a half-truth is at the same time a half-lie; that telling a half-lie is as impossible as digging a half-hole.

Tarasinden Varr
Sessasha's Way

By the law of Morlan, each business in Vindarill had to shut its doors one day out of every eight. The proprietor could choose which day that would be, and it could be different for everyone, but the last day of the eight-day week was most typical. For some reason, Glordan had chosen to close his business on the seventh day. This made for an excessive workload on day six, covering for the seventh when most of the other businesses were open. It also made for very light work on day eight.

"There is a reason for it," Misarda explained as they unloaded a double load of wrapping paper to one of the fish vendors at the waterfront, "but I will let Glordan explain it." When they climbed back into the truck he added, "It does make for a nice day on Mardar. We typically get all the work done before noon."

They got back to the loading dock and parked the truck with barely enough time to splash water on their faces in an attempt to be presentable for dinner. "Dinner on Viadar is always a big deal," Misarda had said. "You don't want to miss it." Mindar could tell that Misarda was right as they walked in.

The bustle and vigor of the warehouse crew was something that could be felt, and the air was thick with the complex aroma of a huge meal. The tables were set differently. The dinnerware was blue with white highlights around the rims, and each place was set with a cloth napkin instead of the usual paper. The dinner tumblers had been replaced with fine goblets that sparkled with a pale pink liquid.

As they waded in among the tables to find a place to sit, Mindar noticed Glordan standing and watching him. As Glordan caught his eye, he beckoned to Mindar who pointed at himself questioningly. Glordan nodded and beckoned again. Mindar worked his way toward him, excusing himself as he passed between the tables, greeting his friends at each table with a touch on the shoulder and a quiet hello and a smile. When he finally reached the table, it was the first time he could see the purpose of Glordan's request.

Across the table from Glordan, engaged in an animated conversation with Jeshwa, the sight of Minxa's unmistakable shock of gray, stringy hair arrested Mindar's breath. Minxa's back was turned to him, so he did not see Mindar stop and stare. Glordan beckoned again, pointing to the seat beside his old friend. Mindar moved mechanically, forcing himself to not fear and to try not to reveal his feelings as he made his way to the appointed seat.

"We have a new guest tonight, Mindar," Glordan smiled. At the mention of his name, Minxa looked up and whirled to face him, his face turning ashen in the same instant.

Mindar forced himself forward. "Hello, Minxa," he said without emotion.

Minxa rose and shook his hand, "Hello, Rindar." He said before he turned and sat down heavily.

"Do you know each other?" asked Glordan with visible surprise.

"We have known each other for many years," Mindar volunteered as he pulled in his chair and sat down. He looked directly at Glordan. "We grew up together on the streets of this city."

Glordan sat down, obviously curious and confused at the same time. "I—I don't understand something here—how long has it been since you have seen one another?"

"I took Minxa with me when I went through the portal the first time—when I left Vindarill," he said. He could feel everyone at the table staring at him as he carefully unfolded his napkin and placed it in his lap. "Minxa brought me back with him just last week, two days before I came here."

"My *friend* Rindar here," Minxa began, "—he left me to die in the cave after we got here through the portal. I was lucky to find my way out."

Glordan's eyes narrowed, but he said nothing. Mindar was not in a position to deny what Minxa had said, but he did not want to play into his petty game of half-truths.

Minxa pressed on. "He can't deny it," he said as he looked around the table. "Ask him. He is too honorable to lie about it."

"I would discuss this later," Mindar started. "This is a long story— and there is some disagreement on what is true about it—between Minxa and me, I mean—but I think it is inappropriate to discuss it here at the table."

"Ha!" Minxa mocked. "Of course it's inappropriate—"

"Stop!" Glordan rose from his seat. "You are both guests at my table, and such antipathy is not fitting here; so we will hear your stories after dinner, when we have eaten together. Either of you is welcome to stay or to leave, but no discord is allowed at this table, especially on the eve of Essendar." He sat down.

Minxa sat speechless. Mindar was appreciative of Glordan's authority, for he spoke like a man who would not be defied, yet with a gentleness and psadeq that inspired submission. Minxa had barely settled himself when he looked up and stood once again. Mindar followed his eyes to see Hanara approaching the table to join them. Mindar glanced over to see Minxa's jaw drop. Minxa leaned over and growled, "How did she get here?"

Glordan bowed and waved Hanara to the seat at the end of the table. "This is our new friend, Minxa," he said to her as she sat down.

She smiled and nodded. "It's a pleasure to meet you, Master Minxa."

"Darana met him yesterday and invited him to join us," continued Glordan, "and it seems that Minxa and Mindar have been longtime friends." The way he said it made their relationship seem genuine, as if their psadeq had never been compromised. "And now it is time to eat."

Minxa looked baffled by Hanara's introduction. When Mindar looked at him, Minxa turned away. Whatever Minxa was thinking, Mindar knew he was not going to share it with him.

Mindar had grown accustomed to the ritual of offering water that preceded every meal at the warehouse, but tonight, Minxa sat to his left. When it came Minxa's turn, he was expected to offer Mindar water.

When Mindar held out his glass and nodded, Minxa's hand was shaking. Whether it was deliberate or not, he would never know, but more water spilled over his hands onto the table than made it into the glass. Mindar felt embarrassed for Minxa, thanked him warmly and continued the ritual with Mirad who sat to his right, trying to ignore the water that had poured into his lap from the table. When Marall had served Glordan's glass, dinner was served.

From deep inside, the Minxa whom Mindar had known as a young man struggled to break through the mordage that held him captive like a prison cell. For the most part, he ignored Mindar, but on several occasions, he laughed and made genuine comments of thankfulness for his invitation to join them at dinner.

✠

When armatan is weak, we are subject to much fear, and unlike other weaknesses, fear consumes us from the inside out.

Tristaron Harrista
The Kirrinath

Minxa had taken the bed beside Mindar. Mindar wasn't sure why, but he wasn't willing to take the chance that Minxa's intent was good. Mindar had nothing of value, except the small collection of coins that he had garnered from the half dozen days he had worked on the truck with Misarda, but Minxa would not have known about them. The six Eladrim guards were at their posts, hovering wisps in the dark corners, but even their presence could not dispel the unease Mindar felt, and he couldn't sleep.

The warm, safe atmosphere of the dorm now seemed threatening with Minxa lying silently on the cot just barely at arm's length from Mindar. "Are you awake?" Minxa whispered at length.

"Yes," Mindar said, "wide awake." He was expecting some sort of response but Minxa lay still. "Why?" he asked.

"Just curious." Minxa's voice was low and casual. He said nothing else.

Mindar lay quietly. The after-dinner discussion with Glordan had been cordial and uneventful. Minxa related what had happened, conveniently leaving out many details and changing others to suit his view of himself and his situation. Some of it was simple self-delusion, but there were many bold lies. Glordan listened patiently until Minxa stopped speaking. Glordan had turned to Mindar and raised his eyebrows.

"I don't know where to start," Mindar had said. "Minxa's story is basically true—" Glordan didn't move. Minxa sat and waited. Mindar then related the story from his point of view, trying to change the lies into truth as honestly as he could without telling his own lies in return. It was harder than he thought, and several times he had to back up and clarify things he had said. It would have been easy to embellish the details to his own advantage.

When he had finished, Mindar had felt a wave of fear pass over him. The truth, as he presented it was much less compelling than the lies Minxa had told. Without the exaggerations and the prevarications, the true story was rather uninspiring and left Mindar looking like a heartless, self-seeking opportunist. He looked up at Glordan.

Glordan had his fingertips pressed together in front of him, and he was staring at them intently. They both waited until he stirred and spoke. "It is odd," he started, "how two stories of the same event can be so different—" He paused to think through his next words. "I would like to believe you both, but that is obviously impossible. So I choose to believe neither, because I cannot know your truths for sure—or your lies." He glanced back and forth between Minxa and Mindar. "It is one of the great noble truths, that truth will always be vindicated in time."

"I am sure it will," Minxa had said smiling. Mindar nodded. He was confident that he had been truthful, but he was not as confident that there was any way that this truth could be verified to Glordan—ever.

"Are you awake?" whispered Minxa from the cot beside him.

"Yes," he said.

"Just curious," Minxa responded.

The hint of sarcasm sent a shiver down Mindar's spine. "Why did you come here, Minxa?" he asked.

"To find you!" Minxa said. Mindar felt his smile in the dark, and it was not a pleasant feeling.

Mindar did not know how Minxa got out of the cave. With no one to lead him out, it must have taken him a long time. In addition, Minxa's eyes seemed fine from what Mindar could tell. The thought sent his mind wandering through the paths that had led them here and then back to Erinshava and Sereline. Mindar had not made it to the library tonight, as he had hoped, so had made no progress in learning what had happened. The thought angered him.

"Are you awake?" whispered Minxa from the cot beside him.

"Yes," he said.

"Just curious," Minxa said again as he turned over. The springs on the cot creaked as he did so.

The silence of the dormitory hall settled in deeply, with the only sounds being that of the slow, heavy breathing of deep sleep and the occasional snoring from other cots. Mindar could feel the weariness settling over him, but he knew Minxa was awake beside him, and he fought to stay awake.

"Are you awake?" whispered Minxa again from the cot beside him.

"Yes," he said.

"Just curious."

Each time Mindar felt the fear rise. Mindar knew the nature of fear that plays on the noga and the hjarg to cause doubt about all the good and right things. He knew that Minxa was playing this game, but he did not know what his purpose was. Mindar was determined to not have to find out.

"Are you awake?" whispered Minxa for the tenth time.

Mindar paused before answering. "Yuh," he said sleepily.

"Just curious."

Mindar slipped into a feigned deep breathing of sleep, fighting hard not to succumb to its desire to take him with it.

"Are you awake?" whispered Minxa once again.

Mindar did not answer. He lay still and continued breathing slowly. He wondered what he should do as he waited unmoving in the still darkness. It seemed like an eternity before Minxa spoke again.

"Are you awake?" he asked.

Mindar did not answer. Minxa shifted on his bed. Mindar guessed that Minxa was turning over so he could see him. Then Mindar heard him draw back his blanket carefully and swing his legs over the side of the bed. He laid waiting for any sudden movement, but Minxa sat still. Mindar did not dare move his head to see if the Eladrim guards were still at their posts. Somehow, he knew he had to play into Minxa's game. There was nowhere to go. If he panicked, they would end up in another tale-telling session where more lies would be told and less truth would be known. Somehow, he knew that he had to wait and that in the waiting, truth would be revealed.

The pillow descended on Mindar's face so fast he barely had time to take a breath and no time to scream. He felt Minxa straddle his chest and pin him to the bed. Mindar had both hands on Minxa's wrists, desperately trying to break his grip on the pillow that covered his face so tightly he could not breathe. Where were the Eladrim guards? Surely they would see this. Mindar's lungs burned. He tried to kick, but there was nothing to kick, and his legs flailed silently in the darkness.

Minxa pressed harder. Mindar scratched at Minxa's arms and felt his nails tearing flesh, but nothing could break Minxa's grip. Mindar struggled harder, helpless in the fading consciousness of suffocation.

Suddenly, in the dark nothingness, everything changed. Mindar could not tell what happened, just that the pillow disappeared and there was air. Mindar gasped and choked. He heard a string of profanity and the heavy blow of a body being hurled against the stone wall of the dorm beside the windows. Mindar lay in bed coughing and gasping. The shouting intensified as several other dormitory residents joined the fracas in the corner. There was someone beside Mindar, stroking his arm and whispering, "It's all right—it's all right."

"Get him on his feet," roared Misarda. Mindar began to recognize what was happening. "One move," Misarda growled, "and they'll have to scrape you from the floor." Minxa stood in front of him, with both hands pinned behind his back by two other workers. Minxa looked up and spit in Misarda's face. Misarda's fist moved so fast that Mindar was not sure he saw it, and Minxa crumpled to the floor. "Get him outta here," Misarda said as he turned toward Mindar.

Misarda knelt beside Mirad, who had been helping Mindar. "Ya alright?" Misarda asked as he put his hand on Mindar's shoulder.

Mindar nodded and coughed. "I think so." He watched as they dragged Minxa out of the dormitory. "What will happen—to him?" he asked.

"We'll throw him out. He won't ever come back in here."

"Can't you turn him over to the polls?"

"Na, the polls won't do us no favors. They're suspicious of this place anyway. Some friend this—this—"

"Minxa," Mindar said.

"Ya, *Minxa*. Well, he's outta here now."

"What happened?" Mindar asked. He was sitting up in bed. The lights at his end of the dormitory were on, and several neighbors stood around watching.

Misarda smiled. "Not sure. Someone woke me up. Told me you needed help."

"Who?"

"I don't know. I didn't recognize him."

"One of the Eladra?"

"What Eladra?!" Misarda was genuinely surprised.

"The Eladra that guard this place at night!"

"What are you talking about?"

Mindar looked up at the amazed, blank faces that surrounded his cot. No one seemed to know.

He shook his head. "Never mind," he said. Misarda helped him stand and walk to the washroom. The cold water felt good. He splashed it on his face and into his mouth to revive his wits and calm his nerves. He was suddenly aware once again how small the margin is between life and death.

As he emerged from the washroom, Glordan met him in the hall. He was leaning against the frame of the door into the dormitory.

"Would you like some tea?" he asked. The look in Glordan's eye gave Mindar the sense that he should not refuse.

"It's very late," Mindar said as he ran his fingers through his hair. "I don't want to trouble you at this hour."

"I am already troubled. We have never had such a disturbance in the warehouse." Glordan's dark eyes were somber and unwavering as he stared at Mindar. "Follow me." Glordan turned and led him out of the dorm, down the hall and into the huge kitchen. The lights were already on, and as they made their way around the preparation table in the middle, he could hear the water boiling in a small kettle. Glordan waved to one of the stools by the counter. "Marall and Mirad will be joining us presently," he said. "Have a seat."

Mindar sat and watched as Glordan moved easily around the kitchen. He retrieved a tea thimble and cups from various cupboards and spoons from the drawer beside Mindar. After measuring the tea into the thimble and securing its cover with a snap, he dropped it into the waiting pot. "Darlander tea," he exclaimed as the thimble hit the bottom, "—from North Strand. It will serve us well tonight."

✠

Revenge is more costly than forgiveness.

Otallan Proverb

Minxa sat in the dark on the curbstone several blocks from the warehouse. By pinching the bridge of his nose tightly and breathing through his mouth, he had managed to stop the bleeding. It hurt, but Minxa was no stranger to pain. What hurt most was his pride. He had gotten so close, and in another ten seconds, Rindar would have been dead. Now he was unhurt, and the element of surprise was gone.

Luck had turned against him again. His nose was broken, and so was his hope. The chill wind coming in off the harbor smelled of rain, and he had no shelter for the night. Minxa wished that he didn't care anymore, but he knew that he did. He sat and waited in a dull stupor of hopelessness, partly the fog of unconsciousness from the fist of the brute who had torn him off Rindar and partly from the overwhelming fear that Rindar might have been right. "You can't escape yourself," he had said. Minxa shuddered as he thought about his plan being thwarted once again.

Getting the map and finding his way back to Vindarill was only part of the plan. Vengeance against Rindar had been another piece of it, but dragging Rindar into the portal had not diminished his anger or slaked his thirst for revenge, and now there were other complicating factors.

Vashtor had found him in the cave, lost and hungry and had agreed to lead him out, but not without cost. Minxa had to forfeit all the silver that Marhan had given him in return for his freedom, and even after that, he was sure he had not seen the last of Vashtor.

After four nights sleeping on the street, the invitation of a place to sleep and a hot meal, promised by the note on the bottle of water given him by the man behind the fish cart, was appealing. On his way to find the warehouse, Vashtor found him again and warned him not to go. He gave Minxa no reason for his concern, and Minxa was still not sure whether Vashtor could have known that Rindar was there. Minxa had certainly not expected it himself.

He was still pinching his nose with his head back when he noticed that someone was approaching. "Sorry I couldn't have been there to help." Vashtor's deep, gravelly voice was unmistakable.

Minxa chose not to answer. Vashtor was one of the last beings he wanted to talk to right then.

Vashtor sat down on the curb beside him. "What happened?"

Minxa did not bother to look at the NarEladra. "Rindar was there," he said. Talking made his nose and head hurt more.

"Really?" The tone of Vashtor's voice carried a hint of a sneer.

"Look," Minxa growled, "everything was going well—except there was one guy, a big one that I did not count on. Where were you?" he added as an afterthought.

"I can not help you in there; I told you that!"

"Why not?"

"The warehouse is guarded by several Eladra. It would be foolish for me to challenge them alone."

"Why don't you get some of your friends?"

"I am assigned to do this alone."

"Do what alone?" Minxa asked. "And if you have to do it alone, why do you need my help?" He released the pressure from his fingers. The blood seemed to have stopped flowing. Minxa lowered his head and looked over at Vashtor, his huge body huddled on the curb in the darkness.

"I cannot enlist other NarEladra."

"Who gave you this task—and what is it?"

"Do not meddle with things you cannot understand," Vashtor said.

"What if I don't want to help?"

"You have no choice; you owe me your life. The cave, remember?"

Minxa looked down between his legs, spat the blood out of his mouth and shook his head. "I gave you the silver," Minxa said. "It was all I had."

"What good are silver coins to me?" Vashtor was mocking him.

"You took them readily enough," he said.

"I saved your life, and you think these little trinkets are a fair trade?" Minxa heard Vashtor shaking his change purse up and down.

"Then give them back to me!"

"No," Vashtor said, "it's not quite that easy. Besides, I still need your help."

"When?"

"I'm not sure. But I will find you when it is convenient."

"Convenient for who?" The words were a reflex. Even before Vashtor answered, Minxa knew the words that were coming.

"For me. Who else?" Minxa felt Vashtor's hand on his shoulder, cold as ice and almost as hard. "You know why I am here, don't you?"

"Not exactly—" Minxa mumbled.

"Lonama's map! It is here in Vindarill, Minxa. You know that."

"What!?"

"Think, Minxa. It must be here. Do you know today's date?"

"Ulrar...second." Minxa hesitated.

"You told me that Rindar stole the map on Ulrar:6."

"I'll never forget…" Minxa looked up.

Vashtor was smiling at him. "You see, we have four days to find the old man with the map, before young Rindar finds him. Can you find young Rindar for me, Minxa?"

"I think I can," Minxa mumbled as he spit more blood out of his mouth.

"Don't try to run, Minxa. You tried it once already, and it won't work any better this time. Meanwhile, find a place to sleep, get some food and some clean clothes." Vashtor stood up, and as he did so, he tossed five silver coins onto the sidewalk beside Minxa. "Spend it wisely—if you can."

Minxa gathered the five coins. A vague desperation flooded over him as Vashtor hissed into nothingness, leaving the cold darkness of the street to wrap around him. Minxa was not sure if he should cry or throw up. He did neither. Instead he stood up and wrapped his cloak around him and headed east toward the waterfront, hoping to find a place to sleep off the last hours of this miserable night.

1Δ Apothecary 1Δ

We believe that Mah'Eladra created all that we see, and worlds far beyond what we see. Why then do we doubt that they are capable of creating beings like the Melendars?

Mortag of Horrinaine
Of Beings

A bright shaft of sunlight spilled across the table, casting a long, early morning shadow behind Mindar's tea mug. The polished tabletop shimmered where the steam curled over its lip and spiraled up slowly to fill his nostrils with its sweet, pungent fragrance. Mindar felt Hanara staring, her penetrating blue eyes searching deep inside his vorn. He was not uncomfortable, because he knew this stare, though he was not sure he knew the person behind it.

Mindar looked around the small, second-floor kitchen. A vague sense of familiarity wafted through his mind as he scanned its details. There were two windows: one behind the sink that looked out over the street in front of the shop and one that faced the brick wall of the building next door. A single light hung over the table where they sat. Everything was in order, and each cupboard was neatly arranged in a manner fitting of Hanara. It was similar in size and décor to Hannahoruan's kitchen in Kinvara.

Mindar tried to rationalize the familiar with its association with Hanara and the similarity of the two kitchens, but there was more to it. Somewhere on the fringes was a significance that eluded him.

"Misarda is a fine man," Hanara was saying. "I could see his concern when he dropped you off here."

"I know," Mindar answered.

"He said you needed a place to stay for a few days."

Mindar nodded as he sipped the hot tea. It had a musty taste, but delicate and spicy at the same time.

"What happened last night?" Hanara waited as Mindar thought through the events of the evening, searching for a good place to start.

"You met my friend, Minxa, last night?"

"Yes," she said, "he has a wild vorn, and his mordage is deep and thick."

"He is angry, too," Mindar added.

Hanara did not answer as she sipped her tea.

"He came to the warehouse on an invitation as I did, but I don't believe he knew I was there. After dinner we spent an hour or so talking with Glordan and Marall. Minxa spent most of it twisting the truth, just enough to keep it plausible so that they could not tell if he was lying."

"Glordan is a man of great wisdom and vision," she said. "He knows the noble truths and knows that they will always be vindicated if we are patient. Apparently he did not have to wait long."

"No," Mindar conceded, "but I almost lost my life allowing truth to be vindicated."

"It is not your time." Her tone was matter of fact.

"Does one know when it is his time?"

"Not always—but those who live in psadeq with Mah'Eladra, who know noble truth and have vision, often know the time. Perhaps it is more that they know that there really *is* a time, so they are at peace with this truth and are not afraid of it. The *when* of it does not matter. "

"Is there a time for you?"

"There is a time for every being," she said with a smile, "every snake, every dog, every horse, every man and woman—and the times are different for each kind." She took another sip of tea before continuing. "The *way* is different for each kind—their vorns are different and so is their psadeq with each other and with Mah'Eladra. They have made it so that we do not have to concern ourselves with the ways for the others—

only for our kind."

"Do you know my time and my way?" he asked.

She looked deep inside him before answering. "I know some, and some of that I cannot speak. I know this: that you are not quite ready, Master Mindar."

"In what way?"

"I don't know that. You must keep your vorn free of mordage that would prevent you from seeing your time when it comes. If you do this, when your time comes, the way will be clear."

"What do you know of the Melendars?" Mindar asked to change the course of the discussion. He could not tell if it was his imagination or whether Hanara shifted visibly when he said the word. Her response was slow in coming, and she stared up into her forehead as she spoke, grasping her mug tightly in both hands.

"It is an ancient legend, indeed, from the time at the beginning of The Beginnings. Mah'Eladra set life into the beings of Tessalindria. With passion and power they sent the beings forth, knowing that they would have to make their own way in our world full of choices, both good and bad. They would have to fight to keep psadeq with each other and with Mah'Eladra, and they must seek this in armatan and kariis.

"To the Eladra, they gave no choice. The Eladra are their servants, an extension of Mah'Eladra's arms. They move freely in their service, but they do not have choice. There were those who rose up in rebellion, thinking that they, too, should have choice, like the man kind and the animals. They denied their nature and in doing so, broke psadeq with Mah'Eladra and the other Eladra. With the Eladra there is no armatan and there is no kariis, there is only obedience and disobedience. That is their nature and that is their end."

Hanara lowered her eyes and stared at him once again. "To a handful of beings, they gave the elements of the Kirrinath without limit. Because their noble truth, wisdom, vision and armatan are complete, psadeq is complete, and there is no need for metnoga, kariis, raatsa and selkah. The Melendars will live until Tessalindria dies. They will be the last to ascend Sessasha's Stair into the Deep Sky. They will draw the stairway up behind them and close the doors of the Deep Sky forever."

"How many are there?"

"Eight."

"Are you one of them?" he asked.

Hanara laughed. "Perhaps. The Melendar do not know who they are."

"How can that be?"

"I am not sure, but I believe that Mah'Eladra made them unaware of who they are so that they would not become arrogant. They are servants who do not know that they are such. They are facilitators of Mah'Eladra's plans and purpose. Perhaps you are one, Master Mindar?"

Mindar looked up from the fragments of tea leaves that lay in the bottom of his mug. She was smiling at him across the table.

"Come, now, we have much to do. The Essendar meeting starts in about an hour at the warehouse. We do not want to miss it."

Mindar gathered the bag that Glordan had given him to hold his scant collection of belongings, and followed her up the stairs at the back of the apothecary. On the third floor there was a small room under the roof. "This will be adequate for a few days, will it not, Master Mindar?"

"More than adequate," he said as he set his bag in the corner.

"Do you know why Glordan asked you to leave the warehouse?" she asked. She was framed in the doorway to the small room, facing Mindar. The light shone through the window past him, reflecting off the smooth polished floor and illuminating her with a radiance that seemed unnatural.

"He said it was for my own safety, but I am not sure I understood that."

"Why didn't you understand it?"

"Well, the dormitory was guarded by Eladrim beings—six of them— so I am not sure where I could go that would be much safer."

"Yet you nearly lost your life at Master Minxa's hands—"

"Yes," he said with a pause, "I was not sure what to think about that either."

"Perhaps there is more to Master Minxa than you know," she said. There was a certain wildness to the way she said it that was characteristic of Hannahoruan. In that brief instant the resemblance flooded him once again. "I think Master Glordan realizes that he cannot protect you—and he endangers the others by letting you stay."

"I have known Minxa all my—I'm not sure what you mean, 'more to Master Minxa.'"

"I am not sure what I mean either. Until we find out, you must be very cautious around this city when you are not here."

"Will I be safe here?"

"For a time—and you will know the time when you have to leave. While I am here, no one can harm you."

"Hannahoruan used to say that about her apothecary in Kinvara— and it was true."

"Hannahoruan?"

"A friend of mine," he answered. "She ran an apothecary like this one in Kinvara, about a thousand years ago. She looked exactly like you—same voice, same eyes, same hair…"

"That was a long time ago, Master Mindar."

"Only a few weeks for me," he said as he sat down on the bed. "I remember it like yesterday."

A long pause followed. Mindar stared at the floor, and he knew Hanara was staring at him. "We will speak more of these things," she said at length. "You can clean up in the washroom across the landing here. We will need to leave for the meeting in about fifteen minutes."

Mindar nodded without looking up. Their discussion had brought back a flood of memories about the last days in Kinvara; about his wife and his daughters; about Erinshava and Hannahoruan. He did not want to wash up. He just wanted to sit and remember.

✠

Food for my belly; a dry place to sleep,
Silver in my pocket; and naught to make
me weep.

Vindorian Rhyme

Two days rest and regular meals had done wonders for Minxa's attitude. He had sold two coins at the Brass Bucket, a waterfront pawnshop that dealt in antiquities. The shopkeeper had been stunned to see ancient coins of such perfection, especially in the hands of a viddik who had not bathed in days and whose costume was contemporaneous with the coins. The shopkeeper had grown suspicious. When Minxa threatened to leave and take the coins with him, the man buckled and gave him three hundred dendra for two coins, in cash. He said it was all he could afford. Minxa was not sure this was a good price, but it would be enough to clothe himself and get a clean place to sleep and eat for several days.

Minxa took up a room above the Rusty Anchor saloon. It was not the best of accommodations, but no one asked any questions, and it only cost forty-two dendra for a night. His room was at the front on the second floor, tucked into the row of businesses that served the waterfront of Vindarill from the street one block away from the wharfs. Minxa couldn't see the harbor from the grimy window with cracked glass, but when he lifted the sash, he could smell it. He washed his face with the cold water from the dingy sink in the corner before he headed down to the saloon for something warm to eat.

The food in the saloon was mediocre but passable, and they served a wide variety of ales and wine. At night, the saloon was cleared for the general revelry of the longshoremen who came there to drink after the day's work, and every morning, they served juice and greasy breakfast to the same crowd as they tried to wake up.

Most of all, Minxa felt at home. Here, no one cared that he was a viddik, and if they did, it hardly mattered since so many of the others were also. The open, anonymous camaraderie of nightlife made life simple for him. There was no one who knew him or anything about his past, and no one who cared whether they knew it or not. No one measured him by his clothing or his accent, but only by whether he had enough money to be able to sit down with a mug of ale and talk about anything and nothing until they were all kicked out at the midnight bell.

During the day, he wandered the streets of Vindarill, trying to reacquaint himself with his old haunts and hoping he would catch a glimpse of the young Rindar. Once he tried to get into the entrance to the tunnels, but was thrown out by the guards. He tried waiting around until the shift they had worked was over, but he never caught even a glimpse of his quarry.

On the third night Minxa was just finishing a bowl of fish stew and rye bread when a giant of a man sat down beside him at the table. "Seen ya couple times here," the man said as he sipped on an oversized mug of ale.

"Been here two days," Minxa mumbled. "I've seen you too."

"Where ya from?"

"Vindarill—you come here a lot?" Minxa felt safer being the one asking the questions.

"Every night for three years."

"What's your name?"

"Nashon," the man said as he tipped his mug back again. His wrists were as thick as Minxa's ankles; and his arms, hardened with muscles from the heavy work on the dock, were covered with tattoos. The sleeves of his shirt had been torn off to showcase the immensity of his shoulders. "And yours?" he said as he lowered his mug.

"Minxa."

"Ya workin'?"

"Not right now, and you?"

"I'm a rigger. Best on the docks." His grey eyes twinkled under his thick brown eyebrows. "Rig the cranes for the longshoremen and stevedores. Ya want somthin' ta do?"

"On the docks?"

"Na," Nashon said with a smile, "just a little errand inshore, just take a couple a' hours."

"Inshore?"

"In the town—we call it inshore." Nashon set down his mug and wiped his lips with the back of his wrist, then laid both forearms on the table as he leaned forward.

"Not interested in working right now," Minxa said, "but I do have a question."

"Yuh?"

"Well, I have a couple of old coins I need to sell—"

"Brass Bucket, just around the corner."

"Been there. He bought a couple, but didn't want to buy more."

"Coins, you said?" Nashon asked. "There's an old place, inshore, haven't been there in years, let's see—Windera Street. Run by a shrewd old scalefish who'll give ya top dendra. Ya gotta know yer stuff, though. Old black sign with a bear paw on it that has his name on it: Koto—sumthing like that."

"Is he honest?"

"Honest, yes—but real shrewd. Tell ya what. You help me with my errand, and I'll show you where it is, help you get yer value."

"When?"

"I have tomorrow off—always take Modar off. After breakfast?"

Minxa stuffed the last piece of bread into his mouth and chewed it as he watched Nashon. It had been a long time since he had trusted anyone. Nashon stared back. He crossed his arms across his massive chest as he waited patiently for Minxa's response. "After breakfast then," Minxa said.

Nashon stood up. "See ya then." He turned and sauntered away, leaving Minxa wondering what he had just gotten himself into.

✠

Any path can become rocky and difficult without warning. Should we expect the path of life to be different?

Oratanga
Passages

Work in the apothecary was intermittent and slow. Mindar tended to customers and kept the shop in order. The little he knew of what he sold did not seem to matter. Hanara had everything ready for people she knew were coming. When someone came in looking for something in particular, Mindar recorded their name and what they asked for, and Hanara would prepare it when she was in the shop.

She was gone most of the time, collecting ingredients from places unknown, and Mindar wondered what she had done before he came. There was no evidence that there was anyone else before him to do what he did. In the times when no one was around, he read the books from the library that Jeshwa brought him, the pages marked with small slips of paper where Jeshwa and Garva had found something of particular interest. There was nothing about his wife or daughters. The legends about the

Melendars were twisted and contradictory, steeped in conjecture with no account offering proof that there was any truth to them at all.

Evening trips to the library were out of the question. Hanara thought that Minxa probably knew where Mindar was. Mindar had no reason to doubt her and no evidence to confirm her suspicion, but after the encounter in the warehouse, Mindar was not in a hurry to find out if Hanara was right.

Misarda stopped by the apothecary with the truck two days after Mindar had started there. They ate lunch together on the bench on the sidewalk in front of the shop. "I wish you were on the truck," Misarda said between bites in his sandwich.

"No assistant yet?" Mindar asked.

Misarda shook his head as he chewed on his sandwich.

"Lots of work?"

"Yeah, but I gets it done. Modars are usually a light day," Misarda said as he nodded toward the huge calendar on the bank building down the street. "Modar," it read across the top—the second day of the week. The month and day below it read "Ulrar:6."

"I've wanted to ask—" Mindar paused as he stuffed his mouth with bread. Misarda waited until he had chewed it sufficiently. "Who woke you up the other night?"

"I told you, I don't know who it was." Misarda looked out across the street. "His hands were like ice. He didn't say nothin', either; he just pointed."

"A big guy?"

"Hard to tell in the dark. By the time I was awake enough to realize what was happening, I didn't care who he was."

"Thanks for the help," Mindar said.

Misarda nodded. "You were in sore trouble," he said with a laugh. "Your friend is quite strong."

"He was a soldier in the Kinvaran army," Mindar said. "A trained killer. Never guessed he would try to kill me."

"That's why you're here with Hanara?"

Mindar nodded. "I'm not sure whether I am in a prison or under protection sometimes. Perhaps there isn't much of a difference when it comes right down to it."

Misarda finished chewing his sandwich. "Believe me, there is a big difference," he said with a quick smile. He paused before continuing. "How did you like the gathering—on Essendar?"

"At the warehouse?"

Misarda nodded.

"It was…" He had started talking without knowing what he was going to say. "I guess it made me realize how little I know about the

Sessashians. Or perhaps it made me aware of how much I thought I knew that was wrong."

Misarda leaned back on his hands and listened as his eyes roved back and forth with the passing traffic. "You've been away from here for nearly forty years," he said absently. "What you thought you knew was from a young man's perspective, to begin with—and then all those years living before Sessasha ever lived..."

"You believe he was the anthara?" Mindar interjected.

"Yes, and that is the distinction. There are many who don't."

"It's not popular to be Sessashian, you know," said Mindar.

"Never has been—probably never will be." Misarda looked over at Mindar. "I have found as I have gotten older that popularity with others is highly overrated. It just got me in trouble—nearly killed. When I took the time to stop and think, I realized that the noble truths, psadeq and the rest of the Kirrinath were far more valuable—and made more sense when I made the effort to embrace them."

"Well, I have a lot of questions," Mindar said, "and we don't have a lot of time right now, but if you don't mind, perhaps we can talk again soon."

"I'll do the best I can. The real experts are Glordan, Mirad and Jeshwa." He stood up and stretched. "What kind of questions?"

Mindar opened his mouth to speak when a sudden movement to his right caught his attention. He looked over to see a raven landing on the sidewalk. "Vakandar?" he said.

The bird strutted in front of him, then stopped and cocked his head before turning himself around and looking critically at Mindar with the other eye.

"What have we here?" asked Misarda.

"What have we—what have we here?" mimicked the bird as he strutted past again. With a fluff of his wings he leapt up onto Mindar's knee. Misarda jumped.

"Vakandar!" Mindar exclaimed.

"Don't have much time, no I don't," Vakandar said as he hopped to the other knee and turned around. "Visha'andar is here," he continued. "Do not fear."

"Fear what?"

"Do not fear—do not fear." Vakandar shuddered his feathers. "Must go—must go now."

"Wait," Mindar said, but Vakandar had spread his wings and leapt into flight. He swooped low over the sidewalk and wheeled back toward them. Mindar felt the huff of his wings as he passed over his head. Misarda ducked. Vakandar swept upward and veered around the corner of the building and disappeared.

Misarda stared after him. "That bird spoke to you!" he gulped as he looked back at Mindar.

Mindar nodded. "He is an old friend—saved my life at least twice."

"The legends—they say this can happen, but I've never—" Misarda's voice trailed off.

Mindar was about to attempt an explanation when Hanara appeared around the corner. She was hurrying toward them at a half run with a keen urgency in her eyes. "This doesn't look good!" said Misarda under his breath.

Mindar stood up as she approached. "Inside, Master Mindar," she said as she pushed by him without looking up. She turned at the door. "Master Misarda, you must go to your truck and wait there. I have urgent need of your services for a brief trip."

Misarda nodded then turned and headed for his truck. Mindar stepped into the sheltered light of the apothecary, and Hanara pushed the door closed behind him.

"What's going—"

"Sssshhh!" Hanara gestured toward the back room.

Mindar sat down in the chair across the small preparation table from Hanara. Her eyes danced in the dull light that came through the one window in the door at the back of the shop. "I have an urgent errand," she said. Her hands were busy with the small vials and bottles she had scooped from the counter when she came into the room. "Eight streets down—" she pointed in the direction she meant, "Windera street, on the right—" She paused as she counted the drops from one vial into the other. "There is a man there, Master Kotorvan. He needs this remedy for his son who is sick with a fever." She looked up. "Have you heard what I said?" she asked as she pushed several crushed leaves into the bottle with a small stick.

"Yes. Windera Street; Master Kotorvan."

"He runs a small pawn shop. It's not much of a business, but he's honest, and he'll pay you in silver. Don't linger in the shop, do you understand?"

"May I ask why?" Hanara's agitation was curious. In all his years—at least with Hannahoruan in Kinvara—he had never seen her act like this.

"You may, but I do not have an answer. Master Misarda will take you there, and he will bring you back. We must not waste his time; he is being paid by Glordan." She capped the little bottle and shook it vigorously. "Two drops under each nostril, twice a day, and make sure he does not drink this. Is this clear?"

Mindar nodded. "Two drops under each nostril, twice a day—and don't drink it."

"Hurry!" she said as she grabbed him by the hand and hastened him out the door. Her strength was surprising and surpassed only by her determination for his haste. She nearly pushed him into the truck.

"What's the urgency?" asked Misarda as the engine roared to life beneath them.

"Eight streets down on the right, Windera Street—"

"I know it well."

"A pawn shop—Master Kotorvan—"

"Been there many times." Misarda eased the truck into traffic. "Is he ill?"

"No, his son has a fever," Mindar said.

"That's an awful lot of hurry for a fever."

"I think there is something else going on," Mindar added. "I mean, why was she so determined to have me do it? She hasn't even wanted me to leave the shop since I arrived."

Misarda shrugged. Windera Street arrived quickly. It was really more of an alley that seemed to have been overlooked by progress. The truck rumbled over the narrow stone pavement, thumping and lurching in and out of potholes that could not be avoided. About halfway down the block, Misarda stopped opposite a dingy little door between the unwashed windows of a small shop. Above the door, a small black sign hung from a rusty iron bracket. The faded, yellow paw print of a bear was encircled by the peeling words "Kotorvan" above and "Pawn Shop" below.

"She said not to stay too long, but could not explain why," Mindar said as he swung his feet down onto the ancient curbstone.

"I'll wait here until you are done," Misarda said as he cut the engine.

A small bell rang somewhere, and the little lever above the door slapped back into place as Mindar pushed the door inward on its rusty hinges. The shop was long and narrow and piled with toys, tools and junk, dimly lit by bare bulbs hanging from the ceiling on cracked wires. Reflecting on the tragedy of materialism, once prized objects now gathered dust in a back-way pawnshop. Mindar waited briefly as his eyes grew used to the gloom, then walked carefully down the rows of societal detritus. There was no sound anywhere, as if the cobwebs in the corners were catching it and holding it from him.

"Hello?" he called into the deadness. "Hello?"

A slight scuffling at the back of the shop caught his attention. He walked carefully toward it, and as he came around a low counter piled high with old magazines, he found its source. An old man lay on the floor, bound hand and foot with twine, and gagged with a mouthful of rag held in place with an old bandana tied around his head. His eyes were wide. Cold fear swept over Mindar.

The man squirmed and groaned behind his gag, and when Mindar bent down, the old man recoiled. "I'm just going to untie you," Mindar said. "Hanara sent me with a potion for your son," Mindar continued as he reached carefully into his pocket and pulled out the vial for the man to see.

The man's eyes softened, and he nodded and turned his head so that Mindar could untie the bandana. The knot was tight, but yielded to Mindar's strong fingers. When he pulled the rag out of the man's mouth, he realized how far it had been pushed in. "Are you Kotorvan?" he asked as he worked at the knots on the cords around his wrists.

The man gasped for breath and nodded his head, unable to speak. The cords had been tied so tightly that they had cut off the circulation in his hands, which were purple and bloated. Whoever had done this had intended that Kotorvan would die.

When the ropes fell from his wrists, Kotorvan closed his eyes and rested his hands gingerly on his belly while Mindar worked on his feet. His breathing was almost normal now, but he lay motionless on his back with his eyes closed.

The knots holding the rope on the man's feet defied Mindar's strength. Thinking that there had to be a knife in the midst of the mess in the shop and realizing that the danger had passed, Mindar rose to go find one. As he did so the bell announcing that someone had entered the shop rang behind him. He stopped. Kotorvan sat up suddenly, his eyes wide with fear, his finger on his mouth begging for silence.

Mindar peered over the counter between two stacks of ancient magazines. Two figures had entered and were making their way toward the back where he was crouched behind the counter. He could only see silhouettes because of the light from the window. They were laughing. "I left him back here behind the counter."

"And the map? How did he get it into the safe?"

"He tricked me." It was Minxa's voice. "Said he wanted to put the goods in before he gave me the map. Slipped it in and locked it on me."

"So you tied him up?"

They were dangerously close now; five more steps and they would come around the counter. The only advantage Mindar had was surprise. Kotorvan was useless, his ankles bound tightly and barely able to use his hands. Mindar took hold of the base of a small lamp that was sitting on the floor behind the counter. He crouched and waited for those last five steps.

As the leader stepped around the end of the counter, Mindar leapt up with all his strength, driving the butt end of the lamp into the groin of the first man and throwing his full weight against the torso. There was a groan and a yell, as both bodies tumbled backward with a crash against a pile of old boxes on the table behind them.

Mindar wanted to run—to escape past the sprawled bodies, but he knew he could not leave Kotorvan. He leapt forward, swinging the lamp with all his strength down on the two men. Each was bigger and stronger than Mindar, and they scrambled away through the rubble, rolling and thrashing, spilling boxes and cartons in the frenzy to escape Mindar's attack.

It was not long before they had recovered from their surprise and realized that Mindar was alone and cornered in the back of the long shop. Minxa stood up and laughed as he brushed himself off. "My old friend Rindar. Rindar, meet Nashon." He nodded toward the giant of a man that stood behind him, scowling in the shifting light of a light bulb that swung back and forth above him. "Thought you could come and steal the map from me—again?"

Mindar felt his emotions leap inside at the mention of a map. "I know nothing of any map," he said cautiously. "I came here to deliver a remedy for the shopkeeper's son."

Minxa chuckled, but there was evil rattling through every fiber of it. "Hah! You expect me to believe that?"

"It's the truth. I would not have known about any map, had you not mentioned it."

Minxa looked at him warily, confounded that Mindar might be telling the truth. "Where is this remedy you brought?"

Mindar pulled the small black vial from his pocket with his right hand. He was still holding the lamp with his left. He held the vial out for Minxa to see.

Minxa stared at it, then looked up. "Get out of the way, Rindar," he growled. "We have a map to get out of that safe." He started to move, and Mindar raised the lamp to threaten him. Minxa laughed again. "The surprise is gone, Rindar. You don't stand a chance and you know it."

As Minxa leaned over to pick up a pot that lay at his feet, the doorbell rang at the back of the shop. The door opened a crack and then shut abruptly with a slam. Nashon swore and whirled around.

The door opened again, a little further this time, and then slammed harder. The doorframe shuddered. Nashon headed for the door, but Minxa kept his eyes on Mindar. The leering expression was gone. The door opened, the bell jangled, and Misarda's voice called, "Nashon!" The door slammed again, rattling the glass in the windows. Mindar could look over Minxa's shoulder and see the door. Nashon was waiting for it to open again. Nothing moved. "What's going on?" Minxa yelled over his shoulder.

"Dunno," growled Nashon.

"Well, get on with it—do something!"

The man was so big that he had to stoop to reach the door handle, and as he did, the door flew open, cracking soundly against his bald head. He staggered back, and the open doorway darkened as Misarda hurtled through it with a packing blanket stretched in front of him. The blanket settled over Nashon's head as Misarda flung his full weight into the blinded man. Nashon crashed backward, and Misarda tumbled on top, his sledgehammer fists raining blows onto Nashon's smothered head. The commotion broke Minxa's concentration, and as he turned to see what was happening, Mindar took the opportunity to move behind the counter. In a matter of seconds, Nashon lay unconscious under the blanket.

Misarda stood up and moved toward Minxa. "You again!" Misarda said. "What are you doing here?"

Minxa dropped the pot he had picked up and stood still. There was nowhere to go. "I came here to buy something that this shop had for sale, but the shopkeeper tricked me and locked it in his safe."

"That's a lie," came a hoarse voice from behind the counter as Kotorvan struggled to get to his feet. He had managed to cut the bonds from his ankles, and as he rose slowly his voice was labored and rasping. "He came in to pawn something that I suspected was stolen. He saw this old box and wanted to trade what he had instead. I told him there was no deal."

Minxa scowled, but the old man went on. "He left, promising to return with enough to buy the box. I suspected that he would have to steal to get enough, so I put it in the safe. I have seen this type before."

Mindar listened as he kept his eyes on Minxa. Misarda stood less than four feet behind him, blocking the aisle and any possibility of escape without having to face the man who had bested him that night in the dormitory at the warehouse.

Kotorvan continued, "When he came back I refused to give him the box—by the law of Morlan I do not have to sell anything—and he beat me and tied me up, vowing to return and take it. He said something about it belonging to a friend of his." Minxa looked at him with eyes full of hatred, and Mindar felt a wave of emotion roll down his spine. "If you—" Kotorvan paused as he realized that he did not know how to address Mindar, "if you had not arrived, I would probably be dead."

Minxa was surveying his situation as Misarda opened his mouth to speak and took a step toward his quarry. In a catlike movement, Minxa leapt backward, rolled over a small bench covered with papers, landed on his feet on the other side, and moved swiftly toward the door. The door opened inward, and before Minxa could open it and escape, Misarda had caught his cloak. Minxa whirled, and for a brief moment Mindar could not tell what was happening. Suddenly everything stopped. Minxa turned and pulled himself through the door, leaving Misarda standing and watching.

Misarda uttered an oath under his breath. "He had a knife," he gasped. By the time Mindar reached him, there was blood soaking the front of his shirt, and his right hand was stuffed in the gashed cloth, holding his chest. "Can you drive?" Misarda rasped as he looked up at Mindar with eyes already hollow with pain. Mindar shook his head.

"I can," said Kotorvan as he limped toward the front of the shop. "At least I can try." His hands were still discolored, and he was rubbing them gingerly.

"Take me...to Hanara's." The pain was distorting his face. "Quickly...keys in the truck."

Kotorvan pulled Mindar aside. "Get the box out of the safe," he whispered urgently. "Take it upstairs with you when you give the remedy to my son." He spoke the safe's combination into Mindar's ear. "Got it?"

Mindar, dumbfounded by the rapidity with which life was changing, nodded and turned toward the back of the shop. Kotorvan was helping the flagging Misarda out the door toward the truck. "Go!" he called. "And get my son and yourself out of here as soon as you can. Go out the back door."

Mindar wanted to ask "Where?" but there was no time. The engine roared to life, and Kotorvan piloted the truck down the narrow alley.

The safe was behind the counter, buried under another pile of junk, and Mindar had to try the combination three times before it would open. When the handle turned in his hand, Mindar found himself holding his breath, and as he pulled the heavy door open, his eyes flew to the box. There must have been other things there, but Mindar saw none of them. He grasped the box, slammed the door to the safe and spun the dial twice.

With the map tucked under his arm, he suddenly felt as if his feet had wings. He took the narrow stairs three at a time, and at the landing, without knowing why, he bolted into the first door on the left. It was a small room. The window had been covered with a dark cloth, so the light from the window was muted and faint around its edges. The small bed just inside the door was mounded with rumpled cloth that moved suddenly. "Father?" The voice was small and weak.

"I am a friend of your father," Mindar said.

"Did Hanara send you?"

The boy's round eyes stared back at Mindar in the gloomy room. "Yes," he said gently, "she sent this remedy for your fever, and asked me to bring it to you."

"Where is my father?"

"He...he had to run an errand."

"What is your name?"

"I am Mindar...Mindar Colloden."

"My name is Jazdar." He lay still, staring up at Mindar, who stood frozen in the doorway, paralyzed by the uncomfortable situation. He wondered how Kotorvan had been able to trust him so completely.

"Where is your mother?"

Jazdar hesitated. "She left."

Something about the way he said the words shook Mindar's hjarg. He knelt down beside the bed. "Shall we try Hanara's remedy?" he said gently.

Jazdar nodded.

"I have to put two drops under each of your nostrils—"

Jazdar rolled onto his back obediently.

"Four drops, and don't drink it," Mindar said as he screwed the top off the small black vial. "Can you walk?" he asked as he put the first drop under the boy's left nostril.

Jazdar moved only his lips. "Think so," he said. "Why?" he asked after the second drop.

"We have to leave here—" The third drop fell onto the boy's upper lip. "It's not safe here right now—breathe through your nose." Drop four found its mark.

Jazdar breathed deeply and sneezed. "Owww!" he said.

"Do it again," said Mindar. Jazdar inhaled again, but with a little more caution.

"It burns!"

"It heals," Mindar said. "Sometimes things that hurt also heal."

"My father says that a lot."

"Your father is a wise man. Can you sit up?"

Jazdar pushed himself up onto his elbows and stopped to inhale again. "I think this is helping," he said.

"I'll wait outside the door while you get dressed." Mindar stepped through the doorway as he screwed the cap back onto the small black vial. There was something unusual about Jazdar—some strength, resolution or insight the boy possessed that made him different. Mindar could only guess at his age. Maybe he was ten, but he seemed too small and young to be Kotorvan's son.

As he stood by the door, he realized that the map box was still tucked under his arm. He held it up and scrutinized it in the light of the single bare bulb that hung above the landing. The case looked identical to the map he had carried for so long. Mindar's mind ran circles around the thought that it had been less than two weeks since he had lost the map, and yet if this was the same one, it had been passed on for nearly thirty generations to come back here. Where had it been? Whose hands had touched it, and how could it have survived unchanged through all those hands? Mindar wanted to open it and look at the map itself, but there was no time.

He was about to turn back to the door when the bell rang behind the desk downstairs. He crept to the door and tapped. As he pushed it open, Jazdar was just buttoning his shirt. Mindar held his finger to his mouth. "Someone just came into the shop," he whispered.

"My father?"

"I don't think there would be time for him to get back here from Hanara's yet."

Mindar could hear the footsteps of someone making their way through the shop. They stopped at the bottom of the stairs, behind the counter. He leaned close to Jazdar's ear. "Is there another way out?"

Jazdar pointed to the window.

"Your father said to go out the back."

"We would have to go down the stairs to do that," Jazdar whispered. He pointed at the window again and beckoned Mindar to follow. The windows swung into the room with a slight creak on the rusty hinges, and Jazdar clambered up onto the shelf in front of the windowsill. "Very steep," he whispered, "but the roof is flat." He swung out the side of the window and disappeared. Mindar climbed up on the sill and peered out. The section of the roof immediately outside the window was too steep to get a foothold, but by standing on the sill, he could just reach the edge of the roof where it became flat. Mindar wondered how Jazdar could have reached the roof.

Jazdar peered over the edge. His tousled black hair and the two dark smudges under his nose from Hanara's potion were comical, but his face was somber with worry. "You better try to close the window," he said. Mindar looked back. The window wasn't meant to be closed from the outside.

"Hold this," said Mindar as he held the map up to Jazdar's reach. He reached back in and did the best he could to pull the two sides forward as he balanced on the sill, holding onto the casing of the window on the outside. When he had closed it as well as he could, Mindar stood up and laid his hand on the top edge of the roof. With a helping hand from Jazdar, he scrambled up to where it was flat. As he stood up, he caught the vague apparition of an Eladra out of the corner of his eye. It stood on the edge of the roof. Long ago he had learned that one never looks directly at the Eladra, but a little to the side. When he did it was very clear.

"Do you see it?" asked Jazdar.

Mindar was startled. "What?"

"I thought I saw you trying to see the Eladrim warrior on the edge of the roof."

"Yes, Jazdar, I saw the Eladra."

Jazdar looked at him curiously. "I've never met anyone else who can see them," he said. "C'mon, there is an old ladder down from the roof." He took Mindar by the hand and pulled him toward the back of the house.

"How long have you been able to see them?" Mindar asked.

The roof was nearly flat with several interruptions where skylights poked up through from the rooms below. It shimmered with the heat from the midday sun. "I have seen them all my life," Jazdar said in a low voice, "but I didn't know what they were until about a year ago."

"How old are you?"

"Twelve."

"And what made you understand what these...shimmerings are?"

"Shimmerings?"

"Well, they aren't really all that visible." They had reached the ladder. It was a decrepit welded-iron affair with rusty handrails that led straight down the back of the building between the windows. Mindar shook it to see if it was solid.

"It's all right," said Jazdar. "I've been down it many times. We have to be careful at the bottom, 'cause we pass right by the back window to the shop."

Mindar nodded. Jazdar swung onto the ladder and started down, and when he was about halfway, Mindar followed. The ladder swayed from side to side as Mindar worked his way down. It was not something he would have trusted under ordinary circumstances, but there was little choice. The explosion ripped through the shop when he was five rungs from the bottom, blowing the glass out of the window to his left. Mindar half jumped and half fell off the ladder. "Quick," said Jazdar, "we have to get out of here!" He grabbed Mindar's hand and tried to pull him up off the tired, hot asphalt that lined the ground behind the shop.

Mindar pushed himself to his feet and started running behind Jazdar. The boy knew his way, probably from many jaunts out the back of his home above the shop. Mindar had all he could do to keep up as Jazdar ran along in front of him.

Jazdar slowed down and came to a stop, bent over and started coughing. They had run several blocks. Mindar breathed heavily and laid his hand on Jazdar's shoulder just before the boy collapsed in a heap on the pavement. He rolled onto his back, his face staring blankly up into the sunlight, bright red with fever and exhaustion.

Mindar knelt beside him and loosened Jazdar's collar as he took in the surroundings. They were in the middle of a narrow alley, one end of which opened onto a busy street and the other against a brick wall topped with coils of barbed wire. They had entered from the side between two buildings. Mindar laid the map on Jazdar's chest and lifted him, cradling the boy's head in his left arm. He was surprised at how light he was.

He made his way toward the street, wondering what he would do when he got there. Just before he emerged onto the street, a police car swept past, its whistles shrieking to warn people out of the way as it headed toward Kotorvan's shop. After the car had past, Mindar stepped out onto the sidewalk, carrying the limp boy. Hanara's apothecary was about three blocks to his left.

People moved to the side as Mindar swept along the street, undaunted by their stares. Misarda's truck stood opposite the apothecary, and the cab was empty. Mindar kicked at the door to the shop, and it opened without resistance, so he carried Jazdar to the small room in the back. Kotorvan looked up as he entered.

"Jazdar," he gasped as he stood to meet them.

"Lay him on the mat on the floor," said Hanara. "Then go lock the front door."

Mindar kneeled with Jazdar in his arms. By the time the boy was on the mat, his father had soaked a towel in the sink and was daubing his face. "Jazdar, my son, my only son—" Hanara's hands were bathed in blood, and she held her right hand firmly over the wound in Misarda's side. Mindar's memory flashed back to the day Dakan had died in the glen outside of Fazdeen. He felt the sickening wooze of shock rolling over him as he headed for the front of the shop. He threw the bolt on the door and turned around the little sign so that it said "Closed." As he reentered the back room, Hanara beckoned. "Hold your hand here," she ordered as she pointed to her own hand. Misarda was unconscious on the table. "Right here," she said as she placed Mindar's hand where hers had been.

Mindar could feel the warm blood, and the smell of it made him sick. He felt the same nausea he had felt when he woke that morning after murdering the old man so many years ago, the same nausea he had felt when he had been wounded in the Verillain Dale, and the same nausea he had felt when Dakan died. Dark clouds rolled in around the corners of his consciousness; and he stood in the fog, holding his hand over the hole in his friend's belly, holding in Misarda's life as his own life swam before him in darkness, trying to give his life to his friend as he had for Sereline.

Hanara returned in the darkness. Her voice was distant. "Hold this bowl—Mindar?" He felt the warm bowl in his right hand—had to hold onto his friend's life...

"The remedy for Jazdar, Mindar? Do you have it?" Her voice was so far away.

"My pocket," was all he could remember. Someone reached in his pocket and took the vial.

✠

The crushing debt of selfishness grows deeper with each self-indulgence that tries to relieve it.

Hispattea
The Essences of Corritanean Wisdom

Minxa bent over Nashon and slapped his wet face. Even the blast that tore the door off the safe had not woken him, nor had the pitcher of cold water. "C'mon, Nashon, wake up! Wake up!" he said.

The giant stirred and tried to open his eyes, but as soon as Minxa could see under his eyelids, his eyes crossed and rolled back into his head. He let out a groan and passed out again. The whistles of an approaching police car warned Minxa that he had no time left. Escape from the front door would be impossible, and the littered floor of the shop with its already narrow aisles would have made it difficult to get Nashon out the back door even if Minxa could have moved him by himself. Minxa stood. "I have no choice, friend," he muttered as he turned to head out the back.

He hesitated for a moment and stepped back to the giant on the floor, rummaging around quickly for his money purse. It was not hard to find, tied to his belt on his right side. Minxa fingered it. There must have been ten coins in it. He was just about to pull it off when the door to the shop flew open. Vashtor burst through.

"It's good that you are here," Minxa lied as he stood up, leaving the purse behind. "I was just about to start pulling him out the back."

"Grab his legs!" ordered Vashtor. "I take his arms."

Minxa bent to grab Nashon's ankles, and Vashtor heaved the giant from the floor by his shoulders.

"Quickly now, out the back!" Vashtor moved like a cat. Minxa tripped twice before they got the man around the counter and once more as they tried to get him through the back door. When they were safely out of the shop, Vashtor reached down and grabbed Nashon's arm and with a quick twist, hoisted him onto his back. "C'mon," he said through clenched teeth. "Follow me."

They ran down alleyways for about a hundred paces before Vashtor slowed and dropped his shoulder, letting Nashon slide to the ground in a heap. Vashtor bent down and straightened Nashon's body so that he was lying flat on his back. Minxa heard more police cars wailing their way toward the shop.

Vashtor sat down on the curb beside Nashon and looked up at Minxa. "What's going on here?" Minxa felt the iciness of his tone.

"I don't know," Minxa admitted. "I came here to sell the other three coins—to get money to pay Rindar for the map."

"Pay Rindar?"

"I found young Rindar last night after he got out of the tunnels," Minxa said, trying to change the mood of the conversation. "I followed him home...I can get to him tonight before he goes—"

"What happened at the shop?" Vashtor interrupted.

"Nashon recommended this shop; said Kotorvan was shrewd but honest. The Brass Bucket wouldn't buy any more coins."

"And?"

"Well, when I came in, the map was just sitting on the bench behind the counter."

"*The* map?"

"Yes, *the* map. I don't know how it got there. I tried to buy it with the three silver coins. Kotorvan's son was there. The sickly little monster told his father not to let me have the map, so Kotorvan refused to trade for it. He said I didn't have enough."

"And?"

"I left to get more money. I borrowed some more from Nashon, and we came back. The old fool had locked the map in his safe, so we tied him up and went to get explosives. We had the explosives, but when we got there, Rindar was there. His friend from the warehouse, the big guy, must have been watching outside, and he caught Nashon by surprise. I barely escaped after wounding the brute with my knife."

Vashtor stared unmoving. "Escaped?" he growled. "What happened to the map?"

"I waited until Kotorvan and the big guy left, and then I came back in. I blew the safe as we had planned—but no map."

Vashtor rose. "You didn't get it? It wasn't in the safe?"

"Rindar must have taken it somehow."

"Somehow?" Vashtor was standing in front of Minxa at full height and looking down at him angrily. He shook his head. "Rindar has it now and so history is becoming. Do you see it, Minxa?" Vashtor smiled briefly as he posed the question, then his face sobered. "We must change what is about to happen. We must get the map tonight, or it slips beyond my grasp. Take the man home," he said as he poked at Nashon with his boot, "then meet me at dusk on the wharf behind the Rusty Anchor. We must find the young Rindar again." Vashtor turned and took two steps before he vanished. Minxa bent down and shook Nashon. The giant groaned and tried to open his eyes. At least Minxa would not have to carry him all the way back to the waterfront.

✠

The gravity of seeing the future is reserved for those rare individuals who are capable of handling that responsibility.

Mortag of Horrinaine
Of Beings

When Mindar opened his eyes, the cool light of evening filtered through the front door of the apothecary. He was flat on his back on a mat behind the counter, and the air was still. He sat up.

"Come," said Hanara. She was sitting on a stool just beyond his feet as if she were awaiting his revival. "Everything is all right now."

"Misarda?"

"Kotorvan has taken him in the truck back to the warehouse. He will be well taken care of there."

Mindar followed her to the small kitchen on the second floor. "And what about Jazdar?" Mindar asked as they climbed the stairs.

"He was exhausted and overheated, so he is sleeping on your bed. He will be fine tomorrow. Had you not given him his medicine before you left, he might have died. Kotorvan will come back to get him and take him home tonight." She turned at the top of the stair and looked directly into his eyes. "There is deep truth here," she said. "The Eladra are here. Two lives have been threatened, and you have been tested," she said as she turned and moved into the kitchen.

Mindar followed. His heightened senses tingled with her presence. "And you came back carrying Lonama's map," she continued as she pointed to the map box on the table. "Where was it?"

Mindar stood in shock. "You...you didn't know about the map?"

"How should I have known?" She turned and stared into his eyes.

"I thought...I guess I thought that you sent me to Kotorvan's because you knew the map was there."

Hanara paused thoughtfully. "I sent you there to deliver a tincture for Jazdar's ailment."

"But you were so urgent!"

"Jazdar's ailment was urgent. Sit down, Master Mindar." She pointed to the chair in front of the map. "I made you some tea," she said as she turned to the stove. "It may be a long night."

The tea was strong and tasted like licorice and cinnamon with an odd bitterness that made Mindar wince when he sipped it. "Faganwort," said Hanara, smiling for the first time that Mindar remembered that day. "It's an ancient herb, all but forgotten in this day of new medicine. It will help you be clearer."

Mindar smiled, sipped the drink again and stared at the map box in front of him. "Would you open it for me?" he asked as he looked up.

Hanara was staring at him, holding her own mug with both hands wrapped around it tightly. "I cannot touch Lonama's map," she said. Her tone and her eyes told Mindar that it would be inappropriate to ask why or to insist on an answer.

Mindar set his mug to one side and laid his thumbs on the cover of the box. He was sure it was the one he had for so long in Tessamandria. He closed his eyes as he carefully lifted the cover, and it was not until he knew that the map was visible and ready to be touched, that he opened his eyes.

"You know this map, Master Mindar?!" asked Hanara. He looked up. It was not quite a question and not quite a statement.

"Yes," he said, "I know this map."

"When did you see it last?"

"When I...when it fell from my grasp—when Minxa pulled me into the portal—back in Kinvara."

"A thousand years, and it finds its way to your hands again." She was staring through him. Mindar could feel her eyes looking at something deep within or beyond him. It was her way, and he had felt her penetrating stare before, but he was not prepared for what she said next. "You must hold it now, until your death. In your death, you will pass it to its rightful, next owner."

"Me?" Mindar gasped. A wave of cold fear swept over him as he dropped the cover back onto the map box and pulled his hands from it. His mind reeled under the staggering weight of the revelation. Before him on the table lay the object of his own death; the compass that was his guide, this marvel of all the ages, this gift of Mah'Eladra to men, that he had had the privilege of carrying and protecting for most of his life. That which had protected him so diligently, now burned as the icon of destruction on the table before him.

"Yes, you," Hanara was saying. "You are the map bearer, and it is your responsibility to pass it on to one who will use it well."

"That's not what I meant!" Mindar stammered. "I mean—" He stopped, unable to grasp the fullness of what he was facing.

Hanara broke through the fog of his thoughts. "The map is a gift of Mah'Eladra, and it was given you when you were young. It has protected you and guided you. The Infinite and Oblivion are shaped differently because of your hand in this world and because of the map. So you should not fear, Master Mindar. When it is passed on, that will also be by the hands of Mah'Eladra. It will be a blessing to you and to him who receives it."

"But it wasn't given to me!" Mindar protested.

Hanara raised her eyebrows. Mindar stood up angrily and pushed himself back from the table. "I took it! I stole it! It was not a gift."

"One cannot *steal* Lonama's map, Master Mindar."

"I murdered a—" Mindar felt himself nearly choke on the words. "I took the map—from a man whom I...killed. From me!" His voice trailed off into the twilight settling on the windows from the Deep Sky.

Hanara did not flinch. She set her mug down on the table and rose to stand opposite the table from him. "Master Mindar," Hanara said firmly, "the hands of Mah'Eladra do not err in their work in this world of ours, but our knowledge of their work is often insufficient to see the kirrin in what they do. If the yielding of this map into the hands of another but costs you your life, is that not a small yielding to the greater good you have done?"

"That's an easy thing for a Melendar to say." The words burst forth in anger before he knew they were coming.

"You know nothing of what you are saying," Hanara said sternly. Her eyes burned. "You know little of the Melendar, and most of that is supposition. I do not know if I am Melendar, but this I do know: that every Melendar, in every path that they walk, tastes the reality of kirrin in every step they take. Without kirrin, there is no Infinite. Without kirrin, there is no Melendar. You are being asked to taste it once in all its completeness; this is where your entire life has been leading you. To deny it now would be the greatest of failings."

Mindar stood still. Raging torrents of anger and loathing, fear and resentment, of great joy and completeness, swirled around him, tearing at his vorn. The psadeq he had fought for with each and every relationship would fall behind, yet his psadeq with Mah'Eladra would become greater still, eclipsing all the others in quality and magnitude. Still, everything he had ever known would be swept into nonexistence behind him.

Hanara did not move. She seemed content to let him wrestle. He reached for the map and then withdrew his hands once again as he looked around the small kitchen. Was this the place where this whole journey had started? What if he had never taken the map when he left? Did he even have a choice, and did he have a choice now? What if he had died in the Verillain Dale, in the cave north of Fazdeen or in the assassination fires of Vindarill? All the peculiarities of life were laid before him as a given, and yet he knew with the same certainty that he had made his own decisions at each point when there was a question about what to do.

He sat down numbly at the table and looked up into Hanara's eyes. They were deep with concern and wonder. "What do I do now?" he whispered hoarsely.

"You move on with your life. Thinking that you know your end should not change what you do because, if it does, it means that you were not doing what was important to begin with."

"Perhaps I did not understand that importance very well," Mindar mumbled. "Besides, I do not know the end—only fragments of it."

"Perhaps not," said Hanara, "and perhaps the fragments that you know, or think you know, will serve to make what you have started complete." She trailed her statement with the rising tone of a question.

Mindar looked up. "How can I know?"

"Does it matter? I ask again: would knowing the details change the way you have chosen to live?"

Mindar paused as the words sank deep into his vorn. She was right. Life was not and never would be measured by the brief temporal pastimes and amusements of daily life, but in the psadeq with Mah'Eladra that would last into the Infinite. He pondered the idea that he had known all his life that he would die, but had never had to believe it. Perhaps he was fortunate to have this knowledge, and fortunate that he could know what it was to face death and not succumb to the fear of it.

✠

To yield gracefully to death is the greatest accomplishment of life.

Taharal Minnas
Knowing Life

Mindar was still sitting at the table with the map unopened in front of him when Kotorvan returned. The deep shades of twilight were all that remained of the day outside the window at the end of the kitchen, and the sky shone with the beautiful deep blue-green luminance that it only has at the end of the day. As he came into the kitchen, Kotorvan flipped the switch by the door that turned on the light above the table.

"Sorry," he said quickly when Mindar looked up. Kotorvan flicked it off again.

"No, turn it on," Mindar said.

As Kotorvan flipped the switch again, Mindar felt the strange melancholy that had gripped his vorn dissipate under its flood. "Is my son still here?" the older man asked.

Mindar looked up into his tired face. "He is on the cot in my room upstairs," Mindar said. "I think he is sleeping."

Kotorvan disappeared through the door, and Mindar heard him go up the stairs, pause for a moment and then come back down. He reappeared at the door to the kitchen and made his way to the table. "May I sit down?" he asked.

"Sure," Mindar mumbled. He was not sure he wanted company, and yet the old man's presence was a welcomed diversion to his thoughts of the last hour as he wrestled with his newfound knowledge.

"Hanara told me to tell you she will have to leave about eleven," Kotorvan said. "There was a death in the circle, and they celebrate the fires of Eshen at midnight."

"Aren't you going?"

"Not tonight. Only a certain number can go, and I have my son to take care of."

"Does Hanara have to go?"

"Yes. She is part of the ceremony."

Mindar sat and pondered what it meant. He felt safe when Hanara was in the shop. It was the same feeling he had had at Hannahoruan's apothecary when Kinvara was falling to Mankar. No one could touch her shop if she was there. It leant more credibility to the possibility that she was a Melendar and more fear to what would happen if she left.

"Do you know where she is now?"

"She is downstairs, putting the shop in order and making her preparations for tomorrow. Do you know what it is?" Kotorvan said as he pointed at the map box.

Mindar felt a look of incredulity flit over his face and then recede as he realized that Kotorvan's inquiry was sincere.

"It's Lonama's map."

There was a long pause. Kotorvan leaned forward with a peculiar intensity. "Are you sure?"

"Yes."

"How do you know?"

"I carried this map with me for nearly forty years," Mindar said, "and I know it like the lines in my hands." Kotorvan was leaning back in his chair, his arms folded across his chest. He was staring across the table in disbelief. Mindar asked him, "How did *you* get it?"

Kotorvan shook his head as if clearing it of vague thoughts. "Lonama's map!" He leaned forward and pulled the box slowly toward him across the table. Mindar felt jealousy tearing at his vorn. He wanted to reach out and grab it back, but the map still belonged to the strange old man across the table. He restrained himself and waited patiently. "I received this box about a week ago," Kotorvan said as he looked up, his fingers on the cover. "An old man with a queer accent—he came in and gave it to me and told me to hold it until I could find the owner."

"A queer accent?"

"Diss map, you keepa dis one. When d'owna come, hees gonna give ya sumpin special." Kotorvan's mimic was clear.

"Bald head—about this tall?" Mindar held his hand up over his shoulder.

"Yes, right. Right odd fellow. You know him?"

"I think so," Mindar volunteered. "Did he say how you would know the owner?"

"You think *you're* the owner?"

Kotorvan's shrewd bargainer's eyes told Mindar everything. He had seen it a thousand times in the bazaars in Kinvara.

"I owned this map for forty years—"

"This very one?"

Mindar paused.

"I have heard there are several," Kotorvan said with a hint of a smile.

"There are eight," Mindar said it without emotion, "and I am sure this is the one that was in my keeping."

"That—other fellow—"

"Minxa?"

"The one with the scar. He said it was his," Kotorvan said, "but he offered me money—a lot of it, actually, but not *sumpin special,* if you know what I mean."

"I offered you nothing," Mindar observed, "but you gave me the combination to your safe and let me carry the map."

Kotorvan's sharp eyes gleamed. "You saved my life, Mindar. Hanara sent you. My son had told me that you were coming—"

"But you were afraid when I came."

"At first. I thought it was the scarred one returning. In the end, I was right in giving you the map—you brought it back to me."

Mindar pondered how all this had happened. The series of events that had brought him back to Hanara's place, too perfectly connected to be coincidental, seemed almost choreographed to the point where Mindar realized that he had done little, other than play his part. The map still belonged to Kotorvan, and yet he knew it still belonged to him somehow.

"What do you want for the map?"

"Sumpin special," Kotorvan was smiling.

"You know exactly what this special thing is, don't you?"

Kotorvan nodded slowly, his gleaming eyes never broke contact with Mindar's gaze.

"And you don't necessarily believe that this is rightfully mine."

Kotorvan smiled. "That's right."

"Wait here."

Mindar returned carrying the empty kaffa bottle that Klaria had given him in the cave. He set it deliberately onto the table between them and looked down into Kotorvan's eyes. "Is this special enough?" Kotorvan's jaw dropped, and his eyes narrowed at the same time. The bottle sparkled in the light that hung above the table, its delicate features casting odd shadows down its sides, deepening the effect.

"Where did you get this?" Kotorvan gasped. "May I?" He pointed to the bottle before touching it.

"Be careful—it's special."

Kotorvan laughed nervously. Mindar nodded in answer to his question.

"I have seen two of these in my life," Kotorvan exclaimed as he lifted the bottle toward himself. "The first was many years ago, from an old friend whose father had given it to him when he died—and this one." The older man looked up. "Where did you get this?"

"It was given to me when I first arrived back in Vindarill."

"Given?"

"Yes. I had nothing, and being a viddik, would get nothing. The old man who gave you the map, gave me this bottle."

Kotorvan sniffed the bottle opening.

"Is this *special* enough?" Mindar asked.

The trader's gleam returned to Kotorvan's eyes. "If it were not—?"

"I know there is little in this world that compares in value to Lonama's map," Mindar conceded, "but then again, the map is only useful to its rightful owner—" Mindar left the thought unfinished. "Besides, if this thousand-year-old bottle is that special thing that Klaria spoke about, then value is not part of the discussion is it?"

Kotorvan sat for a long time, slowly turning the bottle over and over in his hand. Mindar waited.

"If I give you the map, may I keep the bottle?" the older man said at length.

Mindar nodded. "It would be my pleasure, but is it enough?"

Kotorvan looked up in surprise. "What do you mean?"

"I would give everything I have for this map."

Kotorvan smiled. "I think I know this, but the bottle, and my son's life—and my life—are sufficient. It is clear to me that the map is not mine to own, and it is not my place to demand from another man everything that he has; that is the province of Mah'Eladra alone." Kotorvan stood and reached across the table with his hand in a gesture signifying the culmination of a deal. "I must gather my son and go home. I will see you in the morning?"

Mindar shook Kotorvan's hand as the old man waited patiently for his answer. "I hope to see you in the morning," he replied. He hoped it would be so, but for the first time in his life, Mindar understood fully that there was no promise of tomorrow.

✠

We know so little truth about the past. Why should we feel entitled to know anything about the future?

Karendo Marha
Journey to the Infinite

The eerie hiss startled Mindar from his thoughts. The map box remained untouched in front of him as the large form of the Eladra entered his field of view across the table. It was Visha'andar. He pulled the chair from the table, sat down awkwardly and stared at Mindar without blinking.

"This is the night, isn't it?" Mindar asked without changing his gaze.

"Yes, it is."

"And this is where it happens?"

"You remember well."

"No," Mindar sighed, "I remember very little—but somehow I know. Will you be here when it happens?"

"I will be here, though you will not see me. I have been sent to comfort you, but I cannot prevent what happens."

"Do you know what happens?"

"No." Visha'andar's answer was blunt. Mindar knew there was little chance that much more would be forthcoming.

"Do you know much about the Infinite—or Oblivion?"

Visha'andar leaned forward and placed his elbows on the table, and when he did so, Mindar was reminded of how large he was. His arms were bare and muscled and perfectly smooth, each muscle defined for its purpose. His eyes were dark and teeth as white as the stars. "I know nothing of Oblivion, but I have seen the Infinite many times."

"Can you tell me about it?"

"What do you wish to know?"

Mindar was surprised by the willingness of the giant's answer. "Well, I…well, how does one know—I mean how does one know with certainty—" He paused and looked down because he was not sure whether he could really ask the question that burned in his mind.

"You want to know your destiny—the Infinite or Oblivion?"

Mindar nodded.

"You won't know."

"Why?"

"It is the province of Mah'Eladra."

"But on what basis?"

"On psadeq and kirrin. These are the measures of the man kind before Mah'Eladra, but I cannot know for you."

"I do know—but..." Even as he said the words, he felt the shadowed uncertainty of death peering around the corners of his vorn. He knew he could not give in to its taunt, so he changed the subject. "These aren't the measure of the Eladra?"

"We are not measured. We serve."

"I am afraid," said Mindar. He was surprised that he said it, but relieved that he had finally allowed himself to do so. He looked up.

"And I have come to help you in your fear. Do you know what you fear?"

"I think...I thought—well, that I was afraid of death, but now I think that I fear the *pain* of dying." Mindar was playing with his fingers. He looked up. Visha'andar was staring at him earnestly. "Do the Eladra know pain?"

"Yes, but I do not know if it is the same as the pain of your kind." Mindar waited.

"I see many men in their pain. I see them curse others, and I see them curse Mah'Eladra and wither in their anger and hatred. I see them call out in fear, and I see others rise above their pain."

"Can I do that?"

"Yes. You have the El of Mah'Eladra, and you know kirrin."

Mindar and Visha'andar talked together for nearly an hour. With each question and each confirming answer from the Eladra, Mindar understood and grappled with his situation. He was no stranger to death, but his own death was not something he knew how to face, and somewhere in the conversation, the glimmer of understanding began to surround him. Death was just another doorway, another portal. In many ways it was the culmination of the direction he had taken with his life. Life on Tessalindria was nearly done, but life on the other side of this portal was waiting for him. It occurred to him that Mah'Eladra had led him carefully through most his life as he considered each decision and where it would lead. It led here, to this night and this place.

"What will happen if I die?" Mindar asked.

"I cannot say. I do not know death."

"Will I see others? Will I recognize them? The vision of the Tessarandin speaks of the regathering of the vorn and the journey to the Deep Sky." He was staring at the Eladra to see his reaction.

Visha'andar paused and waited, still as a statue, then smiled. Mindar couldn't remember him ever smiling, and it buoyed his vorn. "What is it?" he asked.

"There are six things I know. Only five can be told," said the giant as he raised his index finger. "The vorn is torn apart in death, but it is regathered when the fires of Eshen carry the basa into the sky." His middle finger flicked from his fist. "The Eladra escort the vorn to the Great Margah, but the vorn of the man kind must enter on its own, for the Eladra cannot enter until all their service is done here on Tessalindria."

Visha'andar's ring finger joined the other two. "In the Margah there is—ransom—and he will know the completeness of the vorn. Be afraid but do not fear, for you are washed in the Jualar Springs, and your vorn is complete." With a flourish of his hand, his little finger emerged. "The ascent to the golden stair is made alone, amidst the throngs of the ages."

The giant paused as if listening again before he spoke. "The stair seems a journey longer than it is, but one finds that it is not."

Mindar sat stunned. He was looking straight at Visha'andar's huge palm spread out before him. "Will there be others? Others that I know?"

"I cannot say, but you know."

"Sereline?"

Visha'andar shrugged.

"My daughters?"

The giant paused to listen. "Erolin and Menzor?" he asked as he looked back at Mindar.

"No, Therall and Serinda—" As he said their names, he felt his throat tighten, and he wondered how Visha'andar could have made such a mistake. He had never known an Eladra to get the facts wrong.

"I cannot say. It is not my place," said Visha'andar, interrupting Mindar's thoughts.

"Erinshava? Minxa?" Mindar was not sure he wanted to hear an honest answer to either, though he felt he knew the answer to both.

"What is, was and ever will be, Mindar Colloden," said Visha'andar. "That which is not, never was and never will be."

Mindar looked down at the map. He understood all the words, but he wasn't sure he understood what they meant. Everything from the giant's lips was falling in the manner of the purest of noble truth, poured forth in the delicate balance of the paradox. He had struggled always to grasp both sides of these truths and to realize the profound center in accepting them, but he was not sure that words were adequate to capture them. He sat and stared at the map box before him, not wanting to look up into Visha'andar's eyes.

Visha'andar stood up abruptly. "Do not fear, Mindar, for I will be with you—and so will Vishortan." Mindar followed his finger as he pointed to the corner of the room. The light vapor of another Eladrim warrior hovered in the darkened corner beside the sink. Visha'andar vanished with a hiss when he looked back.

Mindar sat facing the door to the tiny kitchen. The map box waited in front of him, and the single light hung motionless above him, its cone of light illuminating the whole table, but little more. Mindar tried to remember the time he had arrived so many years before. To the best of his memory it was about two in the morning, which meant that he had another hour to wait.

He wondered why Visha'andar had left so abruptly. It was almost as if the Eladra had sensed something was happening and was forced to make a sudden departure. The street outside had fallen asleep with the darkness. Neither Tal nor Meekar were yet to be seen, and the dark stillness surrounded the kitchen like a cocoon. Mindar's mind flicked back over the events of his life. There were so many branches; so many turns that could have been different. He thought about Minxa and the path he had chosen. Both of them had come from the same place, cut from the same mold; and yet, given the same choices, Minxa's life had become so different.

He wondered about whether he had the courage to face this night. His thoughts drifted to Sessasha. He did not know a lot of detail about what he had faced and how he had done it, but Mindar knew enough. He pondered what it must have been like for Sessasha to face death with so much surety that he could suffer as he did for what he thought was right, to the very verge of giving up on psadeq altogether.

Mindar was not sure how long he had been sitting in the deep quiet of this strange night when he first noticed the faint movement somewhere in the building. It was one of those soft sounds that wasn't really a sound at all, just a subtle presence that one might even pass off as imagination. His senses tingled with anticipation, and he felt his heart skip a beat. There it was again, so faint that he could not tell where it was or even what it was. He sat still, not daring to move.

For several minutes nothing stirred. Mindar's heart raced as he glanced at the clock above the door. It was still too early, but something was happening already: another deep thump somewhere else, but closer; a creak on the stairway, and then the silence closed in again.

Mindar had his hand on the map case, but he knew he should not look at the map. The answers to everything lay right there beneath his fingertips, yet it was not for him to know, as if the map no longer rightfully belonged to him.

The silence crept along. He wanted to move and dared not do it at the same time. He wanted water, but knew that there was no need for it. His head hurt with the strain of listening into the quiet kitchen.

"Click!" Someone had laid hold of the doorknob. It turned slowly, and the door opened into the kitchen. Minxa stood framed in the door-way, still as a statue in the bare light of the single bulb, with his right hand behind the middle of his back. His gray hair was matted and his dark eyes sunk deep in their sockets. He looked tired.

"May I come in?" His soft request carried a sense of warmth, under-pinned by a subtle gloating.

Mindar did not move except to nod. When Minxa stepped through the door, Mindar noticed that he was barefoot, and his trousers had been torn off at the knees. He moved without a sound and made no effort to close the door. Two shadows glided in behind him. After they were both in the room, he reached back and pushed the door, and it swung slowly and closed with a click. As Minxa approached the table, his NarEladrim escorts took their places on either side of him and slight-ly behind his shoulders.

Minxa stopped before he reached the table. "I have come for the map."

"It is no longer mine to give you," said Mindar slowly, keeping eye contact.

Minxa smiled. "It's been a long road, my friend and I am not in a hurry. Besides, I wasn't asking you to give it to me; I have come to take it." He nodded to the chair in front of the table. "May I?"

"Of course."

Minxa drew the chair back with his left hand, swung it around and straddled it with his legs so that the back of the chair was in front of his chest. When he was seated, he pulled his right hand from behind his back and drove the point of a dagger forcefully into the solid wood of the table. "Where did you get *this*?"

The dagger Mindar had brought with him through the portal wagged back and forth slightly. "I might ask you the same," Mindar said.

"Ho! I found it in your chest—under your bed." Minxa's eyes flick-ered for a moment before becoming cold again. "Where did *you* get it?"

Mindar sensed the danger he was in. Minxa's tone was utterly ruth-less.

"I brought it with me from Kinvara. I found it in the ashes of Valradicca's smithy the morning after he was murdered. You knew I had it. Dajaan showed it to you in the caves."

"'Every man will die once'... Isn't that what that book says?"

"The Tessarandin?"

"Yes, that one."

Mindar knew the section that Minxa was referring to. Rasler had read it to him several times. "It does say that," he said, "but not in the context of a man taking another man's life. It is more about Mah'Eladra knowing that every man will die and when—not about murder."

"So Mah'Eladra—" a sneer spread across Minxa's mouth as he said the name, "they must have known when Valradicca would die and how."

"They know of everyone's first death. They also know who will then live and who will face the second death."

"And you believe all that?"

"I have no proof, but I choose to believe so that I will not face death twice." Mindar said.

"You are more a fool than I thought. There is one death, and it is final—for each of us. There is nothing afterward."

"For those who choose to think it so, it *is* so. Oblivion and the second death are one and the same for those whose ignorance and mordage make it so." Mindar felt an invincible boldness welling up inside of him. "For those who know otherwise, we will live on in the Infinite—for those whose mordage has been removed, who have had psadeq restored with Mah'Eladra and with others." Mindar noticed that the NarEladrim guards shifted slightly whenever the name Mah'Eladra was spoken. He wanted to look around to see if Visha'andar and Vishortan were with him, but he dared not take his eyes off Minxa.

"Do you suppose that tonight may be the night for you to test your belief?"

"I think so."

"And you are not afraid?"

"I am afraid of you—and I fear the depravity of your vorn. I fear the pain of dying, but not death itself."

"So you have thought about this for a while now."

"We are all going to die, Minxa. I have faced the possibility of death many times, and it is inevitable, even for you. The issue, as I have come to see it, is not whether or when we will stare into the face of death, but if we are prepared to do so."

Minxa leaned forward and laid his hand on the dagger. With a simple twist, he lifted it out of the desk. "I suppose you are right," he said as he tilted the blade so that the light from it glinted into his eyes. "I am not ready for death—I intend to live. I don't give up that easily. You know, Rindar, if you had let me have the map back there on the road—way back there in the Verillain Dale, it would have been so much easier."

Mindar did not speak until Minxa had raised his eyes from the dagger and looked at him. "Perhaps it would have been much harder. Do you know that I nearly died from that wound? I still have the scar."

"And you still have the map." Minxa said.

"Do you intend to finish what you started that day?"

"If I have to—" One of the NarEladra moved suddenly. The gray giant leaned forward and whispered in Minxa's ear, and Minxa smiled. Both NarEladra vanished with a hiss. "Someone else is coming," he said with a smile. "Were you expecting someone?" He laid the dagger on the table in front of Mindar and stood up silently, lifting the chair and swinging it around to face Mindar. It met the floor without a sound. Minxa whirled, and moving like a cat to the door, he switched off the light. Mindar sensed him retiring to the corner of the kitchen behind where the door opened.

Mindar could not see the clock in the dark. He guessed it was close to two o'clock; he sat and waited, listening intently. He could hear nothing.

Klaria had told him that the map would never allow a person to find and meet his other self. He wondered if this were so and wondered if perhaps this situation, since the map had not been used, was outside the map's control, or if, because the map was the province of Mah'Eladra, they could make exceptions if they desired.

Out of the dim twisting of his thoughts he heard the light tread on the stair rising to the landing outside the kitchen. The steps paused, and then the same "click" preceded the slow swinging of the door, and there he stood. Mindar froze. The silhouette of his barely eighteen-year-old self stood in the shadow of the hall light, his left hand held the hazarine as his right hand fished for a light switch. As the light came on, Rindar looked up, scanning the room quickly. As his eyes fell on Mindar, his jaw dropped, and the hazarine came to attention between them.

Mindar knew that the hazarine would not work. He felt the emotion of his discovery almost forty years ago: that the room was not empty. "Come in," Mindar ventured. The young figure hesitated, looking cautiously around the room, his hazarine hand twitching nervously and his dark stringy hair hanging lazily down just above his eyes.

"I have a hazarine."

"I know. I can see."

"I know how to use it." He was still standing in the doorway.

"I don't doubt that you do, but do come in."

"I thought no one was here—I mean, no one was supposed to be here!"

"*Supposed* to be here?"

Mindar could see the nervous energy of youth. He thought back and remembered the anger and the violent power it engendered in him. He tried to assuage it, knowing how that power reacted to fear. "Did you come looking for something specific?"

Suddenly, the youth stepped forward and with a single motion pushed the door shut behind him. "I don't want to talk."

"Why did you come here?" Mindar held up the map box. "For this?"

"This is impossible," Rindar muttered.

"Sometimes the greatest truth is discovered when we are forced to accept the impossible."

A wave of suspicion swept over the eyes of young Rindar. "Put it on the table!" he commanded, waving his hazarine.

Mindar set the box quietly onto the table, taking care to make the motion seem deliberate and unthreatening. He looked up again into the darting eyes behind the hazarine. "Would you like some tea, Rindar?"

The dark eyes stormed, and he took another step closer. "How did you know my name?"

"How did you know about the box?"

Rindar glanced around the room for a moment, assessing the layout of the small kitchen. "I—I was told it was here."

"Did Vashtor also tell you no one would be here?"

Rindar hesitated in surprise. "But that don't matter," he said as he stepped forward again until he stood about two steps from the table. "All I want is the box."

"It's yours to take, but don't give it to Vashtor. It's far too valuable for that."

"I need the money."

"This box is worth far more to you than any amount of money Vashtor could offer you."

"You're stalling."

"Take the box." Mindar pushed the box forward several inches.

Rindar readjusted his grip on the hazarine. "Push it here."

"You need to come and get it."

Rindar glanced around nervously again. Mindar knew that Minxa was in the corner, but dared not look over at him. "I don't wanna do this." He raised the hazarine and squeezed the handle. Mindar felt the lie. He had done it so many times and said the same thing each time.

Rindar squeezed again and swore, then dropped the hazarine and lunged forward, grabbing the dagger off the table and brandishing it in front of him.

Mindar noticed that his hands were shaking. "There is no need for the knife," he said. "All you need to do is take the box and go. Just don't give it to Vashtor." Their eyes locked in a faint recognition, a connection that Mindar could not explain. Something in Rindar's eyes had changed, and they looked as if there was a sudden dim realization of some deeper truth, but there was no time to explore what it meant.

Minxa moved silently out of the shadows, his raised hand carried a small leather sack that he brought down swiftly on the back of Rindar's skull. Rindar never heard him, and he sank to the floor under the blow. Minxa bent only to retrieve the dagger from Rindar's limp hand, and the two NarEladra hissed into place on either side of him. No sooner had they appeared than Mindar heard the same faint hissing behind him.

"This is between you and me," Minxa growled.

"It has nothing to do with either of us," said Mindar. "The map belongs to him." He pointed to the unconscious heap on the floor. "And he will take it out of here later this morning. You know that."

"I came to change what I know." The NarEladra had separated, moving away from Minxa, their eyes fixed on their counterparts behind Mindar with their hands on the hilts of their swords.

"And what, exactly, is it that you know?"

Minxa hesitated. "You came here that night—tonight, to rob this place. Vashtor offered you money and told you about the map!" There was a glint in his eye as he waved the dagger back and forth as he spoke. "But tonight is different. Vashtor did not talk to him this time."

Mindar smiled. "How would he know Vashor's name if Vashtor did not talk to him before he came here?"

Minxa hesitated as a glimmer of truth dawned in his eyes before he turned and glanced at one of the NarEladra behind him. The NarEladra shrugged impassively. "*You* were the one who told him Vashtor's name," Minxa growled as he turned back to face Mindar.

"But he didn't deny it, so why should you?" Mindar asked. "Vashtor has betrayed you, Minxa. He wants the map, but because the NarEladra have no memory of the future, he did what he thought was necessary to make sure he got the map, even without you, and now you are about to betray him because you don't care about the map. You're here to seek revenge."

Minxa's eyes narrowed. "Now you're lying."

"Five silver coins," Mindar said. "Check his front right pocket."

Minxa paused again and took two steps back until he was standing over Rindar's body. Without taking his eyes off Mindar, he rolled Rindar over and fumbled for the pocket, finally plunging his fingers in and pulling out two silver coins. His eyes narrowed as he stood up and approached the light. "Sesh!" he muttered as he examined the coins. Turning suddenly, he hurled the two coins at the NarEladra behind him. Vashtor did not move as the coins bounced off his chest and cheek and fell to the floor. Minxa whirled to face Mindar again. "Tonight I'm changing all this!"

"You keep saying that, but look, I have never been able to recall exactly what happened that night. This would explain it. The silver coin the inspectors found—" Mindar pointed to the limp body on the floor and continued, "The only other thing we know is that there was blood all over the place when I woke up and that I walked out of here with the map. No bodies, remember? Just blood—*two* types of blood! What was the second blood type, Minxa? You want to change history? Put down the dagger!"

"Give me the map!"

"I already told you, it is not mine to give. It belongs to him now!"

Mindar reached out to point down at his younger self slumped on the floor with his left hand. Minxa lunged forward, slashing with the dagger. The tip caught the back of Mindar's forearm, cutting deep into the muscle. The pain shot up his arm like a bolt of lightning. He had not felt anything like it in years, and the wave of shock rolled over him, making him dizzy. Blood was flowing through his fingers where he tried to grasp the wound shut. Behind him and to either side, he heard the unmistakable screech of swords being drawn quickly from their scabbards.

Minxa reached for the map, and Mindar slapped it away with his good hand. The bloodied dagger flashed again, plunging through Mindar's other forearm, and Mindar felt it twist between the bones before Minxa yanked it clear. Mindar sat back heavily in the chair with both arms bleeding and nearly useless. He could feel the weakness from the loss of blood that poured from both arms.

"Get the map; we have little time," said Vashtor. He was holding his sword in front of him. His voice was ugly and angry.

Minxa reached out to take the map again. With all the life force he had left, Mindar rose from the chair and hurled himself at Minxa across the narrow table. He heard the profanity and felt the blade at the same time, coming up under his ribs as he collapsed on top of the table. Minxa rolled him off, and he fell to the floor. He could still see, but could not move, and what was left of his vision was turning gray in a fog of unconsciousness. Everything hurt and nothing worked. He could taste blood in his mouth.

Minxa was moving slowly, but as he reached for the map, a bright sword swept over the table. Minxa yelled, and the NarEladra swore. Mindar faded farther from the room, and the gray fog turned bright from above. He could hear the swords clashing and the deep guttural curses of the NarEladra. Everything swirled and flashed with bright popping sounds. All around, the brightness of the light increased until out of it he could see a swarming movement of intensity that could never exist in Tessalindria. Everything moved in all directions at once, and the depth of it was beyond comprehension.

As the bright movement increased, the pain ebbed away, along with the cacophony of the battle that surrounded his body. A gentle rushing sound came from the bright dance above him, and the rushing sound grew in intensity until it eclipsed Tessalindria completely and Mindar was surrounded. Mindar felt the engulfing power of the brightness and uttered one last word before he yielded to its embrace: "Mah'Eladra—"

✠

There is no pride in death's shadow.

Mythinian Proverb

Minxa had never felt anything like the icy pain of the Eladrim blade that sliced his forearm as he reached for the map. He staggered backward, his anger rising with the frustration of being denied that which he had sought for so long. "Get that map!" Vashtor grunted as his sword flashed against that of one of the Eladra that had appeared suddenly when Minxa first struck Rindar. Minxa's right arm was useless with the cold and pain. The dagger had fallen to the floor.

The battle raged around him as the swords of the Eladra and NarEladra swirled and flashed with searing hisses and thunderous collisions of steel on steel. Minxa looked for a chance to get ahold of the map. As the fighting moved away from the table for an instant, he reached out once again. "No!" thundered one of the Eladrim warriors as his sword swept down. Minxa jumped back and tripped over the crumpled form of the boy who lay unconscious on the floor. He lost his balance and sprawled backward onto the floor.

The fighting continued above him unabated as if his presence was unnoticed. He crawled to the table, nursing the ever-increasing cold in his left arm. The dagger lay on the floor. Another thought occurred to him as he picked it up and rolled backward, stopping beside the young Rindar's unconscious body. In a last fit of jealous anger, he raised the dagger to finally change history forever. He did not see exactly what happened, but lightning blazed across his back and up his shoulder, throwing him off balance and causing him to drop the knife. Darkness rolled in around the corner of his eyes and he pitched forward.

Minxa felt himself land on top of the boy's body. His own blood flowed down across his face and dripped into a dark pool on the floor in front of him. His strength would not respond to his commands. The light faded into gray, and the gray into darkness as the sound and fury of the Eladrim battle fell into the strange distance of approaching death. It wasn't supposed to end like this. He was not ready to die and he knew it, and everything that he had sought, everything that he had believed was slipping away, and there was nothing to hold onto as he slid slowly into the darkness. Before the light faded forever, Minxa uttered one last pleading word: "Mah'Eladra—"

A Word from the Author

I keep having this discussion with my good friend Herm Foley about the location of Tessalindria. He wants me to work with one of the astrophysical computers available on the Web and use what I have discovered about the star constellations on Tessalindria to locate the planet relative to the stars we see here from earth. To this point, as a historian and storyteller about Tessalindria, I have resisted his pleas because of the time and the potential expense of that effort. To me it seems that there are far more important issues related to this tiny planet, issues that are more poignant and germane to our understanding of our universe, ourselves and our origins, than the exact whereabouts of this unique world.

I would rather understand why a planet that is a third the diameter of the earth seems to have a similar gravity and why so much of the history seems parallel to ours in important ways and so wildly different in others. I'm curious to know why the scientists of Tessalindria have, after much rumination and mathematical theorizing, concluded that it is the only place where life could possibly have developed, while those who believe in Mah'Eladra have come to the conclusion that if they are indeed the authors of life, then the universe should be packed with it, as if it were bursting out everywhere, even in the seemingly empty spaces of the galaxy.

I am consummately curious why two-thirds of the planet's inhabitants count with eights and the rest in tens. This oddity has been the source of continual confusion in unraveling the numbers that appear in all the historical references. The tens business seems to have started late in Immerland and spread north to Werenvar and east to Hartana. From there all the northern islands adopted it. I want to know why all the languages are so similar; why many Tessalindrians seem to be able to understand the original language, but no one speaks it. I would like to know more about the origins and the purpose of the portals; who are the Melendar, and why would Mah'Eladra create them; what exactly is the Kirrinath, and how does it relate to the outworld realities, of which we are certainly a part...my curiosities are endless, but for now, I am content to let Tessalindria remain hidden in the stars.

Herm argues that knowing where Tessalindria is in the vast tapestry of our sky might shed clues on all these things, but from what I have found in the literature, I am more likely to find answers to *my* questions first, for any clues to its location seem to be intentionally obscured. Perhaps I am missing something that other researchers will some day find, so for now, we will have to wait. When the time is right, if we are to know this answer, it will have to be given to us.

—F. W. Faller
www.immerland.com
Spring 2004

About the Author

Frederick W. Faller was born on Cape Cod in 1955 and lived there for five years before spending a year in Sweden with his family. There, his mother came in contact with Christian missionaries, thus beginning the spiritual journey that has shaped most of his life. On returning to the United States, the family stayed for two more years on Cape Cod and then moved to suburban Washington D.C. where he lived until completing high school.

He graduated from MIT in Cambridge, Massachusetts, with a degree in earth and planetary sciences (with a focus on meteorology and oceanography). It was during this time that a spiritual awakening moved him through a series of jobs that brought him to the point of being a minister for two and a half years. He remains active and productive in the local church ministry, leading small group Bible studies, teaching, counseling and writing.

Through the years, he has written a number articles and essays on various issues related to Christian faith and life. *A Sword for the Immerland King* was his first foray into fiction, and *Lonama's Map* is his second. These works of visionary fiction or high fantasy are a reflection of his devotion to finding basic truths through his study of the Bible and applying them to the reality of our lives in this complex spiritual world. These two books are part of a larger picture: a series of books about the small planet of Tessalindria, deliberately removed from the religious milieu of our own planet to give fresh insight into spiritual truths.

A man who thrives on the creative process—when time allows between the demands of his family, his job and the work of the ministry—Frederick enjoys the hobbies of blacksmithing and bladesmithing, which spawned the theme for his first book. He has been a sculptor and woodcarver for as long as he can remember. He works as a mechanical engineer for a firm that makes medical devices and has a number of patents, attesting to a broad range of technical inventiveness. For a number of years, has enjoyed listening to and playing folk music. He plays the banjo, hammered dulcimer and single string bass for the occasional evening gatherings he hosts at his home.

Frederick lives in a Boston suburb with his wife, Ellen, and three teenage children: Rachel, Jesse and Samuel.